THE *Ranting* OF AN UNEDUCATED REACTIONARY

OSCAR PHILLIPS

The Ranting of an Uneducated Reactionary

v25.0 r6.1

Shyman and Shyster Publishing

ISBN: 978-0-578-23844-9

PRINTED IN THE UNITED STATES OF AMERICA

Contents

Preface

I was born and raised in a liberal state. As a youngster, like 99 percent of the other kids living in a small suburban town, yours truly was not the least bit interested in politics, although this writer does recall thinking, as a fifteen-year-old boy, that Republicans were the better political party because they were tougher on criminals. Also, I vaguely remember someone saying that "Republicans are for the rich and Democrats are for the poor," which made me skeptical because it implied, unfairly, that the GOP doesn't like poor people and that the latter are never Republicans. My parents were both Democrats but weren't overtly political. The word "uneducated" in the title of this book means that the author never went to college. However, I did make up for not doing so by previously spending four and a half years in high school instead of the usual four, like ordinary students did. For that achievement alone, yours truly should have graduated high school magna cum laude.

In the year 1980, for some unknown reason, I became interested in jets and which ones were the fastest. This interest segued into which countries had the most nuclear weapons. In the same year, there was some news about how a nuclear arms treaty allowed the USSR to have a certain nuclear missile, but the USA was not permitted to have the same kind, which just didn't sound quite right to me. This news coincided with the 1980 presidential election and the candidates' opinions about these treaties, along with other political subjects. When the writer watched Ronald Reagan and Jimmy Carter debate and then with my beginning to think about the issues afterwards, there was an epiphany.

Right smack off the bat, I became a conservative and then began moving to the right. My ideology had been simmering beneath the surface for many years, though. Some, if not most, conservatives start off being liberals, if they don't already have Republican parents shaping their politics, and then commence moving upwards. But yours truly was influenced by no one. This author would have become the same right-winger even if Ronald Reagan had never existed. In 1995, the architect of this fine book was a bit of a political junkie, reading numerous right-wing and left-wing periodicals and the political opinion pages of newspapers. Yet, I never read an entire political book from first page to last and never considered writing a letter to the editor on any matter. And then one day in the noted year, there was a story in the local newspaper about a forum on racism.

Introduction

In August 1995, the local newspaper published my response to a town forum about racism. I cannot recall if this author produced any more articles the same year, but I did write maybe three in the following year. In fact, after the racism forum letter to the editor, the first article that I wrote and subsequently published in 1996 is the first chapter of this book. Though, it was considerably augmented for this publication. By late 1996, the political columns that ran in the newspapers gave me an idea. Having a lot of strong political opinions racing through my mind, I thought that yours truly could do the same as the pros, only not nearly as much. So sometime in early 1997, this wannabe writer fancied himself an amateur columnist (some may emphasize the word "amateur" but that's okay) and wrote about two dozen articles from the year 1997 through 2001. On occasion, the editor would even employ the title that I used for the top of the column.

I penned and published only about five more newspaper political articles in the first decade of the turn of the century and shortly afterward started to tell myself that this author-in-the-making should write a book. In the year 2011, I mailed an unrequested manuscript to a publisher, but they rejected it and rightfully so. Yours truly finally commenced seriously writing this book that you are about to read, in July 2014, though I employed only about five percent of my 1996-2009 writings. The sources that the writer used were political periodicals, newspapers, and the internet. In some of my articles, the names were changed to protect the ignorant. The seven "Opinionated Bits and Pieces" chapters are a mish-mash of random thoughts. ENJOY!

IMPORTANT: What with their predilection for peace signs, love beads, tie-dyed tee-shirts, sandals, and sit-ins; the political Left that dominated pop culture between 1965 and 1975 did have one thing going for them that should be appreciated by us all: their diligent advocacy of free speech. But, just like Father Time, the Left has changed. Today, the adage "freedom of speech" is purely subjective. Many on the current Left want terms like "boat-rocker," "thought-provoking," "rebellious," and "non-conformist" to be reserved for progressives ONLY, because they know that the American people, in general, romanticize individuals who espouse or represent these four labels. Hence, the aforementioned words become complimentary, not stigmatizing, thereby attracting the public to and subsequently encouraging agreement with the progressive message. The Left will never use these labels to describe conservative individuals for this very reason. But, if this author is wrong about something that he said, what's so bad about that? Should one not have the freedom to be wrong? Much of what I write is taboo, iconoclasm, socio-political non-conformity, and controversial, sure to be demonized without anybody presenting an intelligent argument against it. Now, there are those who deprecate, mock, and disagree with what is the polar opposite of my book (political correctness, wokeism), but they will also capitulate to it. To do so, these individuals concede its "legitimacy." Americans who succumb to and eventually respect political correctness/wokeism, which has now become the unofficial *law of the land*, will then become intolerant themselves. Those who take umbrage that a book like this could be published today would not have batted an eye in the 1970s if the very same style of literature came out. It's the current, repressive cultural atmosphere that frightens them away from condoning its release, not so much the book itself. Our country will hopefully and soon revert itself back to the hippie generation where the term "freedom of speech" was in BOLD PRINT, not "quotation marks."

wants government to subsidize their livelihood. To a liberal, a special interest group is a private enterprise that wants government to leave them alone so that they can continue to make a profit. Liberals call this SELFISHNESS but fail to see their own selfishness when they clamor for government social engineering in the name of what THEY perceive to be justice. In liberal-speak, selfishness and greed characterize a policy that espouses individualism and economic freedom. If it's capitalistic, then it's "mean spirited," "cold-hearted," and "cruel." Meanwhile, whatever government policies are "compassionate,""caring," and "humane" just happen to be conducive to socialism.

Although most Americans do not consider themselves to be liberal, if one is not cognizant of a capitalistic philosophy, then one tacitly gravitates toward socialism. The irony is that many, if not most, conservatives don't realize that libertarian conservatism IS capitalism and that liberalism is just quasi-socialism. But there isn't a communist or socialist that doesn't realize this. And for the far left to refer to conservatives as "capitalists", does not help the cause for "economic equality" (a euphemism for socialism) and "social justice" (ditto). Well-meaning liberals by themselves cannot afford to be totally honest, because they sense that the culmination of what they want is SOCIALISM and that the mere mention of the word could scare off potential supporters. But if the United States were living under outright socialism, it would then be libertarian conservatives (subversives) who couldn't afford to be honest because they would be punished by the all-caring, omnipotent State.

To all genuine liberals: If the "throw-money-at-the-problem" way is your line of thinking, then you might as well admit to being democratic socialists. The masquerade is over. But as J. Peter Grace, a Democratic economist, once pointed out back in the late 1980s, "Soaking the rich to solve the problem is a hoax, because even if government confiscated one hundred percent of all annual taxable income over $75,000 not already taxed, it would take in enough money to cover federal spending for only seven days. To generate significant new income tax revenue, the government has to go where the money is, and more than ninety percent of all taxable income flows through brackets of $35,000 per year or less."

CHAPTER **1**

Liberalism is the Road to Socialism

IN THE EARLY 1980s, President Ronald Reagan said that the American people wanted Big Government off their backs. This was essentially true, if the citizens concurred that government was indeed weighing the people down and suffocating them. But what our fortieth president absolutely avoided saying was that the American people do not want the government to provide for them and take care of them, because he knew that wasn't true. Correspondingly, he raised taxes many times in deference to Congress' spending appetite, at the behest of the electorate. Over a short period of time, Reagan was subsequently made a scapegoat by more than a few for a deficit made by the many. Some 75 percent of the public wants a universal health care system, oblivious to the implications, or not caring, that it is socialistic thinking on their part. But if you believe that health care is a right, then shouldn't you also think that jobs with good wages, affordable housing, and not living in poverty are also rights? If the readers don't consider themselves to be socialists, then how can they answer "Yes" to the previous question? It seems that basically the only thing that Americans don't like about socialism is the word itself. Many want health care REFORM. But why, to most of our citizens, does "reform" and having a president and Congress "do something" always mean increasing government and NEVER reducing it?

"Special interest" is a term that one hears in the news a lot. To a conservative, a special interest group is an organized gathering that

Prologue

Back in the 1980s, yours truly was a staunch anti-communist. Not anymore. Presently, I am a NON-communist but consider myself to be one of America's pre-eminent ANTI-socialists. Indeed, ANTI-SOCIALISM is the narrative of the literature that you are about to read. All genuine conservatives are pro-capitalism and all of them are non-socialism; but the vast majority are not ANTI-socialism and therein lies the problem. By having this book published, is it possible that the author can change the world? Absolutely not! Is it possible that I could be the one most responsible for convincing Americans to seriously desire and strongly fight for more liberty? No comment. Actually, the "scripture" that you are about to read was written mostly for profound personal reasons.

Acknowledgments: I would first like to thank my mother and father, because if it weren't for them, I never would have been born. But mostly, I would like to thank myself for taking the time to write my outstanding book, and I wish me the best of luck. Also, thank you, the reader, for purchasing this literary work of art. May God Bless the United States of America!

Does the reader want more proof that liberalism is the road to socialism? Done! Have you ever noticed that liberals harbor a dislike of the term "privatize" which connotes *anti-collectivism* and forces self-responsibility on the individual? Have you ever noticed that NEVER does a liberal even suggest that we should cut back on domestic social spending and entitlements because the aforementioned government funding will bring us to catastrophic bankruptcy and/or socialism. Have you ever noticed that a liberal cannot be "pro-family" without advocating government subsidies (e.g. welfare checks for mothers with illegitimate children)? Have you ever noticed that throughout American history, whenever a Marxist college professor or socialist debated someone, that someone was always a conservative, never a liberal? But then, to be fair, what could a liberal and a socialist possibly debate about? Have you ever noticed that it's always liberals that want to circumvent or abridge the Constitution, the capitalistic pillar of our republic? And are you aware that liberals call the Constitution a "living, breathing document" because they want it to be malleable to their socialist whims? Have you ever noticed that rarely, if ever, does a liberal refer to the USA as a Constitutional republic, but rather, "our democracy"? The entire left calls our nation a DEMOCRACY because if we the people think of it as, treat it as, and brand it as a "democracy" then we will inexorably take the DEMOCRATIC route to socialism. And liberals are absolutely unable to explain why America should NOT live under socialism. A liberal cannot and will not make a fist and throw a roundhouse swing at socialism because said Democrat is well aware that he's going to end up punching himself in the face.

Liberalism eventually transforms into leftism because it can't say "no" to itself! The former's natural inclination ultimately results in government tyranny (albeit the caring, compassionate, and inclusive kind). Since liberalism is *progressive* (just like many diseases), it induces its proxy, the Democrat Party, to become more socialistic. Not only do liberals have no aversion to our taxes being raised, but they almost never inquire precisely what the government is doing with the taxpayers' money (besides waste it), as if it's none of our business. As an apparently wise person once noted, the conservative's favorite holiday is the 4th of

July while the liberal's favorite holiday is the 15th of April. With liberalism, almost always, the word "comprehensive" involves government coercion. Liberals tell the discontented common folk: "Republicans want to take away YOUR [insert government subsidy or entitlement here] to benefit their rich friends." The operative word in the previous sentence is "your." As if it's a birthright. It wouldn't work well politically if they told the voters the more accurate: "Republicans want government to rescind the allowance it presently gives you." Liberal comedian Bill Maher once claimed that President Ronald Reagan's tax cut "strangulated the economy." Like all of those on the left, Maher believes that it's the omnipotent State that stimulates the economy with the money it appropriates and spends. The more that this benevolent State taxes the people and modifies their monetary behavior, the more it can run the economy to perfection. The leftist entertainer evidently infers, as many Americans do, that cutting both taxes and spending would only give us more economic freedom, which in turn, would "strangulate" the economy. To Maher and others, the government and the economy are synonymous, and to starve the great State is to kill the economy. But there ARE Democrats who are ambivalent about government throwing billions of dollars down the proverbial rat hole. That is, they don't like it, but at the same time, the party of FDR fears that fiscal discipline and accountability could result in administrative austerity. That frightens them. You may have observed that liberals never even broach the subject of socialism because they will then be compelled to address it in a positive or negative fashion---and they'd rather not do either one.

In order for post 1965 liberalism to validate itself, it must segue into a subtle form of socialism and then an avowed socialism. To attain the latter, the more one keeps steadily "progressing" leftward and reaching its ideological pinnacle, the more one will need to lie to oneself and subsequently to others. Dodging questions is also a form of dishonesty. Liberals and the far left are fairly likely to avoid giving a "yes" or "no" answer to political questions that call for only a YES or NO reply. They need the answers to socio-economic issues to be in a noncommittal grey area so that obfuscation and the very concept of socialism can thrive. Progressive individuals would rather not recognize that their

advocacy of government social engineering on behalf of the little guy/underdog constitutes narcissism on their part more than it does do-goodism. However, what the reader should ponder is—since the working-class liberal voters look to government to CREATE jobs; does that mean government becomes their Creator? Or is that past tense?

Has anybody ever noticed that only conservatives, never liberals, recite the aphorism, "The road to hell is paved with good intentions?" Well, it's not because the libertarian right has a virtual patent on it. Liberals can't and won't recite it because *good intentions* manifest through government social engineering, which they refuse to disparage even though Hitler engaged in it. And whenever a conservative points out that the second word in the definition of Nazi is "socialist," the progressive left takes umbrage and rebuts that the Nazi use of this term is a misnomer. They're wrong. It is not a misnomer. Those who lean to the left just feel compelled to come to socialism's defense after the description of it as being part of Nazism is divulged. Numerous times, conservatives have written about or verbally condemned fascism, Nazism, and apartheid as being unjust, oppressive, and wrong. But can you name a post-1965 liberal politician, liberal columnist, or any well-known liberal who had said or written a bad word about socialism? The correct answer is NO! You can't. Why not? Because, like a communist is just a socialist in a hurry; a liberal is just a socialist in a closet.

The difference between a liberal and an avowed socialist is that the former's philosophy isn't blatantly socialistic on purpose. The late Rhode Island Senator Claiborne Pell, a liberal, once observed in the 1980s that the USSR's (Union of Soviet SOCIALIST Republic) economic system was decaying and said that one day it would collapse. So naturally, he was a passionate supporter of socialistic economic policies right here in the United States. Pell and other progressive minds claimed that taxes needed to be raised in order to support our infrastructure, knowing full well that their version of the term "infrastructure" was just a Trojan horse for more social spending and entitlements. They believe that raising the debt limit is fiscally RESPONSIBLE, but cutting spending, which is mostly what caused the debt, is IRRESPONSIBLE. When ignorant liberals proclaim that government "manages" or "controls" the

economy, they are perhaps oblivious to their socialistic thought process, but partially correct. That is, it's okay for the all-powerful State to be a traffic cop and judge, not an equalizer or emancipator. But when the liberal/left speaks adoringly of a progressive president who is "going to bring us all together" and promote an "inclusive" agenda, any such attempt is via collectivism and coercion by the almighty State.

"The American people will never knowingly adopt socialism. But under the name of liberalism they will adopt every fragment of the socialist programs, until one day America will be a socialist nation, without knowing how it happened." So said Norman Thomas; the American Socialist Party leader. Fortunately, there are a few of us who disagree with Thomas on the last five words of his assertion, but otherwise, he's pretty accurate. In addition, Mr. Thomas provided us with a rare glimpse of a socialist actually telling the truth. His revealing quote notwithstanding, cogency is the enemy of socialism. To the capitalistic right, verity is quite appealing, but to the socialistic left, it's quite appalling. Nothing about socialism is intelligent or honest. It is merely a utopian emotion that turns into an unmitigated lie whenever struck by reality. Socialism is just liberalism with omnipotent governmental power to command and make the people obey.

CHAPTER 2

Collectivist College Creeps

SINCE AT LEAST the late 1960s, the academic left's doctrine has been based primarily on emotion and arrogance. Leftist lunk-heads on many college campuses disrupt speeches by conservatives (who personify capitalism) in order to prevent others from hearing the truth. For example, spoiled students of the University of California at the People's Republic of Berzerkeley were chanting loudly in order to drown out a speech given back in 1983 by former United Nations Ambassador Jeanne Kirkpatrick. But alas, Ambassador Kirkpatrick was siding with the proponents of liberty in El Salvador, and therefore, didn't deserve the freedom to speak. If a lone college male with a megaphone stood in the middle of a university campus and proclaimed, "I am a Nazi, I love Nazism, and I want so very much for America to live under Nazi totalitarianism," he would be stopped and told that he doesn't have the freedom to make such a "hate speech." On the other hand, if a group of students were to make similar statements about COMMUNISM, they would be applauded by their peers for giving just the opposite of a "hate speech," praised by the faculty as "young people exercising their right to invigoratingly speak their minds" and would be given their own student-funded activity club.

DIVERSITY: The denizens of a university and its supportive town are proud of the DIVERSITY that they have installed at their learning institution. Nobody's going to call them bigots; that's for sure. But would they advocate DIVERSITY elsewhere? How about, for example, the chief

resident at the White House and his or her Cabinet? The entire university liberal/left would reply, "Oh, yes, absolutely." We'd have a President of the United States who is a white man and the vice president is a black woman. The rest of the president's Cabinet and their staff consist of Hispanics, Asians, gay men, lesbians, transvestite transsexuals, dark-skinned albinos, religious atheists, devil worshippers, a few American Indians, and one epileptic midget from Puerto Rico. We'd have a White House that's so diverse that it would need to implement SEVERE restrictions on its diversity.

Now then, would the campus progressives support it? No, they definitely wouldn't, and I'll prove it. I "forgot" to mention that each and every person in this particular White House is a conservative. There are no liberals, no leftists and no moderates. Proof accomplished. Now, let's say that the three branches of the Federal government were to consist ENTIRELY of multi-millionaire, heterosexual white men. There are NO women or minorities. But each and every man is either a liberal or a socialist. Would the liberal/left push for and support such a conglomerate leadership without one iota of DIVERSITY in it, in Washington, DC? Their honest answer is, "Yes, definitely!" Hence, this corroborates that their desire for *diversity* is a veritable sham and a shallow one at that. The university liberals would of course prefer that our nation's capital be a smorgasbord of ethnic origins, race, sexual eccentrics and whatever. But what supersedes that is such government personnel absolutely NEED to lean in a progressive (i.e. socialistic) direction. Liberals feel vindicated when the little guy/underdog joins them in their goal to help the "oppressed" marginalized. The left merely wants surreptitious progressivism under the guise of diversity, the better for the left to succeed. Colleges and universities that have 90 percent white students or more are considered to be NOT DIVERSE enough. The aforementioned belief by the left, however, does not apply to campuses with a 100 percent black student population, meaning no DIVERSITY whatsoever. *Diversity*, in and of itself, really isn't that important to the academic left, unless it's contrived and pretentious.

College students that lean to the left wear their smugness on their sleeves, followed closely behind by the snot from their collective noses.

Logic is to play no part in the noted progressive killjoys' idealistic quest for justice. They like to think that they're being noble whenever they rebel just for the sake of rebelling. Said petulant liberals have been known to wear political buttons which implored Americans to "QUESTION AUTHORITY" (this EXCLUDES communistic educators at elite universities). Now, this writer agrees with the slogan. Authority isn't always right or always wrong. To question authority is to use intellect. Therefore, I add to this slogan, "Question those who question authority" because they too may later on become the authority. Now that's ideal rebellion. The proponents of progressive academia often use the term "blind obedience," because of its fascistic implication, to impugn the motives of those who agree with conservative Republican leaders, like Donald Trump, on political matters. But nobody should ever agree with Trump because he is a Republican or because he was the president. When somebody agrees with a president of any political stripe, that person should be able to explain why our nation's leader is correct.

On the other hand, the college campus brainwashed can more credibly be accused of "blind disagreement" since they, though educated, are unable to explain why a conservative leader is wrong. A much better example of BLIND OBEDIENCE would be a classroom full of left-wing brown-shirts fawning over their Marxist professors and cheering on the great socialist cause despite the millions of deaths and the untold misery that socialism and the pursuit of it has produced since the year 1917. Call these progressive PC zealots what you will: the compassion Gestapo, egalitarian jackboots, the Stepford Wives of Stalinism. Whatever? Student defiance or non-compliance to the current politically correct campus orthodoxy is strictly forbidden. Although, northeastern universities and other havens of leftism DO encourage their students to be independent-minded, as long as these young adults adhere to groupthink. The only distinct difference among similarities between today's Democrat Party-voting college radicals and the dictatorship-adoring youngsters of Germany in the mid 1930's is the lack of virulent anti-Semitism on the part of the former. In the anti-Vietnam war/hippie era of the late 1960s/early 1970s, non-conformity and protest against any type of authority was in vogue. Back then, the liberals in academia reveled in freedom of speech, while the sniveling fanatical left of today's college campus refutes it.

Back then, college radicals demanded that conservative spokesmen come to their university to explain themselves and for lively give-and-take debate with the students and the faculty. Present-day right-wingers who somehow sneak their way onto a podium in an Ivy League auditorium or northeastern re-education campus will just get shouted down by the tolerant left; that is, if the right-wingers don't first get food thrown at them. Left-leaning students don't want to challenge a conservative speaker after his oration, because that conservative would then have the opportunity to challenge them. But no can do; the higher education denizens of the left desire to be enthralled by a utopian vision and socialism-based grandeur. For they are the ANOINTED authority and don't deserve to be challenged or defied. In the college protest heydays of 1965 through 1975, it was the ruling-class political right that was deemed narrow-minded, snobbish, and elitist, as opposed to the free-thinking left with their liberating penchant for anti-authoritarianism, irreverent humor, and dissent against the societal status quo. Currently, these two ideological adversaries have switched the aforementioned character traits.

Progressive college kids jejunely condemn the "I've got mine/I'm on my own" (individualism) philosophy of the capitalistic right as selfishness, but wholeheartedly endorse the "I want what's yours" (redistribution) attitude of the socialistic left. They're all emotion fortified by dishonesty, propelled by a propensity for stupidity which they use to fuel their idealism. These left-leaning college students would like to think that, with their over-reliance on feelings, they can't possibly go wrong. But in their vow not to use reasoning and utilize only self-deceit, the leftist liars of academia fail to recognize their own selfishness when they demand that Washington, DC pay their tuition or provide for them. The lumbering leviathan commonly known as the Federal government is revered by today's "forward-thinking" college students, while "anti-government *hate speech*" (read: anti-socialism language) is to be denounced as disloyalty to the Almighty State. They would never call a liberal Democratic President a "dictator." Such a slur is reserved only for the more conservative Republican who is hostile to statism.

Employing Orwellian doublespeak, these proletariat-loving punks hope to stigmatize hard-line libertarian GOP candidates for public office, precisely because the latter doesn't support the "compassionate" subjugation of the American citizens. Said college kids on the left will call the reader a *fascist* if you are opposed to groupthink compulsion, government-enforced collectivism, societal conformity mandated by Washington, DC, and you disagree with their desire for strong-armed (but well-intentioned) statism for the people. They, themselves, are NOT in the least bit AGAINST the *totalitarianism* of fascism but merely dislike fascism's lack of empathy for the underdog. Collectivist college creeps insist on believing that coercive egalitarianism cannot possibly make the transition to a cruel, uncaring despotism. They erroneously think that in order for the United States to stay far away from Nazism, we need to reject actual liberty. Our progressive youngsters deceive themselves when they infer that an authoritarian dictatorship stems from a free-market, God-fearing America abiding by the Constitution. But it is they who will not condemn ALL statist social engineering, which is where authoritarianism emanates. In a nutshell, the left-wing Politically Correct students that dominate college campuses think that top-down socio-political tyranny derives from the ideology and policies of "those anti government type" conservatives. Wow! Doublespeak, indeed!

CHAPTER **3**

Welcome to the Nanny State

THERE'S A PLACE 2,551 miles southwest of Los Angeles. It's a paradise where the trade winds gently blow, the palm trees softly sway, and most of its inhabitants worship the Almighty (government). In at least the last two decades, the State of Hawaii has become more restrictive, although they have always applied, as the socialist editors at the islands' main newspaper have proclaimed, a *hands-on* government. And it has nothing to do with a certain redistributionist community organizer who was born there in 1961. In Hawaii's efforts to thwart thoughtless behavior, numerous waterfalls (such as Kipu Falls and Opeaka'a Falls on Kauai, where a few individuals have died through their own carelessness and swimming holes, e.g. the "Toilet Bowl," an ocean inlet at Hanauma Bay) have become illegal for people to venture into. Not only will the State of Hawaii NEVER rescind these restrictions, but you can bet your bottom tourism dollars that there will be more OFF LIMITS signs to come. Authorities on Oahu have NOT closed down Sandy Beach (a rough, crashing wave could cripple the average-body boarder) and Kapena Falls (leptospirosis sickness), both, deaths possibly resulting.....YET.

Starting in the 1990s, besides the noted waterfalls on the Garden Island (Kauai), a visit to others also became strictly forbidden. Hawaii's governor, with the help of law enforcement, should order that barbed wire fences or ten-foot-tall cement walls be built around the entrances of said attractions. Yes, such barricades will ruin the beautiful tropical scenery, but at least they would prevent the tourists from frolicking in the waterfall pool and enjoying themselves. The only exception to the authorities closing down the Aloha State's hot spots is the Kalalau Trail on Kauai. Although, there have been far more deaths (over ninety) on this hiking trail than all the waterfalls of Hawaii COMBINED, it will never be shut down by those at the state capital because said adventure is far too famous, prestigious, and popular and would cause enormous public outrage. In fact, this hiking trail on the Na Pali coast has what is regarded as one of the *top ten* most dangerous beaches (more than three dozen people drowning) in the WORLD.....Hanakapiai Beach. And the real nice thing about this beach, I think you'll agree, is that it has no lifeguards. ENJOY, if you go swimming there. Oh, don't forget to thank Hawaii's obviously impartial and highly principled lawmakers and their conscientious integrity for allowing you to. In any case, the once aptly named Aloha State is supposed to be a place of fun and relaxation, not a veritable outside nursing home where your safety is guaranteed. The politicians in Honolulu should be extra careful or they will subsequently make it against the law for each and every citizen of Hawaii to be self-responsible. Indeed, if individuals aren't made to suffer the consequences of their actions, then the state itself will suffer the consequences of those individuals in the court of law. In order to avoid certain litigation in the future, the 50th state's lawmakers will put more restrictions on pleasure-seekers, and rightfully so. It's either this, or the State of Hawaii can have every adult who lives on or visits their islands sign a legally binding note of SELF-RESPONSIBILITY and the governor should then tell the trial lawyers and other ambulance-chasers to go pound sand (at the beach of their choice). But then again, it wouldn't be surprising if the government-adoring denizens of this Pacific paradise, particularly the Hawaiians themselves, accept a tacit authoritarianism to live under, if it's ostensibly for their own good.

In all fairness to the Aloha State, because it's just a group of small islands in the middle of the Pacific and feels isolated because it IS isolated, they tend to look to Washington, DC and local government as nannies. But nannyism has spread over the continental United States as well, in order to save the people from themselves. Many, if not most, of our nation's citizens welcome it. Americans are perhaps aware that since the turn of the twentieth century up until the 1980s, the vast majority of swimming pools at hotels and motels had diving boards. Today, you cannot find even one of these places of accommodation in which their swimming pool has a diving board. Like the State of Hawaii, they're scared to death of lawsuits. My wild guess is that sometime in the 1980s, a little boy tried to do a flip off the diving board and hit his head on it, which sent him to the emergency room. His parents then sued the hotel or motel for having the audacity to have a diving board attached to their swimming pool....and WON! Other places of accommodation took notice of this lawsuit and totally eliminated the diving board, while partly helping to eliminate personal responsibility.

Also in the 1980s and going back some 160 years, American children DID NOT wear helmets when riding bicycles. Nowadays, it's the law in at least twenty-one states. If a *helmetless* fifteen-year-old boy, in one of these states, is riding a bicycle down the sidewalk of a small suburban street where there's hardly any traffic, and a cop sees him, he's in trouble. Conversely, it is perfectly legal for kids, while riding in the back of a pickup truck flying down the highway at 65 miles an hour, to NOT wear helmets or safety belts. If the aforementioned youngsters don't take flight and make it home okay, they could open up a lemonade stand just like American children have done for over a century. But unlike yester-decade, they will need a license. Yup, that's right. Across the country, from the redwood forests to the Gulf Stream waters, there have been many stories of police shutting down little boys' and girls' lemonade stands that were in violation of town ordinances. Perhaps the local authorities would allow them to sell lemonade if these children wore helmets? Some people in New York wanted to ban an ice cream truck from going near a playground or park because it was too tempting for children. This is yet another example of adults absolving their own responsibility in order for the nanny state to protect their own children from life's negative consequences (e.g. ice cream trucks, unauthorized lemonade stands, diving boards and bareheaded bicycle riding).

The former mayor of the city that never sleeps, Michael Bloomberg, wanted to ban large sodas and sugary drinks. There was no word on whether the mayor forbade HIS residents from drinking two or more MEDIUM sodas, or if he wanted to outlaw pizza parlors and donut shops. But there was a rumor going around that Mr. Bloomberg had ordered all restaurant owners who sold soup with a lot of calories and carbohydrates to place signs on their restaurant windows that shouted, "NO SOUP FOR YOU!" Also, New York, Chicago, and Washington, DC have the nation's strictest gun laws but also have the most murders. Gun control advocates have been at a loss to explain this. They probably don't want the American people to know that 1930s Germany also had very strict gun control laws.

Back in the late 1990s and early 2000s, sport utility vehicles (SUVs) were all the newfound rage, despite being a cause célèbre by liberals calling for the nanny state to ban them. It seems that the liberals didn't like Americans enjoying SUVs. These are vehicles that the paternalistic left said were too dangerous to drive, blocked other drivers' views, and wasted gasoline. Oddly, these progressives didn't have a problem with motorcycles (dangerous) and their helmetless drivers (careless). Nor did they mind trucks and vans (blocking other drivers' views) and young people driving around town in their compact cars—mere teenagers who were not going to work or any important destination but just driving aimlessly, apathetically and WASTING GAS. And this writer won't mention our citizens, particularly the elderly, who have gas heat in their homes and their thermostats up too high in autumn. But I digress. What probably happened regarding the SUV was some liberal Hollywood celebrities were reported to have been seen driving the big, gas-guzzling monsters, which tended to silence and undermine advocates of the nanny state to influence the common folk. You rarely, if ever, hear about the once controversial and evil SUV in the news anymore. Present-day liberals will not denounce the SUV like the liberals of yore once did, but they will happily own one—a big, gas-guzzling, expensive one!

The majority of the American people, including most conservatives, support a socio-economic SAFETY NET for those who have hit hard times (born poor, or lost a job, self-irresponsibility, etc.). There's only one thing wrong with this picture. The United States has never had a socio-economic safety net—or at least, not a working one. Whether it is folks living in Appalachia or in urban or rural areas, there have always been those who lived in, or are living in, abject poverty, despite the prevalent nanny state. So where is this "safety net" that we keep hearing so much about? It's been a rhetorical fraud perpetrated on the gullible. It's been the great political dupe that gives the people hope. Some will reply to the author that there IS a safety net but that some unfortunate souls have "fallen through" it. If that's the case, what good is a "safety net" that belies its name, and why hasn't nanny come to the aid of its apparent victims? Let's put it this way: If a certain passenger is on a cruise ship with safety nets all around the entire vessel, and this passenger tumbles overboard and somehow FALLS THROUGH the safety net and the captain or crew witness the incident, should that man, now treading water, be rescued? Or should he be left in the ocean to drown because, after all, this man has already fallen through the "safety net?" If the United States had a REAL social safety net, there wouldn't be any hunger, homelessness, or poverty whatsoever. The ONLY authentic nanny state SAFETY NET that would guarantee our safety, security, and well-being and one that would definitely work, is socialism. And you wouldn't be against that, now would you? Whenever the citizens are not held accountable for their actions, we lose more of our liberty via more government laws. But then again, losing our liberty isn't discernible if nanny state paternalism compensates for this loss.

"If you want government to intervene domestically, you're a liberal. If you want government to intervene overseas, you're a conservative. If you want government to intervene everywhere, you're a moderate. If you don't want government to intervene anywhere, you're an extremist." Syndicated columnist, Joseph Sobran.

CHAPTER **4**

Catchwords on the Left

FROM TIME TO time one will hear certain words or phrases employed by the American left. The following is a guide which should prove resourceful in detecting what the left really means when they utilize such terms. For instance, to have our country move "FOWARD" and reach its progressive pinnacle is to continue the betterment of the people of America. To this day, the majority of conservatives don't even realize that the term "progressive," as used in the political arena, is a euphemism for "socialistic" at all times. There's not a soul on earth that can name an economic policy that is definitely PROGRESSIVE and is loved and desired by progressives, but it is NOT socialistic or conducive to socialism. Under Marxist theory, going from capitalism to socialism to communism is "progressive" because it benefits humanity. *Progressivism* is relying on one's emotion, employing wishful thinking, immersing oneself in utopianism, and then just plain flat-out lying. The adjective "progressive" is particularly useful to the left because of its double meaning.

As a result, the dupe or dolt who is unsophisticated will be taken in by the left's charade and will likely support any cause that employs said adjective. For example, a child going to school and becoming more educated while entering into a higher grade every year is moving in a PROGRESSIVE (proceeding and improving) manner. And that's good, is it not? Likewise, a broken leg that's getting better is said to be making PROGRESS. That can only be encouraging news. Therefore, it behooves

Americans to desire and support, with the exception of disease, but especially in politics, anything that's "progressive." The left's stratagem of using this word has been successful because most voters are gullible and fail to decipher it. This author dislikes crypto-socialists for not admitting to being socialists. But I don't blame them the least bit for not doing so and understand and agree with their tactic. Yours truly would do the same. They and other clandestine socialists (e.g. Gloria Steinem, Congressman Gerald Nadler) are well aware that the best way to help the socialist cause is to not admit to being socialists. They fear, and rightfully so, that they would lose any influence they may have. At any rate, other euphemisms for socialism are "social change," "economic democracy," and "social justice." The pathway to socialism is sometimes known as "fighting the good fight", working for "the movement" or "the struggle", "the struggle continues", "fundamental transformation" and govermental "investment in the people." Circa the year 2022, various progressives longingly spoke of our country "making the *transition*" which is another way of saying that we the people are "moving to a better place for a better future" that in turn, is a euphemistic way of saying that "AMERICA WILL SOON LIVE UNDER SOCIALISM."

Being "heartless" and "old-fashioned" are ascribed to anybody whose "values" do not go "forward" in bringing "change" to the American people (which, of course, is for their own good). "Reactionary" and "regressive" are terms that are attributed by the left to conservatives and right-wing causes that benefit free-market capitalism. If we could go backwards in time through the last one hundred and twenty years, we would notice a sharp reduction in the size of government, and hence, a nation becoming more capitalistic (more free). Well, a REACTIONARY (unlike your typical blueblood, wants-so-very-much-to-be-liked, country-club Republican), is someone who REACTS to our country's "progress" toward "a more caring and humane society." The reactionary does this by advocating "REGRESSIVE" measures (cutting actual spending, not just the rate of growth, pushing liberty via deregulation, and trying to abolish government departments like the IRS). A reactionary is someone who wants the country's leftward drift to not just come to a standstill (which is the mindset of your commonplace conservative), America's

trajectory toward socialism; but rather to take America "BACKWARDS" (LESS domineering government) in a capitalistic direction.

In essence, the term "reactionary" is a political attitude that doesn't necessarily side with or benefit the *marginalized* (the little guy/underdog/downtrodden). Said term is merely a truth that is not conducive to socialism—the ultimate lie. Quite simply, a person who is a reactionary (in an ideological sense) is an anti-socialist. All those on the far left are well aware of this. Unfortunately, most of those on the liberty-loving right are not. The ubiquitous ideological label "oppressive", when used by the far-left, means inducing liberty and freedom upon the American people. Such long-time communist jargon was particularly prevalent during the 1980s. "Fascist" is another catchword that is used to denigrate the conservative right. Actually, conservatism (particularly of the libertarian kind) is far more likely to bring us toward laissez-faire capitalism rather than the totalitarianism the left-wing fascists (excuse the redundancy) would thrust upon this great constitutional republic. But most of those on the left know damn well that they cry "fascism" in order to demonize what they're well aware is actually ECONOMIC FREEDOM / SOCIAL LIBERTY (aka *capitalism*). And the political left LIES like this in order to dissuade the ignorant and gullible ordinary citizen from ruminating in a conservative/pro-capitalism manner, but instead, reflexively reacting in a NON-thinking way which is always conducive to building socialism. The aforementioned progressives (especially college kids) delude themselves when they insist on believing that socialism (caring, sharing and humane) is the exact opposite of fascism (cruel, heartless and intolerant). Like socialism is the stepping-stone to communism, fascism is just a short, quick pathway to socialism. When the liberal/left complains about various Republicans "moving further to the right", what they're really conveying is that the GOP is trying to induce more freedom onto the American people, is adhering to staunch Constitutional conservatism and are not vacillating and capitulating to liberalism like they're supposed to.

We have all heard the catchwords "Big Oil", "Big Tobacco" and "Big Pharma" (pharmaceutical) used by liberals, moderates, and the media in public discourse. Why do they always insert the term "big" in front of the products of said free-market businesses? Why not just call them "the oil

companies" or "the tobacco enterprises?" Do you, the reader, ever hear these talking heads refer to the manufacturers of Kellogg's Corn Flakes and General Mills Cheerios as "Big Cereal"? Do the American people in general label the makers of home cooling units as "Big Air Conditioner"? How about "Big Jewelry," "Big Bicycle," or "Big Kitchen Appliances"? No, they don't. Not yet. But the reason why our political "superiors" make sure to mention the word "big" is because the nefarious oil, tobacco and pharmaceutical companies have taken advantage of the put-upon citizen and have done financially better than they have a right to. They are BIG bullies who need to be cut down to size. You, the little guy, won't be able to take on these giant corporations by yourself and that's when Big Government (the little guy's best friend) comes to your rescue. Hey, I've got a fantastic idea! Wouldn't it be great if Big Government slew (nationalized or at least controlled) Big Oil, Big Tobacco and Big Pharma, thereby eliminating their threatening of you and your resentment of them?

McCarthyism: If the author of this article claimed that folk singers Woody Guthrie and Pete Seeger were both commies, I would be accused of McCarthyism and be automatically dismissed by the largely naïve and ignorant public as being wrong because the infamous and overzealous firebrand (Joe McCarthy) from Wisconsin was also known as being wrong. The public's absence of discernment notwithstanding, the mere association would, unfortunately, stick. The defenders of the late folk singers couldn't simply contradict my accusation because that would be very likely to prompt a research to find out if Guthrie and Seeger really were Reds. That's precisely what the left doesn't want. Instead, they would be far more effective by stigmatizing yours truly with the charge of "McCarthyism" and thereby discouraging any curiosity the public might have had in the first place. But I'll spare our citizens the itch. Although Woody Guthrie was never a card-carrying Party member, he did refer to himself as a communist and wrote over 170 columns for their newspaper. Pete Seeger WAS a card-carrying member of the Communist Party USA from 1942 until 1949 and remained Red thereafter. Before he passed away, his wealth was estimated to be over four million dollars. With the exception of his spouse, comrade Pete Seeger shared his money with no one. Good for him!

CHAPTER 5

Opinionated Bits and Pieces

REGARDING POLITICAL CORRECTNESS (cultural Marxism), there are individuals who are against it but will not take the initiative to disobey it. They are merely timid cultural conformists waiting for a popular anti-PC uprising of fed-up Americans who will finally exhibit more political clout than the PC left has. If this happens, the reticent sheep will then and then only, jump on the bandwagon. But it takes decisive citizens to form a parade and stand up to the fascistic "anti-fascist" brown-shirts on the left. Political correctness along with wokeism/*cancel culture* is a toxic stain that must be wiped out if we want to save our Constitutional republic. This is particularly the case with those working in journalism or literature. For example: A book-publishing gentleman would be aghast that a customer would want him to publish the customer's book that supports Nazism, which the former won't do. But the publisher would have no qualms about producing a book that exalts communism even though he, himself, is definitely not a communist. For it's not the subject matter of either disreputable ideology but the peer pressure of political correctness, which is the scourge of progressivism that deters the publisher. The man is well aware that the conservative, liberty-loving right will never gather up an angry mob of hundreds to harass and threaten this publisher, and that's precisely the reason why he isn't scared of them and therefore doesn't respect them, like he does the leftist bullies. However, what the intimidated book-producer may not be cognizant of is that he has already permitted political correctness/

wokeism to dictate what said gentleman can and cannot do, even though no leftist thought-crime police ever contacted him. In doing so, the pusillanimous publisher is surrendering to what he believes to be imminent cancel culture, by obeying their wishes and allowing the far left to become de facto co-owners of his business, or they could put him out of business. A manuscript sent to the noted publisher can derisively mock Evangelical Christians and will soon be a book on sale at Barnes and Noble. But a manuscript is considered non grata if it ever so gently ridicules Muslims. Proponents of political correctness (pro-censorship) will tolerate a person who demurely disapproves of them…for the time being, just as long as that person tows the line. Currently, the progressivism Gestapo recognizes that any attempt at thought control via government edicts or left-wing harassment of someone for reading the book *1984,* is a tad premature and not feasible. But the publisher, among book distributers like Barnes and Noble and Amazon and others; is undoubtedly a supporter of the First Amendment and very likely disagrees with political correctness. But if he abides by it then this man is well aware that there's a yellow streak running down his back and that he is complicit in the detriment being done to our free (so far) country.

If a religious, white Christian-bakery owner CAN'T, by law, REFUSE a gay couple that wants said bakery to make them a wedding cake with little same-sex figurines on it, does that mean that a black cake-maker CAN'T legally TURN DOWN self-declared members of the Ku Klux Klan who want this baker to fix them up a cake that's in the shape of a noose?

The rape or sexual assault of a woman is a traumatic and horrible crime that more than a few of them have experienced. But the vast majority of women who always vote Democrat will agree with this writer that sometimes a rape or sexual attack should be downplayed if not altogether ignored and disregarded. Like, for example: If a man is a left-wing progressive candidate running for national office and actually is guilty of rape or sexual abuse of a lady, then she, the victim/survivor, should play it smart by keeping quiet for the time being and not rat on

the guy. You, the reader, may ask, "But shouldn't this man, this low-life criminal, be punished by the law?" Well, sure he should, kind of, I suppose. Though, one must take into account that since the alleged violator is a liberal or socialist and could very well become one of our nation's top lawmakers, the noted assailant would at least make up for what he did by his supporting Roe V. Wade, advocating closing the gender wage gap and backing other women's issues (leftist policies). And that's what really matters, when all is said and done. On the other hand, it would be politically and strategically smart for Democratic women to LIE about being sexually accosted by a politically right-leaning man running for public office or becoming a Justice of the Supreme Court, since his ideology (Constitutionalism / anti-statism) is deleterious to women. This being the case, a conservative fellow is to be deemed guilty of the crime until proving that he's innocent. Plainly, the female self-declared victim deserves to be BELIEVED while the accused male (Republican) deserves to be immediately demonized and tarnished for life. Correspondingly, a woman who was once GROPED by a conservative president makes her more of a victim / survivor than if she was RAPED by a liberal president. So, ideologically speaking, it is quite possible and even probable that a male political candidate or lawmaker who is a liberal Democrat and is widely acknowledged to be a sexual assaulter could turn out to be the woman's best friend. As the *Mallard Fillmore* comic strip once quipped, "Always believe the woman!...(unless you like the man's politics)."

There is absolutely no truth to the rumor that Transportation Secretary Pete Buttigieg engaged in a me'nage a' trois with Sam Brinton and Dylan Mulvaney. Mr. Buttigieg is a married man.

Citizens who look to the government as their benefactor are in direct proportion to those who forgive public servants in political office who are scoundrels and liars. The people don't really mind a politician who lies, just as long as his lie is also a promise that he made to them. This lawmaker had initially assuaged their concerns, and that is what's most important. Besides, his constituents also lie when they say that they "will never forgive" Congressman so-and-so for supporting

such-and-such legislation that his constituents disliked, and then proceed to, in essence, FORGIVE this politician by voting for him in the next election. But said office-holder knows that he can easily afford to disappoint some voters, because they adore him on a slew of other matters just as essential to them. The same citizens particulary appreciate the campaigning male candidate who bounds enthusiastically onto the stage (jacket and tie off) while rolling up his sleeves. This symbolizes to the hopeful audience that he emphasizes with the conventional blue-collar toiler, because, look at him, the man is *ROLLING UP HIS SLEEVES*, which indicates that he's ready to get his hands dirty and go to work for the common folk that he loves. Wonderful! The office seeker's campaign slogan is *(Insert name here)* ---"He's for The People." Nothing hackneyed about that cliché. Said political aspirant refers to the electorate as "HARD-WORKING Americans" (buttering up the crowd stands a very good chance of getting them to like the candidate and vote for him) and will probably trot out the trite, vapid slogan, "Washington Is Broken," which implies that he's going to go there and fix it. Actually, our nation's capital isn't broken. It's doing just fine, thank you. Washington, DC would be broken only if it stopped being corrupt and harmful to the republic.

Have you ever noticed that it's always Republican politicians that are asked, in reference to their rhetoric, to "tone it down," never a Democrat politician? Republicans, especially the conservative ones, are going to have to realize that conservatism will always be more controversial, provocative, and "shocking" because it advocates a thought process that is steeped in logic and intellectual honesty and it often embraces an unsympathetic truth. Conservatism is also unlikable because it's seemingly against the little guy/underdog, not socially lenient, doesn't allow for self-deception, and argues against the government subsidizing of wrongful behavior. Any successful attempt to TONE DOWN conservative rhetoric will almost always convert into Democratic policy.

What do the following words and phrases presently have in common? Free-market types; the stars and stripes; the rich; the greeting

"Merry Christmas," the red, white and blue; the Catholic church; blonde hair and blue-eyed; God, country and hunting; Christians; and white people. The answer: They're all pejoratives.

Many of America's left-leaning Jews have a propensity or desire to conflate Holocaust revisionism with the conservative (capitalistic) Right. This is because Judaism, the majority of progressive Jews assume, is supposed to espouse compassionate and benevolent government social engineering which the Right has an animus toward, in the same way that Holocaust deniers possess hostility toward Jews themselves. But yours truly does not believe and will NEVER believe that exactly six million Jews died in the Holocaust. What I do know is that Adolph Hitler hated capitalism, and in 1941, remarked that 90 percent of the components that brought him to power were made up of left-wing elements. With Nazism (nationalistic socialism) and communism (international socialism) merely being two sides of a bad socialist coin, it's very comforting to acknowledge the fact that no American Jew has ever joined the Communist Party USA. You see, Jews are smart people; they know better.

In order for the United States to remain a free country, we must continue to be white-dominated. Capitalism (liberty/freedom) is the *White man's socio-economic system* and bedrock while socialism (subsidation/security) is the minorities socio-political underpinning and eventual goal. Whites espouse and practice individualism and self-dependence far more than minorities do. Blacks, Mexicans, Puerto Ricans, and other Hispanics (excluding Cubans over the age of forty) tend to think socialistically. As in "I want my government to provide for me and take care of me as much as it possibly can and give me free stuff." That's a lot of "me" that they care about. But the vast majority of minorities don't really care about America's $31 trillion dollar debt, as of this writing; nor do they respect and appreciate the Constitution ("a right-wing document written by rich white men"), if they were to be quite honest. What blacks and Hispanics need, which would benefit both them and an already financially bankrupt society, is to have more liberty and fiscal self-responsibility injected into their

lives via drastic social-spending cuts. Such a governmental action would result in said minorities NOT having children that they and the country can't afford. In the not-too-distant future, if most of our voters are not white, identity politics will reign supreme and the nation will quickly descend into a socialist tyranny. What was once thought of as and called "our American culture" will be impugned and maligned as "our white culture" and later on smeared as "our white supremacist culture" and subsequently disregarded and rejected by a timid go-along-to-get-along public. Mark my words.

P.S. Cries of "racism" and "bigotry" about this essay are not only irrelevant, but also a validation of my detractors' belief that what the author wrote is true by their intentional neglect to write or explain any disagreement.

The difference between a white conservative and a white liberal is that the former will claim that a white man's deed of having found a cure for leukemia is more important and praiseworthy than a black woman's deed of inventing a toothbrush that won't snap in two. The white liberal, on the other hand, will insist that what the latter did is equally beneficial to society and that said black woman deserves just as much, if not more, commendation.

The National Rifle Association is not so much detested by the liberal/left because the former "likes guns" per se, but because they appreciate and cherish the freedom for Americans to own guns. In the past, when a crazed, unbalanced gunman opened fire on crowds, killing many innocent people, especially children, a grieving nation projected its wrath on the NRA. Loved ones had died as a result of a mass shooting. The killer himself was either shot to death or was going straight to prison for life and therefore wasn't available for public retribution in order to diminish America's grief. Hence, the nation's bereavement needed an immediate and convenient scapegoat (the NRA) to facilitate our revenge for justice. Analogous to gun ownership, if an extremely irate and malevolent driver purposely runs over and kills a small group of jaywalkers, it is at least somewhat the fault of numerous car clubs across the United States. Men who are members of these clubs have an irrational worship

of automobiles. Many of these adult males harbor a childish obsession with owning more than three cars---powerful machines (some can travel faster than 160MPH) that will easily end a human life by making contact with it. The Federal government should implement a law that PROHIBITS a citizen sixteen years of age or older owning in excess of two cars. The more of these dangerous and unnecessary vehicles that our government confiscates, the safer the American people will be.

The liberal/left earnestly believes that the American people *have a right to a job*, though they are against the American people's RIGHT TO WORK.

The Tea Party is wholeheartedly opposed to corporate welfare but still disliked by some 75 percent of the American people. The redistribution-minded Occupy Wall Street movement is/was more popular than the libertarian-minded Tea Party. It is precisely because the former's doctrine is socialistic that they are rarely thought of as being DANGEROUS and EXTREME like that of the latter group and the robust economic freedom of the United States during the first decade of the twentieth century. The Tea Party is hated because of its insistence on fiscal discipline and its obstinacy in wanting to reduce the national debt, which implies seriously cutting government domestic social spending. It was the Tea Party-inspired gridlock of Congress in 2011, it is believed, which temporarily slowed down the much-needed expansion of the Federal government and the enormous healing powers of its legislation. Currently, the media and the majority of voters are hoping that the Establishment Republicans will rescue the GOP from the Tea Party types so that the former can get back to going along, albeit grudgingly, with the Democrats. Much to the chagrin of the Tea Party, when the government steals money from Peter to pay Paul, most of the American people will always side with Paul.

In a year 2009 speech on the subject of racial issues, Attorney General Eric Holder said that the United States was "in too many ways, essentially a nation of cowards." Some took umbrage, although the former attorney general was correct. But then, blacks like Holder are allowed to vent their frustration or anger regarding whites because they, the blacks, are "second-class citizens." The same cannot be said about whites. For it is particularly the white race (*the privileged*) at whom political wokeism is aimed, made to stifle the opinions of, and subsequently bring down. And it's whites, especially, whom the PC police call on to abide by it. But it is Eric Holder's liberal politics and its tacit endorsement of wokeism that makes us a NATION OF COWARDS. There are just too many white people in America who correctly believe that they need to be cowards in order to take the side of blacks who have said or done something wrong.

A Planned Parenthood doctor should be permitted to legally perform abortions here in the United States for eternity, but only if his or her last name is Mengele. Nonetheless, a seven month old fetus does NOT have a right to a life due to the fact that said unborn baby never spoke out about wanting to live when it had the chance to.

Liberalism is emotional honesty, but it is intellectually dishonest. And for those two reasons, millions of Americans will be attracted to it. In the battle against liberalism, truth and facts will lose much of the time because it's the bleeding hearts' solicitude that deserves priority. In this respect, truth and facts are not necessarily desirable. One facet of liberalism that its proponents are devoted to is the siren call of GOOD INTENTIONS. No matter what the actual result of what liberalism brings, as long as the liberal adheres to good intentions, then he or she cannot possibly do wrong. Example: A family of six, inside their house on a cold winter night, phones their next-door liberal neighbor and tells the man that their home heating unit has broken down and that they're starting to freeze. The compassionate neighbor runs over and quickly douses the house with gasoline and sets it on fire, killing the entire family in the process. Now then, did the man do anything wrong? The answer.....NO, he didn't! Because the now dead family's liberal neighbor was caring and had strictly GOOD INTENTIONS (the nice man was just trying to keep the family warm), he does not deserve to be blamed for the tragedy. If feelings reign supreme, then liberalism will win any debate.

Why do the American people think that it's clever when somebody asks the "clever" question, "Does a tree that falls in the forest make a sound if nobody was around to hear it?" Because the answer to that question is a resounding, common sense....YES. If you were right next to a large tree when it fell, would you hear the noise? Likewise, would the same falling tree make a noise if you WEREN'T there to hear it? Does a car going 55 miles an hour and crashing head on into another car make a noise? How would you know if you weren't there to hear it? This "clever" question about the falling tree is made by the same smart people who ask, "Why is there no cure for the common cold?" But there is. It's called blowing your nose, taking antihistamine, and waiting three to six days. And then they also wonder why we can put a man on the moon but we can't find a cure for world hunger. But we already have a cure. It's called EATING FOOD.

Some liberal citizens have suggested that, in order to save capitalism; the US government must monetarily reinforce Medicaid, Medicare and welfare along with a slew of other entitlements and save Social Security. Liberal individuals say this, even though they condoned the Democrats' raiding of Social Security to help pay for the former three. But the more important point is that it's because of capitalism (economic freedom) that we have citizens needing government subsidies and protection. Since this is the case, why don't we just eradicate capitalism and be done with the problem? If we must implement socialistic economic policies in order to "save capitalism," does this not imply that socialism is superior? Why dawdle by moving ever so casually in a progressive direction, when immediately placing America lock, stock, and barrel under socialism would promptly improve the lives of millions? After all, if we became a veritable full-fledged socialist country some 25 years from now, millions of our present-day citizens, particularly the elderly, won't live that long to experience its joy. Socialism is assured equality and will benefit all Americans, with the exception of rich white men. Meanwhile, capitalism is INEQUALITY and will only benefit rich white men. The conclusion is that socialism is obviously morally and socially superior. No, society can't save capitalism by going in a socialistic direction, but some of us can hopefully convince the rest of us to deceive ourselves that society is doing just that.

A government that does not subsidize the nuclear family is extremely likely to reinforce the nuclear family.

Most Americans who vote Democrat tend to look at the US Supreme Court as being a miniature version of the United Nations. That is, the nine members of our republic's highest judicial court REPRESENT different groups of citizens nationwide. Or at least, they are SUPPOSED TO. For example: The late black judge, Thurgood Marshal, while he was on the bench (and still alive), was "supposed to" represent black America. And he did, because he was a liberal. Judge Clarence Thomas, a black man, is also SUPPOSED TO represent the same but doesn't, because he's a conservative. Then there's Chief Justice John Roberts, who represents ostensible conservative lawmakers that will back away from supporting ACTUAL conservative (read: controversial) decisions because they don't want to cause pandemonium, are concerned about their legacy and strongly desire to be liked by the liberal media. Also, we have Sonia Sotomayor, who sticks up for Latinos (both wise and unwise), plus the deceased Ruth Bader Ginsburg, who went to bat for liberal women, and Elana Kagan speaks on behalf of Jewish people. Also, there was Sandra Day O'Connor, nominated before the more erudite Robert Bork, merely because she's a woman. She was the appointed spokesperson for moderate Americans. The late Antonin Scalia was voted onto the Supreme Court to defend the interests of our Italian citizens. And finally, Judge David Souter, who, while on the nation's highest court, represented men who were once believed to be cogent conservatives, but were actually mild-mannered milquetoasts.

Washington, DC has the highest per pupil spending ($25,000 per student) in the country but the worst test scores and the lowest graduation rates. Yet, after acknowledging this, the majority of Americans under the age of forty will still continue to believe that more spending is the answer to the problem. It's plainly a case of stupidity subsidizing indolence.

Speaking of which, you'll realize that the American people really are stupid when after they watch an important televised political debate, our citizens will select the winner of it as the candidate who "came across as the most human." Perhaps the people initially thought that each debating candidate was actually a pork chop or a box of cereal, and that these debaters had to prove them wrong. In any case, may God save America!

On occasions in the past, the United States has allegedly behaved immorally, which President Obama thought was discreditable to our nation, where he lectured the American people, "That's not who we are." Yet the ex-president has famously stated that he wanted to "fundamentally transform America" in order to, supposedly, get away from customarily "who we are." In other words, Mr. Obama subscribes to our country's long-held beliefs and traditions ("who we are") and now he wants it stopped ("fundamental transformation"). Obama either doesn't notice or doesn't want to acknowledge his self-contradiction. But then again, neither do his supporters.

Many, if not most, American women would prefer their male doctors to be handsome. This allows the former to have a vicarious romance with an attractive man who is concerned about the lady and is taking good care of her. A surrogate (and *perfect*) husband, if you will. It's analogous to the way that women desire male Democrat politicians to also be physically appealing. For an adult female to fantasize about the aforementioned *ideal* representative is, she feels, to gain solace and make her life worth living. But a gentleman lawmaker who is good-looking though a hard-line Republican is negated by his Constitutional conservatism, which is non-responsive to a woman's needs and wants.

Over the past century, neither the Communist Party USA nor the Ku Klux Klan has inflicted any significant and permanent damage on our nation as a whole, although the former has been a far greater influence on more US citizens than the latter has. Thousands, if not millions, of black Americans since the year 1919 have been enraptured and inspired by communist doctrine, not the least bit realizing or caring that communism would actually make their lives infinitely more miserable than the KKK did or could ever hope to do.

The below essay was written in the summer of 2019:

For our next American president, all we need is a Republican who is just ever so slightly LESS conservative than Donald Trump, and the government will grow by leaps and bounds. This growth of government will incur more rules, regulations and restrictions, the better to run the country and society to perfection, which is something that the government is reknowned for. But the economy will take a severe downturn and we will be ankle-deep in fascistic waters. The term "fascism", a precursor to socialism, will become very convenient to the left because they will be able to blame the president's "fascistic" policies (tax breaks for the rich, etc.) for the catastrophically bad economy and most Americans will believe it because they want to. Though, in reality, it was more government control that the left espouses and the people dutifully accept; that's the real culprit. But since most Americans erroneously equate libertarian conservatism with fascism, coupled with the realization that the United States is not currently living under government ownership of the means of production (socialism), our citizens will ignorantly infer that the free-market private sector is responsible for our crushing debt and imminent financial downfall. The phrase "United We Stand, Divided We Fall" should be changed to the exact opposite: "Divided We Stand, United We Fall" if a once capitalistic America continues on its socialistic path.

A black mother in her late thirties is very likely to be PROUD that her fifteen-year-old daughter gave birth, while a white mother also in her late thirties is more likely to be ASHAMED that her fifteen-year-old daughter became pregnant. The reader may respond, "Well, blacks and whites have a different set of values." Yeah, can't argue with you there.

Prelude: Reader, before perusing the below essay on former President Trump, pretend that it's February 2020.

Never Trumpers are not really conservatives as some of them claim. To contrast with America's essentially liberal cultural environment, the aforementioned merely like labeling themselves *conservative* because they're attracted to the contrarian and idiosyncratic nature of conservatism. Besides having contempt for his supporters, Never Trumper Republicans dislike the 45th president more than they do Hillary Clinton. And not just personally but politically! If Never Trumpers actually voted for Hillary Clinton in the November 2016 election, then that proves that they're philosophically closer to liberalism than to conservatism. Hence, they subsequently berate the GOP by extension. Indeed, Never Trumper newspaper columnists and other pundits spew far LESS vitriol at the Democratic Party than they do at their own party. The degree that President Trump succeeds in "Making America Great Again" is paralleled by the spiteful Never Trumpers delight in the fact that the Democrats are trying to destroy him. The enemy (Democrat) of their enemy (President Trump) is their friend.

As of January 2017, Donald Trump was more bold, decisive, and conservative than Ronald Reagan was as president. Though these Never Trumper Republicans are seething that actual conservatism (socio-economic freedom and American sovereignty) and not pseudo-conservatism was thriving under a crude, unorthodox, boorish, anti-globalist billionaire with an overbearing demeanor. To them, it's the former real estate magnate's off-putting personality that matters most, not his predominant pro-capitalism initiatives, his coordination of a January 2017 to February, 2020 robust economy, the foreign policy victories, his installing conservative judges and scoring numerous *America first* accomplishments. The aforementioned RINOs and those on the prominent left desire for the American people to judge #45 by his considerably less-than-graceful words that he speaks, and NOT judge the former president by his deeds that are beneficial to our country. In fact, many of Mr. Trump's naysayers are actually neocons who dislike intensely, the president's successful conservatism more than they are bothered by his brash and objectionable personna. Our nation's Chief Executive's non-diplomatic bluntness and off-putting clarity is just as anathema to the Never Trumpers as it is to the liberal/left. But because of the president's seeming repugnancy, he (Orange Man Bad) doesn't deserve the Never Trumpers approval and isn't going to get it. This will be *The Apprentice* star's just deserts for having the audacity to offend them. The problem with the former real estate mogul is that he exudes confidence, not humility, and doesn't seem to realize how aggravating that is to his haters. But what's particularly irksome and infuriating about Donald Trump is that he sticks to his promises (thoroughly unbecoming for a political leader) and then brags about it, thereby disparaging and outshining past Establishment presidents, both Republican and Democrat, over the last three decades. Plus, our Commander-in-chief is expected to act *presidential* by being a globalist and NOT a blunt, fearless non-conformist espousing American sovereignty, touting economic nationalism and defending himself against a dishonest media.

George W. Bush, on the other hand, was absolutely "presidential" while residing at 1600 Pennsylvania Ave. Unlike Trump, he longed to be liked and never went on the offensive by chastising or badmouthing the liberal press, Democrats, or left-wing activists. Plus, the ex-governor of Texas abided by the "way things are done" while residing at the nation's capital. Bush was what members of the GOP "are supposed to be." But the Donald was never even a politician (the gall of him) before being elected as America's leader and he's been constantly bucking the system ever since. This, besides his being obnoxious of character in the views of the Never Trumpers and getting their knickers all bunched up, makes Mr. Trump categorically unqualified to lead the nation (they would like to think). The least our 45th president could have done before winning the White House in November 2016 was to frequent the elite Washington DC Swamp cocktail parties and drink champagne while rubbing elbows with some Establishmentarian stuffed-shirted snobs.

P.S. Questions for the Never Trumpers: President Jimmy Carter was not, nor even thought of as a "morally defective, narcissistic, lying lout." Yet, he lost the November 1980 election. How come? Did Carter deserve to lose? If so...why? And to pour salt on the wound, this good and decent

man was defeated by an opponent who was an *amiable dunce* that hated poor people and was a bellicose, finger-on-the-red-button cowboy who wanted to start a nuclear war with Russia just because he didn't like their communist system. It's quite apparent that the American voters made a very bad mistake by not RE-ELECTING Jimmy Carter, is it not?

A man named Ariel Castro kidnapped three women and kept them for ten years in his home in Cleveland, Ohio, where he is alleged to have chained them up and sexually abused them. He was arrested and found *guilty* of the offense. While serving only a month of a lifelong prison sentence in 2013 for his crime, Castro hung himself to death. One of his kidnap victims opined about Ariel Castro's suicide, that he "took the coward's way out." No, he didn't! He took the smart way out. With absolutely no chance of parole, Castro probably figured, "What's the use of living?" He's called a coward by his victim and others because the kidnapper/rapist's immediate death deprived them of the satisfaction of seeing him "rot in hell for the rest of his life." Castro's short one month stay in prison means that he has "won" in the minds of many. Indeed, if Ariel Castro was a coward, then that makes someone with terminal cancer who commits suicide, also a coward.

2016 Democratic Presidential candidate and liberal sap, Martin O'Malley, mawkishly apologized to the nation for mentioning the phrase "all lives matter." Black society, with the knee-jerk agreement of left-leaning whites, doesn't like Americans to say that "all lives matter." This is not because it purportedly downplays the death of blacks (it actually doesn't) but because it undermines the narrative of blacks getting killed, unjustly or not, strictly by whites, especially white policemen. Someone saying the slogan *"all lives matter"* only serves to nullify or negate the empathy that black America seeks from white America. Blacks getting needlessly killed far more by other blacks warrant far less national attention because black society doesn't owe blacks. White society does. Thus, the refrain from saying "all lives matter" is not about lives per se, but about the politics of reparation / money atonement (shakedown) for the last three centuries of black America and the "well-deserved" guilt-inducing

condemnation of whites. So in essence, it's not so much , *black lives* that are pertinent, but rather, the vilification of *white America*.

What's so bad about income inequality? It's neither evil nor criminal. But the prominent left that wants to eradicate income inequality is just vicariously jealous for needy Americans who, said progressives think, should be jealous. This subsequently justifies the left's desire for socialistic monetary policies in order to punish the rich and, they claim, help the poor. Any lower-class citizens who actually ARE jealous of the wealthy should realize that they, of lower-class income status, live a far better life than the middle-class citizens of most countries. No, economic inequality is NOT immoral. Only those who want to eradicate it through confiscation and redistribution are.

MLK's dream to the contrary: When various white people judge blacks on the content of their character and not the color of their skin, it bothers the hell out of a lot of black people.

Some prominent Democrats don't want a wall on the southern border but say they will settle for a fence. What's the difference in purpose, you ask? The difference is that a WALL is built to keep OUT the riff-raff while a FENCE, on the other hand, is built to keep the RIFF-RAFF out. Plus, people are quite capable of climbing over a wall but not over a fence. Congresswoman Nancy Pelosi said that walls are "immoral." She is correct. Walls in many countries (approximately five dozen) all over the globe have been built and every one of them is immoral, particularly, Pelosi will agree, the one built by the Israelis. China has the biggest wall (the Great Wall of China, 2150 miles long), plainly making it THE most immoral of all barriers in the world. Many liberals have said that walls are racist. Well, no, walls don't have it in their genetics to be racist. But a wall DOES have feelings and can express joy or sadness. For example, when the gates of the Berlin Wall opened in November 1989, hundreds if not thousands of commoners in both East and West Germany started chipping away at the wall with hammers and chisels. Many of these individuals divulged that they could have sworn to have heard the

wall CRYING as it was crumbling. If the claims that the Berlin Wall was audibly sobbing uncontrollably are true (and they probably are), was it because this barrier, built by progressives, had experienced happiness about its imminent downfall or was it just grief-stricken that it was saying goodbye forever to communist East Germany?

NFL football teams and NBA basketball teams are not diverse enough. *Diversity* is always virtuous, automatically superior and is considered to be *strength*. Therefore, the two aforementioned sports should remove no less than 40 percent of their black players and replace them with whites. A professional football team and basketball team would be much stronger and better if they were more DIVERSE and *"looked like America."* It would especially make for improved race relationships in our country.

Some of my colleagues on the libertarian and traditionalist right think that liberals are just dolts who can't walk while wearing sandals and sip Starbucks coffee at the same time. But most of America's liberals are NOT like that (51 percent to be exact). Though, many liberals and libertarians DO agree on some issues; such as objecting to the U.S. 2003-2011 military intervention in Iraq, opposing the war on drugs in America, protecting our privacy plus civil liberties and being against (or for liberals, at least INITIALLY against) any governmentally-mandatory vaccination. The Libertarian Party itself is particularly known for agreeing with liberals on having open borders. Liberals are also in the same boat with traditionalists on a few issues. They're both, for the most part, receptive to government eminent domain. The anti-statism libertarian right is against it. Liberals and traditionalists supported the raising of the drinking age to twenty-one. The noted two political opponents are in favor of an American National Service Program (basically drafting young men into the military) ostensibly to get them to show their devotion to our country. This isn't urgent or necessary, and even then it's only nominally patriotic. Back in the early 1970s, traditionalists and liberals joined forces in stopping cigarette advertisements from being televised, neither side caring the least bit that they were being paternalistic. Two decades later, this ideological odd couple claimed that *"Joe the Camel"*, pictured on a pack of cigarettes, was too cartoonish and

thus, influenced teenagers to start smoking. Unfortunately, for Joe the Camel and free enterprise, the enemies of the drawn dromedary were never asked the question, "Of the millions of teenagers who have seen the cigarette box character, why is it that some 99 percent of them did NOT feel the least bit persuaded to start smoking?" But then again, such an inquiry would have been considered rude, flippant, insensitive and worst of all, insightful. RIP Joe Camel (1974-1997).

The very best way for the Federal government to help the black people of America is not to.

Nations all over the world recognize that a Republican administration (a conservative one, not a moderate one) in the USA as epitomizing "American values" more than a Democrat administration does. This is because a Republican (*a republic*) national leadership embodies a sovereign and capitalistic (free) United States that defends its interest while a Democrat (*a democracy*) does not.

Coronavirus; the ideological metaphor: Observe the following seething contempt exhibited by liberal news headlines in regards to the *individualism* and "Don't Tread on Me" attitude espoused by the government lockdown opponents, "Health care workers stand up to anti-lockdown protesters." "Meet the nurse that stood up to the protesters." "Nurses hailed as heroes standing up to protesters." And so, folks, it was like this; the protesters were *bullies* and *villains* that the brave, heroic nurses "stood up to." The noted demonstrators were actually just rallying for the government to give them, the people, more freedom. One dishonest progressive (excuse the redundancy) journalist, regarding the pathogen pandemic, referred to the noted liberty-lovers as "extremists" and upbraided them for violating "stay-at-home" orders. Irrespective of the magnitude of the international virus (which is not the point of this paragraph), you'll notice that the protesters were rebelling AGAINST the government while those demonizing the aforementioned non-conforming dissenters were themselves, espousing OBEDIENCE to the government. Contemporary progressivism simply has a predilection towards governmental dominance and supremacy whether it's

compassionate communism, sympathetic socialism or friendly fascism. If the China-spawned infection had happened in the late 1960s/early 1970s, the young Americans in said hippy era who collectively acquired a cultural amalgamation of left/libertarianism, would have been dead-set opposed to the lockdown. The majority of today's liberals; disregard the Constitution and are inordinately fond of a government-enforced virtual confinement if it's ostensibly for the citizens' own good. Which is not at all unlike their near infatuation with the ordered mask-wearing of citizens. To many a pandemic-obsessed liberal, the coronavirus mask is not just a security blanket, but a pseudo-religion. And they detest it when twice-vacinated "anti-maskers" (apostates) rebel against the proclamations coming from *those higher up*. Regardless of the actual effectiveness of the COVID masks, progressives adore a nation-wide conformity mandated by the omnipotent, but supposedly benevolent State. Now the pro-liberty protesters DID think that COVID-19 was real but were merely dissenting against, they believe, an overreaching law. The covid 19 lockdown began in the spring of 2020 and went on for some 14 months in the 50 states. The lockdown opponents were simply yearning to get their freedom back despite the risks. On the other side, supporters of the partial suppression of American livelihood during this time desired to take no chances and were either apathetic (liberals) or euphoric (the far left) about an impending nationwide economic catastrophe and draconian societal restrictions. But then again, freedom doesn't advance humanity. Only social control via a governmental clampdown administerd by an empathetic, beneficent quasi-dictatorship does. Almost the entire liberal/left will agree with yours truly on this.

The overwhelming majority of black Americans will agree that a Democrat politician doesn't actually have to make black lives better via his or her voting record. Democrat politicians only have to be REPUTED to be doing so. And they are.

Isn't it both interesting and yet ominous that North Korean dictator and internationally nefarious James Bond movie villain, Kim Jong-Un, is a communist while socialist and communist sympathizer Bernie Sanders is THE most popular senator among Democratic voters?

When the 90% left-leaning media employs the word "historic" in various news article descriptions, it's mostly to compliment a person, deed or acomplishment that is personified in *liberalism* and not so much as something being unique, important or memorable pertaining to American history. For example, the media would NEVER have called the Supreme Court's newest member "historic" if she was black but a *conservative*. To do so would have been to heap praise on Ketanji Brown Jackson. But no can do. Though, the aforementioned person is certainly UNIQUE, no doubt. Jackson is the only Supreme Court justice ever to be uncertain if he or she was a woman or not. Definitely HISTORIC! The noted woman/man/whatever conceded that "she" wasn't a biologist, and was therefore unable to define what a woman is. Hey, what a coincidence; the vast majority of Americans don't know what their gender is either, since THEY"RE not biologists. Anyway, the real good thing about Justice Jackson is that "she" is not a liar.

The American voters have long been schizophrenic regarding our two main political parties. That is, they want the Tweedledee and Tweedledum parties to have bold, clean, stark differences so that the citizens can have a clear choice as where to take our country. This way, the United States of America can have the changes that we need as long as everything stays the same.

Alright, alright....I agree that socialism is an unjust and oppressive slavery but hey; at least it's not racist like the system of social liberty and economic freedom (read: American capitalism) is.

Over the last couple of years, there has been much news on TV about high-end luxury stores in big cities like Philadelphia, Chicago, San Francisco and Los Angeles, being vandalized and looted by flash mobs and smash-and-grab thieves running out of the stores with expensive items. And ninety-nine percent of the aforementioned criminals were white.

Of the many candidates that ran for president in 2016, two of them were Texas Senator Ted Cruz and Vermont Senator Bernie Sanders. Most of the American electorate found the former to be more repulsive because Senator Cruz is intelligent, a strict Constitutionalist and a man who assertively defends the sovereignty of the United States. But the Constitution is a contradiction of activist government and sovereignty is the enemy of globalism. This is scary to many Americans. Bernie Sanders, on the other hand, frightens and repels far fewer of our nation's citizens because he's a self-declared socialist. A higher percentage of our citizens would consider Mr. Sanders to be more in the "mainstream" of national politics than they would Mr. Cruz. In any case, the Democratic Party DOES NOT have a problem with Bernie Sanders being a socialist. They have a problem with his ADMITTING to being a socialist. But when the American people in general find a de facto Marxist running for president in a major political party to be both acceptable and viable is when they become more brazenly honest. Though, such citizens, particularly the atheists and agnostics among us, should take heed that putting their faith in a progressive politician is to practically worship a false god.

In his run for the presidency in October 1988, George H. W. Bush taunted and besmirched his Democratic opponent, Michael Dukakis, as a "liberal," which caused a wee bit of vexation in the former Massachusetts governor. Fast forward twenty-eight years: The Hillary Clinton of year 2016 leans to the left of the Michael Dukakis of 1988. On Election Day November 8th, 2016; America's 41st president voted for Hillary Clinton. This electoral choice by him elicited disapproval by some in the GOP, but that's alright. George H.W. Bush made up for his 2016 vote by retroactively losing to Hillary's husband in his 1992 re-election attempt for another term in the White House.

Barack Obama's 2008 presidential campaign motto was the word "hope." No matter how bad liberalism makes their life, blacks and liberals will continue to follow the beaten path while believing in "hope". For it is the innate vacuousness of HOPE that offers them hope. Or at least, that's what they hope.

CHAPTER 6

The Socialist King

ALTHOUGH THE REVEREND Martin Luther King Jr. had expressed an admiration for Karl Marx and said that *The Communist Manifesto* was "written by men aflame with a passion for social justice," he himself was never a communist. Martin Luther King Jr. was a democratic socialist. He was working for the socialist cause at least the last three years of his life and actually became a socialist even before he got married. MLK was greatly influenced by an American socialist author, Edward Bellamy, and his novel published in 1888, called *Looking Backward 2000-1887*. In as early as 1952, in a letter written to his then girlfriend, Coretta Scott, who gave him Bellamy's book, King said to her, "I imagine you already know that I am much more socialistic in my economic theory than capitalistic." And he told Miss Scott, "I would certainly welcome the day to come when there will be a nationalization of industry." Plus, "So today capitalism has outlived its usefulness. It has brought about a system that takes necessities from the masses to give luxuries to the classes." About the novel's speaking of the change from capitalism to socialism, Mr. King explained to his future wife, "This, it will be remembered, is one of the points at which socialism differs from communism, the former emphasizing evolution and the latter revolution." Quite simply, Martin Luther King Jr. was an *evolutionary*, not a *revolutionary*.

According to the Southern Christian Leadership Conference which he headed in 1966, the reverend became a passionate enemy of

capitalism. In 1965, Mr. King said in a speech, "Call it democracy, or call it democratic socialism, but there must be a better distribution of wealth within the country for all God's children." Also, "If we are to achieve real equality, the United States will have to adopt a modified form of socialism." The following year, the civil rights leader stated, "There must be a better distribution of wealth and maybe America must move toward a democratic socialism." He once conveyed to the participants at the SCLC's Minister Leadership Training program not to be scared of employing the word "socialism" because "Something is wrong with capitalism as it now stands in the United States. We are not interested in being integrated into this value structure… a radical redistribution of power must take place."

King added, "The movement must address itself to the restructuring of the whole of American society." The "social justice" activist, in his radical book *Where Do We Go from Here*, wrote about a "higher synthesis" between capitalism and communism; a "socially conscious democracy which reconciles the truth of individualism and collectivism." However, the preacher admitted in private that such a definition was really a euphemism for SOCIALISM. But since an approximate fifty/fifty amalgamation of capitalism and communism (which is essentially what the reverend was calling for) equals FASCISM, then that would make Martin Luther King Jr. a de facto fascist. Although the reverend probably didn't know that what he wanted amounted to fascism, he was certainly cognizant that he was a socialist. Choose your poison. Both socialism and fascism are variants of societal subjugation, thereby making MLK a perhaps unknowing advocate of a veritable slavery.

Like all socialists, Mr. King supported a guaranteed annual income, a main tenet of socialism. On the last night of his life, he told a crowd, "I may not get there with you. But I want you to know that we as a people will get to the Promised Land." Translation: "We black Americans will one day be living under socialism." Martin Luther King, Jr. was too religious a man to have been a Red. Although, in using communist jargon, MLK did denounce capitalist America as having "interrelated flaws of racism, poverty, militarism and materialism." He also joined hands with the enemies of freedom. Baynard Rustin, Stanley Levinson, and

Jack O'Dell (aka Hunter Pitts) were communists who were colleagues of the renowned civil rights activist and worked for him as unofficial advisers and confidential organizers until the reverend's death. Also, in an early 1968 meeting that he had with Andrew Young among others, the preacher angrily chastised the future Georgia congressman, "I don't need to hear from you, Andy. I've heard enough from you. You're a capitalist and I'm not."

And then there's the other side of the ideological divide. Some conservative think-tanks, publications, and prominent spokesmen have been telling us that Martin Luther King Jr. was a Republican and/or a conservative. The noted "right-wingers" are not so much being disingenuous as they are being dishonest. Reverend King was never a Republican or a conservative. Although he was not a *registered* Democrat, the progressive preacher expressed that he always voted for the Party of FDR and would have endorsed JFK had the 35th president lived to run again. Many of my brethren on the right are so eager to harness at least some of the black vote over to their side that they adopt wishful thinking and then proceed to lie. These particular "conservatives" are political cowards and they know it.

Many will say that we should still honor MLK with a holiday even though he was a socialist, because he spearheaded the late 1950s / early 1960s protests against racial discrimination and segregation (true). And that he was instrumental in helping to get the Civil Rights Act of 1964 and the Voting Rights Act of 1965 passed (true again). But some questions for the reader need to be answered: Was Reverend King the only one involved in the civil rights movement from 1955 to 1965, or were there others? And in pretending just for a moment that the person, Martin Luther King Jr., never existed; would these two aforementioned laws still have been passed sometime in the 1960s or early 1970s; yes or no? For a decade, starting in 1955, Reverend King did well and good in his praiseworthy battle against racial discrimination and segregation. But those are NEGATIVE RIGHTS that any decent person would and should support. The problem is that the late civil rights leader also became a proponent of POSITIVE RIGHTS, which always involves government coercion and collectivism.

But let's say that in late 1965, instead of being a democratic socialist, MLK was a neo-Nazi (a nationalistic socialist). He glorified Nazism, expressed his loving admiration for Adolph Hitler and his policies, and proclaimed that the Holocaust never happened. This being the case; should there still have been an American holiday named after Martin Luther King Jr.? Yes or no? If you, the reader, answered "no" to this question but answered in the AFFIRMATIVE for a MLK holiday after agreeing that he was a socialist, then how do you explain the incongruity? Is Nazism unjust, oppressive, and wrong? Likewise, is socialism? If you answer "no" or "not necessarily" to the very last question, you are tacitly admitting to being a socialist or communist and should quite naturally therefore be in favor of a national day off to commemorate King. If you, however, answer "yes" to the question of socialism being unjust, oppressive, and wrong, then you should also be AGAINST the holiday for the slain civil rights activist as if he was pro-Nazism the last sixteen years of his life. If you don't do this, then you will immediately realize that you're someone who is more worried about popularity than about being honest and correct. Just like the pusillanimous "right-wingers" who, in a flight of fancy, declare that Martin Luther King Jr. was a conservative Republican.

Michigan Congressman John Conyers pushed for the King holiday right after the Reverend's death. About said law that passed fifteen years later, Conyers opined, "I never viewed it as an isolated piece of legislation to honor one man. Rather, I have always viewed it as an indication of the commitment of the House and the nation to the dream of Dr. King." The "dream" that the Congressman had in the back of his mind was King's goal of socialism for America. And of course Conyers "viewed it as an indication of the commitment" to the DREAM because he, himself, was a socialist just like MLK was. As a collectivist, Mr. King wanted everybody to have their fair share, and why not? As a philanderer, he certainly had his fair share. But just before President Ronald Reagan, in 1983, signed the King Holiday into law in order to appease black America, he was alerted about the reverend's transgressions (adultery, plagiarism, associations with domestic comrades) by the Governor of New Hampshire. Reagan replied to him, "I have the same reservations you have, but here the perception of too many people is based on the image, not reality. Indeed, to them, perception is reality."

What our fortieth president was conveying, in granting the MLK holiday, was "Perception becomes legitimized deception while reality remains a truth that should be ignored." In other words, Ronald Reagan turned yellow in order to validate a pinko. The late religious preacher rightly admonished us to not judge a man by the color of his skin but by the content of his character. His own words notwithstanding; a holiday was bestowed on the Reverend King. Presently, the 1960s civil rights icon is a sacred cow to white Republicans and a demigod to black Democrats. Many feel that MLK particularly deserves nationwide commemoration because he was taken away from black Americans at such a young age (thirty-nine) by a white man (James Earl Ray). White support of this holiday should be viewed as the contrition that it is. So now, once a year, the United States is officially honoring and celebrating a man whose DREAM was the downfall of our capitalistic (freedom) economic system, the best in the world, and replacing it with the slavery of socialism. Anybody care to make a toast?

CHAPTER 7

I Want My Social Program

WHEN IS THE last time that you heard a politician promising to cut or eliminate SPECIFIC social spending programs, entitlements, or government departments (such as Department of Education or the National Endowment for the Arts)? Republican politicians can't stipulate exactly what domestic social spending should be cut, because they are extremely aware that the American people would reject such action. Our citizens don't mind conservative politicians speaking in vague generalities about "cutting spending" just as long as these candidates are not really serious. Indeed, any Republican's pretense of drastically cutting domestic social spending enables the electorate to pretend that they agree. Directly after a November election, the American voters will call for relative "fiscal conservatism," but when their next visit to a ballot box in the eleventh month of a numerically even year gets ever closer, the voters will backpedal.

In the future, the Democratic candidates are going to have less to worry about. Not so for their general election opponents. For the Grand Old Party, evasiveness will predominate. For them to win, it will have to. More and more, the Republicans running for political office are going to have to walk on eggshells. Such was the precarious position of Mitt Romney. In his run for the Massachusetts Senate in 1994, Romney suggested that he would like to eliminate the Department of Education. In his 2012 presidential run, the former Bay State Governor was undoubtedly relieved that no one asked him about this past political faux pas. Besides hemming and hawing, how would he have answered it? Voters will, in the future, be unable to make our liberal lawmakers uncomfortable by putting them on the spot on the subject of domestic social spending increases, because the noted Democrats will say "yes" to virtually every voter demand or request. Conservative and moderate politicians, on the other hand, have no choice but to break out in sweat by saying "Yes" to more social spending or at least try to evade the question.

One of the sacred cows that a candidate or politician cannot say "No" to, is the elderly. Old folks swarm in droves toward the voting booth, more than any other special-interest group. Their main concern is the preservation of the unConstitutional Social Security. Why is it mandatory that I give my money to the government to save for me when I retire? How come I'm not allowed to do that for myself? The overwhelming majority of America's senior citizens are AGAINST the privatization of Social Security. Peculiar, is it not? That is, these individuals are all over the age of sixty-four and are reputed to be locked into receiving Social Security. Money that was withdrawn from their income ever since each of them was eighteen years of age. The geriatric crowd have monthly government payments coming to them for life and tell themselves that it can't be taken away. So why do THEY care if Social Security is privatized for young up and comers? It's because, deep down, the elderly know damn well that they're at the top of a redistributionist Ponzi pyramid and that they, our senior citizens, are basically living off the money of younger people. Give the twenty-something-year-olds the freedom to NOT have to participate in the building of the SS pyramid and there goes a large chunk of the financial foundation for silver-haired retirees. The mere fact that most of them would vociferously object to VOLUNTARY participation in Social Security by workers from eighteen to sixty-four years of age proves that the elderly know it's true. Privatization would only crumble America's number one Ponzi scheme, commonly known as Social Security. And this is because SS is collectively owned and managed by the Federal government. Subsequently, because American citizens DO NOT have a legally-binding OWNERSHIP of "their" Social Security; then that grants the politicians in Washington, DC to LEGALLY take the ill-gotten booty from the people's SS fund and spend it on said lawmakers pork barrel pet projects. Only a private entity that manages the beloved FDR initiated program, which would then factually belong to individuals, guarantees that nobody can confiscate their money. Be that as it may, between the two financial dichotomies, the vast majority of Americans would easily select government-run Social Security in its present state. It used to be, years ago, that only Social Security was known as the Third Rail of politics. Today, it has company, and lots of it, though culpable political spokespeople informing now and future SS recipients that these government redistributionist outlays are "theirs" will at least diminish the guilt, shame, or embarrassment of the individuals receiving the filthy lucre.

As previously imparted, most if not all earmarks, set-asides, pet projects, and just plain subsidies have joined Social Security on the Third Rail of politics in which a candidate merely mentioning the words "*cut*" and "*expenditures*" in the same sentence is taboo. For a politician to even broach the subject of fiscal economics with just these four words "We'll have to eliminate" is political suicide. Former Rhode Island Republican Congresswoman Claudine Schneider once stated that she believes in telling people how to fish rather than giving fish to them. If Schneider believed that, then why was she against cutting any domestic social spending whether it was profligate or not? The Congresswoman was also against raising taxes to pay for it. Another politician from the smallest state in the union was Senator Claiborne Pell. For over three decades he served his constituents splendidly.....by also being irresponsible with their income. But then, Pell was a liberal Democrat and thus, it was desired and expected of him to be fiscally irresponsible. In fact, it would have been irresponsible for the R.I. Senator NOT to have been irresponsible. If a gang of animal rights activists had convinced Pell that he'd have been sensitive and compassionate to support legislation to build government-subsidized nursing homes for fang-less walruses, Pell would have voted for it.

Back in the 1980s there was a minor controversy in the news about how the American taxpayer was paying an exorbitant cost for certain items (like $435 for a hammer) that the US military was purchasing.

It was the decade when the peacenik/pinko left was eager to exploit, for political reasons, the juxtaposition of a Republican presidency with wasteful defense department expenditures. But make no mistake about it; there have been vast amounts of the taxpayers' money that was squandered by our military over the last half century, no matter what political party was in power. Alas, there were billions of dollars in weapons boondoggles that never came to fruition or didn't work, even if they did see the light of day. Not to mention, millions in funding for armaments that our military generals insisted they did not need but were overruled by various spendthrift Democratic and Republican politicians who claimed that we DID need them. "We," meaning that particular lawmaker's voting district and his or her re-election, not the defense of the national interest. And lest we have forgotten, there was the infamous $640 that was spent for a toilet SEAT.

Though, with gazillions of dollars in military waste, I could understand the Pentagon and our political leaders spending ONE MILLION dollars on the actual toilet; that is, metaphorically speaking. But what is even more reprehensible than that of the crooked defense contractors and careless military officers is the hypocritical attitude of the American people. What about the billions of dollars in earmarks, pork barrel subsidies, and non-related tack-ons to spending projects that our public servants indulged in with the tacit encouragement of their constituents? Like, for instance: $336 million dollars was earmarked for Amtrak and $50 million for planting trees on private property. Both of these were tacked on to the November 2012 HURRICANE SANDY relief fund? Huh? One doesn't know whether to laugh or cry. But wait. There's much more for the history books. How about $113,277 spent to preserve "historic" video games or $6 million dollars to build a canal in Idaho for gondolas? Now, this last one is a swell idea, but only if we change the name of the Gem State to Venice.

And speaking of Idaho, there was $1.5 million spent to study the potato. Eye kid you not. There was $75,000 to PROMOTE Christmas trees and poinsettias in Michigan. $60,000 was used for Belgian endive research, which, I think that you the reader will agree is far more important than cancer research. One million dollars was set aside to build a bus stop with heated pavement (can't live without that). Plus, $10 million of the taxpayers' money went to an arts organization in Pakistan to produce their own version of Sesame Street. A much-needed infusion of $702,558 bankrolled the study of the impact of televisions and gas generators on villages in Vietnam. A quarter of a million dollars was spent on preventing wild pigs from attacking exotic plants in Hawaii. Also, half a million dollars was earmarked to finance a research on the effects of cigarette smoking on.....dogs. $1.8 million financed the study as to why pigs smell. Maybe they were eating exotic plants. The American taxpayers generously funded $350,000 for an arts festival in Italy. Now, yours truly wholeheartedly supports this one, but only on the condition that the boot-shaped country changes its name to Idaho. *Capisce?* And last but not least, $120 million per year was sent to certain Federal employees from the years 2006 through 2011. But these people never received a dime of the payments because they had long been dead.

All this is a sort of guns vs. butter issue. To wit, the underlying belief of most Americans is that the US government spending money on a component (the military) whose mission is to fight and kill people warrants a more stern and exacting judgment, particularly when that component WASTES money; for example, purchasing an ashtray for $600. But "appropriations" like the government grant of half a million dollars going to a university to develop a sonar catfish counter, or "allocating" $15,000 for the study of hitchhiking, are nullified by the feeling that such "domestic social spending" is at least designed by virtue to help people, not hurt them. These "investments in people" are then rationalized as being well-intentioned and almost honorable and are therefore not perceived as something, unlike the military, that merits ridicule, contempt, and consequent elimination. But the biggest reason that politicians and the voters won't publicly criticize another's domestic social spending program, no matter how fiscally imprudent and morally bankrupt it may be, is for fear of RETALIATION. These government gluttons are well aware that their denigration of fellow freeloaders will put themselves in public funding jeopardy and their elected lawmakers in a precarious political situation. Such is a bad move for them, to be certain.

The idiom "One man's trash is another man's treasure" notwithstanding: It doesn't matter that one person's social program is "totally unnecessary and very wasteful" or that another's is "real important and absolutely needed." Shine a bad, stigmatizing spotlight on one domestic spending program, and that spotlight can't help but shine on the other "valid" programs standing right next to it. The public would rather not have to dread the impending cuts or elimination of various "entitlements" and *social service departments*. Quite simply, many, if not most, Americans envy government waste on the military/defense department and condone one another's foolishly exorbitant pet project waste. The citizenry couldn't have cared less about the $385 million that taxpayers lost in the 2011 Solyndra bankruptcy scandal, nor the deficit. But while they're all hogging the pork barrel.....(sorry), these selfish leeches are either oblivious to or apathetic about the fact that they are draining $million$ in funding away from the more worthy, credible, and legitimate spending programs (healthcare, housing, food stamps, and the like) that they ostensibly advocated in the first place. Our national debt is subordinate to what really matters... that the three branches of the Federal government keep the people fat, happy, and dumb by throwing more slop into the trough. Oink.

FOOTNOTE: In regard to Claudine Schneider and her being against raising taxes, this author was not admonishing the former Congresswoman for her opposition to it. I, myself, was in agreement with the lady about not raising taxes. The writer was merely pointing out the hypocrisy of the R.I. ex-politician's position from her own economic (liberal) and political perspective. Yours truly doubts very much that Schneider's aim, in relation to her lack of support of taxes being raised, was to "starve the beast" of government spending. Though such a motive on her part would have been praiseworthy, Ms. Schneider was a moderate liberal and wasn't that clever.

CHAPTER **8**

Liberalism Vs. The Far Left

AS THE FAMOUS folk song goes: (feel free to sing along), "If I was a commie, I'd hammer in the morning, I'd sickle in the evening, all over this land. I'd"....Alright, alright....it doesn't go quite like that. But it might as well, since the song was co-written by Pete Seeger, that lovable commie troubadour who for decades merrily went on weaving his way in and out of radical rallies, proletarian picnics, and Red-diaper-baby youth camps. With "America is a free country" having already been embedded into the national psyche, there becomes a propensity to strive for other ideals: social equality and the collective well-being. To the liberal mind—which incidentally is not an oxymoron—socialist and communist organizations should not be ostracized by society since they purportedly desire humanitarian unity for a better nation. This being the case, any seemingly hostile behavior espoused by these over-zealous two doctrines should be viewed as mere justifiable resentment and NOT mean-spirited cruelty. To self-declared *progressives*, yours truly posits the question: If communism is as far to the political left as progressivism can go, does that mean that communism is the pinnacle, zenith and high point of progressivism?

Genuine liberals will agree that the old Soviet Union's OWN particular MODEL of socialism was rotten and did not work. This way, socialism itself gets the benefit of a doubt that liberals would like to think it deserves. They will concede that democratic socialism has some flaws but is nonetheless, inherently good and workable. Communism is simply to be regarded as socialism with a malevolent look on its face. But then, looks aren't everything. In any case, the excesses of socialism/communism are to be offset by their noble aims and lofty goals. If you, the reader, look for and purchase the PERFECT dream house that you've always wanted, but then discover a broken window and a bedroom door that needs repair, you wouldn't tear the whole house down, would you? To some liberals, calling an actual card-carrying communist a "communist" constitutes being a "smear" or "McCarthyism." Liberals condone communism for its "good intentions" but condemn Senator Joe McCarthy (pursuing clandestine communists) and movie director Elia Kazan (outing clandestine communists) for what are also GOOD INTENTIONS. It's as if fighting back against communism was more deplorable than communism itself. When the author's fellow dinosaurs on the political right brand certain individuals and organizations as "communist" like they have over more than seven decades, it makes liberals cringe even if it's absolutely true.

Perhaps you're familiar with the rhetoric of some of my conservative comrades of bygone eras: "Hollywood actors are all communists. He's a commie. She's a commie. The entire Democratic Party is nothing but a bunch of commies." But I disagree with them. John Wayne was a Hollywood actor and he wasn't a communist. Liberals feel uncomfortable when the American right mocks or disparages communism. That is to say, if a conservative seems to be denigrating communisms social transgressions (no freedom of the press, speech, artistic expression, or religion) then the liberal will concur with this. But if what said conservative has in mind is the economics of communism, then the liberal becomes suspicious. He or she starts thinking to him/herself, and correctly so, "When that conservative badmouths communism, what he's really doing is attacking socialism. And when he attacks socialism, what he's really doing is criticizing liberalism." Progressivism contends that Nazis and fascists have innate character and personality problems but communists merely have demeanor and reputation problems. The entire liberal/left insist on believing the socio-political SYSTEMS of Nazism and fascism are intrinsically rotten to the core and can't be rehabilitated, but with the virtuous "social values" structure of socialism and communism, it's just a matter of finding competent and upstanding personnel to manage the latter two. All genuine liberals are compatible with Republicans who are solely NON-communists, but many liberals try to portray vitriolic ANTI-communism as being parallel with racism. Some liberals particularly feel that communism isn't bad, wrong, or evil but just a "different" way of life for a lot of people. If you're a Baptist, do you have to be against and hostile toward people who are Presbyterians?.....Precisely!....So why be ANTI-communism?

Like the term "economic freedom", the *sovereignty* of the United States, to the garden-variety liberal, is acceptable but not particularly desired or respected. Liberals believe that the wholesale embracing of American sovereignty throws a monkey-wrench into what should be our goal of being a humble, complaisant part of a family of nations. When you comply with what the majority want you to do, there's not just the pleasure of popularity, but the satisfaction of acceptance. The noted Americans who lean to the left are, of course, citizens of this great nation, but consider themselves to be, first and foremost, citizens of the world. Liberals like to fantasize that the United States would be a much more honorable and respectable country in the eyes of the world if we didn't have the juxtaposition of so many millionaires with so many poor citizens. That it isn't right or fair that our nation, unlike many others, is well-off and has been living the good life for over a century. To Democrats, unlike our homeland in which they live, it is totally acceptable for an impoverished third world country to close its borders and embrace a strong sovereignty. And that's because nobody envys them. On the other hand, guilt-ridden, non-patriotic liberals don't like to admit that other countries are jealous of America because that's a reflection on them, the other countries, not on us. The United States, however, just for the sin of being prosperous and successful, should open up its doors and unconditionally welcome the plebian masses. Our contrition has long been overdue. We owe it to the world. Also, this nation called "AMERICA" should not be envisioned as an entity unto itself, but merely a name given to this certain piece of land that its inhabitants presently reside on. You see, because the USA is, or supposed to be, part of the global community, progressivism contends that we cannot have an "America first" agenda because that would offend and alienate other nations ("our family"). The left's view is there would be far less resentment of the United States by our global neighbors if we would just show humility by being more like the rest of the world. This implies that the other countries are morally superior to America. So, instead of practicing our independence here on planet earth, because the USA is a leading superpower, it is believed that we should become more humble and quaint while we subsequently obtain the leadership role of globalism. In liberal-left La-la land, this is desirable because it would debase our country and simultaneously boost the status of Third World nations. To the internationalist mindset, American unilateralism is NOT leadership. Only cooperating with our allies or the United Nations and World Trade Organization' desires and directives and then stepping to the forefront is. The liberal/left believes that a non-conformist America going it alone in pursuit of its objectives constitutes being a rogue nation that must be reined in for global communitarian reasons. This intimates that the United States is up to no good if it doesn't consign itself over to a world governing body.

Now don't get me wrong. Even though our country's liberals will disagree with this writer on many issues, I still consider them to be Americans. And make no mistake about it; out of everyone in the entire world, American liberals have been more patriotic about the United States than anyone not living here. But what all of us should acknowledge is that liberals are not communists and vice versa. It's not even debatable. Although, there has been a rumor in some circles that there was a certain liberal Democrat who, back in the 1930s, tried to join the Communist Party USA. But he was rejected by the aforementioned organization for being, they thought, a bit naïve and weird. Yours truly never met the guy and didn't know a lot about him. But I did find out that he went on to become an actor in Hollywood and later, the President of the Screen Actors Guild. After that, he became the Governor of California and then the President of the United States.

CHAPTER 9

Opinionated Bits and Pieces Part 2

THERE IS A building in Washington DC that has been home to every president since George Washington. It's called the White House. This is obviously a racist title for a dwelling that is supposed to represent ALL Americans, not just whites. The man who named it the "White House" was himself, white and he was a bigot, no doubt. If the United States really desired to heal its racial, ethnic, and gender wounds and prove to the citizens of the world that our country really is trying to eradicate its institutional racism and oppression, then we should give the People's head residence a new title. I submit that, from now on, we proudly refer to it as, and demand that our lawmakers change the name of said building to, "The Black, Latino, Gay, Transgender, and Politically Acceptable Whites House" or if that's too long, employ the acronym, the "BLGTPAW House." Who's with me?

The young liberals of generations ago were staunch advocates of the First Amendment. Most of today's young liberals believe that the term "free speech" doesn't apply to speech and opinion that contradicts their "core values" (liberalism). It was the American political left that owned the counter culture since the late 1950s. Think the Beatnik Era of 1957 through 1964 and the Hippie Generation of 1966 through 1973. Participants of these two groups back then were known for being rebellious, iconoclastic, questioning authority, going against the grain, and just plain being anti-Establishment. Some fifty years ago, DISSENT was what the left was all about. Today, the far left still desires the American people to adopt this very attitude, but only as long as they don't defy Democrat authoritarianism or rise up against centralized government and challenge its edicts. Indeed, any *struggle* against progressivism is to be demonized, and conformity as mandated by proponents of the almighty State is insisted upon. To the far left, DISSENT is particularly *patriotic* if one is trying to bring down America.

A bad white cop (and bad apple, Derek Chauvin, with eighteen complaints having been filed against him in the past) in Minnesota on May 25th, 2020, was filmed appearing to bring slow death to a black man, George Floyd, by kneeling on his neck. The vast majority of Americans however, are unaware that, six days later, eighteen black citizens, in a 24-hour period (a sixty-year record) in Chicago, were murdered by other blacks. A black human being in the United States is 270 times more likely to be killed by other blacks than by whites. The death of a black person committed by a white person is to be politically exploited to the Nth degree. But eighteen blacks getting killed in one day by the same race is to be ignored and forgotten, while violence against whites by a mob of hateful blacks brings utter Schadenfreude to the far left. The social movement, that's being funded by billionaire far-leftists (e.g. George Soros) and big corporations yearning to be liked and accepted (via their virture-signaling) by America's progressive pop culture, is known as Black Lives Matter (aka Black Lies Matter). All lives matter! Yes, Ive heard that the latter three-word phrase is racist, but then again, so are stratocumulous clouds. Actually, the truism "all lives matters" gets under the skin of blacks and white liberals because it implies that blacks aren't special and therefore don't warrant the undivided, deferential attention that many believe is supposed to be given to them by whites.

The Black Lives Matter movement is admired by many not so much for its purported goal of saving or improving black lives, but for its clenched-fist salute, which is the symbolic theme of socialism/communism, which BLM fans WOULD LIKE TO THINK saves or improves the lives of black people. The platitudinous "Black Lives Matter" motto insinuates that the onus of blame for, and responsibility to rectify, the plight of blacks and their trouble with the law, is on white people and thus, the subtle vilification of whites is to be included in the equation. But there really are some black lives that DON'T matter. Examples: A black life doesn't matter to a black mother living in the ghetto, who never sets a curfew for her thirteen-year old son. Plus, most black Americans and white liberals don't really care if the head of a five month old black fetus is crushed by powerful forceps being squeezed by a white man. The now dead fetus used to be a black life, but that doesn't matter. The lives and livelihood of black store owners in Minneapolis in early June of 2020, and in Ferguson, Missouri in late summer of 2014 didn't matter to the rioters (mostly black) and their supporters as these stores were vandalized, looted, and destroyed. Nor was any sorrow or regret expressed by the liberal/left when this happened. Also, not one of the rioters or protesters who have complained about "systemic racism" (there's no such thing) and "white privilege" (ditto) has ever and will NEVER, say a bad word about socialism, the ultimate and racially-equal oppression and subjugation. The overwhelming majority of conservatives condemn Officer Derek Chauvin for what he did. Most of America's blacks and left-leaning whites would NOT have condemned Mr. Chauvin if he were BLACK. But especially, in the addition to the former Minneapolis cop being black; there would have been very little, if any, condemnation if the victim, George Floyd, was WHITE. Though, said deceased man's name WILL come in useful to those who chant "Black Lives Matter" in order to guilt-trip white citizens into assuming responsibility for blacks. So, sure, black lives do sometimes matter, but only as they pertain to whites.

What do singers Neil Sedaka, Carol King, Barry Manilow, Barbara Streisand, and Neil Diamond all have in common? They've all recorded Christmas albums. It's a bit of an oddity, and not an unwelcome one that the aforementioned Jews sing what is usually thought of as CHRISTIAN holiday songs. But this writer doesn't begrudge them in the slightest. Yes, I'm well aware that American Jews wrote tunes like "White Christmas," "Winter Wonderland," "I'll Be Home for Christmas," "Rudolph the Red-Nosed Reindeer," and Mel Tormé wrote about his chestnuts being roasted on an open fire in "The Christmas Song." The author is not being the least bit snide or snotty by saying that I feel sorry for Jewish citizens, who are particularly alienated every December, though all rabbis will convey that this is most unfortunate, but Judaism should not change just to accommodate any sadness on the part of Jews during the Christmas season. The rabbis are correct for profound religious and historic reasons. Jewish singers probably approach Christmas carols in a secularist frame of mind, which allows them to "participate" in the Yuletide festivities in a non-religious way. And that ought to be fine with everybody. After all, Christmas tunes are joyous, catchy, and certainly memorable. The only Jew who should be PROHIBITED by law to sing Christmas songs is any early 1960s folk music artist who sings through their nose.

Since each and every liberal will NOT answer the question "Do you think that ALL of the following five systems---Nazism, communism, fascism, socialism and apartheid--- are unjust, oppressive and wrong?" with either a YES or NO response, then that proves that all American liberals are Nazis. You, the reader, may retort "That's outrageous, absurd, inflamatory and just plain false." No, it can't possibly be false (Nazism is the de facto leader of these five immoral, despicable systems) because otherwise, they would have answered the question with a resounding "Yes"; but did not and won't. So, how do you explain that?

The polls always ask the American people nebulous political questions like, "Do you approve of the direction that the country is headed in?" What do they mean by "direction"? Like, in a southwestern direction? Are these pollsters suggesting that our actual land mass, itself, should perhaps drift toward Bora Bora? Or they will inquire, "Do you think that America is on the right track?" Not if it's a railroad track. Polls that do not put our citizens on the spot by asking them PRECISELY what actions our nation should take are vacuous and meaningless. It's plainly a case of ambiguity trumping definitiveness. It's as if these vague questions were purposely designed and used to keep the sheeple fat, happy, and ignorant. The public opinion surveys should ask Americans, "Because the United States is bankrupt due to its overspending, do you think that we should, as a remedy, try to spend our way out of it?" As a result of being conditioned by the inane queries that the pollsters have been asking us for more than half a century, many if not most people will answer the aforementioned question in the affirmative.

The late Hollywood black actor Sydney Poitier was NOT African-American. Though, if white professional golfer Ernie Els, who was born in South Africa, IS an American citizen, then he is an African-American. The same criterion applies to white actress Charlize Theron. There are millions of white people who were born in and presently live in the continent of Africa and they are Africans. Any blacks living in the United States who were born in, say, Jamaica and have only Jamaican ancestry, are NOT African-Americans. If the idolized Olympic sprinter Usain Bolt, a black man, were to become a citizen in this country, he wouldn't be an African-American. The United States has never had an African-American for its vice-president. Although Kamala Harris will laugh (which for her, is way out of the ordinary), at the previous statement, she will not disagree with it. Being African is a national origin, not a race. And as long as some of us enjoy using hyphens, should we start referring to our white citizens as European-Americans if they have dark hair, and as Scandinavian-Americans if they have blonde hair?

The Green New Deal is simply totalitarian socialism being carted in on a gigantic $93 trillion dollar Trojan Horse of "caring about the environment and being deeply concerned about climate change." If one is not a socialist or communist bent on seeing America utterly destroyed, then there is no good reason or excuse for supporting the Green New Deal. For there isn't a soul on earth who can explain how the United States can stop the alleged world environmental catastrophe known as "climate change" from happening WITHOUT this country of ours living under socialism nor moving in an authoritarian-socialist direction. Particularly, it won't be explained by some feelings-and-emotion-dependent teenage chick from Sweden. Greta Thunberg, her actual name, angrily opined about capitalism (economic-freedom / social-liberty), that it's a "racist, oppressive extractivism that is exploiting both people and the planet to maxamize short-term profits for a few." It's a shame that Arvo Halberg isn't still living and middle-aged. He could have comforted the sulky, scowling Greta by giving her a big hug.

During the late 1940s through the 1980s, conservative Americans' suspicion and perceived enmity of the USSR, were labeled Red-baiting hysteria and they were mocked ("those dastardly commies under our beds are out to get us.") by the liberal/left. Has anybody ever noticed that the years 2016 through 2020, liberals wanted to take a rough and tough stand against Russia and its current leader (Putin)? This is mainly because their candidate Hillary Clinton disingenuously but effectively portrayed Donald Trump as being a friend of Vladimir Putin, and then the left merely parroted this narrative for purely political reasons. But it's the exact opposite of the 1980s, when liberals blamed icy Cold War USA / USSR relations on the Republican administration and sided with America's Moscow-funded enemy, the Marxist Sandinistas in Nicaragua. Back then, the entire political left badmouthed and disagreed with President Ronald Reagan more than they did with then, Russian dictators Brezhnev, Andropov, and Gorbachev COMBINED. The difference between then and now is that, to the progressive left, Russian president Vladimir Putin SEEMS LIKE a fascistic dictator and not a romanticized revolutionary (a'la Che Guevara). No wonder Putin is so unlikable. The problem that American progressivism has with Putin is that he is supposed to be an old-time ideological Marxist-Leninist, touting a collectivistic Russian government that, unlike the United States government, strives to provide for and take care of its people and that the ex-KGB agent, disappointingly, hasn't vocally done so. In a nut shell, Vladimir Putin comes across as a Benito Musolini when he is supposed to be the world's next Vladimir LENIN.

Moreover and especially, the left dislikes Vladimir Putin, only because they hate President Trump. If America's 45th president from the start of his campaign (June 2015), detested and denigrated the Russian president as much as Reagan did the Soviet Union (calling them the "evil empire" and wanting to leave the communist regime "on the ash heap of history"), the American liberal/left knows darn well that they would have been aligning themselves with Putin and coming to his defense. The progressives' current animus toward Russia is strictly political and not at all patriotic nor anti-communist. Those who always vote Democrat rarely if ever say a bad word about China or Iran, both who are more of a threat to America than Russia is. But for a century, our domestic soldiers of socialism's (the left) main battle had always been with a capitalistic, sovereign USA, its representative Republican presidents and conservative activists, and NOT with some adversarial superpower. Also, liberals wouldn't resent and lambast Vladimir Putin the slightest bit if Hillary had won by colluding with him and it was an absolute fact that Russia's leader personally engineered her becoming our president (he even publicly bragged about it) and the liberals know it. So it's not any "collusion" per se that they really cared about.

The entire American left actually bore no real malice toward the largest country on earth from the year 1917 to 2015. In the 1980s, they wanted so very much for the politicians in Washington, DC, particularly the Republicans, to make friends with their counterparts in Moscow. Indeed, "the liberal lion," Senator Ted Kennedy, who progressives idolized, COLLUDED with the Soviet Union when he wrote a letter in 1983 to that country's dictator, Yuri Andropov, asking him to help undermine Ronald Reagan's 1984 re-election. Today's liberal/left will never denounce what the late Massachusetts senator did. Quite the contrary, they blithely and malevolently support Kennedy's 1983 transgression. In March 2012, President Obama was caught on camera telling then Russian leader Dmitry Medvedev that he, our 44th president, would have more "flexibility" in accommodating them, the Russian government, after the upcoming November election. This was perfectly fine with liberals and Democrats. Obama's complaisant socio-political stance toward Russia merely induced indifference on the entire left that was even louder than their deafening silence. Presently, our country's top four enemies, in the opinion of the pro-capitalism right are, in order: (1) China (2) Iran (3) Russia and (4) North Korea. The top four enemies that the pro-socialism left is presently antagonistic toward are, in order: (1) The United States (2) Israel (3) Russia and (4) America.

If former Beatle John Lennon, who was living in New York in 1980, were allowed to vote in the US presidential election of that year, he would have voted for Ronald Reagan.

UNITY isn't necessarily good. George W. Bush once proudly said about himself, "I'm a uniter, not a divider." If one were to look back through the years 2000-2008, one would disagree with the former president. But then, Presidents Reagan, Clinton, and Obama were also NOT *uniters.* While these four gentlemen resided at 1600 Pennsylvania Avenue in different eras, millions of Americans liked them and millions detested the noted two-term leaders. If anything, a better case could be made that this quartet of past presidents were *polarizers.* Actually, whether a politician is a "polarizer" or a "uniter" is somewhat irrelevant. It's our nation's chief executive's economic, social, and foreign affairs policies that affect the lives of our citizen and not his or her *everybody-come-together* persona or lack thereof that's pertinent. World history teaches us that "unity" is not always what it's cracked up to be. In mid-1930s Germany, there was "unity" among the citizens, but it was an execrable, inglorious one. Though, here in America we have what could very well be the most efficacious example of *unity* in the world. It's called "the NUCLEAR FAMILY." Elsewhere, in 2016, the voters of the United Kindom elected to end (Brexit) their *unity* with the European Union. This was good for both the people and the sovereignty of the United Kingdom. Presently, the primary issue that all Americans should concentrate on being UNITED on is maintaining our liberty. If everyone in all fifty states were to do this, we could then call our country "The United States of America."

Henry Hyde was an Illinois Republican Congressman from 1975 to 2007. He once offered an opinion about his opposition to having *term limits.* "When that dentist bends over with the drill whirring, do you not hope he has done that work for a few years?" His analogy was flawed. Having a skill or profession which the patient or client relies on for a successful outcome is profoundly different than a person who is an expert on nothing but was likable enough to get elected to public office where he or she opines on issues, speaks to constituents, signs papers, and votes on various legislation. The aforementioned politician can be in office for just ONE term and quite competently formulate or vote for rulings that are wonderfully beneficial to Americans. Or this lawmaker could be a Congressperson for thirty-six years and support and pass bills that have actually been detrimental to the nation, much to the ignorance or apathy of the voters. It is the words of President Calvin Coolidge that the voting citizens of America who DON'T support term limits should heed: "It's difficult for men in high office to avoid the malady of self-delusion. They are always surrounded by worshippers. They are constantly, and for the most part sincerely, assured of their greatness. They live in an artificial atmosphere of adulation and exaltation which sooner or later impairs their judgment. They are in grave danger of becoming careless and arrogant."

Authoritarian dictators Ferdinand Marcos of the Philippines and Saddam Hussein of Iraq demanded the citizens' obedience but did not essentially need their agreement with edicts of the dictators' regimes. But the far left (egalitarian fascists, socialists, and communists) in America want not just the people's obedience to the wise, benevolent State, but also their appreciation and conscientious support of the State's extreme (but caring) progressive agenda. To have this would not only flatter the ego of the far left, but such thought control would be more likely to undermine a citizens' rebellion against a potential socialistic totalitarianism in America's future.

Martin Luther King Jr. once said, "Nothing in the world is more dangerous than sincere ignorance and conscientious stupidity." Well, yes, that's true. But, nevertheless, the black people of America still have the right to vote Democrat.

One particularly cogent sounding, but essentially daft, phrase was President Ronald Reagan's famous words to Soviet Premier Mikhail Gorbachev. Whenever they met to discuss arms control and US/Soviet relations, our president was fond of telling the Russians, "Doveryai, no proveryai," which, in English means, "Trust, but verify." Liberals, conservatives, the non-political, the vast majority of Americans, and even those who hated Reagan were positively impressed with and inspired by his seeming eloquence. However, there was one citizen who wasn't. Yes, just one. The noted anti-communist president calling for us to TRUST our number one nemesis, is negated by his insistence that we verify that the communists in Moscow aren't cheating. When the nation's Commander-in-chief instructs the American people to TRUST the Soviets, doing so is NOT a request. It's a veritable command. He is TELLING us to. There should be no equivocation about it. That being specified, if we're supposed to TRUST the men in the Kremlin, then why do we need to VERIFY that they're not cheating on arms control? We TRUST them, remember?

Let's put it this way: You're the manager of a clothing store and your own mother, whom you completely trust one hundred percent, comes in. Would you have a store detective follow her around and order your employees to watch her, via the ceiling monitors, just to VERIFY that she doesn't shoplift anything? If so, why would you? You TRUST her—remember, stupid! Though, to give Reagan the benefit of the doubt, he may have noticed the intrinsic contradiction of his slogan "trust, but verify." But our 40th president was also aware the public was scared of a possible nuclear war with the USSR and that Americans were anxious for him to "do business with" the Russians and to "try to get along" with them. He correctly surmised that the popular, albeit illogical, "trust, but verify" would suffice in allaying at least some of their fears. If this is indeed the case, then President Reagan simply had to come down to the people's level of understanding.

Has anybody ever noticed that only conservative politicians, NEVER liberal ones, are called "hard-liners?" It's because liberalism leads us in a socialistic direction and there's nothing HARD-LINE about that. But to inject more freedom and more self-responsibility into the lives of the people is to enact a cold, cruel, and uncaring HARD-LINE approach to governing. Also, has anybody ever noticed that the word "bureaucracy" is not in the liberal/left's lexicon? That's because it's a pejorative employed only by the capitalistic right. Lastly, has anybody ever noticed that the connotation of the word "powerful" when applied to a liberal American president is different than when it's applied to a conservative president? When associated with President Barack Obama, who desired bigger government, the term "powerful" signified *hope*. But with President Ronald Reagan and his plan to instill the philosophy of individualism onto society, the term "powerful" conveyed being able to inflict damage on America via governmental *indifference* (i.e. LESS benevolent governmental command and control of the people and hence, less "guidance" of them for their own good).

Back in the 1950s, if a white man called for America to be a color-blind society, he was considered to be a liberal. Today, if a white man insisted that our nation be color-blind, he is considered to be a conservative and probably a racist. Times change, and apparently so do the initial truths.

Some establishmentarian Republican politicians will SUPPORT amnesty for illegal aliens trespassing from south of the border because, as these GOP lawmakers put it, "Hispanics are hard workers." Right! As opposed to American blacks, whites, and Asians, who are NOT hard workers? How is being a "hard worker" or not germane to the illegal immigration issue? Also, does this mean that an undocumented person from say, Honduras, living in America, who is uncommonly lazy, should be deported for lethargic behavior? Timid Republicans that support amnesty realize that saying "NO" to millions of Hispanics (especially disconsolate children with snot oozing from their nostrils) looks too harsh in the eyes of the American people, especially the voters. And so they, the GOP, rationalize their actions by manufacturing an excuse (hard workers) to supersede the law (illegally being in the USA). The craven country club Republicans are unable to explain how dirt-poor, unskilled, uneducated, unauthorized intruders from south of the border who don't speak English, bring in economic exuberance and become a boon to America, like some in the GOP have claimed. Said new arrival of Democratic voters from across our borders forces lawmakers in the party of Ronald Reagan to choose the socio-political perception of kind-heartedness OVER the reality of an absolute national bankruptcy and deep recession. This is done solely for the purpose of said politicians to be re-elected and they know it. To top it all off, these lying GOP milksops, just to prove that they have a heart, will then trot out the timeworn sentimental cliché, "My own ancestors were immigrants who came from Europe in the early 1900s on a boat and they just wanted the opportunity to make a living."

The huge difference is that, back then, those self-sufficient immigrants wanted to assimilate into the American way of life and practice individualism while living in liberty, not reject our culture and values and, especially, not sponge off of any behemoth welfare state. As the notable economist Milton Friedman once explained, "You cannot simultaneously have free immigration and a welfare state." To at least partially live on the government dole is the main reason the poor people of South America came to live here in the first place. They, more than likely, were initially informed about America's generous social benefits when corresponding with their relatives and friends already living in the United States. American amnesty for six million-plus mostly illiterate, impoverished trespassers the world over would be an "act of love" (channeling Jeb Bush) that said unwelcomed freeloaders would surely take advantage of. It would also make Democrats running for election very happy.

Prominent but recreant GOP members like former Ohio Governor John Kasich say that "we can't ROUND UP" eleven million illegal immigrants and deport them. This is a disingenuous dodging of the problem. US authorities are not "rounding them up." The undocumented invaders are not cattle that we are roping into a corral. When US law enforcement finds the individuals who have broken the immigration law, the latter should be deported, whether it's just fifty of them a year or five hundred thousand, in the same fashion that the FBI doesn't "ROUND UP" criminals but instead pursues and catches them one by one. American supporters of amnesty or an open border would be absolutely unable to explain why the United States should not allow unlimited immigration to enter into the US and become citizens forever. After all, the Statue of Liberty does NOT say "Give me your tired, your poor, your huddled masses yearning to breathe free...but absolutely no more than three thousand of them a year." If you, the reader, don't welcome, say, three million illegal alien Hispanics a year for eternity to become citizens, then you're a NATIVIST. Now, isn't that right? The United States should adopt the far stricter immigration laws of another country on this earth. That country, you ask? Mexico. The Americans who are against our own "inhumane" rules of entry will not say a bad word about Mexico's far stricter, repressive immigration policies because they, Mexico, are a nation of ethnic underdogs (non-whites). Republican lawmakers should realize that giving amnesty to millions of unlawful trespassers from poor countries in order to be liked by the liberal media and cordially accepted by the uninformed American voter will only render the GOP debilitated and obsolete, by the year 2030. The Democrats certainly realize it.

Contrary to popular belief, in the 1930s, there were no Auschwitz or any other Nazi extermination camps operating anywhere in the world.

There is nothing inherently wrong with ideological extremism. Most Americans, upon being asked if they think that the reason that we, the people of the United States, should not live under communism or Nazism is because they're both "too extreme" would answer in the affirmative. Such Americans are ignorant. The reason why we should not live under communism and Nazism is because they're unjust, oppressive, and wrong. Period! That they're "too extreme" is irrelevant. If the politicians in Washington, DC were to implement economic and social policies that brought the unemployment rate down to three percent, drastically reduced crime and eradicated poverty and homelessness, but it was an ABSOLUTE FACT that these measures were "too extreme" would you be against it? If so...why? Conversely, if everyone agreed that our nation's course of action was NOT the least bit EXTREME, but did, however, increase unemployment to 25 percent and the rate of crime, poverty, and homelessness skyrocketed, would it be alright with you? It should be. It's NOT at all EXTREME, remember? The late Senator from North Carolina, Jesse Helms, had a one hundred percent conservative record. Barack Obama had a one hundred percent liberal record as an Illinois senator. The majority of the people of our country will agree that Helms was an extremist but that Obama is not. This corroborates the stupidity and dishonesty of most Americans.

You mention to the fiscally apathetic (usually liberals, moderates, and young people) that our government has been wasting billions of the taxpayers' money on pork barrel projects, earmarks, the Bridge to Nowhere in Alaska, Big Dig in Massachusetts, and other economic boondoggles while improving virtually nothing. You then ask them how they feel about it and what should be done about it. The fiscally apathetic will invariably answer, "Well, there's ALWAYS been wasteful government spending throughout American history." And there you have it. Their reply is not a denunciation of wasteful spending but a shirking of it. You understand; it's not like Washington, DC just started flushing billions of dollars down the proverbial toilet a scant few months ago. No, they've been doing it for over sixty years, and so we should all be used to it by now. What's the big deal? Why stop something that's been so natural and part of our culture?

Liberals don't like conservative columns and editorials in our newspapers, and vice versa, but for different reasons. Left-leaning individuals in our country don't like reading the truth and moreover, don't want other citizens to read it because it may influence them. On the other side, right-leaning individuals don't want to read a bunch of lies and moreover don't want other Americans to because it may influence THEM.

Some of my brethren on the ideological right have it all wrong. They think that the majority of black Americans automatically stuck up for President Obama because he's black. Not true. Blacks habitually came to his defense primarily because Obama's a left-leaning Democrat. They also circled the wagons around Bill Clinton, the country's first black president (as he was lovingly referred to by many blacks circa 1998) during the Lewinsky scandal. And these particular black people did so because our 42nd president was perceived to be a liberal. Liberalism (bigger government) represents HOPE to many blacks. Now, "hope" is really just PASSIVITY. Though, there are those who would like to think that PASSIVITY is actually a strategy for happiness. They are sadly mistaken. But the worse the liberal politicians and their policies make the collective life of black Americans, the more that the latter will hold liberal politicians in high esteem. For instance, young blacks with the help of vouchers (which conservatives love) who go to private or charter schools are far more likely to go to college and/or do well in life than those who go to public (government) schools. White liberals are vehemently against vouchers and want America's black children to go to public schools. Many, if not most, black parents dutifully agree with white liberals on this issue.

The next message of enlightenment from yours truly will NOT help "black society" but it will help black INDIVIDUALS. There really is a colossal difference between the two. This writer's advise to black America, particularly the young, is to espouse individualism from the get-go. As a black person (or any other race) you might as well think of yourself as an INDIVIDUAL due to the fact that you will never stop being one. Following this advice is the best way of achieving middle-class status. And in doing so, you won't be living "the white life" nor "the black life" but the *American life*. As soon as a black turns eighteen, he or she should set out on his or her own and leave the confines of the city or desolate small town behind. Better yet, you should become a conservative. But under no circumstances should you let your friends or relatives know. Otherwise, you will be ostracized and/or hated by your peers. Does this author guarantee if a black became a conservative, that he or she would become successful or wealthy? Nope. Absolutely not! But I do guarantee that they would HAVE A BETTER CHANCE of doing so because the noted black individuals will intelligently comprehend their circumstances and what they need to do. And that is not to be like the others. Compare the blacks who always vote Democrat with the ones who always vote Republican and find out which group is living a better life? And then after you do that, try not to lie to yourself with the reply, "Duh black Republicans just be kissin duh white man's ass" or words to that effect. You, yourself, have been brown-nosing the Democratic Party for so long that you have practically become their permanent colostomy bag!

When the far left bases their political aims on emotion, feelings, and utopian desires; they believe that they can't possibly go wrong. And from strictly that standpoint, they're correct. It's when some anonymous person defies and challenges the left with logic that the latter will immediately attempt to stigmatize (a la Saul Alinsky) that person as a "right-winger." It is then that the left depends on the ignorance of the public as to what a "right-winger" wants. Progressives realize that when they smear the right-wing (pro-capitalism) messenger, they smear the message. The result enables the impressionable young and other adherents of pop culture to hitch their wagons to whatever seems to be "cool" and popular (the leftist agenda). It's a convenient escape hatch where no serious thinking is needed. What the people should know is that the goal of the left is to punish certain Americans and then afterward, build a better society for all citizens. This "better society" just happens to reside, at least theoretically, in socialism. The goal of the right is the search for the truth through honest and intelligent analysis. This truth just happens to reside in liberty-based capitalism.

The difference between the old, stuffy, puritan right and the new politically correct/woke left is that the former didn't look forward to being offended.

A bit of colloquialism has practically descended into cultural Marxism that the vast majority of America hasn't recognized. That is the current practice of referring to females in the spoken word as "guys." When speaking to a bunch of teenage girls, many, if not most people, would address them today as "guys" even though it's exactly what they ARE NOT. This isn't just the politically correct thing to do, but it is also trendy and hip. Calling them "girls" is passé, slightly insulting, almost sexist, and worst of all...true. So from now on, the female basketball teams in high schools are to be referred to as the "*guys* basketball team." Also, when a mother-to-be gives birth to a baby that has a vagina, it would be both proper and accurate to say that she just gave birth to a BABY GUY. Ladies on television talk shows are always called "guys" by each other and their guests. Likewise, when conversing with an audience of men and women, the speaker must address them as "guys" instead of "people." Nowadays, it is considered insensitive and demeaning to call people, "people." In fact, it virtually guarantees that there will be some person in the audience yelling at the speaker, "What do you mean, you people?" So remember, if you ever give an important speech to an audience of hundreds, be sure to refer to them as "guys." There may be ladies present.

In the opinions of millions of Americans, a devout libertarian conservative Republican president who presides over a Federal government that gives society more socio-economic freedom by not providing for or being responsible for its citizens, deserves to be and will be called a dictator by them. But a staunch liberal male Democrat president accelerating omnipotent government to take away their liberty (but with an altruistic attitude), with more laws, regulations, and restrictions will rarely, if ever, be branded a dictator by these same Americans. And this is because the Democratic president doesn't deserve it. Indeed, the man is just validating that he cares about his people, and there isn't anything wrong with that. Our society's dislike of dictators is exceeded only by our liking of a powerful, ostensibly benevolent, though domineering State. Sometimes, it seems that the government's total control of our citizens is necessary in order to liberate them from the shackles of freedom.

The difference between a liberal and a leftist is that the liberal is a do-gooder who pretends to be patriotic while a leftist is a subversive who pretends to be a do-gooder.

Poor Benito Mussolini: Every time that the Left spouts "fascist" in order to demonize President Trump and prominent conservatives, they always bring up the name "Hitler" or sometimes the Spanish authoritarian dictator, Francisco Franco, who the left erroneously labels a fascist, or they even bring up…"Joseph Stalin"?? But almost never does the left mention the preeminent fascist in the world for a century now, Mussolini. Although, there WAS an American liberal who, back in the 1930s, said about the European despot, "I am much interested and deeply impressed by what he has accomplished and by his evidenced and honest purpose of restoring Italy and seeking to prevent general European trouble." Besides the previous quote, President Franklin Roosevelt also refered to Mussolini as an "admirable Italian gentleman." The Italian dictator (1922-1943) was once a member of the Italian Socialist Party and called Karl Marx "the greatest of all theorists of socialism." Il Duce (his nickname) was also an atheist and admirer of Vladimir Lenin. He eventually became anti-egalitarian and disenchanted with his aforementioned political party's class-warfare strategy of achieving power in Italy. Later on, after taking command of the boot-shaped country, like a communist but with a nationalistic bent, Mussolini created an oppressive police state that controlled banks, enterprise, and the citizens. Although the Italian tyrant personally didn't like Adolph Hitler, he became a "friend" and ally of the German despot for geopolitical reasons. And just like the Führer, Mussolini detested a right-wing socio-economic system called *capitalism*. But as a historically vile, loathesome villain to be despised and politically exploited, Benito apparently just doesn't cut it. Heck, many on the far left have denounced their Uncle Joe Stalin even more than they've verbally shunned the late bald-headed Italian autocrat. Mussolini just plain wasn't as infamously evil as the Berlin-based, mustached madman and hence, progressives exploiting Il Duce as a cudgel of incrimination wouldn't be as effective in their demonization of the pro-liberty Right. That's undoubtedly the reason why the American left rarely ever shines a political spotlight on him. Poor Benito Mussolini: the forgotten fascist.

It's alright to engage in a flight of whimsy about a potential avant-garde shake-up in the way that our lawmakers do business at the nation's capital just as long as we get back to the political normalcy that we're so accustomed to. There was a news item telling us that Democrats desire EXPERIENCE in a candidate for political office, while Republicans want an OUTSIDER. In this context, the word "experience" is a codeword for "the status quo" while an outsider is a rebellious UPSTART who is trying to bring CHANGE to "the way things are done" in the Washington, DC Swamp. The "experienced" member of the status quo represents relative *safety*. The outsider, however, and his plan to "shake things up" connotes future uncertainty. To the Americans who vote Democrat, the experienced politicians really are, said citizens do regret, a "good ole boys" network. But in being so, at least this network, which includes the thoroughly disliked but tolerated and ultimately accepted *lobbyists*, remains reassuring to non-Republicans by NOT doing something radically different to the system that the latter has become accustomed to. Many a voter who resents and has complained about the STATUS QUO is a person who actually supports it. The Democratic electorate, for the most part, doesn't want moral integrity and righteous ethics in their representatives if it means the same for themselves. Liberals are weary of the phrase "Drain the Swamp." Now, they don't enthusiastically support the *Swamp*, but nor are said Democrats opposed to it. Though, they ARE suspicious of and will subsequently object to, anybody who wants to tear down an entity that shares the fiscally reckless and ethically irresponsible attitude of liberalism. For it is precisely this *culture of corruption* in Washington, DC that facilitates liberalism and hence, the almighty benevolent State!

In order for the American people to truly enjoy and appreciate well-intentioned, good-hearted socialism and be forever thankful for it, they are going to have to be locked into it from which there can be no escape.

In the early 1800s, the overwhelming majority of people in America were not the least bit oppressed by slavery. Furthermore, many in that majority actually found slavery to be downright helpful. Today, a predominance of the super-sensitive will consider the preceding two sentences to be utterly inflamatory. But all of these emotion-dependant snowflakes and their obligatory virtue signaling after their reading of these statements, will come to realize that they didn't disagree with what yours truly initially said (and they won't). Indeed, that the first two sentences are so bitingly true is the main reason that they're so inflammatory.

"BIRTHERISM" isn't racist. And after reading this paragraph, anybody who says that it's racist is a liar. The noted term designates the belief of various Americans who said, during his 2008 presidential run, that Barack Obama wasn't born in the United States. Now, such a belief may be classified as "dislike" of him, certainly "suspicion" of the former president and maybe even "paranoia," but it's not racist. The "birtherism" hearsay was first started by Sid Blumenthal, a supporter and assistant of Hillary Clinton in her 2008 attempt for the presidency. But those who voted for Hillary and initially denounced the canard will adamantly deny that what Sid Blumenthal did was racist. How come? If you'll notice, Jesse Jackson, Alan Keyes, Al Sharpton, Herman Cain, and Ben Carson are black men who also, at one time, ran for president, but absolutely NOBODY accused any of these five of NOT being born in America. This proves that *birtherism* isn't racism but merely a nationwide unfounded rumor devised by a liberal Democrat.

To my comrades on the pro-capitalism right; this author supports implementing nationally the *Fair Tax* plan that many of you desire. But bear in mind that most Americans will be against the Fair Tax if it doesn't include collectivism and redistribution. Commensurably, when our citizens envision economic "fairness," they are NOT thinking of governmental *neutrality*. The American people will consequently believe that if your tax plan doesn't go in a direction of installing socio-economic equality, then it cannot possibly be FAIR like the title claims.

The individual is the societal entity of innate superiority because a person mainly focuses on oneself. The aforementioned notion is followed by, in descending order: The family, the community, the town, the county, the state, then last and certainly least, the Federal government. The view of today's liberal/left and most voters is that the real order of societal superiority is the precise opposite.

Any socio-political conflicts between whites and blacks before the year 1966 was, generally speaking, white people who were the "bad guys" and black people who were the "good guys." After 1965, and in regard to personal character, the two racial groups switched sides as to who were largely more virtuous and law-abiding.

Charles Manson was a *"doomsday"* leader of a 100 member cult. David Koresh was a cult leader and head of an 80 member heretical fringe group called the Branch Davidians. People who are attracted to a cult leader's "wisdom" and "charismatic personality" are apt to be indoctrinated because they are overburdened with feelings of loneliness, emotion, and are intellectually-speaking, a few sandwiches shy of a picnic. Citizens that despise Donald Trump and call him a "cult leader" and his supporters "cult followers" are liars who resent the fact that he's so popular. 75 million Trump supporters with their love of America and having a liberty/freedom socio-economic philosophy, far from constitute being a small, unconventional, pseudo-religious sect. If there's any individuals who would be members of a cult, it's the citizens that continue to believe in (and do so religiously) SOCIALISM despite its history.

Can you read between the lines of subtle communistic jargon? Observe: "When the government itself is chaotic and an absurdity, if it rules without helping and commands without leading, how can we persuade every citizen to obey the law and confine self-seeking to a circle of the total good? How can a society be strong or even be saved unless led by the wisest?" Saved? Saved from what? And about Hillary Clinton in her 2016 presidential run, the radical writer added: "Only she has the courage to take on a herculean summons to marshal us all to betterment." Remember now, "ONLY she" can "marshal us all" to betterment. Evidently, Obama couldn't and didn't. But do the writer's statements not reek of government control and coercion? Although the person (last name, Rosenblum) who wrote this is more than likely a communist, I haven't the slightest idea what his or her religion is. But then again, neither do you, the reader.

The slogan "Make America Great Again" or "MAGA" connotes PATRIOTISM/ CAPITALISM. MAGA" is essentially *paleoconservatism*. When Joe Biden and other liberals supplement the word "MEGA" before "MAGA", it changes the the latter term to then mean STRONGLY *anti-socialism,* although, the left will never publicly divulge this. "MEGA" is a more potent, insidious modifier to the pejorative "MAGA." The gist of this verbal attack on the pro-Trumpers is that the American people should be petrified of terminology ("MAGA") that only forbodes individualism and self-responsibility for them and thus, the inducement of more actual liberty. For genuine liberty is scary because it doesn't tangibly take care of the peoples' problems and provide them with hands-on comfort. To "Make America Great Again" is to provide the citizens with far less government control of them. Doing so only portends a "you're on your own" capitalistic socio-economic country built by MAGA (i.e. conservative) Republicans in Washington, DC. This is thought to be dangerous because it doesn't subjugate society in a caring, compassionate and equitable way. No human being should have to live within economic freedom and social liberty, because they're both main components of the *MAGA philosophy* and are therefore inhumane.

CHAPTER **10**

The Bell Hooks Syndrome

AUTHOR AND FEMINIST, bell hooks, (her first and last name are, intentionally, not capitalized) gave a lecture at the University of Wisconsin, on white supremacy and multiculturalism. The two are not really that indistinguishable from each other, since both advocate group-differentiated rights and harbor resentment toward certain people. Anyway, at the conclusion of bell hooks' address, this writer walked up and asked her if a black American (which, incidentally, she is) would live a better life living under socialism. Hooks replied with an enthusiastic, "Oh yes, absolutely!" And then I asked, "What model of socialism? Would it be like Cuba's?" And she responded, "Yes, like Cuba's." Listening to ms. hooks, beforehand, I could sense that the feminist author was probably a socialist because she would repeatedly cite individuals and agendas that were "progressive" (a euphemism for "socialistic") and often mentioned "the struggle," jargon used countless times in communist periodicals. Bell hooks told us, "The white dominant Christian church relies on Biblical verses to justify racism." Now, this is an utterly baseless and bigoted remark. But, nonetheless, she did receive a standing ovation from the mostly white audience at the end of her speech. The college newspaper article about her said that bell hooks "does not capitalize her name because she considers the issues more important than a name or personality." This is a smart move on the feminist author's part. Otherwise, if she DID capitalize her name, people would have thought that bell hooks was being pompous and pretentious and wouldn't be able to take her seriously.

For years, the University of Wisconsin falculty has invited only left-leaning academes to speak to the predominantly white student audience, presumedly because these speakers are humanitarian do-gooders, just like the Wisconsin University falculty. For example, we've had socialist and co-author of the Clowerd-Piven strategy, Frances Fox Piven. She and her partner, Richard Clowerd's strategy and aim were to overload the welfare state and subsequently bankrupt the United States. They semi-succeeded (America is not a socialist country......yet). Then it was Marxist historian and clandestine former Communist Party member, Howard Zinn, who came here. Expelled CIA agent and communist sympathizer, Philip Agee visited, as did Democratic Socialists of America co-founder Michael Harrington, plus Black Panther revolutionary, Stokely Carmichael and status-seeking socialist professor, Cornell West have imparted their wisdom on the Wisconsin University student body. And last but not least, twenty-three-year veteran Communist Party USA member and social justice pioneer (obviously), Angela Davis. Unfortunately, Gus Hall was evidently too busy to make an appearance. Oh well, our loss.

For Black History month, which is when Ms. hooks arrived, why didn't the university invite college professor and author, Walter E. Williams (also black), for a lively debate with her? It's because they know that Mr. Williams is a conservative intellectual and that he would have torn her apart. The inhabitants of the University of Wisconsin and most college campuses are passionate supporters of diversity (excluding diversity of political opinion). That is to say, the professors and various department heads at Wisconsin U. and other learning institutions want to INDOCTRINATE the idealistic and susceptible young minds, not educate them with different philosophical perspectives. Not only this, but the left academia, in general, that dominates higher learning institutions, seeks out and enjoys having their own kind come in and preach to the choir. In the process, these "forward" thinkers validate their ideology so that they can continue to soak in a cocoon of self-content.

The last thing that an elite university wants is to have some intelligent libertarian *classical liberal* such as Professor Williams venture onto their campus and then proceed to factually and rationally punch holes in their dreams of a compassionate, collectivistic utopia. Like Mr. Williams and other scholars on the capitalistic right, progressive professors and lecturers are also intellectuals. The caveat is that their intellectual dishonesty is to be intrinsic and not optional. You see, the aforementioned educators envision themselves as being smarter than the working class, and they really are. With their more advanced minds, the ivory towers of the academic left believe that it is incumbent on them to help engineer a more humane, superior system for the masses in which to live. The socialism that they've conjured up is not the run-of-the-mill kind that the forlorn, oppressed citizens are purportedly wistful about, but is instead "scientific," which gives it the gravitas and grandeur that these erudite educators would like to think makes socialism more tenable. The professors and lecturers then hope that their portraying socialism as being "intelligent" compensates for the truth about it. But when their envisage runs into a wall of logic and reality, verbal deviousness for the purpose of persuading becomes indispensable. Liberal college youngsters are susceptible to brainwashing, not because they're liberal per se, but because they're glutinous blobs of feelings and emotion. These gullible, impressionable, and ancillary university students, who are influenced by their self-aggrandizing but wise professors, are the new, idealistic generation, and they're going to rectify all that the elders have so incompetently screwed up. The trouble is that they find it impossible to be idealistic WITHOUT the movement toward centralized government. The noted college kids then "discover" the all-encompassing healing powers of SOCIALISM and think that they just happened upon a beautiful thing. Said neo-Marxist morons erroneously tell themselves that if America goes in a socialistic direction then it cannot possibly go in a fascistic direction. They eventually find out that socialism has been tried in other countries with no success, to put it mildly. But then again, those other countries didn't have idealistic, American youths running their socio-economic systems.

Sure, conservatism is cerebrally stimulating, but it is liberal/leftism that's comforting to the conscience, particularly young guilt-ridden college students with rich parents. The mere pretense and vacuity of youthful liberalism becomes noble and worthy in their quest to perfect American society. Uniformity of the political/ideological thought process becomes just as essential at our American universities as it did in the public schools of Berlin circa 1934. Many of our immature but enlightened college students advance in life by becoming "communists." Are they really communists? No, the vast majority isn't, and the Marxist professors know it. Said students just sometimes casually but privately adopt the "communist" moniker because its disposition and outlook are the opposite of the "stuffy" conservative status quo that they've long resented and have been yearning to spite. But if such "communist" youngsters of higher learning thought about it for a minute, they would realize that they call conservatives "fascists" precisely because, and much to their dismay, conservatism is NOT fascism nor even favorable to it. The noted collectivism-adoring collegians would really rather not be informed by America's educators that for the United States to go in an absolute LEFT-wing socio-political direction, is to arrive at fascism first, then socialism and lastly, communism.

Actually, most of these ultra-idealistic college kids are just CONTRARIANS who will shun communism once they reach adulthood at the age of thirty. In conclusion, Ms. bell hooks notwithstanding, what higher learning students, particularly minorities, should comprehend is that socialism (which "multiculturalism," political correctness, and "diversity" are conducive to) is not enchantment, but instead, enslavement. We really should refrain from going the route that the likes of bell hooks want to take us. Finally, not to be left out of the academic discourse, Wisconsin University President Larry Mendenhall offered "The learning communities must resist the kind of thinking that allows us to close our hearts and minds to our fellow travelers in this world." Well, so far, the University of Wisconsin has done an excellent job of inviting and accepting fellow travelers to lecture on its campus. And I'm sure that Mr. Mendenhall and his successors will continue the tradition.

CHAPTER **11**

The Politics of Compassion

AT A TOWN hall meeting in the 1980s, former Democratic Congressman Jack Reed was asked if he thought that redistribution from the rich to the poor was a socialistic economic policy. It is, of course, although said politician had no choice but to say "no" to the question, which he promptly did. The gentleman answered this way because he didn't want it to look like he backs a policy that he admits is socialistic and realized that his advocacy of redistribution is what keeps liberals like him in office via the voting booth. It also tells Mr. Reed and like-minded officeholders that they're being compassionate and sensitive to the needs of the poor and needy.

We've all heard that "Republicans don't care about the poor" (read: "They'll cut back on government hand-outs."). Liberals like to say that the GOP will "widen the gap between the haves and the have-nots." Hey, what a coincidence! That's the same thing that Karl Marx and his followers said about capitalism. One fallacy many Americans believe is that the presidency is supposed to implement measures to eradicate poverty and hunger. Well, let's say that instead of a Republican president, America had a left-leaning Democrat for president. Now three years into President Liberal's term, would there still be homelessness, unemployment, and hunger? Of course there would. To this, the bleeding hearts would say, "Well, yes, but at least there's less of it than there would be under a Republican president." Even if that were true, poverty is still there, now isn't it? This can only mean that, like a Republican president, the Democrat president "isn't doing enough for the poor." Unbeknownst to most of the public, a politician's "caring about the poor" is merely a sympathy and a moot point unless it manifests itself through government responsibility and control. Quite simply, in the socio-political arena, if it isn't socialistic or conducive to socialism, then it isn't COMPASSIONATE.

Although famous compassionate rocker Bruce Springsteen lives on a horse farm in New Jersey, has a mansion in Beverly Hills, and is worth two thirds of a billion dollars, he is not a limousine liberal. The singer/songwriter also owns at least three more homes in the USA (where he was born), but owns no homes ninety miles south of Key West. Springsteen performed in a 2009 documentary feature film written and directed by Howard Zinn, a communist. The multi-millionaire musician once declared, albeit erroneously, that it was "the right of every American to have a job, a living wage, to be educated in a decent school and a life filled with the dignity of work." He also stated: "Right now, there is a fight going on to help make this a fairer and more equitable nation." Such opinionated tunes would have been music to the ears of Norman Thomas. The Boss has done a lot of concerts all over the country. Obviously, he is a fellow who has traveled far and wide. Bruce Springsteen currently fancies himself as a latter-day Tom Joad, but he's more like a contemporary Pete Seeger, only without the hammer and sickle. Or better yet, a Dean Reed without the dimples.

A few decades ago, Hollywood actor Martin Sheen slept with some filthy hobos on a city sidewalk in the winter and used the television medium to tell Americans that there are poor people in the United States. In the near future, Sheen intends to be even more informative by going on nationwide news to tell us that the sun is hot. Detractors of this article would respond that the actor was just being compassionate. If that's so, then why didn't millionaire Martin act the part of giving at least one homeless tramp a scant two hundred dollars so that he could buy some clothes, eat a good meal, and bathe and sleep in a cheap motel for a night? Now, I'm aware that lying down on a ventilation grate next to a rich celebrity can be a very comforting and rewarding experience for a vagrant, a warm memory that would be cherished for years and sidewalks to come. But it would have been a little warmer if Mr. Sheen had given the vagrant his coat.

One man who could have given Martin Sheen a run for his money in the limousine liberal department was former Rhode Island Senator Claiborne Pell. In the late 1980s and early 1990s, Pell, a Democrat in his mid-seventies, was worth about 22 million dollars and was one of the richest in the Senate at that time. Why did Rhode Islanders continue to hold this compassion charlatan in such high reverence? Did he give any of his own money to the poor and needy, and if so, how much? And if one doesn't know or care if he had or not, then on what grounds does one consider Pell to be "compassionate"? Is it because our rich ex-senator, while in office, voted to give himself a much-needed pay raise with our earnings? Or is it the pork and paternalism that he brought home from Washington for three decades compel us to overlook any "vices" of his with compliments like "compassionate" and "in touch with the common man?" This is a validation of the outright pretense and shallowness of liberalism.

Let's play "Find the Compassion," shall we? There are three parties involved in this game: A liberal politician, a wealthy woman, and a poor man. With the law on his side, the politician confiscates money from the affluent female and gives it to the poor man. Now then, where is the COMPASSION coming from? Is the poor man being compassionate? No, he's merely accepting the money. How about the rich lady? Nope, she's not volunteering the money over, it's being taken from her. Then, the correct answer must be, the liberal politician? Wrong again. He didn't take his money out of his own pocket. The "empathetic" lawmaker voted to have the government seize the wealth of the affluent woman and give it to a total stranger. So where is the compassion? Answer: It's found only in volunteerism and philanthropy. And these two good deeds emanate only from the SELF. But then, you see, many in American society don't place volunteerism and philanthropy on the same pedestal of goodness as they do a collectivistic and redistributionist government. The people don't mind commending VOLUNTEERISM (like the Red Cross and the Salvation Army) and PHILANTHROPY (charities and donations). But these two acts of kindness are random and sporadic and not enough to attain the blanket coverage, cure-all presence of an omnipotent nanny state. Thus, with America's demand for more "public assistance," volunteerism and philanthropy become more expected and taken for granted and, as a consequence, less admired and appreciated.

Rich liberals, by having the government take their money instead of the former giving it away, can think of themselves as being compassionate but still retain their innate selfishness. Indeed, the further one leans to the left, the more one tends to frown upon philanthropy and volunteerism. Communists despise the noted two endeavors, socialists dislike them and liberals dismiss them. The first two of these three ideologically left-leaning groups disapprove of philanthropy and volunteerism because they undercut government responsibility. Our society unfairly and disingenuously regards rich Democrat politicians who NEVER give to charity as being more caring and compassionate than Republicans who always do. The nation's belief is that a politician can't "have a heart" without possessing a socialistic governing philosophy. But what many, if not most, of our citizens don't realize is that a capitalistic (free) country can't possibly be responsible for the economic welfare of its people. It is NOT a civil right to have food, clothing, shelter, and a job. It is merely a right to have the liberty to attain them.

What should be understood, and what many liberals seem to be ignorant of, is that man cares mainly about himself, not others (egoism). Be that as it may, conservatives are more philanthropic and donate their time to help the poor far more than liberals do. But egoism has nothing to do with what race, ethnicity, religion, or gender a person is. The far left (socialists and communists), on the other hand, are well aware of this egoism and are determined to put a stop to it. If the far left had their druthers, American individuals would NOT be left alone to satisfy their own wants and needs, but would instead be made pawns via the State, to "build a better society." Most of the American people associate the term "empathy" with the Democratic party not realizing or caring that the aforementioned emotion is actually just a superficial and meaningless term unless it manifests itself through *progressive (read: socialistic)* economic policies. Subsequently, too many of us are of the mindset that Democratic politicians deserve to be appreciated and looked up to. They don't need to do penance via philanthropy. Self-responsibility-pushing Republican lawmakers do.

As odd as it may sound, what isn't inherent in free enterprise capitalism comes by nature of it. And that's altruism and generosity. Contrary to what the pseudo-compassionate left thinks, from an economically freer (more deregulation and privatization) country, evolves a more caring, charitable public. Look at it this way; if we were to simply live under Big Government on steroids (quasi-socialism), everyone would then have a legitimate reason to refrain from giving to charity or volunteering their assistance. Yes, of course, it would be kind of them if they did. But if someone were to ask any particular American why he or she won't help others in need; that American could rightfully claim, "Its' not my job to, it's the governments." They're supposed to be taking care of that. If I were to help out, I'd be undermining the government's job and absolving them of their responsibility." And this person wouldn't be giving an excuse, mind you. It would be a REASON, a darn good one, and it would be the truth. But then the reverse is also true: If it's not the government's responsibility to care for the people, and it isn't, then that behooves millions of individuals to do so on their own free will. Less government, not more, breeds compassion. The fact that the capitalistic USA, judging from its past, is one of, if not THE, most altruistic, alms-giving country in the world, substantiates all this. That concludes this heart-warming article about compassion.

CHAPTER 12

The Right Way to Think

WHAT IS POLITICAL conservatism? If I had to define it in just one word, that word would be CAPITALISM. Libertarianism is the foundation of capitalism, while traditionalism is the framework that counters and smoothens out the rough, hedonistic edges of capitalism. Personal autonomy and self-responsibility are very much synonymous with capitalism (pecuniary liberty), and conservatives champion these to the hilt. Traditional values and institutions such as marriage, the nuclear family, religion, competition, hard work, and private ownership epitomize conservatism and they are the backbone of "our way of life" (socio-economic freedom). People often, and sometimes unknowingly, equate patriotism with actions or principles that are conservative. If you're a flag-waving, parade-loving American you are, wittingly or not, supporting "America." And in the minds of the far left, that means CAPITALISM. The aforementioned progressives dislike genuine pro-America patriotism because it makes it more unlikely that our citizens will resent their country and consequently, for dissent to breed. To them, REAL patriotism is an obedience to and glorification of the benevolent, father-like State. A benign dictatorship, if you will. Conservatives, on the other hand, are the enemy of the glorious State and in leftist opinion they deserve to be vilified.

What the socialistic Left calls "the far Right" is really just conservatives abiding by the Constitution and adhering to its principles. As you know, or should know, conservative terms like "privatization," "vouchers," and "charter schools" connote lack of government control. Have you ever noticed that the liberal left harbors an animus toward the noted three? Have you ever noticed literature that praises and supports capitalistic economic policies are always written by conservatives (Milton Friedman, George Gilder, and others)? The Constitution is a "right-wing document." That's with or without "quotation marks." It is what begat capitalism. Have you ever noticed that a lawyer or judge who is a "strict Constitutionalist" is always a conservative, never a liberal? Why is that? And with socialism/communism being the exact opposite of capitalism; who were more friendly toward the old Soviet Union and the communist line, the liberal or the conservative? Right-wing vs. left-wing: Right-wing basically means capitalism, and left-wing basically means socialism. It really is that simple.

Unfortunately, no right-wing politician has ever educated the nation's citizens about this, and that's a disgrace. But it is not only the Tea Party who has been let down by the GOP. The Libertarian Party has, for decades, been disappointed with the Republican Party, NOT with the Democrat Party. The Libertarian Party has long been the more serious, radical cousin of the GOP and exists to primarily goad them further to the right (toward, if not actually arriving at, laissez-faire capitalism). On the other side, the Green Party has for many years been disappointed with the Democrat Party and NOT with the Republican Party. The Green Party has long been the more serious, radical cousin of the Democrats and exists to primarily goad them further to the left (toward, if not to, democratic socialism). Essentially, when the conservative right speaks about "the American people," the former is thinking of the latter as an entity of INDIVIDUALS. But when somebody on the liberal/left verbally refers to "the American People," he or she is thinking of them as being ONE BIG UNIT. Incidently, there is no such thing as "right-wing social engineering." OR, there is, although it's being enforced, not by governmental fiat, but by liberty/freedom which obligates virtue and self-responsibility upon the citizens.

The government-fearing militia is on the far right. Timothy McVeigh was a twenty-seven-year-old right-winger who turned into a terrorist and a murderer when he killed 168 people in the Oklahoma City bombing of a building of his doing on April 19, 1995. Most American conservatives support the death penalty and advocated Timothy McVeigh's well-deserved execution. The majority of American liberals, on the other hand, wisely abstained from voicing their opinion about the death penalty (they were privately against it) for this particular young man. Then there's the conspiracy-obsessed BLACK HELICOPTER crowd who fret rightly (pun semi-intended) or wrongly about "shadow government," the "Deep State" and the "New World Order." For perhaps over a century, far-right wingers have been sometimes foolishly paranoid about the Rockefellers, the Bilderberg Group, the Illuminati, the Freemasons and others. In the 1950s, the John Birch Society was a reputable, patriotic, pro-capitalism organization, until its founder accused Republican President Dwight. D. Eisenhower of being a communist agent. Today, the JBS, a mere skeleton of its heyday, has been mostly fixated on the Trilateral Commission and the Council on Foreign Relations and their alleged subversion plots. The new kids on the right-wing conspiratorial block, is the quirky and off-the-wall Q-anon. There's not much to be made about this On-line cult except that it has made some false, outrageous claims that should be taken with a grain of salt.

But this right-wing writer (lame pun intended) disagrees with some of his ideological comrades by positing that the far right and the far left are not the same. That is, they are not part of a circle in which the far right and the far left travel in different directions, but they both go too far and end up meeting and metamorphosing into the same ideological monster. This is plainly not the case. Communism, as all of us know, is as far left on the spectrum as the left can go. And it is totalitarian, is it not? So if the far right is the exact opposite of the far left, and it is, then how can the far right be totalitarian? It can't. If we, the American electorate, were to take our country as far to the democratic left (more government) as we could possibly go, we would end up living under socialism. This would eventually and in all probability descend into some type of totalitarianism (complete government control), which would require the capitulation and subsequent obedience of the citizens to the authoritarian State. But if the voters of America were to steer our country very far to the democratic right (as in, far less government), we would end up living under laissez-faire capitalism, which could, though not necessarily, descend into anarchy (no government, extreme individualism). Contrary to popular belief (rebellious, angry, left-wing punk rockers notwithstanding), anarchy of the ideological kind is on the far right, not on the far left. Paleo-conservatism, nationalistic libertarianism and Ayn Rand objectivism are on the right-wing fringe. With the exception of outright anarchy, which would be absolute chaos, anarcho-capitalism is as far to the civilized right as one can go. Privatizing Social Security plus abolishing the IRS, the Department of Education, and the National Endowment of the Arts, among others (I'm starting to drool on my keyboard), are all good examples of, and even better propositions from, the far right. In a nutshell, the capitalistic thing to do is the right thing to do (ideological pun semi-intended). Incidentally, what would be so bad about democratically taking our country to the respectful, law-abiding, non-violent far-right? And one which would be a socio-economic system with infinitely more freedom/liberty than we have now but with a rule of laws, Bible-based moral values and a small secularist State that observes neutrality and abstains from governmental social engineering.

Basically, the conservative right believes that REAL FREEDOM produces prosperity, while liberals insist on believing that government does. The far left mendaciously tries to portray conservatism as the road to fascism, which is more repressive government control of the people because conservatism doesn't go in a socialistic direction, which, in turn, is more repressive government control of the people. At any rate, the motto of American capitalism is and should be, to help yourself first, and then after you do that, help others. But in order for this to happen, the government needs to get out of the way. The United States has always been a right-wing (capitalistic) or at the very least, a center-right country. Ronald Reagan has been America's most capitalistic president since the 1930s. The ironic thing is that many conservatives don't realize this, but the socialistic left does. The left employed all sorts of pejoratives (cruel and heartless) to describe our fortieth president and his philosophy, but never once used the adjective "capitalistic" that they were thinking. Why not? It's because naïve or ignorant individuals, upon reading or hearing the progressives use the word "capitalistic" to define Reagan, would think to themselves, "Well, wait a minute, this is a capitalistic country, so isn't the president and the rest of the politicians SUPPOSED to carry out economic policies that are conducive to capitalism?"

As a result of this revelation, these individuals may then start reading between the lines of leftist demagoguery and start voting for lawmakers who uphold libertarian economic policies, thus taking America further away from the direction of socialism. Though the second most philosophically conservative/capitalistic president (after Calvin Coolidge); Ronald Reagan did not govern as an economically pure one in his two terms. Unfortunately for America, Reagan was far less conservative in the 1980s than he was the decade before. As a candidate for president in 1979 and 1980, the former California governor said that he wanted to abolish the Department of Energy and the Department of Education. As president, Reagan never even made an effort to do the aforementioned, nor did he practice austerity regarding the budget. In fact, in reference to his administration, the former actor and California governor once sheepishly explained, "We are not attempting to cut either spending or taxing levels below that which we presently have." Too bad he wasn't lying. As an economic conservative in the nation's highest office, Reagan gets a B minus for a grade. And worst of all, at no time during his presidency did the Great Communicator ever communicate with the American people that libertarian conservatism IS free-market capitalism and that contemporary liberalism really is the road to socialism. Federal government from 1981 to 1989 didn't shrink, it grew!

Today's conservative politicians must do what our fortieth president neglected to do, and that is, to rub the truth in the collective face of the American people, whether they like it or not. Prominent members of the libertarian right, particularly self-professed *conservative* politicians, need to put the nation's citizens on the spot about our country's fast-moving tidal wave toward socialism. This is the very narrative exemplified by the Tea Party. But the liberal/left won't tell you that it's the Tea Party's main concern and that's because the noted progressives wouldn't be able to smear the Tea Party by honestly defining them. It is solely up to the pro-capitalism, anti-socialism right (you can't expect moderates to) to resist using tact and nuance when telling our voters (it's THEY who elect our lawmakers) about the moral and economic depravity of socialism or we will inorexorably continue to slide toward it. Or, what's going to stop us from doing so? "That liberty is indivisible, and that political freedom cannot long exist without economic freedom," So quoth William F. Buckley Jr. It's the RIGHT WING that espouses socio-economic liberty and the moral structure that embraces it. We're always right (no pun intended), but we're rarely, if ever, wrong.

P.S. For context, the above article was written well before Donald Trump became president.

CHAPTER 13

Those Left-Leaning Loonies

NOT JUST ANYBODY can be a Left-Leaning Loony (or LLL). One has to make bizarre, unbelievably inane statements and have the ability to evade being captured by a giant butterfly net while running around in a straitjacket. Communist revolutionary Stokley Carmichael, who once gave a lecture at the University of Wisconsin, doesn't qualify. Nor does Russia apologist former RI Senator Stillborne Pell, or that fellow-traveling clown, the Reverend Jesse Jackson, who said that as a waiter and just before leaving the kitchen, he spat into the food of white patrons that he didn't like and then smilingly served it to them. The noted "God-fearing, religious" preacher once joined Vietnamese and Nicaraguan United Nations delegates at a gathering in New York, sponsored by the Communist Party USA to celebrate communist North Vietnam's conquest of South Vietnam. Jackson also went down to Cuba, gave Castro a hug, smoked the dictator's cigar, and shouted out, "Hold on Castro, hold on Cuba, hold on Nicaragua!" Nope, Jesse gets rejected. As does prominent 1960s radicals Abbie Hoffman, Jerry Rubin and Timothy Leary. No, it's nuclear freeze peacenik, Dr. Helen Caldicott, who gets to be a member of the L.L.L. club. That's right, folks! Now, Caldicott doesn't possess the same scintillating intellect as Jesse Jackson (but then again, who does?), though, like all prominent progressives, her speeches are jam-packed with factuality and absolutely no emotionalism. She once compared President Ronald Reagan to the infamous Reverend Jim Jones, the communistic cult-leader. The noted political activist proclaimed that "Cuba is a wonderful country. What Castro's done is superb." Plus, Caldicott has imparted that "Every time you turn on an electric light, you are making another brainless baby." Now, why the heck was she informing us of something that everybody was already well aware of? Anyway, Helen of Australia was a leader of the Physicians for Social Responsibility. The woman once exemplified her social responsibility when she scared the living daylights out of some young, elementary school children by telling them that in the event of a nuclear war, they would become "charcoal steak" and said that their eyes would "literally melt down your cheeks." After a film the physician had seen about America's MX intercontinental ballistic missle, she gave her description,..."It rose slowly out of the ground, surrounded by smoke and flames and elongated into the air -- it was indeed a very sexual sight and when armed with ten warheads, it will explode with the most almighty orgasm."----The lady neglected to tell us that, while watching the film, she emitted the words *"OH-MI-GOD"* four times in a row. In any event, Helen had no criticism of the Soviet Union and their nuclear weapons. However, she did once compare capitalist America to Nazi Germany and associated the U.S. Trident nuclear submarine with "Auschwitz" and "a gas oven full of Jews burning up." Dr. Caldicott: take two Quaaludes, get plenty of rest, and don't call me in the morning. Oh, and one more thing----kindly dispose of the vibrator.

There are thousands of these leftist wack-job life forms roaming loose in our country (most of them not wearing a straight jacket). One of them who definitely deserves membership in the Left Leaning Loonies club is Barbara McKenna. And no, it's not because she's a feminist. Gloria Steinem is a feminist and a socialist, but she is not a loony. On a cool September evening, McKenna gave an instructional and informative speech in a compact auditorium at the University of Wisconsin to rally support for her presidential campaign on the Citizens Party (aka the Quirky Weirdo Party) ticket. This author sat within a small audience that consisted of the usual sort: bohemian beatniks, pacifistic peace creeps and emotion-dependent, idealistic ignoramuses. They were the kind of people who would assert that the Almanac Singers and the Weavers were better than the Beatles and the Beach Boys. The noted leftists are quite content sitting cross-legged and barefoot on the wooden floor of their cabin, smoking pot and munching on alfalfa sprouts while listening to wind chimes. The females of the species commonly buy their frumpy, antiquated clothes from a thrift shop that plays continuous protest-folk music. They strive to dress as UNATTRACTIVELY as possible, most of the time succeeding. Although, their personal hygiene, for some reason, wasn't really that bad. Anyway, said womenfolk usually have long frizzled hair, wear little if any make-up, and refuse to shave their armpits. The males also like to dress in slovenly fashion by wearing old sweaters that were eaten away by moths and sneakers that were in vogue back in the 1950s. Both genders are fond of turtleneck shirts and will dress only in the style of DDD (dark, drab and dreary). I surmise that they wear this garb in order to identify with the "struggle" of the oppressed hoi polloi who will one day break off their chains and overthrow the bourgeois capitalist pigs. Whatever! But there's one thing that's for sure; any woman who doesn't shave her armpits is no Republican. But I digress.

Benjamin Langston was the Citizens' Party vice-presidential candidate and was the first to speak. He was bald and had long hair, simultaneously, and spoke in a slow, doleful monotone. He was really quite sad because all yours truly remembers about his speech was his repeating of the line, "it's really quite sad." After having sat for a short while and melancholically caressing her forehead the entire time that Langston spoke, it was Barbara's turn. She told us that, contrary to everyone's belief, being President of the USA was "really very easy." So the president-want-to-be had everybody stand up (yes, the writer went along with this), close their eyes, put their hands in the air, and say out loud three times, "I want to be president." We then sat down, and the lady asked everybody to raise their hands and each one say what that individual would do if he or she were president. The typical left-wing, but not the slightest bit immature, twaddle came out: "Turn the Pentagon into a hospital," "nationalize the banks," "nationalize the corporations," "nuclear freeze," "provide guaranteed employment." At the end of this claptrap, one guy raised his hand and said, "And with all that we make this a socialist country." After someone booed,

Barbara mumbled, "That's not what socialism is," then quickly changed the subject. At one point, Ms. McKenna declared, "I suddenly had a realization that this system doesn't work for women. It's deliberately and consciously set up not to work for us." That's true. Have you ever noticed that there are no wealthy women who have satisfying careers or run successful businesses anywhere in America?

While in an emotional wrath, Barbara had some in the audience dumbstruck by the display of her hatred of men. Three times in a time span of two minutes, she blurted out something about "soldiers sticking rifles up women's vaginas." After Barbara (no relation to Helen) repeated it the third time, I said to myself, "For Christ's sake, doesn't this woman have a husband or boyfriend?" She also accused the dovish Democrat nominee for president, of being "militaristic." But if only Sigmund Freud was still living! Who knows, maybe he owned a rifle. Anyway, soon afterward, Ms. McKenna told everyone to stand up, join hands, and along with her, sing a song called, "We Are Women, Proud and Free." The Citizens Party presidential candidate said that she especially wanted the men to sing along because, deep down inside, we're women too, and that we must let our womanhood out, which I'll have to admit, is certainly more proper than letting our manhood out. But that did it. This man left the room. Yours truly went along with the "I want to be president" charade, but the author wasn't going to let Barbara get her "revenge" by humiliation. On my way out, I felt a bit sorry for my male ideological opposites who undoubtedly thought that they had to stay and tolerate it in order to show their allegiance to the Cause (the movement toward socialism).

Now, many leftists are working for "social change," but they're not loony or neurotic. Barbara McKenna, on the other hand, shouldn't be contemplating the presidency; she should be down in the fruit cellar talking to Norman Bates' mother. Perhaps she could use a good psychologist?.......Paging Dr. Freud!

CHAPTER **14**

Opinionated Bits and Pieces Part 3

OF ALL THE phenomena and conundrums in life that have confounded many a scientist the world over, no one has figured out why President George W. Bush, in the year 2005, picked Harriet Miers to be the next Supreme Court justice. When our 43rd commander-in-chief nominated her, it elicited much silence and befuddlement from liberals but even more WTFs from conservatives. Now, though Miers was never a judge and had no experience in Constitutional law, she was apparently qualified to become the next High Court justice due to the fact that the lady served two years as top aid to the White House Chief of Staff and that she wholeheartedly supported the re-election of her boss and friend, George W. Bush. Also it was Democrat Senator Harry Reid who suggested to the POTUS that he choose Harriet Miers, which W promptly did. But all speculation aside, this author would never venture that what then President Bush did smacks of cronyism, because that would give cronyism a bad name.

From the 1920's through the 1980s there were thousands of Americans making numerous ideological pilgrimages to the USSR (which is not to be mistaken for Shangri-la), and sometimes getting married there. These same citizens would then often take their American vacations at resorts in the beautiful Catskills, where they would be entertained by various show business artists.

This paragraph is specifically for "social justice activists." That's WITH or WITHOUT the quotation marks. Some questions: Can a person be a social justice activist and at the same time be dead set against socialism? Can we, the American people, live under genuine socialism and possibly NOT have a system of social justice? Is a citizen who is an outright communist automatically a *social justice activist* albeit, a flawed, sometimes objectionable one? And finally, analogous to our nation's inclination toward socialism; someone drives from their home state of Virginia with the important GOAL of arriving in California. But the driver only makes it to Colorado, has a change of heart, turns around and drives back to his or her home state. Is what this person did worthwhile and commendable or was it a just waste of time, effort and money?

There have been some horrific shooting massacres (schools, a movie theater, a nightclub) over the last few years where innocent people have died as a result of being shot by the gunman. But just think; if American lawmakers simply made the possession of guns illegal, nobody would be able to shoot and kill another person. Likewise, if only they also made the possession of narcotics (e.g. heroin, cocaine, opium) illegal, nobody would die of an overdose from them.

The TRUMP vs. CLINTON 2016 presidential race: (a.k.a. the Donald vs. the Hildabeast.) It has been widely opined that the noted two individuals were the worst candidates to run for the presidency in American history. Mr. Trump had been occasionally crude and often boorish while Mrs. Clinton had been dishonest and chronically corrupt. Though both have flawed personality traits, one of the main differences between the noted political two-some is that Trump is authentic. But the billionaire hotel mogul with the coarse language and brash personality has certainly made some controversial statements in the past. For example, while being filmed stepping off a bus eleven years earlier, the 2016 Republican presidential nominee was overheard bragging (via a live microphone) to another fellow, that he, the Donald, once without her permission, grabbed a woman's cat. A lot of upset and outraged

Americans, particularly feline pet owners, didn't take too kindly to Mr. Trump's boasting about his audacity. The former host of the TV show *The Apprentice* also continually declared that he wanted stronger southern border enforcement ("Build the wall") which is for the sovereignty and security of the United States. But such action would call for an illegal-immigration law that's even more strict and rigid than that of the country of Mexico.

Elsewhere on the trail to win the White House in 2016, Hillary Clinton mentioned that she wanted an America that is "hopeful, inclusive and big-hearted." She is well aware, no doubt, that such wistfulness cannot be enacted without socialistic legislation. Oblivious to her Freudian slip, the Hildabeast stated, "I'm going to do everything in my power to get this country back up." "Back up?" Back up from what? Evidently, the last eight years, that's what! She also told her followers "We have come too far to turn back now." That's not true. Yes, Obamacare has bankrupted healthcare insurance companies and has caused the premiums of millions of clients to skyrocket. Race relations had worsened during the two terms of Barack the Unifier. And the economic growth GDP never reached three percent under the 44th president as it did with all forty-three of the previous ones. But we hadn't gone too far that we couldn't turn back, as was made evident in the flourishing years of 2017-2020.

Though the late journalist William Safire once christened her a "congenital liar," Hillary Clinton was fortunate that those who voted for her mostly associate VIRTUE with ever-expanding government and not so much with the former Secretary of State's character or she wouldn't have won the popular vote. On the other hand, the woman is not so fortunate that she went up against an anti-Establishment populist with a dynamic public persona. About only five percent of the American people realize that if the First Lady of the 1990s had not Donald Trump, but any of the other sixteen Republican candidates as her November opponent, she would have easily WON the presidency (her declining to campaign in Michigan, Wisconsin, and Pennsylvania, the Benghazi fiasco, and top FBI agent James Comey re-opening the e-mail investigation of the Hildabeast, all notwithstanding). Ted Cruz would have lost to her, because he's a Constitutional conservative. Hillary would have certainly beaten Establishment favorite Jeb Bush. She would have absolutely run roughshod over the meek and mild moderate, John Kasich. The aforementioned former Ohio governor is kind of like Jeb Bush, only without the immense charisma. In any case, America is extremely lucky that Bill Clinton's lovely wife didn't succeed.

The further one leans to the left, the more that person becomes obsessed with the Federal government controlling the lives of others via collectivism and coercion instead of getting on with his or her own life. But then, like the old saying goes, misery loves company.

The Achilles Heel of conservative individuals is, well, individualism. Just by its very nature, conservatism is passive because it doesn't demand governmental activism. You don't see the libertarian right marching in the streets, committing crimes of arson and destruction while chanting for the Federal government to give the American people more liberty and to STOP being responsible for their lives. A conservative American is just an island of one---playing mostly defense while the entire offense of the left works and *progresses* in angry unison. Although, the left DOES band together in sometimes non-violent mobs. Knowing that 90 percent of the media, the sports and entertainment industry, academia, the young and various corporations wanting to be popular and scared to be protested, are on their side, the left is aware that politicians will subsequently capitulate in order to at least appear to be in solidarity with the "in crowd" (the pop culture) and not be detested or harassed. Many a Republican individual in public office has forsaken their philosophical *"going it alone"* credo, and have succumbed to socio-political conformity in order to be liked and re-elected by the unworldly multitude of voters.

Fox News is paradoxically the most hated news broadcast because it is the most liked. The left detests Fox News because it tells Americans the truth and doesn't bury bad news about Democrats and the deleterious consequences of liberalism. Fox news is a right-leaning (pro-capitalism, anti-socialism) news organization. But its conservatism seems to particularly stand out when Fox News is juxtaposed with the others (ABC, NBC, CBS, MSNBC, and CNN). So it's one conservative narrative against five liberal ones. That's what's known as being "fair and balanced."

Socialism, even with of its PERCEIVED absence of racism, will be far, far worse for blacks than economic freedom/social liberty (capitalism) with its ALLEGED racism. A person who constantly cries "RACISM" is a person who has never and will never say a bad word about socialism, which is a hundred times more unjust, oppressive, and crueler than racism.

The word "Brit" is short for "British" and the word "Jap" is short for "Japanese." While it's perfectly okay to call a person from England a "Brit," it's not okay to call a person from Japan a "Jap." Why is this? It's because the noted *Brit* is white and considered a "first-class-citizen" and is therefore nonplussed by the term. But a Japanese person is a minority and a "second-class-citizen" and not being white, feels that the term "Jap" is a put-down. That must be the reason why. What else could it be? This underdog/little guy status is also the reason why it's alright to call an Italian (a Caucasian) a "wop" or a "guinea" but not alright to call a Mexican a "spic." Likewise, it is acceptable to call an Italian a "grease ball" but unacceptable to call a Mexican the same. The American people are allowed by societal decorum to "punch up" but not "punch down," no matter what the truth is.

Back in the 1930s, unions were useful in protecting workers' rights, negotiating with management for decent pay for their members, and trying to eliminate unsafe working conditions. Today, union heads at the national level are a bunch of socialists who plunder membership fees to pad their own wallets and give campaign donations to liberal Democrats running for public office. To be fair, some of the dues that members pay to their unions actually ARE implemented to fund litigation for an unfair or dangerous workplace environment, and that's fine. But for the most part, unions are obsolete because the Labor Department has supplanted any usefulness that the unions had, more than a half a century ago. Presently, most union members have a bad predilection toward being more thankful to the national-level union leaders than they do to the employers who provide them with jobs. Both the members and union heads should realize that their constant, sometimes extravagant demands could put a business out of business. Don't misunderstand; yours truly does not wish for every union to descend into oblivion. I, myself, used to be a member of an organization called "The Union of Ayn Rand Rugged Individualists," but after only a year and a half, I quit because we never held any meetings.

The population of Detroit, Michigan today, is 84 percent black and 8 percent white. In the year 1970, it was 55 percent white. Over the last five decades, Motor City had gradually become dominated by black left-leaning politicians, including former clandestine Communist Party USA member, Coleman Young, who was mayor from 1974 through 1994. Given this ideological drift of the city, life would be made so much better for the black residents of Detroit, right? WRONG! The dishonesty, fiscal recklessness, and moral corruption of liberalism had caused white city dwellers to flee. This subsequently compelled the black leaders who took over the reins of running the city to compensate (they hoped) for the loss of the white tax base by throwing more money at pensions, unions, and welfare rolls, resulting in extreme squalor and bankruptcy to the tune of $18 billion dollars. If the city of General Motors and Motown Records were run by ALL black politicians since the early 1970's but each and every one of them was a resolute CONSERVATIVE (not *moderate*) Republican, the city's pervasive poverty never would have happened.

The terms "incendiary," "inflammatory" and "polarizing" almost always denote a hard-core truth spoken by a conservative that agitates the general public. But pro-socialism rhetoric by the liberal/left, though it may be deemed to be misguided and overzealous by the American people, is never thought of as being the first three adjectives because socialistic economic policies, at least emotionally, are uplifting and promising.

Democrats religiously believe that the government is entitled to more of the taxpayers' money at any given time, but particularly after it proves its ineptitude at managing the money that it has already taken from them. When America's most popular political party controls Washington, DC the government will continue to expand. However, when the Republicans are in charge at our nation's capital, the government will....also continue to expand, but just a little bit slower. The conservative members of the GOP know that they can count on most of the voters to wince and cry, "You're trying to balance the budget on my back" and "You're trying to make me the scapegoat for the debt that you politicians brought upon us," if any Republican seriously tries to cut domestic social spending. Both parties are well aware that attempting to turn off the spigots of welfare checks, food stamps, and Medicaid will result in riots in Chicago, Oakland, and New York City but not in Omaha, Topeka, and Oklahoma City. They'll have no choice but to capitulate to socio-political blackmail and refrain from installing such austerity measures. This writer is not saying that rubbing the truth in the collective face of the American people will definitely stop us from ending up like Greece. But I am saying that alerting them to it is the only thing that can potentially dodge financial ruin and that the bromide, "just raise taxes on the rich" is just that and not the panacea that too many (68 percent) of our citizens would like to think it is.

Is it just this author, or did anybody else notice that on January 20th, 2013, while sitting down and watching his inaugural parade, that Barack Obama and his lovely wife, Michelle, simultaneously gave the raised clenched fist salute? Question: Is this unbecoming of a US president and what does their raised clenched fists signify?

Liberal movie director Woody Allen once said about then President Barack Obama, "It would be good if he could be a dictator for a few years because he could do a lot of good things quickly." It's not often that you hear a liberal speak in a refreshingly honest manner. Though the majority of black Americans agree with Allen, most left-leaning whites dislike his revealing candor. A die-hard libertarian as president would make a lousy dictator (yes, I know that a libertarian dictator is an oxymoron, but ignore it for the moment) because he would inject more freedom into the lives of the American people. Such an injection would NOT make our citizens obey and therefore, in the minds of left-leaners, wouldn't be for their own benefit. Contemporary liberalism silently contends that a dictatorship is potentially good because it's the vehicle that drives social engineering. This latter action must be done correctly, of course, and its' "director" can't be a mean, corrupt SOB like Hitler, Mussolini, and Stalin were. As most blacks and progressives insist on believing, it is government that does "good things quickly," not individuals. The conservative right dislikes all types of dictatorships. This is not the case with the liberal left. With them, virtually no local or state problem is too small or insignificant for the Federal government to get involved in. This is how you build a benevolent dictatorship, just like the kind that Woody Allen wants and Fidel Castro had (minus the government-induced rampant squalor, tyranny, and over 4000 deaths by firing squad ordered by Castro). While he was alive, the "President" of Cuba was worth $900 million. Though he never gave a dime of his own money to the poor and needy of the island country, in the minds of many on the American left, Fidel Castro more than compensated for his selfishness by being a communist.

It was one of our Founding Fathers and third president, the great Thomas Jefferson, who declared, "When the people have the right information they will make the right decisions." Well, Jefferson wasn't alive in November 2008 and so he didn't know what the hell he was talking about!

Former Ku Klux Klansman David Duke, the pastor Jeremiah Wright, and Nation of Islam leader Louis Farrakhan are men who, with their past controversial remarks regarding Jews, would not get the Jewish vote if each of them ran for president. SURPRISE! Newsflash from The Past: Mary Lee Fray, who used to be Bill Clinton's campaign aid when he was Arkansas governor, said that she heard Hillary Clinton yell at the gentile governor, "You fucking Jew bastard!" Former Arkansas state trooper Larry Patterson, who was the governor's driver for six years, claims that he heard Hillary use anti-Semitic slurs like "Jew-boy," "Jew bastard," and "motherfucking Jew" over ten times, and spew the word "nigger" about eight times. Any Jewish or black person who says that he or she doesn't believe these bygone news items is LYING. But during the 2016 race for the White House, they realize that they NEEDED to lie if Hillary got the Democratic nomination for the presidency. This is because Jews and blacks wouldn't have felt good about themselves nor been thought of as respectable by anyone if they agreed that the stories were true but were supporting and voting for her anyway.

Isn't it interesting that America's most conservative (capitalistic) president, Calvin Coolidge, was born on Independence Day? Is it also not interesting that the publication of the premier free-market book *The Wealth of Nations* by Adam Smith, the signing of the Declaration of Independence, and our country changing its name to the "United States of America," coincided in the same year, 1776? But don't you think it's downright mystifying that the learning institutions of Columbia University, Howard University, Brandeis University, and Morehouse College, among others, have not yet banned the books *The Wealth of Nations* and *The Road to Serfdom* by F.A. Hayek, because said literature has violated the campuses' hate-speech codes?

The main difference between the political left of the late 1960s/early 1970s and the current left is that the latter doesn't like it when somebody defies the government. And it's always those darn anti-government right-wingers (read: pro-capitalism, anti-socialism zealots) who continue to engage in this disobedience.

Even though the "Christmas for blacks" holiday known as Kwanza was invented by a paranoid Marxist who spent four years in prison for torturing two women, the last week of December, Kwanza, is revered and celebrated by well over seventy-three black families across the nation. But what's really good about the holiday that was created for the enjoyment by the black people of America, is that it's not racist like the Christmas season itself. YES, THAT'S RIGHT! The first day of the Christmas season, which essentially begins the day after Thanksgiving, is called *Black Friday.*

Why isn't it called "White Friday?" Are those responsible for this racial slur insinuating that blacks are the only ones who hurry in and out of stores carrying jewlry, large TVs and other electronics? And then there's the very first sentence of the holiday song, "White Christmas." The man who is responsible for the lyrics more than likely wore a pointed white sheet over his head as he wrote them. Plus, why are snowflakes white and not black? And I'm not talking about the snowflakes on college campuses whom, the day after the 2016 presidential election; were hunkering down in their safe spaces petting bunny rabbits, drinking cups of warm cocoa and molding lumps of Play-Doh, all in attempt to overcome their sorrow. Then, to top it all off (I'm on a roll), there's the Yuletide tune, "Baby, It's Cold Outside." It's been alleged that this song is misogynistic and could lead to date rape. Now, the writer doesn't know about that, but I do know that the aforementioned tune is racist. "How so?" you ask? I haven't the slightest idea how so, but it just is and that's all there is to it!

On the choice of Democrat vs. Republican, the voters are often asked the loaded rhetorical questions, "Who do you think cares about you more?" or "Which political party is looking out for you?" (Translation: Who is more likely to have the government provide for you and fiscally bail you out?) Instead, the voters should be asked, "If a politician is dead set AGAINST government taking care of your financial problems, can that lawmaker still be considered caring?" But that politician's feelings (caring) toward the American citizen are irrelevant. Only the policies of right vs. wrong; in this case, self-responsibility vs. government responsibility is what matters. Otherwise, you, the reader, should agree with and abide by the extremely BAD advice that somebody gives you if that person SINCERELY CARES ABOUT YOU.

In early 2009, the Federal government bailed out the General Motors and Chrysler car manufacturers. This bail-out was supported by progressive Democratic president Barack Obama and establishmentarian Republican, former president George W. Bush. Sixty-three percent of America's Democrats, more than twice as many as the Republicans, approved of this government extrication of a free-market enterprise, while twenty five percent of the GOP also gave it the thumbs up. Some folks think that this deed smacked of CORPORATISM, but that's only because that's precisely what it was. All on the libertarian right were against the bail-out, joined by most on the Wall Street-bashing left. More "you're on your own" economic liberty forced onto the nation would induce less government in the marketplace, which in turn, would induce LESS corporatism. Real, honest-to-goodness capitalism is freedom, and freedom bails out nobody.

In relation to the subject matter above, there IS a difference between a corporatist and a genuine free-market espousing CEO (Chief Executive Officer). The latter is concerned almost entirely with liberty, competition and profit while the former is more or less engrossed with the social engineering of society (think Facebook, pre-Elon Musk Twitter and Google) usually, but not necessarily, with the complicity of the State. Incidentally, over seventy-five percent of the political donations from corporations go to Democrat candidates.

Many Americans either think or have stated that "our values" should prevent us from using torture (like water-boarding) on hateful terrorists who want to kill us. Perhaps it never occurred to these Americans that it's precisely because of our good, decent, Judeo-Christian values that the Islamic fascists hate us so much. Yes, Americans themselves should adhere to "American values," but these values and "civil liberties" do not and should not apply to overseas murderers who don't like or respect us for our values and civil liberties. Indeed, in their attempt to bring down America, they could use "our values" against us. Although, if we used WATERBOARDING to get pertinent information out of captured crazed killers, they would certainly respect us a lot more because we didn't display "our American values" while dealing with them.

If an absolute stranger, dressed in casual clothes, walked up on stage with a microphone in his hand and says to the audience, just two words, "Socialism sucks!"---you sitting in the audience will know right off the bat that he is a conservative. Now how in the heck could you possibly know that about this STRANGER? Most individuals would not be cognizant of it, but their instant acknowledgment of his conservative ideology was by DEDUCTION. That is, they automatically realized that the stranger MUST be a conservative because a moderate, and especially a liberal, would never have said "Socialism sucks." As for capitalism, moderates and liberals will CONCEDE that it has done some good for America, while conservatives PROCLAIM that it has done a lot of good.

It is futile for the Republican Party to hope that America's millennial generation will turn conservative. Young people adapt their political inclination to whatever seems to be popular (mostly liberalism) and appears to have more cultural clout. Some of us will remember that when President Ronald Reagan became very popular in 1982, the 1950s short haircut for young men came back into style, along with the clean-cut "preppy look" in clothes. Conservatism among the young was in vogue back in the 1980s but was also just a passing fancy. Since today's millennials are not as educated as the young people of the Reagan era, who, in turn, were not as educated as the 1950s generation, they are less likely to intellectualize and thus, more likely to be influenced by a debased pop culture and the cerebral apathy of liberalism. Just as the main reasons that millions of obviously intelligent women voted for Obama for president in 2008 were because he was charismatic and had a nice smile, our current young adults voted for the same "Dear Leader" mostly "because he's so cool." Like the common citizens of mid 1930s Germany, our progressive youngsters were enthusiastic advocates of THE STATE during the Obama era. They subsequently took glee in lying (politically) to others. That's when Obama's millennial fans realized that they, themselves, had become veritable socialists. Only idealism reinforced and bankrolled by the government, and not truth and logic, is what they espouse. The gradual implementation of socialism will thrive when ignorance is being taught to our youngsters via pedagogic neglect by teachers, much to the consternation of the Republican Party.

The majority of the American people believe that when Barack Obama was elected president in the year 2008, the reason why some ninety percent of black Americans were joyful was because they were proud to see a black person win the White House. The majority is wrong. There is incisive analysis to suggest otherwise, and here it is: The primary reason that some 90 percent of blacks were proud and elated (some crying) is that Obama leans to the political left. Their PRIDE and happiness were contingent on the fact that the newly elected president would steer our country in a profoundly socialistic direction. As an advocate of big government, Obama was seen as coming to the rescue of blacks and providing them with guidance, comfort, and security. That the former Illinois Senator is black was just complimentary icing on the cake. It was 70 percent ideology, 20 percent race, and 10 percent oratory that made for the initial emotional attachment of Obama's political supporters. Indeed, instead of being a one hundred percent liberal, if our 44th president were a 100 percent conservative Republican who was also 100 percent black, as opposed to being half black, as he actually is, Obama would have received only 15 percent of the black vote.

In hindsight, directly after the nation voted in a black conservative Republican as the nation's top CEO on Election Day 2008, a guesstimate of about 85 percent of our nation's blacks would have been not just emotional but angry, distraught (some crying), and NOT the least bit PROUD. "How could white America do this to us after all we been through over the last two centuries?" they would have dejectedly inquired. Blacks would have informed white America that Obama, being a "far-right-winger" (read: an anti-socialist), is antithetical to their historic plight and only serves to negate his becoming the "First black President of the United States." They would have angrily told our mostly white electorate that their voting in as president a conservative black (aka a traitor, sell-out, and Uncle Tom) not only doesn't come close to making amends for America's racist past, but is also a slap to the collective face of present-day blacks and pours salt in their wounds. Society should take notice of how most blacks are insulted by and disgusted with Supreme Court Judge Clarence Thomas (who, unlike Obama, is 100 percent black) and hate his guts even more than various white liberals do.

A self-declared communist shoots and kills a rich, conservative Republican CEO and when arrested and asked by law enforcement why the noted comrade did it, he proudly proclaims "Because I hate Republicans and freedom, that's why!" But of the Americans who are on the liberal/left and constantly carp about *hate crimes*, most of them will NOT agree that what the communist did was a *hate crime*.

Have you ever noticed that Republican politicians make a super-big deal out of CUTTING TAXES ("I want to give the American people back more of their own money") but won't mention a damn word about CUTTING SOCIAL PROGRAMS and "entitlements" plus ELIMINATING various departments (the Department of Education, etc.)? But my right-wing brethren among ordinary citizens are missing the point when they lambaste the Republican Party for not taking a leadership position and specifying to the American people what precisely the GOP is going to do to guide the nation out of any economic debt morass. Prominent party lawmakers know darn well that the American voters really are fond of socialistic economic policies (government providing for and taking care of the people and NOT cutting domestic spending) and dislike capitalistic policies (the exact opposite). For Republican leaders to tell the people this provocative truth is to throw ice-cold water in their collective face. Plus, the Party of Abe Lincoln and Ronald Reagan is abundantly aware that to even attempt to cut domestic social spending would be the political kiss of death and that there will be a mass exodus of their members and independents to the Democrats, the party of safety and security (government), and away from the Republicans, the party of risk and uncertainty (freedom).

On the other hand, the intellectually honest Tea Party holds the American people's feet to the fire, and the American people abhor that. When the Tea Party calls for a respect for and adherence to the Constitution and small government, the progressive left calls them "extremists." In response, very few if any GOP leaders will come to the former's defense. Granted, the Republican establishmentarians might refer to the liberals' big-spending, government-growing agenda as "wasteful" or "unworkable" but won't label it as "extreme" because they fear that the electorate will vehemently disagree with the GOP's use of the latter denigrating term and it would undoubtedly jeopardize Republican elections to office. Candidates in our country's second most popular political party realize that they are going to have to walk on eggshells and avoid scary rhetoric like "The government is not responsible for your livelihood" and "You're on your own" plus "You need to be given more personal liberty even though you won't like it." When liberals disparage "trickle-down-economics", they are really just demonizing economic freedom. When this happens, "conservatives" in Washington, DC will de facto agree with the liberals by their, the "conservatives," disinclination to publicly DISAGREE with the noted left-leaning Americans and explain how they're wrong. In regard to their not educating and warning America about its trajectory toward socialism, the Republican Party stalwarts should heed William Shakespeare's famous quote, "A coward dies a thousand times before his death."

There are two bottles of lethal, fast-acting poison on a table. One sip of the liquid and each will kill the victim in less than one minute. The first bottle has the word "poison" labled on it and was put on the table by a Nazi Party member. The second bottle has the label "medicine" attached to it and was placed on the table by a member of the Communist Party. But what this writer can't figure out is...which bottle is more dangerous? Or are they equally perilous to one's health? I was hoping that the reader would know.

Many naïve, wishful-thinking individuals believe that socialism will work in our country because we Americans have the ingenuity, innate know-how, patriotic attitude and that can-do spirit other nations never had and still don't. Hence, because the very concept of socialism is so extremely attractive, it should be viewed as if it's an exotic elixir that was purported to heal the ailments of the denizens in the Orient, and that we should give this potion a try here. Our leaders in Washington, DC, will simply implement a six-month experiment plan for socialism to work its magic. If the plan somehow fails; the US President, with the agreement by our nation's citizens, will just sign some papers that call for the immediate termination of the plan and we will go right back to being a capitalist country the very next day. It will be like buying clothes from a store, changing your mind about them, and then (with the sales slip) returning the clothes just a few days later. No big deal, and easier done than said. So do not be concerned my friend; this Marxist inspiration will absolutely work here in the USA because we put the first man on the moon and it was an American (Jonas Salk) who found a cure for polio in our country. Back in the real world, socialism is like a disease that is, well, progressive, in that it gets exponentially worse. Although, what happened in Venezuela should nevertheless be ignored by Americans. The nirvana-seeking citizens among us absolutely love the mandates that socialism mandates. The people must be made to mind. Liberal legislation that leads to socialism and its promise of security, well-being, and equity is never deemed to be too EXTREME. Only those who resist it are.

It is quite possible that angry left-wing actor Samuel L. Jackson holds a socio-political animus toward white people. The Hollywood movie star said that he voted for Obama because the 44th president is black. Jackson received no criticism of this racial remark because he, himself, is black. But if a white Hollywood celebrity said that he voted for Mitt Romney because Romney is white, the former would have been labeled a racist by both black and white America. Our current pop culture accepts and respects perturbed, pugnacious blacks making racially tinged remarks because the latter are the "oppressed" and chronically disgruntled second-class citizens. On the other hand, because white people are the "privileged," they are supposed to validate their contrition for being white by also voting for a black Democrat even if it's just only BECAUSE he's black. Whites do not deserve equal treatment on the subject of race, but they do deserve their comeuppance. Or, at least, that is what our society has been conditioned to think.

Mona Charen and S.E. Cupp are liberal journalists who, among many other dishonest Never Trumper Republicans, side with liberalism on most everything but continue to disingenuously call themselves "conservatives." They do this because the WORD "conservatism" has an aura of respectability, integrity and nobility that the word "liberalism" just doesn't have. As many of us know, or should know, it is ideology (conservatism: = conducive to capitalism vs. liberalism: = conducive to socialism) that dominates and shapes American politics, as it should. For the sake of the country, it would be much better that the POLICIES of any president, that matters far more than his or her personality or political party. Yet, Mrs. Charen and Mrs. Cupp, along with most people of their political ilk, voted for the ex-Delaware senator for president in 2020. Two decades ago, the noted two females were nominal conservatives. Today, Charen's visceral hatred of Donald Trump has dissuaded her from saying anything negative about Joe Biden's tremendously detrimental policies (and she IS aware of them) or the radicalization of current liberalism. The 1980s/90s former conservative has expressed that she both accepts and welcomes the freeloading ten million illegal aliens and their $150 BILLION dollar yearly cost to American taxpayers. Charen has many times called Donald Trump an "insurrectionist." She's a liar. Said woman is fully cognizant that Mr. Trump was NEVER convicted of insurrection nor ever even CHARGED with insurrection by any judicial court.

But her entrenched, seething hatred of the 45th president's personality manifests itself into her being outright dishonest and spiteful. Doing so, she believes, enables her to get poetic revenge on certain voters of the 2016 presidential election. In this writer's opinion, Mona Charen has become an emotional wreck who will label the GOP "crazy" but has not, since at least 2020, and will not lambaste the Democratic party even though she knows damn well that it's currently a quasi-Marxist organization that has been doing major damage to our republic since January, 2021. Charen now has such a dislike of REAL conservatism that it has transcended into a veritable acceptance of socialism. So much so, that the left-leaning columnist has referred to Joe Biden's disastrous socialistic enactments as "rational." The genuine and successful conservatism of President Trump has caused her to become politically perturbed. S.E. Cupp used to be a pseudo-conservative a decade ago but is now a full-fledged liberal and she knows it. PLUS, Ms. Cupp was originally attracted, albeit superficially, to *"conservatism"* because it harbors shock value and political notoriety that would bring her the attention that she craved. Said woman has refered to certain Republican politicians (e.g. Maryland Republican governor Larry Hogan) as "conservative" sheerly because they're really moderates. The bespectacled political commentator does this because she currently disapproves of AUTHENTIC conservatism and takes what she knows is absolute meek and mild *moderation,* and simply labels it "conservatism." This way there will only be a slight difference between the phony *"conservatism"* (in reality, *moderation)* that Cupp desires in a Republican politician, and the actual liberalism that the lady herself espouses. She knows that *moderation* will eventually segue into liberalism. In any case, unlike her ideological twin sister, Mona; Mrs. Cupp is a status-seeking, social-climbing butterfly whose main cause is to be accepted and approved of by the mod, in-crowd of woke pop culture and liberal social gatherings. She is well aware that proclaiming the TITLE of *"conservative"* elicits at least a small degree of respect from others, but having actual liberal opinions retains one's popularity. The noted TV host has apparently endorsed the notion that it is far more honorable to be shallow than it is to be disliked by the esteemed left. Both liberal journalist have been enthusiastic members of the Trump Derangement Syndrome club since 2017 (seventy percent of their political columns are about Orange Man Bad), and have badmouthed ONLY conservatives, and never the Democratic party, wokeism, the far-left, liberalism and Biden's extremely destructive policies, both foreign and domestic. And that's because they both support the modern Dems' socialistic agenda. But if these two detractors of Donald Trump had a modicum of credibility and self-respect, they wouldn't have voted for the one-time real estate mogul nor Obama's sidekick in the November 2020 election. Charen and Cupp would have stayed home on Election day because the couple were ostensibly revolted by both the Donald for being....well....the Donald, and by Joe Biden for being a de facto progressive. But their actually having voted for Joe Biden and not ever saying a negative word about his presidency proves that the two female Never Trumpers are not conservatives as they claim, but liberals. If they say they aren't liberals, they're lying.

An organization called ANTIFA is against fascism or would like you to believe that they are. In any case, the fascistic members validate their anti-fascism by firebombing buildings and committing other acts of violence and commanding obedience to their communistic demands. They do NOT really care about civil rights but are just a large cluster of Marxist thugs who hate America. Those who constantly carp about non-existent "systemic oppression" will more than likely support government command and control of white citizens. If blacks and everybody else also need to be subjugated (and they will), then so be it. What naïve Antifa supporters should realize is that communism is basically just a fascism that empathizes with the "marginalized" (the little guy/underdog/downtrodden). But the biggest difference between communism and fascism is that they're spelled differently.

Why is it that that progressives never speak publicly about their desire for government ownership of the means of production? It's because it would be too darn conspicuous. The public generally agrees with Democrats who spout off about the unfairness of unregulated enterprise, but any talk from left-leaning politicians calling for "government ownership" gives even an amenable public pause and a justifiable reason for concern. Enter Maxine Waters: The Congresswoman from California and granddaughter of Albert Einstein unleashed an embarrassing Freudian slip when speaking to some oil company executives about her predilection for nationalization of their businesses. When the reader watches this less than two minute scene on YouTube entitled "MAXINE WATERS OUTS THE DEMS SOCIALIST AGENDA." Right after the Congresswoman three times refers to herself as "this liberal", listen to what she says and then observe the expression on the faces of the two Democrat colleagues sitting right next to her. Afterwards, remember that it's the fascistic government command and control of industry that comes first. The *ownership* part will come later.

Whenever the capitalistic right tries to induce more economic freedom upon the American people by CUTTING BACK on governmental command and control of them, the liberals will accuse said liberty-pushing right of trying to implement AUTHORITARIANISM. A plan or policy championing economic freedom/social liberty does NOT lead to authoritarianism, and within the progressive mindset, that's precisely the problem. But our citizens, for the most part, and in their sheer asininity, will agree with the noted leftists. Most stupid or intellectually dishonest Americans believe that, if the Federal government is injecting more freedom onto the citizens, it's thereby forcing more self-responsibility on them. Since such action is deemed heartless, uncaring and cruel, it is then to be equated with authoritarianism. Simultaneously, a probable majority of voters would like to believe that a benevolent subsidization/subjugation of the people (read: empathetic authoritarianism) would be a worthy ACCOMPLISHMENT.

Is something wrong with this picture? There are Yiddish-speaking people all over the globe with about eighty percent of them members of a diaspora subgroup called the "Ashkenazis." Now, regarding some 150,000 of the aforementioned having been combat soldiers in the Third Reich, the reader may ask yours truly why today's Hebrew leaders haven't changed the noted ironic, disconcerting title to something else......anything else? Well, this author doesn't know why they haven't. Perhaps you should Ashkenazi Jew!

Corporate inversion is corporations relocating their operations overseas in order to escape from US corporate taxes, the highest in the world. Corporate executives tend to look at it as wise business acumen and self-preservation. Liberals tend to think of it as "unpatriotic" and some of them have labeled it as such. Liberalism/progressivism rationalizes that it is UNAMERICAN for wealthy job creators to attempt to flee from repressive taxation, redistribution and coercion which are used mostly for the purpose of social do-goodism. Such a mass exodus from the USA would make our economic climate look dreadful and uninviting, and also damage any credibility that liberalism has; not to imply that it has any. Rule of thumb for Americans to ponder: More and bigger government means LESS jobs and reduced prosperity for all, while far smaller government means the exact opposite.

In general, the American people ignorantly and foolishly believe that "the far Right" and *the far left* in our country are morally equivalent in the same precise way that most liberals and many moderates in the 1980s looked upon the United States and the Soviet Union as also being morally equivalent. It's terribly unfortunate that much of America believes that it needs to be dishonest and then neutral in its attempt to be *fair-minded*. There's too many individuals who erroneously think that they're being "fair-minded" when they really just want to seem impartial by avoiding taking sides in order not to alienate others, particularly on controversial though important issues.

Martin Luther King Jr. once said that black supremacy is just as dangerous to America as white supremacy. Being a black or white supremacist is a personal belief or attitude and far from being the American way of life or "system" that effects most of us. The extremely few white or black supremacists that exist in our country simply do not harm the nation as a whole. Although, a collectivistic totalitarianism certainly would. But the media will only focus on and play up, white supremacy. The practically interchangeable terms "white nationalism" and "white supremacy" are codewords used by the disingenuous left for the purpose of denigrating *social liberty* and *economic* freedom (*read: conservatism* / capitalism). Whatever type of rotten, tyrannical socio-political system that the two Caucasion groups may desire, it would't be anywhere near as bad as socialism or communism. Being a proponent of the latter two is far more egregious than it is to be a white nationalist or white supremacist. Plus, the noted duo of Marxist "religions" are a million times more popular and attractive than any white elitism is and are therefore to a much greater extent, insidious to American society. For a government-induced oppression and near-destitution of ALL of the people is NEVER more just or morally superior to an unfairness towards or mistreatment of merely SOME of our citizens.

The 1976 movie "*All the President's Men*" would have never been made because the book of the same title never would have been written. To this day, there are those who erroneously believe that the book and subsequent movie were produced in order to expose malfeasance and criminal activity at the top levels of government and hold our public officials accountable. They are mistaken. The book was written strictly because its primary subject matter, President Richard Nixon, was a Republican. Had the POTUS in 1972-1974 been a liberal Democrat, his felony----a cover-up, wouldn't have been----well----UNCOVERED----by the journalists/authors. The enmity of various individuals over the decades towards Richard Nixon has been mostly of a political nature and not so much a "pro-law and order" disposition on their part, just like the ideologically-based acrimony that produced the lies about Donald Trump 2016-2023.

P.S. The above subject should not and does not excuse what the 37th president did.

According to leftist-orthodoxy etiquette, one is not allowed to verbally address a transgender person as a "him" or "her." Though, it is perfectly acceptable and appropriate to refer to the aforementioned identity-challenged as a "whatever." But the indispensable question remains: Does your regular, everyday man or woman need instructions on how to have sex with a transgender person?

Minorities will not be allowed to play the fool on TV commercials. One commercial has a young clownish white man clumsily trying to prop something up in a store and a black woman walks in and asks about him to the others, "Is he okay?" Another advertisement has this young idiotic Caucasian male with his tongue stuck to a frozen metal pole with his black friend laughing and mocking him. A third television ad has a black woman slapping a cigar out of the mouth of a silly white man. If the black actor in each of the three commercials wanted to switch roles with the white actor and vice versa, they wouldn't be allowed to. It is now an unwritten law in TV land that the white man has got to be the buffoon/loser and the black person the wiser superior/winner. This is because the producers/directors realize that they are supposed to do what the left that dominates pop culture, wants them to do. For the makers of commercials to disobey woke and cancel culture demands, there will be a public shaming of said persons.

CHAPTER **15**

The Fems

THE TITLE OF this article has absolutely nothing whatsoever to do with men who are hairdressers, interior decorators or antique dealers. It's about feminists and what they really want. There are people who support equal rights and equal opportunities for women, and then there are the feminists. After the Judge Clarence Thomas vs. Anita Hill Senate hearing of 1991 and Thomas's eventual confirmation to the Supreme Court, one feminist woman, Janice Sinclair, in the letter to the editor of a newspaper, wrote, "Don't ask me if I believe Anita Hill. Ms. Hill has defined her abuse and I accept that. I have never questioned the validity of her charges. Don't ask me to explain why she followed Thomas to another job, why she called him. And don't give me your view as to why you think she stayed. And your conjecture is full of woman-hating and self-protection. This appointment [Thomas] was a validation of your harassing behavior!" Most feminists share the same feelings as Ms. Sinclair, though only a few can articulate them at such a high level of calm intellect as her.

In a nutshell, the long-established maxim of "innocent until proven guilty" should not have been considered for this particular Supreme Court nominee because Clarence Thomas is a conservative and is against abortion. Feminists proclaim that the government has no right to tell a woman what she can or can't do with her own body, yet they remain steadfastly opposed to the legalization of prostitution. However, according to these feminists, government does have the responsibility to subsidize a woman's abortion. Hmm, let's see now; a woman should have the freedom to have an abortion, but the taxpayer shouldn't have the freedom of NOT having to pay for it? Yup, sounds fair to me! Actually, it's plainly a case of: Give us your money and then mind your own damn business. Henceforth, the feminists' new pro-abortion motto will be, "Government, get your stinking hands off my body but stick a wad of cash in my uterus!" Now, some people favor funding of abortion only in the case of rape or incest. This is also wrong. One's own personal problems, tragic as they may be, should not be made the financial responsibility of others. If a man's uninsured house burns to the ground, should the American taxpayers be forced to buy him a new one? Some may reply, "But it's his fault that he didn't insure his house. It's not the woman's fault that she was impregnated from being raped." No, and it's not the taxpayers' fault, either. So why penalize taxpayers by making them pay for it?

Pro-choice feminists, in 1991, took umbrage at President George H. W. Bush's desire to withhold funding of "family planning" (an ironic euphemism for abortion) health clinics whose physicians consult with their clients about having an abortion. The feminists called it the "gag rule" because it, presumably, didn't allow the doctor to speak freely. But let's throw this in reverse. Let's say that our 41st president wanted a law that stipulated that as long as these health care clinics were receiving government subsidies, then the doctor was OBLIGATED BY LAW TO ADVISE their patient on whether she should choose abortion, and that this doctor COULD NOT REFRAIN from speaking POSITIVELY about abortion even if he personally opposed abortion. The pro-choice crowd would not have objected to this, and they know it. Therefore, it was not about *freedom of speech*, per se, that concerned the pro-choice feminists but rather their using "freedom of speech" as a ruse to obtain taxpayer funding of abortion clinics. Incidently, the PRO-LIFE, anti-abortion protesters are NOT against the right for a female to have a tattoo on her body. And so it's not so much a case of "the government can't tell a lady what she can or can't do with her own body" (e.g. get a tattoo), but rather that she doesn't have the right to have a human life inside her womb terminated. Has anybody ever noticed that every pro-choice woman keeps shouting that "it's her body" but never says a word about the *baby* that's inside "her body?" Her implicit claim is that SHE is the only facet of the abortion debate which consequently EXCLUDES any other human entity (husband, boyfriend, baby).

Perhaps hoping to penetrate the conscience of America, feminists have long promulgated the mantra, "RAPE IS NOT SEX." Uh, yes it is, and it is all the time. No, it sure as hell isn't mutual lovemaking, but NEVER is rape NOT sex. Since the era of bra-burning, feminists have been uttering the aforementioned catchphrase not so much to condemn the rapist, per se, but to demonize and stigmatize by metaphor, our patriarchal system in general. To hard-core feminists, the punishment of the rapist (who is merely, the former will contend, a by-product of "the system") or even the physical and psychological trauma of the victim, takes a back seat to the politicizing of the assault itself. The *politics* of rape is what's most important to them. But ask the feminists to define "rape" and they will correctly reply that rape is "sexual intercourse by force" oblivious to their own contradiction. Feminists are also fond of saying that rape is always an "act of violence" on part of the rapist. No, not necessarily. For instance, a young college man at a frat party, inserts something into the drink (aka slipping a Mickey) of an unknowing college girl. He carries her unconscious body into a dorm room, locks the door, slowly and calmly unbuttons her clothes, and then inserts something......not into her drink. Now this is definitely rape, but how is it violent? The answer is: It's not. And nobody will be able to explain how it is.

The feminists would also call this an "act of power and control" committed by the frat boy. Once again, it's not necessarily. Is it possible that the horny college kid just "isn't getting any" and he figures that it's an easier way to have sex with the "girl of his dreams"? No relationship, no futile pick-up lines and no hassle. Call the young man "undersexed" or "oversexed" if you want to, but his assault with a friendly weapon on her had absolutely nothing to do with any feelings of having "power and control over women." If a female high school teacher has sex with a fifteen-year-old boy, it is considered to be rape (statutory). But was he raped because the lady teacher "wanted to exert her power and control" over the boy? No, he wasn't. It could be that when the lady teacher herself went to high school, she never engaged in any mattress mambo. Either that, or she did have many a dalliance with sophomore boys but just wants more of it. Former President Bill Clinton was alleged to have raped a woman in 1978 and was accused of sexual harassment of another in 1991 while he was Governor of Arkansas. Most feminist womyn privately believe these allegations but will not reveal their beliefs nor publicly condemn Clinton because he's a Democrat who veers to the left. But irrespective of man's bad behavior toward the female species, as long as American women, particularly ardent feminists, are of the mindset that sex is something that is being done TO them and not WITH them, then any notion that they are the "inferior" gender is not entirely unjustified.

Men are first-class citizens while women are second-class citizens. To many feminists, the institutions of marriage and the nuclear family are equated with the subjugation of women. And since capitalism embraces "the family" along with the professed social and economic inequality of women, then our present system should be replaced with something that will purportedly bring about socio-economic equality. With the passage of the referendums of government-funded abortions and nationalized day care centers helping to induce the growth of the State, the nuclear family will eventually dissolve and free women from its oppression. Comparable worth, if ever enacted, would also be a big step in the leftward direction for the liberation of women. In the near future, if a policy or agenda doesn't lean to the political left, then it will be branded as misogynistic.

Enter prototypical queen socialist/feminist, Gloria Steinem; the hat-wearing dead communist, Bella Abzug; and loopy commie-loving clown, California Congresswoman, Maxine Waters, among others. Because of their progressive (socialistic) agenda, liberalism/leftism and not women's values and rights, per se, becomes their main priority. For example, many feminist women feel ambivalent about pornography. Like the conservative traditionalists that they reluctantly side with on this issue, these female left-wingers would like nothing better than to see the smut and sexploitation trade eradicated for good. But unlike their strange political bedfellows, radical feminists don't mind the way that porn subverts traditional family values. This is because "traditional family values," being a capitalism linchpin, undermines the feminist goal of government-controlled egalitarianism. Henceforth, when a liberal Democrat male politician allegedly commits the "sexual indiscretion" of rape or harassment of a woman, any public condemnation of the incident should at least be toned down, if not mentioned at all.

And that's because, in the minds of the feminists, this progressive candidate for public office needs to be elected or re-elected if he wins the Democratic primary. But if a conservative Republican male politician merely neglects to open a car door for a lady, then Katy bar the door, indeed. There's going to be hell to pay for his wanton act of war on women. Perhaps the Grand Dame of gender equality and admitted Marxist, Gloria Steinem, would come to this lowly Republican lawmaker's defense by claiming that he just made a *bad pass* at the lady. After all, it's what Steinem, the leading activist for gender fairness, opined after hearing about then Governor Bill Clinton's, ahem, "meetings" with Paula Jones and Kathleen Willey. But then again, for Gloria to do so wouldn't promote feminism. Correspondingly, false sexual harassment charges against Supreme Court Judge Clarence Thomas in 1991 were to be "BELIEVED" while liberal Democrat Senator Ted Kennedy had accolades bestowed on him from the vast majority of feminists.

Whether he was slobbering over an unwilling woman on a restaurant table (the horizontal waitress ran away screaming) or swimming away from a drowning one, you can bet your life jacket that Ted Kennedy easily won the votes of most Massachusetts women and received the loving support of nearly every American feminist who detested sexual harassment. The late Sandra Day O'Connor, a moderate, and the first woman to be elected to the Supreme Court, was pro-choice. And yet she was scorned by Steinem and other feminists and called "a man in women's clothing." Why? It's because O'Connor didn't lean to the left. And as a "presumed" female, she was supposed to. In order to be a REAL feminist, a person cannot lean to the right. On America's socio-economic ladder, men are at the top and women are at the bottom. This isn't "fair" and it certainly isn't equal. But what the feminist left's goal of socialism will accomplish is to bring men down to the middle rung of the ladder while at the same time, boosting women up to the same level. Or how else would they achieve EQUALITY? In summation: Liberalism benefits socialism benefits women. Conservatism benefits capitalism benefits men. What mascara is to make-up, socialism is to feminism!

CHAPTER **16**

The Threat of Freedom

PRELUDE: THOUGH THERE is a slight difference between the two, the author reserves the right to use the words "freedom" and "liberty" interchangeably, as is his prerogative. It's a free country.

The Three Cs (the Constitution, Capitalism and Christianity) are the bedrock and linchpin of freedom/liberty. Nevertheless, many Americans actually detests liberty because it's politically imprudent and socially apathetic. Although George Bernard Shaw was a socialist, he did speak the intelligent truth when he stated, "Liberty means responsibility. That is why most men dread it." Most of those who vote Democrat yearn for a sanctuary to escape from self-responsibility. A few decades ago, Republican candidate Alan Keyes, while running for the presidency, gave a speech at the University of Wisconsin. In a brief chat that a few of us had with him afterward, I asked Mr. Keyes if he thought that liberalism is the road to socialism. He replied with "liberalism IS socialism." But then he added the rather intriguing notion that socialism is not just a socio-economic system but that it is also a STATE OF MIND. How compelling. Let's examine the American mindset that's been bankrupting the nation for more than half a century.

In 1994, the Democratic Congress was kicked out of office as a result of their being perceived by the voters as smug and arrogant in their spiteful opposition to the Republicans' government-shrinking Contract with America, and the Democratic ties with a then-unpopular President

Clinton. But in the very next year, when the voters learned that the Contract ACTUALLY WOULD CUT government domestic spending for the first time; they flinched and ran back to the 42nd president and his fellow Democrats for guidance and protection from conservative Republicans who were trying to give the people too much freedom. Subsequently, the GOP ran for the political tall grass and tacitly accepted the "blame for the government shutdown" of November 1995 (when they should have taken the credit for it) by way of their disinclination to tell the American people the truth: there is nothing in the Constitution or Bill of Rights that says our government is supposed to provide for and take care of its citizens. If our men and women really craved freedom, they wouldn't mind in the least bit the government shutting down for a week, instead of feeling that this temporary cessation would, somehow, cause their life to be figuratively snuffed out. These are the very same folks who, for the most part, accept the status quo and desire mandates from Washington, DC. Those that always vote Democrat will usually not associate virtue with actual freedom but with government growth. The American people, in general, will agree that freedom isn't free. But most of them really do take it for granted. Since we've been cognizant of our socio-economic freedom for over a century now, the endeavor for another ideal...*equity*...consequently becomes a just as noble (but unattainable) goal that requires a hands-on government rectifying life's inadequacies. Because freedom isn't benevolent social engineering, we will soon come to believe that LESS freedom, not more, benefits humanity.

"The era of big government is over." It's not, and over the last six decades, it never was. But this statement by President Bill Clinton in the 1990s did provide the American voters with the opportunity to kid themselves while they continued to indulge in voting to make more economic redistribution the law. True freedom is uncertainty and therefore never reassuring. And as long as there is personal liberty, there will never be a guarantee of safety. "Those who would give up essential liberty to purchase a little temporary safety deserve neither liberty nor safety," said Benjamin Franklin in 1759. The advocates of the great, omnipotent State on the left would like us to believe that life is too complex and that it demands the guidance of us (read: more rules, regulations, and restrictions) by our superiors (politicians). Consequently, they deplore leaders of government who commit crimes or acts that are morally or ethically shameful (Richard Nixon, former House speakers Jim Wright and Dennis Hastert, Senator John Edwards, Bill Clinton). Not so much because these political leaders have broken the law, per se, but because their perfidy tends to undermine a servile public's faith in "good, strong government," thus diminishing the people's cooperation with its central planning. It's difficult for the people to genuflect at the altar of Big Government when their leaders are such scoundrels.

Freedom allows people to care only about themselves. The liberal/left calls this citizen behavior "selfishness." Millions of appallingly ignorant and morally corrupt Americans would love for our government to enact a Federal clampdown on said "selfishness." By and large, the American people do not yearn for economic freedom. They yearn for economic security. Our citizens have tasted economic freedom, and quite frankly, they're sick and tired of it. Take the Tea Party, for example. The Tea Party is made up mostly of libertarian conservatives who are strong advocates of American-style capitalism (socio-economic liberty). Far more Americans detest the Tea Party than those who like this unstructured gathering of individuals. Like the Tea Party, the House Freedom Caucus, particularly when going up against moderate Establishment Republicans, are portrayed as "hardliners" which implies that only a political/ideological moderation agenda, and not a liberty-based one, is the natural, humane and correct direction to take. The Freedom Caucus is considered "too extreme" because actual freedom is.....well.....too extreme. A *hardliner* is not just hostile toward collectivism but also strongly opposes the Republican Party "getting along with the Democrats" by acquiescing to their ideological agenda. The largest political party and the most popular in the United States is the Democratic Party (12 million more registered members than the GOP). This indubitably suggests that the donkey Party, which easily owns the *popular vote,* and their liberal (we'll take care of you) philosophy is likable to a greater degree than the elephant Party with their conservative (you're on your own) reputation. A Democratic candidate for national political office will undoubtedly be a lawyer. And being a practitioner of laws, that Democrat lawyer is more likely to increase rules, regulations and restrictions on society ostensibly for the purpose of bringing about a more just and egalitarian social order. A private enterprise businessperson, on the other hand, is probably a Republican. As a candidate for political office, the aforementioned citizen is likelier to have a liberty-based attitude which would cut back on centralized government control and its manipulation of the people that's purported to be for their own collective good. For this reason, Democrat politicians are usually more trustworthy in the minds of the public while freedom-touting conservatives wanting to cut domestic social spending will always be viewed to a much greater extent as a threat to society.

Capitalism IS freedom. When the left bashes capitalism, they're really just badmouthing freedom. The LESS personal liberty that the government mandates for the American people, the faster the nation will advance toward a dystopian society under the observation of omnipotent government, which will inevitably beget martial law and subsequently a police state. To most on the American far left, freedom is somehow, some Orwellian way, an oppressive tyranny because it ISN'T government control of the people. On many college campuses, free speech for conservative students is detested because it allows them to make negative political comments regarding the underdog/little guy crowd that the proponents of socialism purportedly are trying to help. Freedom is risky because on the economic playing field of life, it is....well, freedom. To elucidate, when various lawmakers in Washington, DC pass a new government program, mandate, legislation, or introduce a new department, our society warmly looks at it as being an "accomplishment" or "achievement." These actually decrease the people's liberty, and many of them sense that. But in an excellent example of self-deceit, the sheeple envision these repressive actions by our TRUSTED representatives as being "bold" and "courageous" because the new laws initially provided them with an aura of security. It's government "doing something," and to most of the American citizens, that's always a good thing, even if it's actually detrimental. The public's casual mockery of our "bumbling, incompetent bureaucracy" is exceeded only by their loving support for it. But it's forever the Republican Party, particularly conservative (capitalistic-minded) members that are derided as the party of "NO." That is, they say "NO" to the masses clamoring for the Federal government to relieve them, via statism, of the individualistic economic liberty (self-responsibility) that they find so tedious and repulsive. It seems as though it's the conservatives who are becoming America's neo-SUBVERSIVES. That's most unfortunate.

Freedom / liberty doesn't "look out for you" like Democrat politicians do and it "doesn't care about you", just like "conservative politicians don't." Conservatism is freedom (inhumane) while liberalism is security (humane). The latter comes to the people's rescue, the former doesn't. Though the American people will have a casual political flirtation with freedom and go out on a date with it every once in a while, they will remain steadfastly married to safety (liberalism). With CONSERVATIVE Republicans and their off-putting, liberty-based, self-reliance philosophy, the voters, for the most part, have more confidence in Democrats to better handle Medicare, Medicaid, Social Security and other entitlements and social programs. And generally, the public looks to government to CREATE jobs or at least pretend to create the business climate for it. But, incongruously, this does not mean that they want FEWER rules, regulations and restrictions. The gist of the public's reasoning is that the aforementioned "3 R's" represent a government hands-on approach of our economy. Consequently, this gives them a feeling of comfort and reassurance. But our citizens would like to think that it also, albeit supplementary, CREATES JOBS. The ramification of America's desire for government control of the economy is analogous to certain food consumption. To wit: consuming ice cream, candy, and soda are enjoyable at first, but is bad for one's health in the long run; ditto government accountability for one's livelihood. Spinach, kale, and brussels sprouts, however, taste terrible to many if not most, but are actually good for everybody's health over a long period of time; likewise, the nationwide practice of individualism and self-responsibility. In a case of "He who lives by the sword, dies by the sword," a lot of supposedly free-market businessmen and corporation CEO's side with and fund far left organizations and vote for Democratic lawmakers who promise to have government not just subsidize or bail out their own industry, but place more regulations and restrictions on their competition. Actual *liberty* will make each individual's life better because it compels that person to practice individual accountibility which induces him or her to make the right decisions. Furthermore, in order for one to live the good life, one has to be cognizant that neither liberty nor freedom will guarantee a citizen the good life. They aren't supposed to. With REAL *liberty/freedom*, you reap what you sow.

There's a famous line in the 1953 classic Western *Shane* in which the title character states, "A gun is as good or as bad as the man using it." If one substitutes the words "a gun" with the term "freedom," it would perhaps be a better way to define the latter and America's ambivalence about it. The citizens of our country certainly find the WORD "freedom" appealing but have reservations about its actual practicality, since freedom doesn't manipulate or coerce for the common good. Mankind does. Liberty ALLOWS. Poor people having children that they can't afford are against allowing the taxpayer more economic freedom, because it would undercut income redistribution. On the other hand, a homeless bum has a lot of liberty because he has no personal responsibilities. He abandoned them to be free. Having pets is a restriction on a person's liberty because it compels the owner to take appropriate care of them. And having a spouse who is an invalid will certainly clamp down on the caretaker's freedom. Bringing up children properly (which excludes those who live in Section 8 housing) is a bit of a curtailment (more responsibility) on the parents' liberty. Raising mentally retarded kids is a restriction on one's freedom even more, not just because the aforementioned need more attention, but because retarded children (especially the severe ones) make the mother and father more reluctant or embarrassed to be seen with them in public.

Living in a mansion surrounded by a moat is no better or worse an example of liberty than living under a highway bridge with other vagrants. Both are equal in their extreme but honest representations of freedom. Another example of real liberty is when a child reaches adulthood. As most are well aware, many kids start getting rebellious at about the age of fifteen and complain about Mom and Dad's SUFFOCATING rules and curfews. When the son and daughter turn eighteen, they are finally FREE. They now have the freedom to go off on their own, which, in a very short time, could become a problem. It appears that these youngsters don't have the money to finance their freedom. Suddenly, the trade-off between "suffocating rules" and comforting security doesn't seem so bad. With freedom/liberty, life is what YOU make it. With solicitous, egalitarian central authoritarian control, life is what government makes it. A high percentage of American blacks, Hispanics and women would opt for the second statement.

Special interests on the socialist left want our government to subsidize them and slap regulations and restrictions on other Americans, not caring if it reduces freedom. The State of Texas is doing fiscally well because it's being run by conservative politicians with a capitalistic philosophy. California is an economic basket case because it's dominated by liberals. Their state finances will only get worse when the voters elect more liberals to office. And they will. Republican governors in conservative states will contact an industry in a liberal state and try to poach their jobs to bring back to the former's state. This doesn't happen vice versa because that would only be a waste of time for a Democratic governor. Officials in Texas have been trying to lure businesses from California to relocate to the Lone Star State. The Golden State governor, Gavin Newsom, and his minions in Sacramento would like nothing better than the Federal government to rescind the freedom of Texas to make such an attempt. One can reasonably expect that sometime in the near future, Mr. Newsom will ask (meaning *beg* or *demand*) Washington, DC to bail out their bankrupt state. Some three thousand miles away from the West Coast, the residents of New Hampshire, back in the 1980s, were proud of their motto, "Live Free or Die." Today, New Hampshire is at least a Democratic-leaning state, if not solid Democrat. What happened is that the liberals living in next door Taxachusetts fled the Bay State and took their ideology with them. The same applies to the bohemians from the communes of Vermont. They all wanted to enjoy the low-tax, give-me-liberty-or-give-me-death political atmosphere of the

Granite State. And then they proceeded to vote against it. Currently, New Hampshire doesn't abide by their old motto anymore. The progressives have taken over and implemented so many regulations and restrictions that New Hampshire residents can hardly make a movement, including the one in the bathroom. Democrats, via the government, will "help you." Liberty, via libertarian Republicans, will NOT definitely help you. Liberty has never tangibly taken care of anybody's problems.

Over the last century, the word "freedom" has UNFORTUNATELY had a positive connotation. Looking at it through their perspective, communists have long detested REAL freedom because they think that it doesn't guarantee a better life for the common man. They're correct. Real freedom is cold and uncaring. When the far progressive left (socialists and communists) utilize the abstract term "freedom" in their jargon, it's usually followed by the word "from" within their utopian desires. Hence, they want "freedom FROM poverty," "freedom from homelessness," "freedom from unemployment," and freedom from, well, actual freedom. Since the 1800s, immigrants from foreign lands have dreamt that coming to live in "America, Land of Liberty" would make them millionaires. And after they arrived here, they continued to dream. Or maybe these newcomers inferred that living in a free USA would at least assure them a middle-class income? No, it doesn't, nor should it. Okay, then. Perhaps they deduced that a free and prosperous America could minimally guarantee that its recently arrived residents will not be sharing cheese balls with rats inside of a hotel garbage dumpster? Sorry, no can do. Freedom is like having your own back-yard swimming pool. You have the freedom to enjoy swimming in it. You also have the freedom to drown in it. Nowhere in the Bill of Rights is it de facto written that liberty/freedom is a bowl of cherries.

Real liberty forces our citizens to be financially wiser and more fiscally responsible. Though this makes for a robust economy, it isn't very enticing to more than just a few of them. Many, if not most, Americans want so very much to believe that it is government benevolent command and control that makes their lives better, not actual freedom. They're oblivious to the notion that if government can make their lives better by taking away their liberty, then these naïve citizens, by the same conceptual token, would be obligated to support such a government action. A few decades ago, VOUCHERS were a very attractive idea to many voters. Today, this same word is anathema to most of them. To insert vouchers (financial freedom of choice) into public schools, Medicare, and other governmental expenditures is to weaken government command and control, not strengthen it. The American people are averse to this. They believe that vouchers smack of individualism and are a not-so-subtle indication that each of them would be ON THEIR OWN. Barack Obama had more than once heatedly disparaged the "you're on your own" value of Republicanism. In 2008, he said, "George Bush called this the ownership society, but what he really meant was the 'you're on your own' society." In 2012, our commander-in-chief, Obama opined about the Republicans, "Their philosophy is simple: You're on your own. That's the cramped narrow conception they have of liberty, and they're wrong." He added, "We are greater together than we are on our own."

Wiser words have never been more eloquently spoken since Henry Winston bought the farm. What should have been asked of the former community organizer, if a reporter dared, was, "Mr. President, if the majority of American citizens insist on being on his or her own, what's going to stop them?" Barack Obama (aka the Socialist Stench or SS) believes that only massive government activism with its supposedly giving one a "fair shot" at life, which the SS often spoke of, will the marginalized underdog succeed. This suggests that, with living in freedom, they're not already getting a FAIR SHOT. The more that the powerful and caring government subverts liberty, the more that the sorrowful and "oppressed" little guy will get a *fair* shot. Obama's own Orwellian "cramped, narrow conception" of liberty was to "FUNDAMENTALLY TRANSFORM" it. He was bashing economic freedom and subtly calling for collectivism, and he knows it. Unfortunately, most of the republic's sheeple either didn't realize it or didn't care. When the population of our country pines for paternalistic statism, and the 2009-2017 redistributionist-in-chief was only too happy to oblige, then that grants the government the license to dictate what the people can and cannot do.

The omnipotent State would have the right to subjugate them, and any American would be wrong to say that it doesn't. Until this happens, the nation's citizens will care only or mainly about themselves. But to the Anointed One and his flock, this can not be tolerated. As president, Obama's narcissism and intellectual dishonesty prevented him from seeing the depraved folly of his determination to force some 330 million strangers to be concerned about and collectively work for the common good in the future. In Obama's warped double-think view, when the United States of America is living under the slavery of socialism, then, and only then, will its people be truly free. That is, right after the Statue of Liberty is torn down.

CHAPTER **17**

Day Bee Lion

"YOUNG BLACKS, WHOSE recklessness produces oceans of misery, feel little of the kind of guilt that changes behavior. One reason for this is that they have been taught by reflexive "civil rights' rhetoric that they are mere victims, absolved from responsibility by the all-purpose alibi of 'white racism'. The problem of black America is not an insufficiency of elected officials prepared to regard blacks, alone among American groups, as permanent wards of government compassion. The problem is that millions of blacks are victims of irresponsible blacks." So writes columnist George Will. The black people of America enjoy the status of being perceived as victims and use this to emphasize the responsibility of government to solve their problems. A black person becoming a doctor, scientist, or engineer, undermines the "victim" status that American blacks are supposed to aspire to. Oh, they're victims, alright, but not of "racist" America; instead, they are victims of being spoiled by "government responsibility" resulting in 72 percent illegitimacy and the erosion of family values. In 1964, black out-of-wedlock births were 24 percent. With the "advent" of the Great Society a year later, the black illegitimacy rate skyrocketed to three times as much in just four decades. Today, most black Americans under the age of forty are illegitimate.

Just like the present, there was a bitterness, resentment, anger, and hopelessness of black America in the 1940's, but the difference is the aforementioned feelings weren't part of blacks' CREED back then. Today, this creed epitomizes the "authentic" (real or genuine) young urban black male. It particularly helps his "authenticity" if he dropped out of high school and did some time in prison. A young black man having to hold up his pants while walking is AUTHENTIC. A young black man who is a doctor is not. According to FBI statistics, blacks are seven times as likely as people of other races to commit murder, eight times more likely to commit robbery, and three times more likely to use a gun in a crime. If an urban teenage black girl when speaking about a teenage black boy says about him, "He got an attitude", that is not a put-down but a compliment. Said black girl is really conveying that she likes him and wouldn't mind having this black boy's baby. Plus, she doesn't need for him to marry her. Indeed, the noted female wouldn't have high regards for him if this young black man DID want to marry her. Poor teenage black girls long to have babies due to the fact that they (1) have low esteem, (2) are capitulating to peer pressure, (3) because it's a rite of passage and (4) it fills a void in their lives. Subsequently, these young ladies usually have nothing but the utmost respect for the black male who impregnates them and then doesn't pay for the upbringing (dat gubmint's job) of their child.

The unmarried poor black girl doesn't realize it, but the boy who knocked her up just ruined her life. She, however, would like to think that her pregnancy is an improvement. Having a child that the young unwed can't afford provides her with a convenient alibi (she has to stay home and take care of her baby) for not having a high school diploma or career employment. The aforementioned teenage mother lives with her single mother, who in turn, lives with HER single mother. It's a generational cycle. She's a mother by the age of seventeen, grandmother at the age of thirty-five, and great grandmother before she turns fifty. When said lady reaches the Social Security recipient age of sixty-two, it is at that point that she will be able to collect government checks. And nobody can say that this woman isn't AUTHENTICALLY black if she lives in Section 8 housing, had her first bout of morning sickness before she entered high school, and/or gave birth to her third bastard before she stopped being a teenager. Most young black folks follow this path because they never had an at-home father and their mother didn't set them straight by disciplining them because she, herself, had no self-discipline. Many believe that it is both racist and insulting to strongly encourage poor blacks to get married before they have children. Alas, if some present-day urban blacks still proclaim that they're proud to be black, they should be asked,..."Why?"

What the black left-leaning leaders of America make darn sure not to mention is that in the year 2012, for example, the poverty rate for black MARRIED couples with children under the age of eighteen was 11 percent. For single black FEMALE householders with children under eighteen in the same year, the poverty rate was more than four times as much (47.5 percent). The economist and author Thomas Sowell, who incidentally, is black, states, "The current self-destructive misdirection of energies in black ghettoes cannot be explained by 'a legacy of slavery' or 'racism.' For one thing, this level of self-destruction in black communities did not exist half a century ago when racism was worse and the black population was generations closer to the era of slavery." But then, the problem with Mr. Sowell is that although he APPEARS to be a black man, he is not a "genuine," "real" or "authentic" black, because Thomas Sowell is a conservative. A few years ago, there was a story about Supreme Court Justice Clarence Thomas's visit to a National Bar Association convention and how a lot of black lawyers there were against his showing up. The story said that these attorneys saw his conservative views as his self-hatred. The majority of black Americans will agree with the lawyers. Because he leans to the right, Clarence Thomas (he a traitor) does not represent them, and as a black person, HE IS SUPPOSED TO. The late Supreme Court Justice Thurgood Marshall was a "genuine, real, and authentic" black because he was a liberal. Although, there have been those who have stated that black America is not monolithic, the gist of most non-whites' disposition toward black conservatism ("self-hatred") is that the black population SHOULD BE monolithic for the sake of their cause.

The progressive left doesn't like charter schools or separate private schools for black boys and another for black girls. They fear that such students would practice individualism and go on to become successful and especially independent in life. But with their mother's advice plus government schools and its influence, a black child's attitude is shaped early in his/her life when he or she is socio-politically brainwashed. Blacks have also been taught from the get-go, by relatives and friends, to take what they can get out of life. This manifests itself in their causing riots and exploiting them by breaking pawn shop and appliance store windows and stealing the merchandise. And then what's even more egregious is that they vote Democratic for the handouts. Blacks grudgingly accept that the white race is presently the majority and dominant race in the USA. In resistance, blacks seek comfort in interrelating by referring to each other as "brother" or "sister." It's their way of bonding in an indifferent and uncomfortable, if not seemingly hostile, racial environment. This is analogous to conservative men who refer to their fellow male ideologue as "brother" when going up against the liberal cultural establishment that's dominent and influential in America.

The Crab Barrel: A magazine for black Americans once mentioned that the crabs-in-a-barrel mentality among blacks is a myth. They lied. Whenever a black individual, especially from "the hood," merely looks like he or she is going to be a success in "white society," that person gets torn down by his/her peers. When a crab in a barrel starts to make his way out of it, the other crabs get jealous and drag him down. The other crabs realize that doing this probably won't help the rest of them get out. But that's okay. It's not right or fair that the lone crab gets to escape. Either they all escape simultaneously, or none do. Likewise, many a prominent black leader has vocally beckoned the black people of America, to "join hands and cross over the line TOGETHER." Most Americans fail to grasp that these leaders have the strategy of "collectivism" in the backs of their minds whenever they declare that. The crab barrel syndrome is prevalent in most urban public schools, but not in charter schools or private schools for black boys or girls, much to the chagrin of left-leaning black leaders. In the public high schools of major cities, whenever black children are clean-cut, studious, and get all A's and B's on their report cards, they're called "Oreo cookies." A boy would be taunted with, "He think he white" or a girl denigrated, "She think she better than us." Actually, she is.

More crabs? If a black man escapes the ghetto lifestyle and becomes a self-made millionaire (he acting white), it's not uncommon among black city-dwellers to desire or call on him (excluding a rich black celebrity) to "give back" to the community. Why is this? Did this black individual steal something from the community and now they want him to return it? Or did he just leave town without their permission? Have you ever noticed that when a poor WHITE man becomes wealthy, he is not asked or expected to "give back" to the white community? Does the now successful white man say to himself, "The white people in my neighborhood a generation ago are the ones who made me a rich big shot, and so now, since I'm also white, I owe them big time. The residents in my old community are my people because they are white and so I am obligated to come back and help them?" No, he doesn't say that. But it's as if the only reason why a rich black man is "special" is because the black community in which he once lived made him so. And now he OWES them; otherwise, this rich black man has "forgotten where he came from." So, the least he could do is to feel guilty. You might say that, hoping to influence the guy's attitude via peer pressure, some black males want to blackmail a black male...(sorry). But financial success tales among whites are fairly common. Rags-to-riches stories among blacks are not ordinary. And in the opinions of many blacks, they aren't supposed to be. While whites are more individualistic, blacks are far more racially cliquish.

"The white liberal differs from the white conservative only in one way: the liberal is more deceitful than the conservative. The liberal is more hypocritical than the conservative. Both want power but the white liberal is the one who has perfected the art of posing as the Negro's best friend and benefactor; and by winning the friendship, allegiance and support of the Negro, the white liberal is able to use the Negro as a pawn, or tool in this political 'football game' that is constantly raging between the white liberals and white conservatives." So spoke Malcolm X. But to supplement what the early 1960s black-nationalist leader stated, most of today's blacks don't mind the least bit that white liberal politicians desire blacks to be beholden to them. Furthermore, conservatism is antithetical to black America because it rubs an uncomfortable truth in their collective face, which is something that liberalism doesn't do. Many Americans misconstrue conservative disapproval of the detrimental behavior of blacks as dislike of blacks themselves. On the other hand, it is very difficult for white liberals to disapprove of something that they are reluctant to acknowledge. But white liberals WILL compensate for their lack of criticism of deleterious black behavior by advocating that the government subsidize it. White conservative politicians are more likely than white liberal politicians to treat blacks as equal to whites. It's no wonder that so many blacks don't like white conservative politicians. Although, there ARE a few blacks, particularly the ones that consistently vote Democrat, who politically DISLIKE but respect white conservatives while they politically like but DISRESPECT white liberals.

Then there are the black holders of political office who are "not black enough" (translation: they're not liberal enough). And as long as we're on the subject of COLOR, there are black Americans, among non-blacks, who strangely but commonly refer to themselves as "people of color." It's an interesting oddity that even though isn't the least bit pretentious, does prompt six questions: (1) Do not all people (excluding the Invisible Man) have skin that has a color? (2) If whites are not "people of color," then doesn't that mean that a black person who is an albino, IS NOT a "person of color" especially if he or she is whiter than most whites? (3) Are these "people of color" special? If so, should they be treated differently than white citizens? If they're NOT special, then why utilize the ostracizing three-worded term? (4) Blacks and white liberals are prone to think that a Republican President is likely to be a "divider" when he should be a "uniter." This thought subsequently inquires: Is the nationwide use of the haughty and contemptuous "people of color" label more likely to UNITE the American citizens or DIVIDE them? Which one? (5) If black folks desire or insist on being called "people of color" then doesn't that make them COLORED PEOPLE? The answer to that question is a definitive YES. Let's put it this way; is a box that's made out of cardboard.....a cardboard box? And (6), if a white person CAN'T be called a "person of color" then doesn't that render this very term exclusionary, elitist, and racist?

Actually, the author is being coy. The last sentence of question number #3 is a rhetorical one. You see; the minorities that designate themselves "people of color" believe that its connotation makes racial and ethnic minorities uniquely esteemed by virtue of being the victims of *"systematic racism."* Their societal status in the socio-political arena is consequently elevated by being perceived as the put-upon underdog that decent people sympathize with. The prestigious "people of color" title gives those with black or brown skin a certain *je ne sais quoi* that white people just don't have. It is their sympathy-inducing humbleness coupled with their pride of being a "victim of society" that attracts, they would like to believe, respect, admiration and support from the white majority. Conservative blacks are not usually thought of as or labeled "people of color" (the term has a more ideological undertone then it does a racial one) because the noted pride-infused moniker is reserved particularly for minorities who are perpetual malcontents or racially pure ("we NOT fake blacks") and therefore culturally superior to black conservatives.

It has been duly noted that the Democratic Party conventions have a lot more blacks and minorities in attendance than there are at Republican conventions. But, then again, the Communist Party USA's conventions, rallies and lectures for more than a century received a much higher percentage of black attendance than the GOP has had. In their disingenuousness, the liberal/left would like the American people to think that the Republican Party is trying to keep blacks and other minorities out of it. Quite the contrary; all political parties in America today should welcome anybody and everybody into their organization, because that would make them more powerful and their philosophy and ideas more formidable. Any political party, whether it's the Republican Party or the Trotskyite Socialist Workers Party, would be politically foolish to even attempt to exclude potential members of any race. Besides, an individual chooses his or her political party, not vice versa. But the reason why blacks, women and other minorities gravitate toward the Democratic Party is because they are attracted to the socialistic (government will pamper me and take care of my problems) message of said political party. Consequently, it's why the ignorant among us think of the Democrats as being "inclusive" and "diverse."

It was the Democrat Party, affectionately known by most black Americans as "the Party of the Welfare Check", who actually brought our nation slavery, lynching, segregation, Jim Crow laws, poll taxes and literary tests. Yet, over 90 percent of blacks on election-day vote Democratic. Many of them have proudly proclaimed, "We loyal Democrats!" Well, of course they are. But the trouble is, is that they're loyal to the Democratic Party in the same way that a heroin addict is loyal to his supplier. On the other hand, some blacks have complained, "The Democrats take blacks for granted." My answer: That's right, they do. And why shouldn't they? What are blacks going to do about it if the Democrats DON'T stop taking them for granted? Blacks have absolutely no choice but to meekly accept it. Although, a few blacks do sense that the Democratic politicians are playing them for fools. But black citizens also know that, for them, it's a case of "You scratch my back (I get government goodies) and I'll scratch yours (I vote for you)." These particular black Americans will gladly trade any self-respect for government assistance. Black citizens either don't realize or don't care that when they vote for Democrats, they are adopting a loser mentality.

Black Americans like to annually employ the month after January to celebrate the glorious victimhood decades (largely pre-1970) of injustice and unfairness. Black History Month itself has been negligible in improving the lives of black society. But then again, it's not for them. Black History Month is targeted mostly at America's white citizenry. February is used primarily to guilt-trip current white society on how American blacks were treated from over fifty years to three centuries ago. Whether it's the antebellum South, the Scottsboro boys, Rosa Parks, Stepin Fetchit, or their sulking about Selma, blacks love to bring up the past, not just because they find soaking in their self-pity to be cathartic, but also because by focusing on what white America did to their racial ancestry in the past, black folks don't have to think about or deal with what blacks are doing to themselves in the present. Henceforth, every second month of the year should from now on be called "Divert Whitey's Attention Month."

In order to obtain political recognition and favoritism (identity politics both), guilt-tripping has always been part and parcel of black individuals' modus operandi because without it, they would lose the debate. For instance, many of these LOYAL DEMOCRATS say to

Republican lawmakers, "You don't know what it's like to be poor." These particular guilt-tripping blacks would never have ventured such a prejudice charge against a born-with-a-silver-spoon-in-his-mouth liberal Democrat who has never "walked the walk" of being impoverished and therefore shouldn't "talk the talk" about a remedy. Thus, making the allegation of the Republican's "not having been poor" irrelevant unless it's to induce guilt. It never dawned on these certain blacks that being a conservative Republican does not necessitate being financially well-off, but merely demands reasoning and intellectual honesty. But then once more, that's why they're LOYAL DEMOCRATS.

Blacks validate and vindicate their culture and behavior by calling it "acting black." This way, any perceived misconduct on their part becomes legitimized. An example of "MISPERCEIVED conduct" is white citizens locking their car doors because their traveling through a black ghetto. It is not because of any racism on the part of the former. It's because they associate a much rumored and statistically-supported high crime rate with that area. Black people are some forty times more likely to commit a crime against white people than vice versa. When a taxi driver who is white passes by a black man hailing a ride, to pick up a white man doing the same fifteen yards away, it's not due to racism but to his cognizance of the much higher black crime rate. This is the case even if the taxi driver is a guilt-ridden liberal, or for that matter, a black Democrat. The Reverend Jesse Jackson once said, "There is nothing more painful to me at this stage of my life than to walk down the street and hear footsteps....then turn around and see somebody white and feel relieved." He should have taken a taxi. The Reparations for Slavery idea is another guilt-tripping charade that some blacks would like to see whites fall victim to. Perhaps the reader should wonder why the SUBJECT of Reparations for Slavery is even brought up at all when there is a Democratic president and redistribution is already going full blast. Two questions: Will the more than a million of America's black millionaires be receiving reparations? It's money owed to them for the miserable slavery life that their great, great grandfathers had to go through, so shouldn't they receive it? And, if a citizen is just half black, will he or she get only fifty percent of the reparation alloted, as opposed to the

100 percent due to an entirely black person? And finally, regarding the black American slaves in the early 1800s who are still alive today, this author's postulation is that they should be financially compensated and apologized to by their now-geriatric white masters before they both pass away. Otherwise, it will be too late for closure.

SLAVERY: Slavery is a manifestation of humankind evolving. Therefore, it must be judged in its historical context. In sixteenth-century Europe, people were burnt to death at the stake if they were accused and found guilty by the court of being witches or devil worshippers. In seventeenth-century America (like in Salem, Massachusetts) such individuals were hung. Today, this type of punishment for what is most definitely non-criminal behavior would be deemed utterly barbaric. And it is....but not back then. Three and a half centuries ago, death by fire or hanging was a perfectly just and acceptable fate for these "deviants" in the minds of the ordinary townsfolk. Fast-forward to circa 1820s America. White citizens during this time period also thought that the witch hunts in this country of some 140 years earlier were cruel, and they were aghast that mankind could have been so ignorant and inhumane. However, to them, slavery in America of black people who were brought over from the continent of Africa was perfectly normal, natural, and "with the times." One century and two decades later (the 1940s), whites were pondering over how their forebears could have been so unkind by making slaves out of their fellow human beings, albeit a different race.

Yet, to them there was nothing unfair or indecent about forced racial segregation or discriminating against people based on their skin color. The moral of the story: Mankind, at least in the industrial West, evolves and grows wiser. If blacks were by far the dominant race in America some two hundred years ago, they more than likely would have made slaves out of whites who came here from another country. Indeed, in the year 1830, there were over 3,700 slave MASTERS in the United States who were BLACK. And black slaves being subjugated by members of their own race is even more egregious and reprehensible, is it not? But, alas, black America doesn't want slavery to be an indictment of slavery, per se, but an indictment of white people. Many black Americans in the 1980s disliked and resented President Ronald Reagan for trying to induce, for the reason of self-reliance, more freedom on them. In essence, they denounced our 40th president as a "slave master," precisely because he was AGAINST centralized-government social control of them. Though Ronald Reagan once stated that government is not our master, it is our servant; most blacks living in this country would beg to differ.

Today's "loyal Democrats" (they're back) would gladly welcome being subservient to the benevolent State. This is a mentality that most of our nation's black people living in the nineteenth century didn't have. Present-day blacks apathetically accept the Democratic Party's virtual degradation of them because, said minorities figure, at least the Democrats are lenient toward black folks wrongful behavior and seem to provide (metaphorically speaking) them with food, clothing and shelter. Theirs is an American journey from slavery by a few white men (the blacks' legacy) to the slavery by omnipotent, collectivistic government (their manifest destiny). But black Americans should realize that just as a white man has no right to make a black man his slave, a black man has no right to make a white man his caretaker. The only way for white society to actually help blacks is to do something to them that they're not going to like, and that is to inject more liberty (i.e. less government responsibility) into their lives, which is what happened to our nation's black people back in 1865.

FOOTNOTE: Some blacks will respond to this writer's article by saying, "He don't like black people." That's incorrect. The sentence is supposed to read "He DOESN'T.....like black people." But one's own feeling toward another race is irrelevant. Only the truth is. These same black Americans would never accuse white liberals of disliking them, because the latter has an indulgent and pampering demeanor toward blacks that conveniently will not hold them accountable. Incidentally, the vast majority of American blacks NEVER say the word "doesn't" in a sentence. Why is that?

CHAPTER **18**

Opinionated Bits and Pieces Part 4

CONGRESSWOMAN NANCY PELOSI said that women, blacks, Hispanics, and Asians "reflect the great diversity and strength of our nation." She's right! They really do reflect the great diversity of our nation.

Americans that are scared to death of a government shutdown, even if it were just for two days, are the same ones who are very fond of the nanny state. Similarly, citizens who are intellectually and morally dishonest tend to venerate the powerful (government) and dislike the unpopular (self-responsibility advocates). In a totally related issue, people who accuse President Trump of lying many times are the same individuals who are POSITIVELY GLAD that President Obama LIED when he stated "I will not sign a plan that adds one dime to our deficits---either now or in the future." Plus, most Americans really don't hold it against Obama prevaricating when he told them that he would make government more open and promote freedom of speech. Everybody has heard that "All politicians lie" and that's almost entirely true. But the reader should realize that any falsehoods that are conducive to steering America in a conservative (capitalistic) direction are profoundly superior to LIES that steer us in a progressive (socialistic) direction. The left believes that the end justifies the means. By the same political token, what's good for the goose......

Former military officer and Secretary of State, Collin Powell, died on October 18th, 2021. Powell was a liberal Republican who voted for the Democrat nominee for President in November of 2008, 2012, 2016 and 2020. All the same, Powell was a good and decent American. Moreover, he was also a human being.

Nazism and fascism are FACTUALLY bad and rotten to the core. So is socialism. But despite the sophomoric smears and outright lies by the liberal/left, there are no factual Nazi or fascist lawmakers in the Federal government. In the view of more than 99.99 percent of the American people, that would be utterly intolerable. On the other hand, our society practically welcomes the presence of dozens of socialist politicians (mostly clandestine) at our nation's capital. Although, roughly half of our nation's voters (Republicans, Democrats and independents combined) may find socialism to be an essentric outlier, they nevertheless deem it to be reasonable and well nigh acceptable. Is this very attitude not a harbinger of our future? Alas, the American people have resigned themselves to this future, evidently.

Many Americans will NOT find the political slogan "Empowerment of the People" too endearing if it really means their having to espouse and practice *individualism* and *self-responsibility*. Since politicians are people (although some are actually snakes) and they are put in power by the citizens of America, then this latter collective has handed power over to the aggregate (the 50 states) of the country, via the voters' representatives (our elected lawmakers) to give, not power to individuals, per se, but supposedly "Power to the People" in totality (government of the people by the people). And so, government IS the people. Therefore, in order for "Empowerment of the People" to work nationwide, there must be centralized command and control of society.

Bleeding Heart Conservative: Yours truly is disheartened (no, really, I am) when I see businesses go out of business, especially the small-profit operations. Though this humble author may never enter an eccentric boutique-type store, I do hope that they financially make it and make it big. The writer appreciates and supports free-market enterprise but at the same time, I don't like it when it produces *"victims."* It saddens me when Walmart moves right next door to a small village of Mom & Pop stores just trying to make a buck, though the giant retailer has every right, for the most part, to do so. It is particularly depressing when yours truly hears about a multi-millionaire CEO getting a pay raise directly after laying off employees from his company. And then there's the executive that was fired but given a $ixty million dollar $everence package (golden parachute). It is individuals like these who have done more damage to the reputation of capitalism than any communist could ever hope to do. What has been said in the past is profoundly true…the worst thing about capitalism is the capitalists.

When the American left preaches INCLUSIVENESS for our society, it is extremely important to them that it includes IDENTITY POLITICS and its consequent polarization.

The number one reason why former NFL player Colin Kaepernick isn't hired by a professional football team is because the owners and head coaches consider his keeling during the national anthem to be an antagonistic cancer that would repel pigskin fans from coming to their stadium (loss of revenue). But the aforementioned part-time "social justice activist" won't promise the owner that he will refrain from kneeling and henceforth becoming toxic public relations baggage for any football team. A stadium is private property, and so he does NOT have the right to be disobedient. One wonders why Kaepernick doesn't just take his soapbox politics off the football field and speak elsewhere to the proletarian masses. This longtime admirer and supporter of Fidel Castro's Cuba said that he is against…..wait for it….."systemic oppression." Whoa, ha ha ha! Funny guy, that Colin! When I first heard about him spouting this howlingly hilarious knee-slapper, I laughed until I stopped. But no reporter will even ask the ex-quarterback if he thinks that socialism and communism are unjust and oppressive, because no reporter wants to put him on the spot and quite likely reveal to the American people what Kaepernick really is all about. Otherwise, the author will bet the entire nation $20 million dollars that the malcontent sport star would dodge the reporter's question by refusing to answer it with either a YES or NO. If yours truly loses the bet, I'll pay it off by using the money that he made from exploiting the "system." But the filthy lucre will first have to be confiscated from the noted perturbed, rich athlete via the State (thereby making it legitimate) and promptly given to this writer. I'm sure that Mr. Kaepernick will approve.

Have you ever noticed that conservative Americans are more law abiding than our liberal citizens but that it's the latter who call for more laws? And then, if various said laws come to fruition, the liberals will subsequently become softer on the punishment for violators of these laws. There should be a law against left-leaning individuals who help to enact certain penalty legislation only to, later on, treat it frivolously. But I don't think that these liberals should be punished. We just need more laws to stop them.

Blacks in the United States claim to be racially profiled and treated unfairly by numerous arrests at the hands of law enforcement. But they are arrested disproportionately more and imprisoned because they commit a higher percentage of crimes than whites. Armed with this common knowledge and government statistics, the police suspect blacks of being up to no good more than they suspect whites of being up to no good, resulting in the law "harassing" blacks in greater numbers. However, twenty-year-old WHITE men are "harassed" and arrested far more by the cops than seventy-year-old BLACK women are. So here's the question: In comparison to the latter age/racial/gender group, don't you think that America's twenty-year-old white men are being unduly PROFILED and jailed by the police and consequently, don't you think that they're being treated racially UNFAIR?

Even though some Democrats of a century and a half ago started up the Ku Klux Klan, today's Democrats don't approve of white men and white women dressed in white robes with pointy hoods surrounding a burning cross. But our contemporary Democrats DO approve of white men and white women dressed in white robes and surgical masks surrounding a young pregnant black female lying on an exam table with her legs in stirrups while inside a Planned Parenthood clinic.

Why do we tip? Some have said that it's the feeling of guilt of having one person (such as a waiter) serve another (a patron). But questions arise for the reader: When the teenager wearing a paper hat at a fast food joint brought you your food, did you tip him or her just like you did the server at a sit-down restaurant? If not, why not? Or is your being generous to someone helping you contingent on your having to sit down first? You eat (sitting down) at a greasy spoon that's packed with customers. Your waitress is running around with her head cut off serving you (among others) and obliging your commands. The bill comes to $20.00 and she receives a $3.00 (fifteen percent) tip. You dine at an expensive steakhouse and your waiter just brings over the filet mignon that you ordered and does nothing else for you. The check is $60 and you give him a $9 tip, which is THREE TIMES MORE than you gave the waitress at the greasy spoon when she worked THREE TIMES HARDER for you. Why? If you say that the steakhouse food is better, then why didn't you go tip the cook? Otherwise, you're really just forking over nine bucks for the building interior's classy ambience and the waiter's impersonation of a cigar store Indian. You're at a shoe store sitting down (again) on a chair while the shoe salesman kneels at your feet like your the King of Siam, takes off your shoes (his nose two feet away from your smelly two feet) and at your request, brings you five pairs of shoes that he puts on your feet (that's one shoe on one foot at a time, wise guy) and laces up and then awaits your Royal Majesty's decision. At the end of his ordeal, you mention to the dude that you don't like any of the shoes, get up off the throne and promptly walk out. Now then, did you tip the shoe salesman? It's the least you could do considering that you didn't buy anything. That poor fellow worked harder for you than a waitress at a greasy spoon.

In June of 2015, a twenty-one-year-old white man used a gun to kill nine black people in a church in South Carolina. A few days later, the media presented a picture of him holding a Confederate flag. Most blacks and white liberals blamed the horrific murder on the Confederate flag, the lack of gun control and systemic racism. All authentic conservatives blamed said crime on the noted young white man. Most black Americans and white liberals were against his receiving the death penalty. Most conservatives favored this murderer getting the death penalty.

The US Constitution is the enemy of the people because it epitomizes FREEDOM. Ergo, freedom doesn't install economic security or social equity, both which benefit the people. In essence, this anachronistic document carelessly unleashed onto our country in 1788 by rich, old, privileged white men IS the *enemy of the people* precisely because it's an enmity to socialism, which would be a new and refreshing change to our democracy. The Constitution and capitalism are SO YESTERGENERATION. They're shibboleths for those old-fashioned Republican types imprudently looking to the past. Alas, those who look backward will be left behind. For socialism is the future and a bona fide shining beacon high on a hill that represents a brighter tomorrow for all of us!

The numerical figure "six million" has long been bandied about as to how many Jews died in the 1933-1945 Holocaust. In fact, this very number has become virtual gospel to God's Chosen People. To even challenge it by suggesting that the actual death rate was less than the established "six million," constitutes being "anti-Semitic." Although, a gentile who says that "It was more like five and a quarter million that died" is not the least bit denying the Holocaust, he is nonetheless, questioning the sacrosanct "six million." Now, in and of itself, this isn't deplorable or condemnable. But to Jewish people, the absolute agreement with the infamous number is a veritable litmus test for non-Jews to verbally emote in order to show that they are SINCERELY sympathetic to what Jews went through. God's Chosen People want so very much to think that they are genuinely liked by gentiles in the hope of diminishing any discomfort with or distrust of them. Of course, if the Nazis killed, not six million nor six thousand or even six hundred, but just SIX Jewish human beings during the entire reign of the Third Reich, then that is six Jews too many.

If Christians want to put up a picture of the Ten Commandments on the wall in a government building, which is presumably owned by the American taxpayers, they shouldn't be permitted to. We cannot allow Christianity to impose its moral values on the rest of us. But if our Muslim citizens desire to build a mosque at Ground Zero where, prior to 9/11, the Twin Towers were in New York City, then we ought to refrain from aggravating them and answer "YES" to their request. The nation must prove to the worshippers of Allah that we non-Muslim Americans really are nice people, due to the fact that the followers of Islam don't presently realize it. Our country should also NOT insist that Muslims who live here assimilate into the American way of life, but instead, we ought to warmly welcome their culture and religion and adapt to them as if they were our own. This way, we the citizens of the United States will be steadily making preparations for our future.

When, after five and a half years in public office, a liberal Democrat senator makes the lives of his black constituents a lot WORSE via his voting record, at least 85 percent of black voters in his state strongly desire for him to be re-elected. When, after the same amount of time as a politician, a conservative Republican senator makes the lives of blacks in his state infinitely BETTER via HIS voting record, at least 85 percent of them will be hell-bent on seeing him get thrown out of office. Any white person who thinks or says that black voters are not smart people is just plain WRONG.

HATRED: HATE is to be associated with conservatism ONLY. And even if (and that's a big IF) there is hatred on the liberal-left, it should be excused and played down because the end results of the leftward direction is socialism, which, the left would like to think, is the exact opposite of *hate*. Though, it IS entirely alright with the left if somebody HATES America. Indeed, said progressives hope for this type of *hate* and even encourage it. But what constitutes hatred, and should we have laws against it presenting itself? Plus, who are the arbiters in America that will decide what type of hatred is permitted and what kind of punishment, if any, shall the purveyor of this emotion receive? For instance, is it okay for somebody to hate Mondays? Is it alright for New York Yankees fans and those of the Boston Red Sox to hate each other? Do Cubans living in Miami, Florida who hate Fidel Castro deserve to be rebuked? Does the radical left deserve to be chastised for hating the religious right? Many believe that Nation of Islam minister, Louis Farrakhan, hates Jews and whites. If he does, is it, in turn, justified that the insignificant Muslim preacher, himself, be hated by Jews and whites?

Our citizens on the far left cry "HATRED" to smear and tarnish those who vehemently resist their socialistic agenda! But the noted progressives, themselves, are mainly apathetic about Islamic terrorists who HATE the United States and want to destroy it. Unlike the left, the vast majority of those on the far right do not hate our country. The former merely project their own hatred on those who, using facts and rational thought, disagree with the left, *Veritas odium parit* — (truth begets hatred). But then again, from their perspective, the left SHOULD embrace hatred (yes, that's right). You can't tear down and punish America with *love* running through your veins and a *song in your heart* when you're trying to install tyrannical authoritarianism. Mendaciously labeling American whites and their customary lifestyle as *racist*, is left-leaning blacks way of manifesting their seething hatred of white people. If a white conservative male politician's economic and social policies factually help black citizens, then that makes whatever personal hatred he has towards blacks MOOT, does it not? It's been documented that blacks, twice as much as whites, are likely to commit officially designated HATE crimes against the other race. Should this very statistic compel our judicial courts to double the punishment for blacks? If a rabbi who has vociferously stated numerous times that he absolutely HATES Nazis, murders a man that the rabbi knows for a fact, is a non-violent, law-abiding member of the American Nazi Party, is that a hate crime? That Nazism is HATRED, per se, is not the problem in the minds of the left. The problem is that Nazism is hatred of CERTAIN people, (Jews, gypsies, homosexuals, etc.) that don't deserve it. But to the far left, socialism-based hatred (communism) is righteous and good not just because it hates the wealthy, liberty, and the truth, but because it at least purports to help the "marginalized" in life. These fanatical progressives believe that their strong desire for an ostensibly *compassionate and caring* centralized government inoculates them from any criticism of their own hatred. Or as a political enemy of the late Republican 1964 presidential candidate Barry Goldwater might paraphrase him, "Hatred in defense of socialism is no vice." The Southern Poverty Law Center and other leftists who proclaim to be against HATE refuse to call the Communist Party USA a HATE group because the latter hates spiritually contented and financially secure citizens. *Smith and Jones Lesson*: Smith hates a certain race, ethnicity, and class of Americans. Jones hates altogether different types of our nation's citizens than that of Smith. But Mr. Jones wants the government to control and hurt the people that he HATES, whereas Mr. Smith DOESN'T desire government to control or hurt ANYBODY whatsoever. Although he does harbor hatred, Mr. Smith is a better man than Mr. Jones. Now, the majority of liberals and neo-Marxists in the United States will disagree with yours truly on this because Mr. Smith doesn't want government involvement.

Doctrinaire progressives HATE economic freedom and certain social liberties because such lack of governmental social engineering allow for individuals to pursue what's best for him or her and not necessarily for society. Unlike any possible hostility on the far right, the socialism-fueled hatred of the far left culminates in totalitarianism. The politically correct left likes to say that "there's FREE speech and then there's HATE speech." And it is they who will designate what is and isn't HATE. For example, you CANT say that you hate the late lefty folk singer, Pete Seeger. But you CAN say that you hate Bob Segar, rock star of the late 1970s (as long as he doesn't sing heartfelt folk songs about trade unions and the left's beloved pinko and political activist, Joe Hill). To the leftist PC Gestapo, saying "I dislike socialism" is HATE SPEECH, but saying "I HATE capitalism" is not.

Suffice it to say, the AIM of any actual HATRED on the right, albeit conceivably misguided, is to build America up while the AIM of true HATRED on the left is to tear America down. Most of the time, the term "hate", is exploited by the user as a political sledgehammer to bash those who disagree with his or her ideological opinions. The individuals who employ such tactics HATE honest public discourse. Quite a few on the fascistic left are now labeling any conservative talking points as "hate speech" in order to shut down the truth or pro-capitalism message under the guise of "trying to stop hate." And then there's the infamous HATRED that, starting in the year 2016, afflicted the one cerebrum shared by all progressives in America, called "Trump Derangement Syndrome." Many Americans have heard of Pastor Jeremiah Wright, whose church Barack Obama was a member of for twenty years and initially joined for political reasons. And then there's former KKK member, the infamous David Duke. The first man has been known to hate whites and Jews, and the second one a reputation for hating blacks and Jews. But it's not so much the FEELINGS (hate) that is pertinent but rather, if Wright and Duke had their druthers (each was Supreme Ruler of the USA), what unfair laws, if any, would each man implement pertaining to whites, blacks, and Jews? HATRED itself, matters nowhere near as much as its manifestation.

There have been liberal protesters marching near the offices of various Republican lawmakers. The former were holding picket signs saying, "Hands off My Obamacare." But the operative word "My" is a misnomer. It's not "their" Obamacare. It's the governments. The aforementioned citizens would rather not take note of the dichotomy but instead personalize what's officially known as the Affordable Care Act. The protesters and their supporters do this in hope of convincing the American people that the conservatives are trying to steal from them, (repeal it), something (Obamacare) that is rightfully theirs. If the glorious State is thought of as being "the people," then the gullible will be seduced and hoodwinked into believing that an attempt to cut government is an attack on them, the people. Whenever naïve, ignorant individuals refer to something OWNED and run by the government (e.g. Social Security, Medicaid, and Medicare) as "MY," they're hoping that it stymies any desire by the staunch self-responsibility-pushing Right to rescind it.

Starting in the late 1950s, civil rights activists correctly proclaimed that RACE DOES NOT MATTER and SHOULD NOT MATTER. Currently, those on the left disagree with and challenge this belief via their mantra of "race does matter." Generations ago, blacks didn't have NEGATIVE RIGHTS, and wrongly so. Today, progressives want the government to grant blacks POSITIVE RIGHTS and desire blacks to be given preferential treatment over whites. The caring left doesn't care if this causes resentment in whites nor a worsening of relations between blacks and whites. Indeed, they expect and desire it to.

Perhaps you, the reader, can help me out with something of which I am totally ignorant. Which one was worse.....the government-sponsored communism of the Soviet Union in the 1940s, or the government-sponsored racism of the United States of America in the same decade? Plus, did these two unjust, oppressive systems negatively affect ALL of the ordinary citizens of each country, or just a small minority of them? Lastly, although yours truly is deeply befuddled, I do know that Joseph Stalin was a Communist Party member of and the leader of the USSR in the 1940s. But during the very same ten years, who was the leader of the USA and what political party was he a member of?

The entertainer James Brown was a Republican. So it's not at all surprising that the late singer/dancer, who supported President Ronald Reagan and performed for more than five decades, was called "the hardest- working man in show business." This author's message to the Grand Old Party is: like James Brown, you're going to have to work harder, work longer hours, and pay more in taxes. Millions of Democratic voters are depending on you!

Have you ever noticed that every time that our nation's capital has a debate and subsequent vote on a looming government shutdown, the Democrats will DARE the Republican party to CUT domestic social spending, but the GOP will NOT DARE the Democrat party to INCREASE the latter? This is because both sides are well aware that the majority of the electorate DISLIKE the GOP's capitalistic economics (individualism/self-responsibility) and are actually very fond of the Democrat's socialistic philosophy (governmental "*investments* in the people").

It wouldn't make any sense for an American Nazi to proclaim: "I am a Nazi and I want so very much for our country to live under Nazism. But I definitely do not want to live under socialism. I detest socialism." Ditto a communist with respect to communism. For these two, the Hatfields and the McCoys of the far left, to say this and be dismissive of socialism, would be like an Olympic swimmer stating, "Hey, I really love to swim! I'm just crazy about it! But I hate the water. I can't stand getting wet." No can do, folks. It's a contradiction in terms. Hence, if there's anybody closer to being a Nazi, it's the liberal who has never and will never say a bad word about socialism. Liberal individuals figure that if the Marxist invention really is unjust, oppressive and morally and economically wrong; then how does post-1965 modern-day liberalism manifest itself? It doesn't. It can't. Therefore, liberals have absolutely no choice but to refrain from making a negative statement about socialism. Otherwise, it would only be an indictment of themselves.

Does not the plight of America's children make your little ole heart go pitter-patter? Many of us have heard the news that somewhere in the USA "our children" have been going to bed hungry and starting school in the morning on an empty stomach; that "our" poor children have been struggling with "food insecurities." As I write, tears are falling from my eyes. But this isn't anywhere near as much a matter of malnutrition as it is a more than fifty-year history of too many mothers and fathers shirking their responsibilities. It's the parents' job to make sure that their progeny are eating well. As for the term "our children", in regard to society, there is no such thing as "our children." To insist otherwise is just a plaintive cry for collectivism. The United States, itself, doesn't have any children. But the parents living in it do.

Political opponents use the term "hypocrite" more as an ad hominem attack then to define their adversary's position on an issue. For example: Religious, pro-family Republican lawmaker John Doe, is trying to pass legislation that is advantageous to the nuclear family, but he, himself, is committing infidelity. His opponents will say nary a word about the legislation itself, but instead, concentrate on John Doe being a HYPOCRITE. But his being a hypocrite doesn't make for a bad bill. Whether or not a person is a hypocrite, is entirely incidental. It's what he or she wants for others in regard to public policy that matters. The American people have a very bad habit of listening to the messenger and not the message. In the case of politician John Doe, many people would like to make him and his transgression the subject so they won't have to think about what Doe says, and perhaps not have to accept the potentially good law that he wants. In a nutshell, John Doe's hypocrisy provides them with a convenient escape hatch to dismiss the truth as a potential remedy. Society's view is that it's much more egregious and damnatory for the conservative-right to be hypocritical because, unlike the liberal/left, they're supposed to be moral/ethical straight-arrows who are valiantly defending "our way of life." Since, in comparison, the liberal/left is more likely to "tear down America," any hypocricy on their part isn't as prominent or incriminating.

According to an entertainment magazine, Donald Trump, Hillary Clinton, and Maxine Waters took note of former Chicago Mayor Lori Lightfoot's acting role in a movie made by director Tim Burton. So the three of them, being inspired, have agreed to star in a remake of actor/director Clint Eastwood's 1966 movie, *The Good, the Bad and the Ugly*. President Trump stated that he's doing it because he will need the money. Hillary said that she would absolutely love to be in the film when she gets paroled. And Congresswoman Waters told the magazine that she's ecstatic to partake in the movie and that for appearing on the big screen, she will wear a much finer and prettier wig than usual in order to compensate for her looks.

Conservatives have long had a reputation for disliking France. But there's one Frenchman that we, the capitalistic right, have been quite fond of, and that is Alexis de Tocqueville (1805-1859). The aristocratic de Tocqueville was a political scientist whose philosophy was CLASSICAL LIBERALISM (basically economic libertarianism) as opposed to contemporary liberalism (basically quasi-socialism). He was most famous and somewhat influential for writing, after a nine-month stay in the United States, a two-volume book called *Democracy in America*. The first volume was published in 1835 and the second one five years later. The brilliant nineteenth-century aristocrat from France was way ahead of the curve in conceptualizing the attitude of today's progressives: "We can state with conviction, therefore, that a man's support for absolute government is in direct proportion to the contempt he feels for his country." And the mind-set of many current US citizens and most if not all Democrats, he wrote, "Americans are so enamored of equality that they would rather be equal in slavery than unequal in freedom." Here's more of Alexis de Tocqueville: "What good does it do me, after all, if an ever watchful authority keeps an eye out to ensure that my pleasure will be tranquil and races ahead of me to ward off all danger, sparing me the need even to think about such things, if that authority, even if it removes the smallest thorns from my path, is also master of my liberty and my life; if it monopolizes vitality and existence to such a degree that when it languishes, everything around it must also languish; when it sleeps, everything must also sleep; and when it dies everything must also perish." Plus, in his psychoanalyzing par excellence, circa late 1830s, which perfectly encapsulates the mentality of present-day American society in general, de Tocqueville wrote, "Our contemporaries are constantly wracked by two warring passions: they feel the need to be led and the desire to remain free. Unable to destroy either of these contrary instincts, they seek to satisfy both at once. They imagine a single, omnipotent, tutelary power, but one that is elected by the citizens. They combine centralization with popular sovereignty. This gives them some respite. They console themselves for being treated as wards by imagining that they have chosen their own protectors. Each individual allows himself to be clapped in chains because that the other end of the chain is held not by a man or a class but by the people themselves."

To augment the previous subject: Americans of all political opinions are rightfully opposed to a cruel, uncaring dictator who wants to lord it over society so he can enrich himself and his cronies by using the power of the State for life. But a "leader" who is a lovable and benevolent despot and is only establishing a dictatorship solely to nurture and help the common citizen should perhaps be given a chance. Unlike the first noted dictator, the second one at least has some redeemable qualities. We would like to think of the latter "dear leader" as just a father-like hard driver who is simply caring about his people and is trying to instill equality in our country. What's so bad about that? Besides, it's not so much the *subjugation* per se, that matters, but our ruler's personality and promises. So if the omnipotent State is being responsible for fulfilling as much as possible, your needs and desires, then why are you against it controlling you? For what material reasons do you need liberty, anyway? You, the reader, may respond, "I don't care how many people say that he's benevolent. He's actually a tyrant and I'm against him being the ruler of our country." Yes, that's true, you are. But because of the numerous pleasantries and benefits that the ostensibly kind authoritarian is promising you is so very attractive, it's going to be God-awfully difficult for you to fight back against him. Maybe you should just let your defensiveness down a wee bit and live for today. And you probably will.

After the 2016 presidential election, many voters on the tantrum-throwing, emotional left asked the Republicans to stop calling them "snowflakes." And so yours truly is honoring that request. To you, my political brethren, from now on when you label the noted liberals "snow-flakes", I ask that you please leave out the first syllable.

When certain Americans clamor for new government legislation from Washington, DC to "create jobs," they fail to see the irony. Said citizens don't connect the dots on a liberal (socialistically stagnant) vs. a libertarian conservative (capitalistic dynamism) economic policy. They would like to think that when an Establishmentarian GOP politician acquiesces to liberalism, it makes for sound economic policy. Consequently, the common folk insist on believing that more government spending and legislation, while employing the "reasonable" sounding label of being "fiscally responsible", creates jobs and a robust economy, when actually, it's the exact opposite. These are the same dishonest people who call on the Republicans to accept Obamacare and to "just fix the flaws in it." But they will not criticize the Democrats nor the 44th president, himself, for failing to "fix the flaws" of HIS signature "achievement" in three years after its launch. Barack Obama's obsequious fans want Republican fingerprints on his Affordable Care Act so that when it sinks like the *Titanic*, it will be thought of as a BIPARTISAN bill that just didn't work, rather than a Democratic calamity that ruined America. The Anointed One's flock should take notice that the only way to make socialism better is to make it capitalistic. But, since that's the case, why follow a socialistic path in the first place?

American females and black Americans are second-class citizens, though this is largely inconsequential. For the term "second-class citizen" is more of an innocuous classification of them than it is a veritable social downgrade. No matter. A woman can become president or she can be a rich CEO in which the lady is more powerful than most

American men and unlike them, revels in a life of luxury. The United States does have a *patriarchy* (for over five centuries now) as do all the nations on earth. But our "patriarchy" is about as oppressive to American women as their being second-class citizens is (for the most part, it isn't). Many black Americans have become multi-millionaires and they are more powerful and live a far better life than at least eighty percent of the country's white citizens. There is no American "system" or "institution" keeping blacks and women down. There's only the Constitution, which begets liberty that can lead to wealth, which in turn, engenders livelihood and power for both female and black individuals.

The late Senator Arlen Specter of Pennsylvania was a moderate liberal. Former Congressman Charlie Crist of Florida is also a moderate liberal. In a take on Ronald Reagan saying that he didn't leave the Democratic Party (in 1962), it left him, both gentlemen had expressed that they left the GOP because it had "gone too far to the right." They lied. Arlen Specter was at first a Democrat who became a Republican in 1965 and then a Democrat again in 2009. Because the party of Abe Lincoln had "gone too far to the right" with the 1980 election of the "fascistic and dangerous extremist" Ronald Reagan who, with support from his minions, ushered in the conservative 1980s, Specter should have, at that very time, fled the GOP and sought sanctuary with the Democrats. But he didn't. Why not? Before he joined the Democrat Party in 2012, Charlie Crist was merely an *opportunist* (look up this word in the dictionary and you'll see his picture right next to it) who, in 1986, became a Republican politician because he noticed that Florida Republican lawmakers simply held more political power in the Sunshine State then Democrats did. In 2009, Republican Crist called President Obama's infamously wasteful stimulus bill ($787 million) a "godsend." Though, while running as a GOP member for the Senate in 2010, Crist proudly referred to himself as "a Reagan conservative" and then proceeded to endorse Barack "Fundamentally Transforming America" Obama for president two years later. Very few Floridians noticed this. But if any political party has gone too far in an ideological direction, it's the Democratic Party. This has occurred much to the delight of the renowned and esteemed socialist, Senator Bernie Sanders.

Two Questions: (1). What's the difference between the libertarian right and the liberal/left?......The former is against ALL TYPES of government social engineering. (2). What's the difference between the communist salute and the Nazi salute?......The former is a clenched fist with forearm or the whole arm pointing straight up while the latter is straight-handed with the whole arm pointing at a 15-degree angle. The first (clenched fist) salute supports and celebrates the social movement toward hateful and punishing INTER-nationalistic socialism, while the Nazi salute symbolizes its advocacy of a hateful and punishing *nationalistic* socialism. If, say in 1938, the Nazis changed their style of salute and adopted the CLENCHED FIST, their rivals, the communists, would have switched over and newly embraced the straight-arm/straight-hand salute in order to differentiate between the two doctrines.

Riddle: When do certain Americans first realize that they are bona fide socialists? Answer: As soon as they, when thinking of political/ideological issues, become well aware that they are lying to themselves.

Political *gridlock* at our nation's capital could very well be a godsend, while *bipartisanship* could be deleterious to American society. There are too many of us who foolishly believe that if conservative lawmakers just get together with liberal politicians and pass a bill deemed to be ideologically MODERATE (though it will actually lean liberal), then it automatically becomes good legislation because "both sides found common ground." It doesn't! Only libertarian-conservative bills that force more liberty and individualism on the American people and produces LESS legislation should be considered GOOD legislation.

Selfishness: Most political Americans will attribute "selfishness" to CONSERVATIVE Republicans and their animus toward redistribution and collectivism. But when labor unions make exorbitant demands of a manufacturing company that puts that company out of business or induces them to set up shop in another country, are these particular labor unions not being *selfish*? When various myopic Americans don't give a damn about the geopolitical threat from China and the fate of our Constitutional republic; is that not *selfishness*? When certain people who vote Democrat insist that our government bail them out of their financial problems caring nary a whit if it contributes to bankrupting the nation and, especially, leaving their children and grandchildren to handle America's crushing debt; are they not thinking only of themselves and being *selfish*? In today's America, *"selfishness"* is to be defined and thought of as wealthy citizens wanting to keep their own money. *Selfishness* and *greed* are NOT, unfortunately, to be regarded as poor and middle income Americans coveting the earnings of the wealthy.

Citizens on the liberal-left that pooh-pooh the Americans who claim that the 2020 presidential election was stolen from Donald Trump, will themselves insist that George W. Bush stole the presidential election in the year 2000. The thing is, the pro-Al Gore voters/protesters of two decades ago easily outnumbered the present-day Republicans who expressed that Trump was cheated. Indeed, those that supported the November 2000 Democrat nominee, endeavored to keep their "Bush robbed Gore" charade in the spotlight for eight years. As for the people who voted for Hillary Clinton in November 2016; after hearing her a few months later, say about Donald Trump, "He knows he's an illegitimate president", they did not and will not call the Hildebeast an "election denier" like they did the forty-fifth president. So now it's the Trumpian stalwarts of the Grand Old Party's turn. Like the old saying asserts, "What goes around, comes around."

One woman making minimum wage complained, "I need a better wage for myself because right now, I'm relying on aid, and $7.40 is not able to help me maintain taking care of my son. I'm a single parent." What this means is that if the woman was paid the $15.00 an hour that she desires, and then had two more children, her new hourly wage ($15.00) wouldn't be enough. Employers would then be compelled by the law to pay their workers a salary based on how many children they have and how much aid (money) the government determines they will need. Most Americans support raising the minimum wage, thereby proving out of ignorance or apathy, that they really do think socialistically.

An American is wearing a COVID-19 mask while standing alone, high on a hill in a countryside prairie, ten miles away from the nearest human. There is a one percent chance that this solitary individual is a conservative, a four percent chance that said person is a moderate, and a ninety five percent chance that he or she is a liberal.

The conservatism of today is essentially the conservatism of the 1950s (excluding any racial and discrimination issues). But current liberalism is different than the mere personal *pro-civil rights plus redress-problems-of-the-poor-and-needy* liberalism of the 1950s. Present-day liberals realize that the *personal* liberalism of more than six decades ago will not suffice in bringing about total social justice. Hence, it is only natural and righteous that they become strong advocates of centralized-government social engineering which has always been liberalism's manifest destiny.

Is it just by coincidence that Joe Biden's slogan/agenda "Build Back Better" is astonishingly similar to Chairman Mao Zedong's slogan/plan "Great Leap Foward"? And not just because the first, second and third words of both of them each have the same amount of letters (respectively 5, 4 and 6) or that the noted slogans have the same total amount of syllables (4).

In 1992, Vice-President Dan Quayle misspelled the word, "potato." In 2008, then Senator Barack Obama, while running for the presidency, said that he campaigned in fifty-seven states and six years later, flubbed the spelling of the song "Respect." Now, neither Quayle's nor Obama's verbal gaffes were that egregious. Who, among us adults, still look up the words, "receive" and "necessary" to make sure that we are spelling them correctly? The difference is that the liberal media and their minions sought to ridicule and portray the Republican Quayle as being a dunce but merely joshed Obama because he's a Democrat. For decades, the media has tried to stigmatize the Republicans as being stupid. One can only assume that they do this in order to counterbalance the Democrats being liberal. But the media failed.

The liberal/left loves to fantasize about and portray anything politically progressive as being "bold" and "brave." Government expansion and subsequent societal control (progressivism) is rationalized as being "bold" and "brave" ostensibly because its "ambitious" objective is the protection, security and the caring of the people. Since having *ambition* is a good thing, then any plan that is ambitious is automatically a good plan. Essentially, our country's gradual movement toward an all-concerned centralized government is to be thought of as "bold" and "brave." Likewise, one can justifiably assume that America's implicit permission to be eventually subjugated by the omnipotent State is to be labeled as "courageous." Whenever the liberal/left praises an agenda or policy as being "bold," "brave," and "ambitious," they're selling it to the public as something that is NEW and EXCITING and, very likely, EFFECTIVE. For the most part, the public buys it and then hopes for the best. Any support by America's citizenry for progressivism is, in reality, just dishonesty and moral cowardice under the guise of being BOLD and BRAVE.

Relating to the paragraph above; in case you didn't already know, it is government that will improve your life by "Building it Back Better" than it was before. And so, during the process, you the reader will..... *Have Government's Back*....and in due time, the noted almighty, omnipotent State will have your back.....and then some.

Many Americans that think there's economic *inequality* in our country. There sure is! Just like in all countries. A man worth 2 billion dollars is extremely UNEQUAL to a man worth 20 billion dollars. A super-wealthy celebrity is far richer than a doctor who makes a quarter million dollars a year. A woman with 150 thousand bucks in her savings account has ten times more than a woman who has managed to save only 15 thousand dollars. But the aforementioned monetary *inequality* is nowhere near as deleterious to the United States as *redistribution* is.

To my conservative readers; you should more regularly employ the term "capitalistic" when saying the words "right wing" and similarly attach the term "socialistic" when speaking about the *left*. And so, in essence, it's not "the right vs. the left" per se, but rather "the *capitalistic* right" vs. "the *socialistic* left." This way, you dilineate what the political terms "right" and "left" are really all about. If my compatriots on the Constitutional-right don't go along with this, then they are allowing the public to remain ignorant. The entire liberal-left is well aware of this and it's precisely the reason why they avoid verbalizing said ideological descriptions of the *right* and *left*.

The more that liberal Democrat politicians DECREASE our freedom/liberty, the more that conservative Republican citizens will object and try to reverse course, the more that the Democrats will respond that the GOP has "gone too far to the right", the more that most of the American electorate, in their utter stupidity and intellectual dishonesty, will AGREE with the Democrats' aforementioned response.

In 1965, there was a movie that came out with only white people in it. This film that starred rich white people and no blacks in it whatsoever was obviously racist because the name of the movie was *The Great Race*. Said movie title is what the white producer and white director (both of them rich) evidently had in mind while thinking about themselves and all whites. You, the reader, will reply, "That movie didn't involve racial issues at all. It was solely about some cars, at the turn of the 20th century, trying to reach a destination first." Well, if that's the case; then why didn't the producer or director (both white and rich) entitle this movie, *Cars Trying to Reach a Destination First*?.....Answer me that!..... Also, you ought to be ashamed of yourself for implying that the early 1900s America had no racism. And I won't bring up the racist film classic *The Wizard of Oz,* which had a scene of a pretty, white, teenage girl being chased by a bunch of little flying monkeys!

The vast majority of Americans who vote Democrat ABSOLUTELY, ONE HUNDRED PERCENT DO NOT want to live under an authoritarianism that ISN'T propped up and reinforced by socialism.

CHAPTER 19

Underdogs and Stereotypes

THERE HAS ALWAYS been a universal mindset in America to intuitively come to the defense of the underdog/little guy no matter if they are right or wrong---good or bad. The predilection of emotion is that the underdog/little guy has got to be the winner regardless of the situation at hand. Americans feel much better when this happens. Thus, dishonesty is crucial, and so it must be employed in most if not all social matters in order to attain fairness (equal social outcome) and subsequently rectify the underdog's lottery in life. To elucidate: What if the world's number-one golfer was to go on nationwide television and brag to millions of viewers, "I'm the best golfer in the world. I'm better than everybody else. I'm number one!" Could you just imagine the public outcry? "Why, that conceited bastard! He thinks he's so big. What an obnoxious jerk." But you'll notice that in their emotional protest of the golfer's boast, the people never denied what he said. That's because he didn't say anything that was false. But his speaking the truth has fallen by the wayside as society focuses on his elitist, off-putting behavior. Perception wins, while the fact gets ignored and lost in the shuffle. But let's say that a pro golfer, officially ranked 579th in the world, makes the same (and being quite serious) statements about himself. Unlike the Number One golfer's true statements, this underdog's intentional falsehoods are pardonable and practically acceptable because of his lower standing in the game of golf and life. Although he is knowingly wrong, the 579th-ranked golfer still deserves our sympathy while the world's best golfer, who was totally correct, deserves condemnation. In essence, the lowly, pity-inducing liar becomes the good guy and the truth-teller becomes the villain.

Some Americans disapprove of PATRIOTISM and NATIONALISM because of our "elite" first-class nation status. The aforementioned feel that the United States (the big guy) is flaunting its "superiority" in the face of smaller third world countries when we merely "pledge our allegiance to the flag" or sing "Proud To Be an American." To our disapproving citizens, it is perfectly alright that the denizens of a poor banana republic are patriotic, their president overtly nationalistic and who constantly brags of his own nation's "exceptionalism" because they are the LITTLE GUY/UNDERDOG, and as such, will not, unlike the USA, be perceived by other countries as "rubbing it in." Likewise, it is absolutely okay for a small country to practice economic nationalism in its attempt to provide jobs for its own citizens. But for a superpower like the USA to do the same for our residents would somehow make us bullies. We're supposed to think *internationally* and do what's best for third-world nations (become a pushover). Only about 99 percent of the leaders of the nations in the world are "nationalistic," meaning that they care about the lives of their own citizens more than they care about others. On the other hand, America needs to be cut down to size and humbled, like for example, being the loser in trade agreements with other countries. It just doesn't feel right if we win. It isn't fair that our country has a roaring economy and the majority of others don't. We must be doing something criminal. In the mentality of the far-left, their pretext of "helping the little guy/underdog" goes in synergetic alliance with their intentional *harming of America*. Most Jews in the United States consider themselves to be the underdog religion and subsequently identify with other underdogs. Unlike the Catholic Church, which represents the patriarchy of our country, the alienated Jews partake in social change that benefits the LITTLE GUY.

In 1973, 29 year old tennis player Billie Jean King beat 55 year old Bobby Riggs in a super-hyped three game match advertised as "The Battle of the Sexes." Ms. King was the number one female tennis player in the early nineteen seventies. Mr. Riggs was the number one male tennis player way back in 1939. The lady's triumph over the 1930s' champion was proclaimed a "Win for Equality." Although there's absolutely no hyperbole in this celebrated boast, it would have been far more substantial if Ms. King had played and won against a man with the same tennis ranking as her in the year 1973. But society's *"belief"* that "women are just as good as men in sports" had to be validated even if the noted "belief" had to be concocted.

Elsewhere on the gender front, private clubs that are for MEN ONLY come off as sexist and elitist, but this is not the case with clubs that are for WOMEN ONLY. The female species needs a refuge for gender bonding and to escape from the repression of the male patriarchy for a few hours of respite. But men do not need nor should they seek a place for MEN ONLY, because to do so is a put-down and repudiation of women. A lady can boast, "We women really are more intelligent than men!" and draw yawns. But when a prominent American male says, "We men are intellectually superior to women," all hell will break loose in the media and he will be branded a "sexist," a "misogynist," and a "chauvinist." The truth of either statement being irrelevant, this double standard exists and is essential, because the female is the UNDERDOG or second-class citizen, if you will. This also applies to race. It is considered enlightening and endearing all across America for blacks to boisterously shout "Black is beautiful." But for a white person to quietly mention "White is beautiful" is bigoted, disgraceful, appalling, and some word that begins with the letter "R", but I forgot what the hell it was. Anyway, a black man can say that he likes being black and a white man can also say that he likes being black. And in today's *woke* society, that's all the latter is permitted, because he is not the little guy/underdog that we're supposed to pamper and feel sorry for. Likewise, any American can proudly proclaim that "women and minorities are the strength and backbone of our great nation" while leaving white men totally out of the picture. But NOBODY is allowed to opine that "white men are the strength and backbone of our great nation" even though it's far closer to the truth. Society's view is that when a woman or black person brags about their prowess or special attributes, then they are emoting because they're *proud* and *valiant* in the collective face of a country commanded by white men. Such an emotion coming from the "marginalized" is welcome. But for a white man to brag about the same, then society considers it to be pompous and condescending, and therefore unacceptable. Since a white man isn't societally frustrated, it is uncalled for him to *vent,* because he has no "oppressor" keeping him down.

On television shows and movies from Hollywood, the little guy is regularly victorious. It would be malicious and unfeeling to have otherwise. In TV comedy, it's cruel humor and mean-spirited to make jokes about the poor, but not so to make jokes that demonize the rich, because they are not the little guy/underdog, don't merit pity and therefore, deserve to be maligned. Because society sympathizes with the poor, the former believes that it is incumbent on them to deflate the status of the well-off. No stand-up or late-night comedian makes liberalism the butt of jokes, because liberalism purports to be for the little guy/underdog. It is for this reason that only the *individualistic* economic philosophy of conservative Republicans is ridiculed and never the *collectivistic* philosophy of the Democrats. If there is conflict between an impoverished urban dweller and a wealthy person in a drama, it is the latter that HAS TO BE the villain. In Hollywood movies and television, if a black man is blamed for a certain crime, he really is innocent (he was either framed by a racist cop or it's a case of mistaken identity) 95 percent of the time. The reality is that the opposite is true. The overwhelming majority of the time, the black person actually IS guilty of the crime he or she is accused of.

In Make-Believe Land, the scriptwriters always have the military general as being the bad guy and his foe, the humble corporal, forever the good guy. Ditto the landlord (constantly crooked) and tenant (mainly honorable). In a TV series about lawyers, it's always the defense attorneys who are the good guys that we root for, almost never the prosecutors. This is because the former in known for sticking up for people at the lower end of the social spectrum. In a Hollywoodized physical fight between a man and a woman, all the time it's the woman who "kicks butt" (yup, just like in real life). In a clash between a pretty high school cheerleader who is, of course, elitist and stuck-up and the dowdy, not so attractive girl; who do you think, at the end of this battle, the loser is going to be? If little sister challenges her big, braggadocio brother to a contest, guess who's going to win? In reality, the latter would be victorious by far. Okay, how about an adolescence-oriented movie concerning sorrowful slobs vs. egotistical snobs in a competition at summer camp? Take a wild guess as to who will triumph? And if a horror flick at the weekend matinee shows a giant, menacing creature from outer space chasing a cute, adorable seven year old orphan girl from a broken home; and would easily bite the small child's head off if it caught her, the monster would one hundred percent ABSOLUTELY FAIL......unfortunately.

But it's practically an unwritten law that, in the perception of the American public, the UNDERDOG must win virtually all battles. If he doesn't, then it goes against the grain of feelings regarding what is fair, just and decent and becomes REACTIONARY. Real freedom and the truth (capitalism) are reactionary because they don't constitute hands-on government coming to the rescue of the UNDERDOG/LITTLE GUY. Because socialism isn't freedom or the truth, it is NOT reactionary. George Bernard Shaw once wrote, "The reasonable man adopts himself to the world; the unreasonable one persists in trying to adopt the world to himself. Therefore, all progress depends on the unreasonable man." It's not at all surprising that the late playwright and activist articulated this very thought (or feeling). That's because he was a socialist.

It was actress Jane Fonda's radical second husband, Tom Hayden (aka Tommy the commie), who said about his son, a white man, marrying a black woman, "It's another step in a long-term goal of mine; the peaceful, nonviolent disappearance of the white race." Is it not the least bit peculiar that Mr. Hayden, a Caucasian, would hope for the vanishing of his own race? From a progressive standpoint---no it isn't. You see, the late Tom Hayden realized that whites are the privileged status quo and blacks and other minorities are the humble, pity-inducing LITTLE GUYS. As a scholar of political history, he was well aware that American blacks and Hispanics are a socialistic race and ethnicity (they espouse collectivism and redistribution); and that American whites are the predominant capitalistic race (they espouse individualism and self-reliance). It was Hayden's view that our nation's blacks, Mexicans, Puerto Ricans and other Hispanics with the guidance of socialism, would get their revenge by becoming the privileged status quo and that whites would get their comeuppance. Cubans are excluded because they are staunchly anti-Castro and mostly vote Republican, especially Cubans age forty and older.

Roughly ten percent of natural-born Hispanics care about the sovereignty of the United States and the illegal immigration issue. This is about twice as much as the Hispanic Americans who would switch their votes from Democrat over to the Republican Party if the GOP decided to support amnesty. The majority of people on the left advocate amnesty for illegal Hispanics not just because most of the latter are likely to live off the government (it's the main reason why they came here in the first place), but because Hispanics are a non-white minority. They are the forlorn LITTLE GUY who our society ought to sympathize with. Would the same left-leaning Americans who want to grant amnesty to illegal aliens of Hispanic ethnicity trying to get into Arizona, also back citizenship for millions of ILLEGAL Canadian white people sneaking over into Minnesota? The correct answer is: No, they wouldn't. This is because Canadian whites don't elicit nor deserve our sympathy or support because they aren't the pitiful UNDERDOG. Hence, no social injustice was committed by NOT granting them amnesty. Also, whites are more likely to be self-dependent, which is antithetical to leftism. Would the Hispanics and their backers object if the former were NEVER to become certified American citizens, but WERE allowed to live here forever and enjoy all government services and benefits for the rest of their lives? No, they would not object and would happily accept that. On the other hand, what if illegal Hispanics were to be made LEGAL American citizens for eternity; but were NOT PERMITTED to vote nor receive any government services or subsidies, EVER! Would they object to that? They most certainly would. Thereby proving that it's not so much *"citizenship"* that illegal Hispanics covet, but rather the generous welfare state providing for and taking care of them, that is their main objective. Yes, Hispanics and other poor people all over the world seek to come here to find work, live a decent life and hopefully become rich. But that is strictly their secondary reason for trespassing into our country. Illegal aliens are costing the US taxpayers $113 billion dollars a year. But I digress.

STEREOTYPES: There's a 1980s pop song in which the lyrics say that human beings are the same wherever you go. Bull-feathers! It's a small world, perhaps, but people are different. There has long been a misconception that the word "stereotype" denotes a FALSEHOOD. But on the contrary, many, if not most, stereotypes have, through honest observation, been accurate to a large degree. Like, for example, here in the USA, Indians (from India) have been stereotyped as managing convenience stores and motels (with check-in offices smelling like curry) and the Vietnamese operating nail salons. In the 1930s and 1940s Hollywood movies, the Chinese living in America were portrayed as owning and running Laundromats. Today, the Chinese own and run the United States. But those on the politically correct left cry "stereotype" in order to dissuade the listener from believing the truth about various groups of people; particularly if it's the little guy. Said progressives do this ostensibly in order to EQUALIZE life and make it "fairer" for minorities. This isn't necessarily a rotten thing to do, but it is necessarily disingenuous.

Now, there are both NEGATIVE and POSITIVE stereotypes. Hispanics have been stereotyped as liking spicy food, being in gangs and driving low-riders with half a dozen people in them. How did this stereotype happen if there wasn't some truth to it? Plus, that Asians are smarter and do better than others in college. Upon what is this opinion based? Gay men have long been famous for the stereotype of being effeminate, even though the vast majority of them are not effeminate. Then there's the little-known stereotype of American Jewish women usually having kinkier hair than their gentile counterparts. Jewish females with such frizzled hair are far more likely to be socialistic (Congresswoman Debbie Wasserman Schultz) than Jewish women who don't have frizzled hair. The Jewish lady is inclined to be a socialist if she dresses up by wearing a turquoise Indian-bead necklace over a dark turtleneck blouse. Or there's the age-old stereotype of Jews being cheap, stingy, or miserly. Based on what historical observation? Also, the Mormons are stereotyped as being "pro-family" with many kids (sometimes being taken care of by many wives). The Mafia is "stereotyped" as only Italian men (fond of wearing gold neck chains). It's never Albanian or Norwegian men who are portrayed as being members of the Mafia. How come?

And then there's the "stereotypical myth" about black men being "bigger" than white men. It's not a myth. Said notion is true. Or at least it's true when it's in the flaccid state (and in all states including Alaska and Hawaii). But because this racial belief is seen as a POSITIVE or flattering stereotype, it will never be rebuked by gratified black men, socially conscious white men, and women. Plus, there's the issue of WATERMELON. This writer never understood why it had become a stereotype for blacks. It's not like they eat it every day. Indeed, in many parts of the country and at certain times of the year, watermelon is out of season. But the NEGATIVE, albeit false, stereotype that IS acceptable to almost all people regardless of their politics, race or ethnicity, is the DUMB BLONDE. This is because the blonde, especially a female with blue eyes (like the sultry actress Marilyn Monroe) is envisioned as usually being more physically attractive than brunettes and redheads. The "dumb blonde" bosomy actress Jayne Mansfield allegedly had an IQ of 163, which, if true, quite literally made her a GENIUS. But because of society's envy of their perceived fine looks, blondes need to be "dumbed down" for their own good and for society's self-esteem.

More POSITIVE stereotypes that, in the opinions of certain Americans, need to be undermined are those of the Republicans being more clean-cut, well-groomed, and successful. Just like rich people are better-looking than poor people, members of the GOP are, for the most part, better-looking than Democrats. Republican women dress up nicer and are apt to be more beautiful than Democrat females. Conservative college girls are prettier, have better figures, and are likely to have smaller noses than their liberal counterparts. Both male and female conservative Republicans are almost always smarter and inclined to have nicer teeth. One relatively unknown stereotype (or CHARACTERISTIC, if you want) is that the typical college male recent graduate is half a foot taller, weighs fifty pounds more, and is handsomer and healthier than the 5 foot, 7 inch, 135 pound (high school educated only) young man working at a blue-collar job.

In conclusion: The progressive mindset seeks to humble and discipline seemingly entitled Americans by making them share in the humility of a minority of citizens that the left believes our country at large should emphasize with. But a nation that implements laws and policies in its determination to help solely the LITTLE GUY/UNDERDOG by making life for them more fair, plus prohibit the speaking of both stereotypical truths and falsehoods, does so at its own peril. For tyrannical totalitarian socialism is its manifestation.

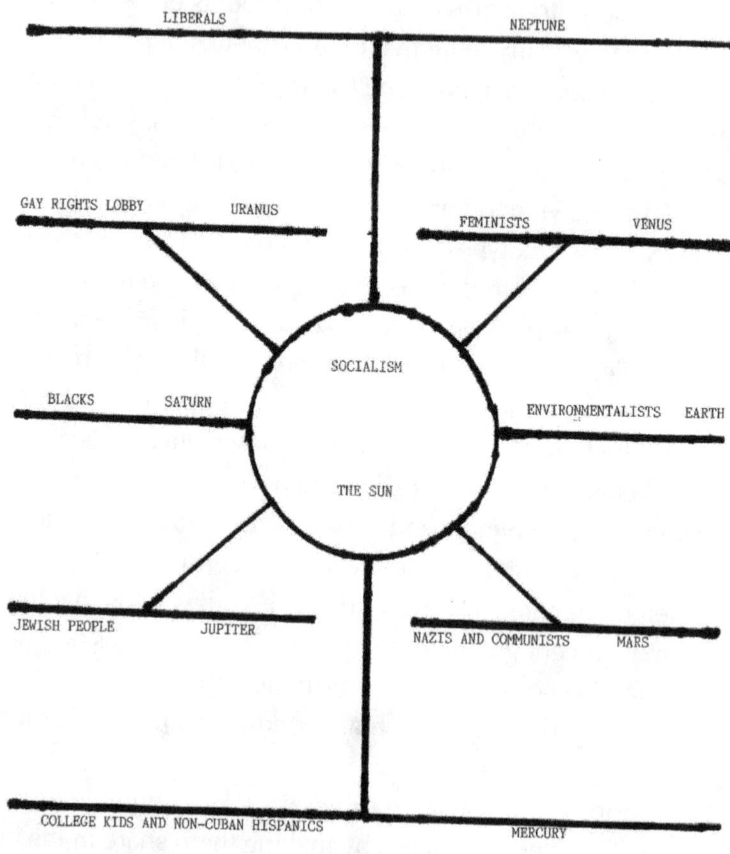
OUR SOCIALISTIC PLANETARY SOLAR SYSTEM
LIBERALS
NEPTUNE
GAY RIGHTS LOBBY
URANUS
FEMINISTS
VENUS
SOCIALISM
BLACKS
SATURN
ENVIRONMENTALISTS
EARTH
THE SUN
JEWISH PEOPLE
JUPITER
NAZIS AND COMMUNISTS
MARS
COLLEGE KIDS AND NON-CUBAN HISPANICS
MERCURY

CHAPTER **20**

The Four Marx Brothers

AS EVERYBODY KNOWS, Nazism, fascism, communism, and socialism are variant forms of government social engineering. Liberals are NOT against ALL TYPES of government social engineering. Conservatives are. Or at least this goes for those brave capitalistic right-wingers that don't yearn to be liked by the ignorant masses who wouldn't mind living under some type of centralized control of society. Nazism and fascism are the bad boys or *brothers*, if you choose, of government command and control of the people and deserve to be immediately scorned and rejected. On the other hand, socialism and communism are the good boys/brothers of command and control of the people and deserve to be understood and forgiven. Karl Marx was the man most associated with giving birth to the leftist social engineering mindset, in the mid 1800s. He and his partner, Friedrich Engels, left behind four sons/disciples named Nazism, fascism, communism, and socialism. In this chapter, yours truly shall discuss the famous Marx brothers quartet, albeit with different personality disorders.

NAZISM: Though it may be hard to believe, Adolph Hitler was even more obsessed with race than present day black Americans and white liberals are. Hitler didn't believe in individualism (intrinsic in capitalism) but rather conformity and obedience to the State (his government). Today, the pejorative "anti-government" is part of the political left's lexicon in demonizing libertarian conservatives. The Nationalist SOCIALIST German Workers Party (NAZI) began in 1920. The Führer, who was alleged to have had homosexual tendencies, was a Nationalist Socialist who hated capitalism and Christianity almost as much as he hated the Jews. The German dictator also disliked socialists who didn't believe in the *"superiority"* of the Aryan race. Nevertheless, in a speech given on May 1, 1927, Adolph Hitler declared, "We are socialists, we are enemies of today's capitalistic economic system for the exploitation of the economically weak, with its unfair salaries, with its unseemly evaluation of a human being according to wealth and property instead of responsibility and performance, and we are all determined to destroy this system under all conditions."

Coincidentally, though quite appropriately, May 1 (aka International Workers Day) is a global holiday celebrated by the worldwide left (labor movements, trade unions, communists). In 1941, the pagan dictator of Germany recalled that 90 percent of the components that put him in power were made up of left-wing elements. Indeed, the infamous tyrant once stated, "Emotionally, my political opinions were left-wing. The socialist aspect was at least as important as the nationalist one." The Führer was pro-choice on abortion and supported government funding for the arts and nationalized health care. Because Hitler directed the German State to rescue them from the depression, the citizens, particularly the young, became enamored of their dictator and were subsequently influenced by his vicious blame-the-Jews anti-Semitism. Just like today's American young people and Democratic voters are, German youngsters, starting in 1933, were smitten not just with progressive (socialistic) economic policies, but with the groupthink and authoritarian social conformity that the State commanded. The swastika that the Nazis initially employed in 1920 was first adopted by the communist Soviet Union in 1917. The two entwined "S" letters of the Nazi swastika stood for "socialist solidarity." In order to at least slightly differentiate from the Nazi swastika, Red Russia switched over to the hammer and sickle (though still intertwined just like the swastika) for their national emblem in 1922.

What the liberal politicians and others on the American left want is for the naïve and gullible citizens to think is that the "far right" connotes Nazism and fascism. Quite the contrary; the far right (paleo-conservatives, laissez-faire capitalists, Ayn Rand objectivists) advocates cutting back substantially on government coercion and statism, which are a major part of what defines Nazism and fascism. But the totalitarianism of the latter couple is not at all the reason why the progressive left is against them. Otherwise, they would also be vehemently against communism. The leftist mindset thinks, and correctly so, that Nazism and fascism are slavery of the people for the benefit of the STATE. But the slavery of socialism/communism, in spite of its history, claims to be for the benefit of the people. With the PROMISE of the last two aforementioned systems, there is, at least, hope. But with the reality of Nazism/fascism, there is no hope. That's because these two social orders never shared in the same egalitarian, messianic aims as socialism/communism which, the liberal/left would like to think, are intrinsically good and, unlike Nazism/fascism, are at least purported to be for the little guy/underdog. Emotion-based progressivism believes or insists on believing that mean and cruel Nazism/fascism is on the starboard side of the ideological spectrum (just the opposite of the caring and sharing socialism/communism sect). The left is mistaken. But, what with their adoration of the great State, their strong desire for governmental edicts and a willing conformity to wokeism, the apparent belief of todays' progressives is that Nazism really wouldn't be so bad if it weren't so darn anti-Semitic.

FASCISM: A half century ago (or the late 1960s and early 1970s) liberalism was essentially a libertarian do your own thing, care about the poor and disenfranchised, pro-free speech, pro-peace/anti-war, question authority liberalism. In the year 2020, it adopted an authoritarian (slowly formed over the decades) disposition and has mutated into a veritable quasi-fascism. Though, there was a time this writer was puzzled as to why the left, particularly in academia, labeled conservatism "fascism" and called conservatives "fascists." Many are familiar with their juvenile insults from the 1980s: "Ronald Reagan is a fascist." "Our country is now living under fascism." "Reagan's fascistic and belligerent war budget." "The scrambled eggs that President Reagan has for breakfast are fascist." This last one is an absurd exaggeration, of course, but you get the picture. For sure, these progressive smear merchants weren't your garden variety, everyday liberal Democrats, because GENUINE liberals don't speak that way. So, what gives? All conservatives and liberals agree that fascism is totalitarianism, as is communism. Why would a freedom-touting conservative be called a "fascist" when he or she has publically denounced both of these totalitarian systems? My colleagues on the right would answer, "The leftist name-callers believe that communism is fair and compassionate and that fascism is the exact opposite." Well, yes, but there's more to it than that, because the actual end results of fascism and communism are virtually the same.

Conservatism/libertarianism IS capitalism. So what does the economic structure of fascism, a precusor to socialism, have in common with that of capitalism? The answer is....nothing....with the exception of OWNERSHIP, or lack thereof. What they have in common is that neither capitalism nor fascism has government ownership of the means of production, and in essence, government ownership of the people. Communism does. So, when the mud-slingers of the far-left cry "fascism", they are not just trying to smear conservatives with a LIE, but they're also bemoaning the "reactionary" right's resistance and attempt to halt government's impending ownership (albeit ostensibly benevolent) of the citizens. To progressives, because totalitarian fascism's lack of ownership renders it ILLEGITIMATE, it has no moral right to control our society. However, totalitarianism WITH goverment ownership (communism) of the people is purportedly beneficial and consequently merits the authorization to control them. It is therefore, LEGITIMATE and from that standpoint, prudent and acceptable. Quite simply, a FASCIST is a tyrant who wants to boss you around and doesn't mind his own damn business. A COMMUNIST, on the other hand, is just trying to help you, which makes him a statesman who IS minding his own business, as he is expected to.

To illustrate: You, the reader, drive a car. (For instructional purposes, forget for the moment, that a car is *personal* property.) A communist dictator in the country that you live OWNS your car. You don't. He has the title to it. You don't. Now, the communist will permit you to drive HIS car, but he has the right to tell you where you are allowed to drive and if you can make any modifications to it. Since the Marxist tyrant owns your vehicle, he, in essence, owns you. The man has total authorization and control. The reader goes to another country where you now live under a fascist dictatorship. That car you drive is YOURS. You, not the government, own it and have the title to it. But just like his Red counterpart, the fascist despot controls you and tells you everything that you can and can't do with YOUR car. The difference in your attitude toward the two autocrats is that you're far more likely to respect the communist. You realize that you can't really blame him for wanting to control you, because it's HIS car. When the noted Comrade gives you orders, he is NOT being mean, cruel or bossy but simply doing what he's supposed to be doing. This Leninist statesman is just caring about his property so you won't have to. Is that positively convenient and fantastic for your livelihood, or what? Indeed. There's a fairly good chance that you will venerate the communist and appreciate his giving you permission to drive a car that HE owns and is responsible for. But, unlike the aforementioned "Dear Leader," the fascist is out of line. That is, where does he get off telling you what you can or can't do with YOUR car? It's in your name. You have the title to it. If this fascist really cared about you and your car, he would OWN the both of you. In sum, because communism is puported to be empathy, it is desirable and acceptable. This is not the case with fascism. It was the late lefty literary icon, Susan Sontag, who conceded that communism is merely "successful fascism" and "fascism with a human face." The long-departed Benito Mussolini is the world's prototypical fascist. He was also a socialist. Former Vice-President Al Gore, among other liberals, once said that he wanted a "partnership" between government and big business. No thanks! That was already tried in the late 1930s/early 1940s Italy. So we need not try it here. Besides, Al is a nice guy and doesn't deserve a public hanging. Fascism is essentially an amalgamation of 50 percent capitalism and 50 percent communism. This desired "partnership" of the powerful State with private enterprise is a dialectic that the former will inevitably triumph over. It is adherence to the Constitution that is America's bulwark against becoming fascist, and it's the left that despises the Constitution.

Fascism is born out of governmental *expansion,* NOT governmental *contraction.*

COMMUNISM: It's extremely rare and almost impossible for a pontificating political aficionado to cry "fascist" for what seems like every other sentence, without that person being at least a fellow traveler if not an outright communist. In the late 1930s, there was a small 2800-member army of American volunteers known as the Abraham Lincoln Brigade. They were proud and eager young men who went to Spain to fight in the Spanish Civil War against the quasi-fascistic dictator, Francisco Franco. At least eighty percent of the Abraham Lincoln Brigade were pro-Stalin communists with an allegiance to the USSR (Union of Soviet Socialist Republic). Woody Guthrie was a 1930s/1940s folk singer and song writer ("This Land Is Your Land") who was somewhat famous for playing an acoustic guitar with the words "This machine kills fascists" emblazoned on it. He was, of course, an *anti-fascist,* besides also being a communist. Guthrie's ideological protégé and prominent heavy metal guitarist Tom Morello, is also an *anti-fascist*. And he proves it by having a hammer and sickle sticker on his guitar and occasionally wearing a red star on his cap and shirt. As everyone knows, communism is as far to the left as leftism can go. For the capitalistic United States to go in a progessive direction until we could go no further, the next stop will be to live under fascism, and then socialism and finally, reach the pinnacle of perfection, communism. To be a communist, it is one's duty to lie. It is wrong and immoral for a communist to be truthful. If the devotees of Marx, Lenin, Trotsky, and Alinsky aren't going to lie to themselves and especially to others, then they have no business being communists. Although, the history of people suffering under communism is worse than that under its more moderate left-wing cousin, fascism, it is the former that is exalted because of its professed egalitarianism. Plus, to the American left, communism at least has something that Nazism and fascism do not have....POTENTIAL. These latter two isms are automatically unjust and oppressive for their lifespan; not so with communism. Communism just needs smart, proficient, diligent and devoted Marxist-Leninists with an expertise in a socio-economic master plan to run it for the long haul – but they can't be incompetent or corrupt. Furthermore, it's the humility and lack of ostentation of communism that attracts left-wing romanticists to it. This, by itself, will of course absolutely guarantee communism's eventual success---they hope. To the entire liberal/left and the American people in general, the *systems* of Nazism and fascism are intrinsically rotten to the core and they can't be improved. This is NOT the case with communism. Even considering its history, more than enough of our nation's Democrats won't condemn the Marxist religion because they would like to think that mere earnest on their part will bring out communism's alleged intrinsic goodness.

Communists in America call for "progressive" legislation, plead for our nation's voters to elect PROGRESSIVE candidates for political office and constantly, in their literature, refer to themselves as "progressives." So here are the questions that ordinary liberals should answer: Are communists PROGRESSIVES? Yes or no? And if the United States were to live under communism, would we all be living in a PROGRESSIVE society? Yes or no? A liberal would have no problems being friends with a communist even though he disagrees politically with his far left pal. But why can't the same liberal be friends with a Nazi or fascist even though he or she also disagrees with THEIR politics? It's because liberalism and communism share the same COMPASSION axis, one that Nazism and fascism do not have. As for socialism, the difference between a closet socialist and a hardcore communist is that the latter has no qualms about publicly lying. But the closet socialist, who is less dogmatic, feels the need to refrain from blatantly lying because that would only tell himself that he's no damn good. His desire is to remain secretive in order to not even have to address socialism. A person who is merely a socialist is a *pinko,* NOT a *Red*. A communist is the latter. Like the color *pink* is just light *red*, socialism is just communism LITE.

SOCIALISM: Those on the left either believe or would like to think that if America doesn't embark on a *socialistic* course, then that means that our country is going in a *fascistic* direction. But au contraire, if society takes the socialistic route then we will indeed rendezvous with fascism....at first. Fascism is the initial control of the people while socialism is the subsequent ownership of the market. A socialist is a person who will disagree with a communist on a few issues. I surmise that 60 percent of the American left is genuine liberals, 30 percent are socialists (mostly clandestine), 5 percent are communists, 3 percent are fascists, and 2 percent are Nazis. With fascism and Nazism being, for the most part, disowned and disregarded, it is the liberals and communists' in-between relative, the socialists, who mostly provide the influence and guidance for the latter two. Socialism is the raison d'être of the entire left. In the leftist vision of America, drastically REDUCING the strangulation of government rules, regulations, and restrictions is OPPRESSIVE. With socialism, there will be a nation-wide *fairness* because of a government enforced societal conformity. To socialists, communism is structurally sound; it's just that its façade needs a lot of work. They desire to believe that the old Soviet Union wasn't an evil but an embarrassment; that the USSR.'s way of life was an aberration of true socialism. American socialists liked the BASIC (not entire) economic system of 1917-1991 Russia and they like the BASIC social freedom of the United States. But like a communist is just a socialist in a hurry and a liberal is just a socialist in a closet; an avowed, self-declared socialist is just an honest liberal.

Certain Americans are socialists because they have a love/hate relationship with their country. That is, every once in a while these disconsolate and malevolent citizens like to tell themselves that they actually love their country. This gives them some emotional respite. The socialists correctly believe that their detesting of America will initially facillitate the tyrannical social order for the Marxist political system to work in the future. So, the United States must first be penalized (subjugation) and THEN it can be liberated (compassionate collectivism). A socialist is anybody who will NOT agree that socialism is unjust, oppressive, morally wrong, and economically wrong. Because, if it isn't; then there's no reason why that individual shouldn't become a socialist. And the reader will not be able to think of any. For progressives (a euphemism for "socialists"), feelings and emotion are sufficient enough for their lofty goal of "building a better society." Logic, intellectual honesty, and the truth are their enemies. Socialists ultimately become dedicated liars because they need to. With their penchant for do-goodism, socialists believe that their deeds can't possibly be wrong. Any bad results emanating from the doings of socialists is to be superseded by their own presumptuousness. It is the lack of integrity that is socialism's Achilles Heel. But socialism's proponents don't mind this lack of integrity because they, themselves, have none. Many avowed socialists think that America can make socialism work because we're rich, perhaps unaware of the fact that we're rich because we've been capitalistic for over 150 years.

For every American to live under socialism (one that especially benefits blacks and Hispanics) is to live an ordinary, quaint, and humble life. It's an entity of humility that causes no resentment, jealousy or dislike of others. And within progressive romanticism, that's most endearing. Socialists are elitists quite simply because they are utterly convinced that they cannot possibly be elitists. In the opinions of many on the far left, having the United States live under absolute socialism would be an attractive WIN-WIN situation for them. In other words, if America were to "advance" to a kinder, gentler, altruistic society even superior to that of Cuba (if that's possible), then the socialists, with their good intentions vindicated, could say that they WON and were correct all along. On the other hand, if our nation turned into a miserable hell hole with life far worse for everybody, then the socialist left would still WIN because "the United States is finally getting its comeuppance. For much too long, we were living the good life while other countries weren't, and now we're getting our just deserts. Good! The reason why there have been poor people in America is because there are uncaring, rich private citizens living here. And from having the benevolent government seize their assets, the rich have been rightly punished. WE WON!" The reality is that with socialism, it's the leaders that run the glorious State who become rich, while the middle-class withers away and the destitute find it harder to climb higher on the economic ladder.

"Democracy and socialism have nothing in common but one word, equality. But notice the difference: While democracy seeks equality in liberty, socialism seeks equality in restraint and servitude." – Alexis de Tocqueville. Socialists have long exploited the precepts and ideals of democracy and used them to build an "evolutionary" road to a "better and equitable life for everybody." But socialism's proxy, the Democratic Party, doesn't and won't make life better for the common people.

Nevertheless, the common people figure that at least the proponents of socialistic policies, the Democrats, purport to do so, and that's something that conservative Republicans (liberty pushers) don't even have the decency to do. Many Democratic voters have already rationalized that we need the kind-hearted coercion of socialism to make us mind. It's for our own good. It is the very promise of "scientific" socialism that makes it "superior" to capitalism (economic freedom), in which there is no promise. And it's the dilapidated left-wing economies of countries whose living conditions that hateful progressives choose to ignore but it's their versions of egalitarian authoritarianism that America's left-wing jackboots desire for the USA to emulate. But a country is strong only in direct proportion to its individual inhabitants standing on their own two feet, not from redistribution. Unfortunately, there are a lot Americans who would rather not acknowledge that a growing centralized government is not utopian or sustainable without strict, authoritarian control. But then again, to them, the term "compassionate despotism" is NOT an oxymoron.

What makes socialism so extremely attractive to those on the American left is that not only is socialism the Great Emancipator, but it is also the Great Punisher. I think that the late columnist Joseph Sobran summed it up quite nicely: "It makes no difference that socialism's actual record is terribly bloody; socialism is forever judged by its promises and supposed possibilities, while capitalism is forever judged by its worse cases. We still give socialism's proponents credit for good intentions instead of condemning their blind arrogance and greed for power over others. Socialism fails to see that desire is unquenchable, it fails to comprehend its own desires and the conflict it reintroduces into what was civilized life. It seeks to protect by coercing, never dreaming that it is the very thing civilized men need protection from." The socialists should rid themselves of their alienation and learn to bear the truth about our capitalistic society, no matter how pleasant it may be.

CHAPTER **21**

See Jane Act

AT A TOWN in New England where the actress, Jane Fonda, was scheduled to shoot a movie; there were bumper stickers that read, "I'm Not Fonda Jane." It seems that a bunch of Vietnam Veterans didn't take too kindly to what Ms. Fonda did during the Vietnam War and decided that it was now *THEIR* turn to protest *her*. In July 1972, and at the age of thirty-four (no youthful indiscretion), Jane went over to the North Vietnamese side and became acquainted with the enemies of American imperialism. She made anti-American radio broadcasts, not unlike Tokyo Rose. The actress was filmed laughing it up while sitting on some Vietcong soldier's anti-aircraft gun. Not that it's a stark contrast, but in a four-year time period, Jane went from sex symbol (think *Barbarella*) to phallic symbol. Anyway, upon returning from her liaison, Fonda called the US soldiers, who were imprisoned by the North Vietnamese communists, "liars and hypocrites" for claiming that they were tortured. Indeed, in speaking to the media, she added that the American "POWs appear to be healthy and fit; all of them called publicly for an end to the war and signed a powerful anti-war letter." John McCain and other prisoners would have begged to differ.

In July 1973, Jane gave birth to a son, Troy, whom she allegedly named after a Vietcong terrorist who once tried to kill Defense Secretary Robert McNamara. The Hollywood movie star purportedly gave her next child the first name of Marxist actress, Vanessa Redgrave. It was also rumored that, in the spring of 1974, Jane returned to have her son christined by the

North Vietnamese communists. In 1975, the political activist once again visited Vietnam to celebrate and congratulate the new dictatorship. Jane Fonda, right up through the mid 1960s, was, like her famous actor and father, Henry, just a plain, non-dogmatic, liberal Democrat. But in 1968, while living in France, she became intensely radicalized by some French communists and North Vietnamese sympathizers. A stage hypnotist trying to hypnotize his audience for entertainment purposes will fail to hypnotize some 95 percent of his audience, but there will always be that five percent who will fall into a deep trance. Likewise, the overwhelming majority of liberals are NOT susceptible to communist propaganda and indoctrination. But Jane had an epiphany while falling into a deep pro-communism "trance"---hook, line and sinker. About a year later, in an argument that she had with Henry, the leftist daughter tried to mollify her father by telling him that she wasn't a communist.

But by 1970, she wasn't at all reticent. Indeed, the fellow traveling actress was quite outspoken. On July 18, 1970, in an interview that Ms. Fonda did with *The People's World*, a publication of the American Communist Party, she said, "To make the revolution in the United States is a slow day by day job that requires patience and discipline. It is the only way to make it. All I know is that despite the fact that I am one of the people who benefit from a capitalist society, I find any system which exploits other people cannot and should not exist." On November 21, 1970, Jane Fonda told a college audience, "If you understood what communism was, you would hope, you would pray on your knees, that we would someday be communists." A few days later, she proclaimed to a different crowd, "I, a socialist, think that we should strive toward a socialist society, all the way to communism." Also, in this month, Ms. Fonda was arrested for smuggling illegal pills. In posing for her mug shot, Jane used the CLENCHED FIST salute. During that era, the clenched fist salute signified not just defiance of American capitalist oppression (aka "fighting the fascist power"), but solidarity with the peace-loving, proletarian masses that were being exploited by the imperialist US multinational robber barons.

On December 11, 1971, she informed students at the University of Texas, "We've got to establish a socialist economic structure that will limit profit oriented businesses. Whether the transition is peaceful depends on the way our present government leaders react. We must commit our lives to the transition." In 1972, Comrade Jane proclaimed, "I am not a do-gooder. I am a revolutionary. A revolutionary woman!" She added, "Revolution is an act of love." Love is what this revolutionary actress felt for Latin American communist, Che Guevara. Though, this feeling of love probably wasn't mutual when Che, Fidel's best friend, explained that, "A people without hate cannot triumph against the adversary." Plus, "To establish socialism, rivers of blood must flow. The victory of socialism is well worth millions of atomic victims." However, Guevara did display his immense love for black people when he stated that "The Negro is indolent and lazy, and spends his money on frivolities, whereas the European is forward looking, organized, and intelligent. The Negro has maintained his racial purity by his well-known habit of avoiding baths." This author has surmised that Jane the Revolutionary felt affection for the Marxist from Argentina because she once gushed, "My biggest regret is I never got to fuck Che Guevara." Yes, Jane should have had sex with Che, and why not? Back in the 1960s, penicillin was easily available. Besides, it's very doubtful that Guevara ever avoided taking a bath.

Like Ms. Fonda, the folk singer Joan Baez also made a trip to Vietnam in 1972. She was there to discuss human rights and deliver Christmas mail to American prisoners. Six and a half years after her experience there, Ms. Baez, no right-winger, had an article published in US newspapers entitled, "Open Letter to the Socialist Republic of Vietnam." This letter criticized the four-year-old communist regime's oppression, numerous human rights violations, and the holding of over 150,000 political prisoners, and pleaded with the Vietnamese government to change its behavior. But before publishing it, Joan Baez contacted Jane Fonda and asked her to sign Joan's open letter. The far left actress wrote back saying that she, Ms. Fonda, was unable to substantiate the liberal folk singer's claim and insinuated that Ms. Baez was lying: "I don't know if we can expect the Vietnamese people to turn free those millions of people overnight, people who were involved in a war much more hideous than any repression." Fonda added, "I hope you will reconsider the assertion of your ad: that the Vietnamese people are "waiting to die." Such rhetoric only aligns you with the most narrow and negative elements in our country who continue to believe that communism is worse than death." Joan responded back to Jane, "What we're (sic) really saying is that I'm betraying seventeen or eighteen geriatric Stalinists who are running the government – not the people." The singer continued, "I've said it for twenty-two years, till I'm blue in the face – I believe in people, not systems. I don't have any ideological yoke around my neck that binds me to human rights violations." OUCH! Most of the prominent names on the American left would not sign Joan Baez's 1979 plea to the Vietnamese government. But eighty-five of said left-leaning individuals DID, including labor leader and civil rights activist Cesar Chavez, liberal actress Lily Tomlin, and socialist actor Ed Asner.

There's a well-known saying: "Deeds speak louder than words." But Jane Fonda's political statements of the past validate, at least for her, the precise opposite.... *Words speak louder than deeds*. Indeed. Joan Baez, like millions of other Americans, was against the Vietnam War for a valid and credible reason. Joan protested our involvement because she thought that thousands of young American men were needlessly losing their lives in a war that was unwarranted. That we weren't defending any US interests. Plus, the United States invaded Vietnam, not vice-versa. As the slogan of that era inquired, "What are we fighting for?" But the famous folk singer did NOT side with America's enemy and thus, is not a traitor. Jane Fonda, on the other hand, is an excellent actress. In 1973, she married Tom Hayden, a far left radical. There have been majestic, awe-inspiring humanitarian visionaries throughout history----Lenin, Trotsky, Stalin, Mao, Pol Pot,.....and now, Hayden. His lovely wife, Jane, and most feminists believed—and to this day still believe—that it's perfectly acceptable for a woman to be dominated by a progressive man as long as it helps the socialist cause (the male domination is only temporary).

In fact, the feminist Fonda was docile and subservient to her domineering husband of sixteen years. According to writer Patricia Bosworth, Tom Hayden forbade his wife to have a washing machine or dishwasher—too bourgeois. He made Jane sell her nice house with a swimming pool and move into a two-bedroom shack that smelled of mildew. They slept on a mattress on the floor. Presumably, the wealthy couple lived like this to exemplify their solidarity with the forlorn downtrodden that had nothing to lose but their chains in their *struggle* against the capitalist oppressors. Miss Bosworth added that whenever Ms. Doormat (Jane) "did something that displeased him – she was receiving too much attention – he encouraged her to discuss her shortcomings in front of him and other friends. And Jane meekly obliged." But in the 1980s, the feminist activist got revenge against her progressive husband for the mean way he treated her, by bankrolling, to the tune of $17 million, his Campaign for Economic Democracy with the money that she made from her exercise videos.

During the US-Vietnam combat era, Jane Fonda was just a delusional communist. Today, she is no longer delusional. It's sheer speculation on this writer's part, but from 1968 on, Henry Fonda's somewhat immature daughter naively believed, irrespective of the war in Asia, that the revolution was imminent. That major social change in the USA was palpable and that she, the famous Jane Fonda, a willing celebrity participant, was "helping to build a better America for ALL, not just some, of its people." The lady probably laments that the supercharged political climate back in the early 1970s seduced her into verbally revealing her true ideological beliefs.

Since the end of that war, Ms. Fonda has been lucky that it never occurred to any interviewer to ask her, "Do you think that communism is unjust, oppressive and wrong, yes or no?" The avowed revolutionary woman would be in a real quandary. That is, does Ms. Hanoi disown and disparage an idealistic goal that she committed to with blood, sweat, tears, and a gazillion dollars, hence, admitting to herself that what she did was all for naught and wasting over a decade of her life? Or does the unrepentant and defiant actress purposely divulge her Red politics by answering the question "no" in order to spite "those anti-communist bastards" and not let them feel triumphant? When ever asked about her 1968 to 1975 role in the Asian conflict, the leftist activist feigned persecution and hoped for public sympathy by claiming that the far right was attacking her simply because she was against President

Nixon and the Vietnam War.

That's a fine audition, Comrade Fonda, but no applause—or at least, not from this critic. During the protest movement of 1964 through 1975, many, if not most, American citizens who were opposed to the war were apathetic about which side (USA or Vietnam) was to blame for this conflict, or they blamed both sides equally. This wasn't the case with the leftist actress and a few others. Fonda and her ilk thought that communist Vietnam was the good guys and the United States were the bad guys. PERIOD! There were no issues of ambiguity or moral equivalence. The noted Hollywood celebrity was against the eight year American involvement in the far East conflict, for strictly ideological reasons. If the Vietnam War had ended early as 1970 but with America VICTORIOUS, Jane would have been extremely angry and distraught. Vietnam would have been like South Korea, a free country with happy citizens living under democratic capitalism.

Now, like she did right after the war in 1975, Henry Fonda's radical daughter may still have visited Hanoi. Only this time, it would have been to offer the Vietcong her heartfelt condolences. About her early 1970s overseas trips, Jane has explained, "I do not regret that I went. My only regret was that I was photographed sitting in a North Vietnamese gun site." The lady speaks the truth. Though, to give her credit, Ms. Fonda HAS told some Vietnam War veterans that she was sorry for upsetting them. That was nice. Since the year 2000, Jane Fonda has been calling herself a born-again Christian and about her infamous Vietnamese anti-aircraft gun photograph of 1972, she states, "I'll go to the grave with regrets about that picture." Okay. And then where to after that?

CHAPTER **22**

Opinionated Bits and Pieces Part 5

NINETY-NINE PERCENT OF the native-born black citizens of America would NEVER want to live in a country in Africa (for more than a year) that is dominated and run by English-speaking black people and has NO RACISM in it whatsoever!

"That's not who we are" is the new mantra used by the liberal left (after hearing Barack Obama repeat it a few times) to deter Republican law-makers from, among other issues, cutting back on both *legal* and *illegal* immigration hence, hoping to spotlight the GOP's alleged disdain for *diversity*. But said progressives don't want diversity so much for *inclusion* per se, but for ideological reasons. That is, the liberal left knows damn well that an incoming spate of the "marginalized" and "disenfranchised" to be, especially from the third world, will think socialistically ("Ooh, boy! I can't wait to get all those food stamps.") and vote accordingly (i.e. select Democrats). Now, if millions of both legal and illegal immigrants were overwhelmingly conservatives though of different racial and ethnic backgrounds from all of the other 194 countries on planet earth; that is NOT considered to be genuinely multi-culturally "DIVERSE." But in response to the 44th President's initial statement....Who precisely, are we? We are a Constitutional republic that hasn't any laws in the Bill of Rights declaring that America is inclined to take in people from other countries. The sentence "Give me your tired, your poor, your huddled masses" isn't US doctrine but merely a sentiment from the poet Emma Lazarus, which was engraved on a plaque inside the Statue of Liberty. Like the poem by Lazarus, this tall monument on Ellis Island doesn't have jurisdiction over or any bearing on immigration policy nor should it. When America DOES allow others to enter and become citizens, they should be independent, self-supporting and assimilate into our society. About the USA, Congresswoman Nancy Pelosi proclaimed, "our diversity is our strength." No it isn't! The Constitution, the Declaration of Independence, the Bill of Rights and socio-economic freedom ARE OUR STRENGTHS. *Diversity* absolutely is NOT automatically strong by any means, or a hallmark of our nation, and it would be detrimental for the country if our leaders were to make it the law. Nazi Germany wasn't diverse but WAS very strong and powerful. Just like today's China. Diversity on its own is fine and dandy, but only if it's strictly incidental and non-binding.

P.S. White immigrants (legal and illegal) from other countries are more likely to practice individualism and self-responsibility in America than non-whites, and for this very reason are preferable. Hence, it's the reason why fair-minded conservatives seem to "like whites more than they like Hispanics." But a Mexican from South of the Border who, economically speaking, practices independence and thinks capitalistically should absolutely be favored over a Caucasian from Canada who doesn't and won't.

The difference between a far leftist and a liberal is that the former hates America while the latter merely resents it. Genuine liberals don't approve of the extreme elements of leftism (political correctness, cancel culture, violent mobs occupying cities, etc.) though feel the need to tolerate it. But liberals do like the socialistic economic philosophy of the far left and will side with them the vast majority of the time for that very reason. The difference between Americans who vote Republican and those who support Democrats is that there are no Republican voters who dislike or despise their country and want to see it punished or destroyed. For it is the veneration or mere appreciation of government dominance and decree, NOT dislike of them; that could lead to tyrannical authoritarianism and the people's submission.

While attending the joyful opening of a new museum in New York in 2015, Barack Obama's extremely lovely wife, Michelle, because of her seething resentment, felt the need to speciously get in a dig at the presumed racial attitude of the museum's management. In presenting the supposed thoughts of black children not wanting to visit a museum, she chastised her hosts, "Well, that's not a place for me, for someone who looks like me, for someone who comes from my neighborhood." Actually, kids of any race and from any neighborhood are rarely interested in the arts (it's an adult thing) but Mrs. Obama was trying to make it look like the museum curators do not want black children visiting their museum because they, the curators, probably don't like blacks. She went on to "guarantee" us that black kids living near the museum "would never in a million years dream that they would be welcomed in this museum." This is an irresponsible and baseless charge that the mother of two young daughters can't prove. Again, kids of all races are probably not as "welcomed" as adults because the former are far more likely to be unruly in a "dull, boring place that's for grown-ups." But Michelle was alluding to, at least in her mind, a "white culture" experience that is largely foreign to blacks, especially children. The woman was callously guilt-tripping and shaming the curators for indulging in an activity that most blacks just personally don't care to partake in. She would like to think that the noted museum managers engaged in racial ostracism so it would validate her resentment, if not dislike, of white people. And about herself as a youngster, Mrs. Obama stated, "So I know that feeling of not belonging in a place like this," which is not at all unusual for any youngsters no matter their pigmentation. What the former president's obviously gracious wife was insinuating is that museums are somehow exclusionary because they don't appeal to black people as much as they do to whites. She's not totally wrong. But the four S's of sports (swimming, surfing, skating, and skiing) are also like museums in that they almost entirely aren't a part of the culture of black America. They are considered "EXCLUSIONARY." In addition, like the curators of museums, white practitioners of the four S's are not expecting many blacks to participate in their activity, but nor do they not welcome blacks. As for Malia's and Sasha's mother, when the happy and hospitable Whitney Museum curators GO HIGH, she GOES LOW. Suffice it to say that Michelle Obama, who publicly shows off a pretty impressive façade of being a nice person and has been proud of her country at least once in her life, is actually a bitter and spiteful woman. But then again, she's probably a crypto-Marxist, just like her husband.

Of all Americans who have ever joined hands with others in a large crowd and sung the song "We Shall Overcome" while swaying from side to side, what many, if not most, of them have in the back of their minds while singing this tune is "We shall undermine and we shall install socialism in our country, hopefully in the near future."

It Is Perception Which Matters, Not the Truth: Adolph Hitler, himself, never spray-painted any Jewish-owned business store windows. He, his own physical self, never killed anybody between the years 1919 and 1944. The man never even stepped foot inside an extermination camp. When Hitler was a 13 year old boy, he helped a little old lady cross a busy street. Actually, the author just made up the last sentence and has no idea if it ever happened or not. But if it did happen, then the teenage Adolph did a good, commendable deed. Now, many if not most Americans, upon reading the latter statement, will go into a tizzy and become "outraged" that "anybody could ever say such a thing!" But you will notice that they never refuted what I said. Various people will become sanctimoniously "outraged" because they are supposed to. It's the decent thing to do. The self-righteous would like to believe that their contrived emotion is superior to intellectual honesty. To them, merely their PERCEPTION (*optics)* of my "sticking up for" the notorious dictator is a warranted indictment and suffices shame on yours truly. For it is *perception* and not insightful analysis that is to be the arbiter of what is right or wrong. It is semblance, not facts, that is to be deemed reality. It's mostly PERCEPTION that should be considered relevant. Logic and truth really don't matter that much, unfortunately.

It is considered correct, appropriate, and acceptable to refer to hip-hop and soul songs as "black music," but, unless used as a pejorative; it's condescending, elitist and unacceptable to refer to country-western tunes and the last five decades of rock n' roll as "white music." This is because, since blacks are percieved as the downtrodden underdog that we're all supposed to feel sorry for, it is absolutely okay to designate certain artistic property as being officially "theirs" in order to conciliate blacks and give them something to be proud of and call their own. But for whites, who are "privileged" and "already have everything," such special treatment isn't allowed. Also, because whites already enjoy a higher social status, they, unlike blacks, can afford to feel alienated for a change. It's only fair. Relative to this, it is thought to be RACIST for a white person to opine, "I dislike hip-hop music" but NOT racist or even deserving of mild reproach for a black person to loudly declare, "I hate classical and opera music." In nightclubs across America, there are no more disc jockeys playing catchy, danceable, guitar-driven pop rock songs (white music) but only drab, monotonous, non-melodic "black music." Rap / hip-hop, with the possible exception of death metal rock and hardcore thrash punk, is THE most NON-melodic music in the industrialized West that there ever was. Today's young people have been conditioned to think that for a disc jockey to spin records with music performed only or mostly by white artists is racist and exclusionary but won't even entertain this notion for nightclubs that play STRICTLY "black music." Why is that?

There is a man who owns and operates a factory that employs many Jews. It is a fact that he is an anti-Semite. As long as this factory owner keeps his opinions on religion and politics to himself; doesn't express any anti-Semitic views to Jews or even non-Jewish employees, and treats his Jewish workers in a fair manner, no worse or better than he treats others, it becomes perfectly alright that this man is anti-Semitic. The same rules of fairness and logic apply to a Marxist college professor pertaining to his or her attitude toward conservative students, particularly in grading them fairly. In America, one's own provocative opinion on a religious or political issue should be deemed tolerable by society as long as its manifestation doesn't tangibly have a detrimental impact on the lives of others. Something for the reader to ponder: Is it possible for a gentile to state something about God's Chosen People that's deprecatory, but it is also NOT antisemitic? Plus, can something be said about Jews that is definitely antisemitic, but it is also TRUE? If so, should this TRUTH be denounced, dismissed and disregarded? Yes or No?

Most followers of the late radical Saul Alinsky, and others on the far left, don't want to inquire, converse, or debate. They just want to demonize the capitalistic right in order to stop the facts from prevailing. Alinsky's tactic of isolating and destroying a conservative who is using logic and intellectual honesty works much of the time because the sheeple in popular culture, where the left has more clout, are mostly recreant liars who just want to go along to get along. Accordingly, practitioners of Saul Alinsky's methods will not label this author's essay on Martin Luther King, Jr., as "taboo" because that's exactly what it is, and because that very word would only elevate my article and make it more attractive. The liberal/left would like the public to dismiss the MLK column under the guise of it being "racism" even though the former knows darn well that it's really iconoclasm. This way, the left hopes to smear the column in their effort to deter readers from agreeing with it. It will probably work, because most American citizens would rather be *liked* than be LIKENED to a controversial truth. Establishment Republicans will yield to pressure from the Alinskyites (as in backing out of a speaking engagement on a university campus). What the noted GOP politicians are doing is timidity masquerading as tact and integrity. In their reneging to show up in a hostile environment to give their speech, the establishmentarians tell themselves that they've won, at the same time realizing that they've actually lost.

From now on, we Americans must refer to each injured soldier returning home from war, as a HERO. It doesn't really matter that he committed an act of real heroism or actually didn't. If a nineteen-year-old did not kill any of the enemy or save his fellow soldier, but was merely riding in a Jeep that hit a land mine which blew off both of his legs, he is to be called a HERO and showered with accolades. When the American people welcoming back the young man thank him for his service to his country and label him a HERO, they hope to stave off any post-traumatic stress or suicidal thoughts that the teenager might have. His parents and other welcoming folks will be banking on the belief that such complimentary words will compensate at least a little bit for the type of fun and enjoyment that their wounded warrior will be permanently missing out on for the rest of his life and that his two-legged friends will be having. This will particularly be the case if our country deemed the war in which the young man fought to be not winnable or unnecessary.

Loretta Lynch is a black woman who graduated from Harvard University and was the Attorney General of the United States from the year 2015 to 2017. But if she's so smart and is absolutely appalled that many blacks in America were hung to death over the last two centuries, then why didn't the former Attorney General change her last name soon after she turned eighteen years old?

Why are money chain letters illegal? They would work if these chain letters WERE LEGAL and the five citizens that you mailed a one-dollar bill to were legitimate, honest, and KNEW that it's legal. Though there are a few who have claimed that money chain letters are not mathematically viable (Note To Reader: Whether money chain letters factually *"don't work"* or do, is not the point or theme of this essay and so don't bring it up). then why did the Feds outlaw it? What are they worried about? Instead of making the money chain letter a product of prohibition as if it were alcohol back in the 1920s, why doesn't the government just label it a "game of chance" and let the participants try their luck at it? Like the stock market where one could lose thousands or millions, or dollar-to-play games (also legal) at a carnival, there's no guarantee that the player would win. A money chain letter is NOT a scam because it doesn't have a person promising to give you a product or do you a favor in return for money, and then reneging. Furthermore, the money-requesting letter mailer will only be getting one dollar from the envelope receiver. That's hardly a worthy endeavor for an intentional rip-off. Currently, money chain letters don't work simply and logically because 99.99 percent of the letters' recipients don't participate in them. But the reason why the money chain letter is against the law is because it could generate ample income for the recipient that the government can't oversee and treat as taxable. In addition, the priggish citizens desire that these mailed envelopes be confiscated by the law because the letters inside are mysterious (they're probably Satanic) and seem sinister due to the fact that Big Brother doesn't regulate or authorize them. Moreover, the term "chain letter" itself, sounds scary and has the reputation of possessing an "unseen evil," if you will, and so its adversaries look to the government to protect them from it. And the aforementioned deferential advocates of statism are ever so grateful when the government does save them from the dangerous threat of the nefarious chain letter.

Most of the snobbish people who become piously perturbed about a stranger not making a return on the five dollars total that he or she mailed out in chain letters will tacitly endorse, by NOT being against it, our government validation of the loss of millions of dollars by Americans on lottery tickets and gambling casinos. The same haughty anti-chain letter poltroons feel that it is their patriotic duty to support a government clamp-down (via tattling) on the mailing of five $1.00 bills by a few citizens, but they are dead set AGAINST the government PROHIBITING individuals to plunk down twenty bucks on a Quick Pick ticket at a convenience store or departing with $2,000 at the poker table. The "gaming" in Las Vegas and Atlantic City should NEVER be prohibited by law, but the mailing of the God-awfully wicked chain letter has got to be stopped ASAP or the whole damn country will go to hell in a hand-basket! Plus, the noted sniveling, tattling snobs would gleefully support the fine or arrest of a chain-letter mailer asking individuals for a dollar, but will sanctimoniously DEFEND THE RIGHT of a homeless bum to stand on a street corner with a cardboard sign saying "Hungry" and "God Bless" while collecting cash from drivers. To top it all off, these supercilious snots feel no sympathy for the countless people who engage in LEGAL Multi-Level Marketing programs and then drop out after four months because they lost $500, not $5. Nor will the holier-than-thou insist that the government put a halt to MLM because it "doesn't live up to its promises." But those who ABHOR private NONCOMPULSORY collectivism usually ADORE governmental COERCIVE collectivism. Though, it is the VOLUNTARY collectivism of LEGAL money chain letters that would benefit the poor and middle class. It's also the prerogative of individuals to give a stranger one dollar, potentially enriching that person in due time, without the government monitoring or knowing about it, that the anti-chain-letter proponents find so disturbing. No sir or madam, it doesn't bode well for monetary gifting in the United States when a very possible majority of citizens are terribly frightened of a money chain letter and ardently support the omnipotent State trying to suppress it. Now what does that tell you about the American people's instinctive disposition toward real liberty?

Liberal lawmakers who are politically hostile toward private and charter schools and are STRONG ADVOCATES of public-school education will most assuredly send their own children to private schools.

An American man who has had a lot of female sex partners is admiringly regarded by society to be a Don Juan, a Lothario, or a Casanova. But an American woman who has bedded many men is dismissed as being a nymph, slut, or whore. If various men are called PROMISCUOUS, it's a commendation. But when certain women are labeled with the term, it's a denunciation. This is an unfair double standard that has been around for too long. But another double standard that's not as well-known is the one that currently exists in the workplace. Because men sexually harass far more than women do, they will receive harsher punishment. Certain behavior by males is more likely to be construed as sexual harassment than the very same actions taken by females. For example: Women in a business environment can ogle or leer at men and it will be extremely unlikely that someone will file a complaint. Not so, vice versa. If a guy standing on a workplace floor is telling a dirty (sex) joke to another man, and a lady just happens to walk by and hears him, US law and workplace decorum will consider his joke-telling to be a form of sexual harassment. It doesn't matter that he wasn't referring to any certain female employee. If the risqué joke made her feel uncomfortable, it's sexual harassment. If men and women workers are sitting in a factory lunchroom watching a buxom newscaster on TV, a woman employee is allowed to respond, "Wow, look at the melons on her, will ya!" If a male employee said that, it would be his last lunch there. Workplace etiquette dictates that only women are permitted to have a bawdy sense of humor. It is possible, but not probable, that this was the situation with conservative Supreme Court nominee Judge Clarence Thomas, when he was accused in 1991 of saying "Who put pubic hair on my Coke?" at his previous job. If the Justice really did make the comment, he more than likely chalked it up to being mere jocularity among adults. But in the judge's now-famous Supreme Court hearings the same year, Mr. Thomas knew he had to deny it and WHITE LIE his way to the bench because the mostly male Senate would be politically compelled by the mostly non-conservative female voting public to cite what he, Clarence Thomas said, as sexual harassment.

"The best argument against democracy is a five-minute conversation with the average voter," said Winston Churchill. More than a few Americans have commented that if somebody doesn't vote, then that person should not complain about political matters when things don't go their way. To augment this, if those very individuals making this comment are not, themselves, for TERM LIMITS, then they should not cast stones at the people who don't vote, since neither of them do anything to help "throw out all the rascals, crooks, and bums." Although many of our citizens who DO call for term limits will have no problem voting for a political candidate who is AGAINST term limits. The American voters: Full of sound and fury, signifying nothing!

Why is it defensible, rational and socially acceptable (in the opinions of an overwhelming majority of Americans) for black citizens to vote for a *black* presidential candidate SOLELY because he's black (e.g. Obama) but isn't the least bit defensible, rational or socially acceptable that white citizens vote for a *white* presidential candidate SOLELY because that person is white? The answer is: For the same reason that it's alright for everybody to wear a sweatshirt that says "Black Lives Matter" but not the least bit okay for someone (especially a white person) to wear a sweatshirt that says "White Lives Matter." Because blacks are the "oppressed" pitied, proletariat that all of America (especially whites) should empathize with, the noted minorities are to be mollycoddled, put on a societal pedestal and reflexively favored over whites, in regards to racial and socio-political issues. In essence, the two races should NOT be treated the same, the public believes, because it wouldn't be racially fair.

Various Americans, if they ever met up with a member of the American Nazi Party, would be seething with rage (or at least make a good effort to) and "get in his face...and really tell him off...and call him every name in the book...and give it to him with both barrels." In doing so, they feel instantly liberated. Said people now know, for a fact, that they really are against Nazism and have obviously proved it. But would the same Americans harbor the same feelings and take the exact same action if they met up with a member of the Communist Party USA? If not, why not? Communism oppressed and killed five times as many people than Nazism did. The nationwide characterization of Nazism has always been that of unmistakable evil, and rightly so. Presently, this is rarely the case with communism. Which should be given the benefit of a doubt. I mean, sure, communism is a totalitarianism that has made some mistakes (albeit extremely minor) along the way, but, unlike Nazism, it at least earns a modicum of respect and appreciation for its potential to do wondrous things for humanity and should be judged accordingly. This is the reason why the noted Marxist-Leninist religion continues to be enamored by the limousine liberal and champagne socialist residents of Matha's Vineyard and the Hamptons, along with their Ivy Leaguer offspring.

QUESTION: Which one of the following persons, presently staying in the United States, is MOST LIKELY to commit an act of terrorism here? You must choose only ONE of these answers.

1. A blonde from Sweden.

2. A vacationer from Aruba.
3. An atheist from Christmas Island.
4. A taxi driver from Malta.
5. A malnourished guy from Hungary.
6. A pugnacious Muslim from the Middle East.
7. A yak farmer from Mongolia.
8. A guy named "Chad" from Chad.
9. A villager from Martinique.
10. A yacht salesman from Bangladesh.
11. A Babushka woman from Russia.
12. A poultry lover from Turkey.
13. None of the above. Because they are all human beings, each and every one of these individuals is EQUALLY likely to commit an act of terrorism in our country. Any other answer amounts to racial profiling and is patently unfair. PROFILING is a form of PREJUDICE, and since prejudice is wrong, then the person who prejudges is automatically wrong.

The correct answer is, of course, number 13.

I don't mean to talk down to you, the reader, but can we all dispense with chiding individuals for "talking down to" someone? When you're telling somebody a truth that he or she is ignorant of or apathetic about, then it becomes essential to "talk down to" them. Teachers and professors "talk down to" their students all the time. The same goes with parents in regard to their children. What does one think that the *bully pulpit* of the presidency is all about? For more than a century, American presidents have used the bully pulpit to educate our society on what they, the former, think is morally right. When Barack Obama was running for president in 2008 and expressing his opinions to a crowd, the Reverend Jesse Jackson, speaking to a person sitting next to him, was caught on microphone upbraiding then Senator Obama, "See, Barack's been talking down to black people." If candidate Obama was at all didactic in conveying to folks what he thought was wise advice about important matters that affect them, is there anything deplorable about that? Has the Reverend Jackson ever been on a podium and "preached" to black adults about right and wrong? If so, was he at all *patronizing*? If the American people need to learn by being "talked down to," then so be it.

Most Americans on the far left dislike our country's religious right more than they do the mentally disturbed Islamic extremists. But then, that's only because the last noted group is trying to hurt the United States. The Oklahoma City bomber Timothy McVeigh was a right-wing radical and Bill Ayers is a left-wing radical. But both of these men abandoned these titles when they became what are known as *violent true believers*. In the case of the former, it is perfectly okay and immensely preferable to be "anti-government" as long as it means strictly "anti-socialism" or "anti-statism." But harboring only that attitude wasn't good enough for McVeigh. He believed that he had to bring death to many innocent people (in 1995) even though doing so didn't inherently help his cause. Less than six years later, death was fittingly brought to Timothy McVeigh. The very much "pro-government" and infamous 1969 bomb-planting revolutionary, Bill Ayers, is today a free (and lucky) man and is a former university professor. He is unrepentant just like McVeigh was. What any ideological or religious zealots should realize is that once they kill in order to ostensibly help certain people, their beliefs and causes become irrelevant. They have now become murderers, which should impress and influence no one.

Many Americans who always vote Democrat often call for the citizens of our republic to join in UNITY. But their vision of "unity" is when conservatism is vanquished and a leftist (socialistic) agenda rules the country. For a nation-wide coerced conformity and subjugation IS *unity*.

A radio talk show host once asked why blacks support President Barack Obama after six years and the Democratic Party for more than fifty years when doing so, if anything, made the lives of black people worse. Well, it's like when a super idealistic eighteen-year-old man joins the Communist Party of America. If he quits the Party after only six months because of disenchantment, then that short term becomes merely a youthful indiscretion on his part. But if the young man remains a member for, say, ten years, then doing so would only induce him to stay many more years. Otherwise, this now twenty-eight-year-old would have to tell himself that he dedicated a decade of his life (wasted time) to something that's been a complete farce. In the subsequent years, the man, now in his early forties, will then feel compelled to stay in "the Party" for the rest of his life "believing" (read: lying to himself) in a philosophy that even the old "Marxist-Leninists" in the Kremlin during the Cold War laughed at and didn't believe in. This is analogous to blacks and their addiction to the Democratic Party. In the minds of most American blacks, the damage that the Democrats have done to them since 1965 does not and should not matter. The BIG LIE to their selves will need to continue if blacks would like to retain at least a modicum of hope and self-respect.

When politicians use the term "comprehensive" in their speeches, it usually means two things: (1) The noted public-service leaders don't know what they're talking about and (2) It will more than likely involve "responsive" (pervasive) government.

In a speech at a fundraiser, Minnesota Democratic Congresswoman Ilhan Omar, in alluding to the 9/11 jet airliners' destruction of the two World Trade Center buildings resulting in 2977 deaths in the year 2001; described the aircraft's Islamic hijackers/attackers and their actions as "some people did something." The woman was concisely correct. Likewise, something else also happened some six decades earlier. What happened was, something in Europe called the "Holocaust" somehow occurred in which some folks did some stuff to some other people and that some of these other people died as a result. Anyway, during this time, someone named Hitler was rumored to have been the cause of the stuff that happened. If that's the case, then my own wild guess is that this Hitler guy was probably not as nice a person as Mother Teresa. Hopefully, this Holocaust thing that some people apparently believe was kind of awful, won't happen in our country, because there is a fairly good chance that it wouldn't be very pleasant. But whatever! I'd like to wish Ilhan Omar a nice day and that the rest of her life is one of everlasting joy and tranquility.

Liberals are stupid people. They will flee their liberal home state (e.g. California, New York, Maryland, New Jersey) to escape from what liberalism has done to it (higher taxes, excessive spending, over-regulation etc.). These self-proclaimed progressives delightedly move to what they know to be the opposite: a conservative, low-tax state, in order to live a better life. But said liberals will tenaciously continue to vote for left-leaning political candidates running for public office in the hope of turning their new place of residence into a liberal state so that they can live a better life.

If Martin Luther King Jr. hadn't been assassinated on April 4th, 1968, he probably would have died sometime later on in his life.

To gravitate toward socialism may give one pause, although doing the former does, one will have to admit, ostensibly provide a sense of prospective safety and security. To make socialism itself work, we just need to BELIEVE IN IT. Or as the liberal-left likes to term it, *"reimagine"* (read: self-delude or adopt an advanced form of emotion/fantasy-based irrationality). On the other hand, any march in the other direction toward laissez-faire capitalism or anarcho-capitalism is to venture into unknown territory. The main negativity of these two examples of extreme freedom is that, unlike socialism, there is not even a pretense of REASSURANCE by either, which is what the American people crave. Omnipotent government is a bulwark against the unknown. Without governmental social engineering which is purportedly for the benefit of the people, we are susceptible to the unknown. Living under absolute, 100 percent freedom and liberty (with reasonable laws) is tremendously threatening and dangerous in the minds of a majority of the population. But in the case of living under out-and-out totalitarianism, dealing with such a threatening and oppressive socio-political environment is deemed as only a possibility. It might happen, but then again, it might not. Give totalitarianism a chance and let's see. But what will be particularly vexing and egregious about living under such a society even worse than those of the old Warsaw Pact countries of the past, is that many if not most Americans will retrospectively claim (scapegoat), regarding our current oppressive predicament, that the "rich didn't pay their fair share." Furthermore, for us to have forestalled the impending authoritarianism; Americans, in exhibiting utter stupidity, will contend that the Federal government should have exerted more command and control of the citizenry via more rules and restrictions. In other words, the people's obedience and submission to the *Almighty State* is needed in order to prevent America from falling under tyranny and subjugation. This nation's Commanders-in-Chief, Ronald Reagan 1981-1989 and Donald Trump 2017-2021 were both far from even close to becoming authoritarians. The difference is that the former was an inspirational, mild-mannered Great Communicator while the latter was a callous, polorizing non-conformist. Be that as it may, about a half dozen times, President Donald Trump, who in this author's opinion had been a better (read: more conservative and successful) leader than Ronald Reagan, had proclaimed, "America will never be a socialist country." But our 45th president was wrong! And the American people will prove him wrong before the year 2030.

"Remember, democracy never lasts long. It soon wastes, exhausts, and murders itself. There never was a democracy yet that did not commit suicide. It is vain to say that democracy is less vain, less proud, less selfish, less ambitious, or less avaricious than aristocracy or monarchy," stated our second president, John Adams, in 1814. The Constitution was not designed nor intended to reinforce the predilections of the majority of American citizens, but to safeguard the God-given rights of a minority of them. Republicanism, which protects the autonomy of the individual, is an impediment to a democracy, which protects the hegemony of mob rule.

If a renowned, distinguished conservative gentleman were to write, and being totally serious, that each and every black American adult is an alcoholic, the entire progressive left would NOT desire to censor his statement precisely BECAUSE it isn't the least bit true or believable.

Indeed, they would gladly welcome the man's absurd and laughable assertion, because it would undoubtedly undercut and damage any influence that conservatism may have. It's when a conservative who speaks the TRUTH that, fascistic progressives (e.g. leftist brown-shirt students on college campuses) will try to stop him from getting his message out. The late author Joseph Sobran once said that "The attempt to silence a man is the greatest honor you can bestow on him. It means that you recognize his superiority to yourself."

The term "white supremacy" is employed mostly as a social and political cudgel against whites and to suppress any white disagreement with what blacks want or desire from society. Words like, "individualism", "objectivity", "traditionalism", "exceptionalism" and "nuclear family" connote *white supremacy* and deserve to be banished from the national dialogue. Correspondingly, to be against "whiteness" (*a negative*) and lovingly support anything that denotes "blackness" (*a positive*) is to engage in the very best of virtue signaling. Something that is "too white" is to be disparaged because it's wholesome, clean-cut and deferential in a red, white and blue kind of way. But the opposite, "blackness", is immersed in humility and recalcitrance and thus, should be esteemed. For the most part, if actions or policies are conducive to undercutting our socio-economic liberty-based fabric, then they are considered to be *Woke*. But moreover and especially, if something is at all favorable to bringing America toward the left's goal of authoritarian socialism, then it cannot possibly possess *white supremacy*. However, it will possess massive amounts of *Wokeness* (black ideological puerility). Or as all dictionaries describe "*woke*", "Something in American black culture that is preposterous and is to be taken seriously." Anyway, since conservatism/capitalism is the polar opposite of socialism, then the aforementioned duo is to be associated with *white supremacy*. Perhaps the kinsfolk of both WOKENESS and WHITE SUPREMACY can one day get together and form a partnership?

Republican commentators on television, David Frum and Michael Steele, used to be nominal conservatives. Today they are de facto liberals. Like Never Trumpers plus members and supporters of the Lincoln Project (a group of liberals and moderates disingenuously calling themselves "conservatives"), these two individuals agree with liberalism most of the time. In addition, the noted speech writer for George H.W. Bush and the former Chairman of the Republican National Commitee rarely aim any of their criticism or hostility toward the Democrat party or liberalism. Moreover and especially, they couldn't stand President Donald Trump because he exemplified a successful conservatism of the ANTI-establishmentarian kind. In the late 1990s, Mr. Frum was a conservative and a dozen years later, turned into a liberal who detested the anti-socialism Tea Party, supported Obamacare and voted for Hillary Clinton in 2016. Nowadays, Mr. Steele proves that he's still relevant by appearing only on liberal talk shows where this "Republican" never says a bad word about liberalism or the Democratic party but instead just smiles in agreement when the liberal host attacks conservatism and the GOP. Frum and Steele both voted for the Democratic presidential candidate in 2020. Anybody who sought to elect Joe Biden is lying through their teeth when they refer to themselves as conservatives. An honest-to-goodness conservative would NEVER vote for a quasi-socialist. But Frum and Steele did so in order to GET BACK AT the Republican party for not adopting their version of what conservatism, they believe, is supposed to be. And that's a pale pastel, ever so slightly to the right of a mild form of liberalism. If the reader wants some sort of measure of what REAL conservatism is and ought to be, just think of political talk radio hosts Mark Levin, Andrew Wilcow and the late Rush Limbaugh.

Messrs Levin, Wilcow and Limbaugh avidly supported the former real estate mogul because, as president, he was in actuality pushing authentic conservatism. Never Trumpers, on the other hand, realize that they aren't really conservative but enjoy refering to themselves as such because this mildly provocative ideological label gives Never Trumpers a notoriety that they enjoy having. The aforementioned are flattered by the attention of being called "right-wingers" but secure in the knowledge that they're actually not. They're merely captivated by the WORD "conservative" because in the socio-political arena, the noted term has a dissonant yet somehow appealing reputation for non-conformity and controversy. Many Americans are attracted to *conservatism* merely because they deem it an outlier from the nation's jejune, conventional (read: liberal) public discourse. Actual conservatism isn't really liked that much, but its prominence IS refreshingly different and enticing. Current (or former) Republicans S.E. Cupp, Michael Steele, George Will, Michael Gerson, David Frum, William Kristol and Mona Charen, among other prominent Never Trumpers, take delight whenever there are denunciations of, not just the 45th president, but the Republican Party and particularly, hard-line conservatism. But the noted individuals will take umbrage if someone tells the unkind truth about the Democratic Party. IF conservative Senator Ted Cruz, and not Donald Trump, was the Republican presidential choice in Novembers of 2016 and 2020; with the possible exception of Will, the seven of them would have voted for the Democrat, and they know it. Now, the word "conservative" is more prestigious than the word "liberal." However, the Never Trumpers creed is to mostly support liberalism though label themselves "conservative" merely as an honorific. Though, they're really just Washington Swamp cock-tail party establishmentarians. After hating on Donald Trump, their second most important political mission is to remake authentic (read: "hard-line") conservatism into a more palatable concoction for the voting public by diluting it with liberalism. Plus, one can reasonably extrapolate that these seven political apostates are presently hoping that the Democrats regain the House and retain Senate in 2024. No Donald Trump haters have ever asserted (and never will) that the former President wasn't conservative enough. Indeed, it's precisely because Mr. Trump conducted himself as an ideological patriot and implimented right-leaning (less government, America first) successful policies, that is the bane of his detractors. Five of the noted deprecators (Gerson is now deceased) actually ARE liberals and are lying if they say they aren't. George Will is a moderate who has for decades been known, in various conservative circles, to give lip service to conservatism though eventually relinquish to liberalism. In essence, Will has long been a....*liberal sympathiser,* if you will (pun intended). Since 2016, all seven have never said, and won't say (except for Gerson, who isn't speaking) a negative word about Democratic party policies, liberalism, socialism, Joe Biden and any prominent Democrat. And so it isn't like the aforementioned group of six are against the 45th president ONLY. No.... Donald Trump is just a pretext to their NOT liking strong Constitutional pro-liberty CONSERVATISM, which Trump and hard-line conservative office holders embody. The six of them either don't realize or don't care that they're being petty and narcissistic when they help effectuate detrimental change (socialism) to our country by voting for liberal Joe Biden in order to spite and, they hope, punish the more right-leaning former real estate mogul all because they don't like him. What these half dozen individuals and their minions really want (they won't tell you and so I will) is for Republican party politicians to espouse centrist establishmentarianism that will eventually go along with liberalism, but that they will simply catagorize the noted subterfuge as *conservatism*.

Fidel Castro was a Red worth $900 million and led a luxurious lifestyle that included an 85-foot yacht. Barack Obama is merely a pinko and is worth just $70 million, although he does own an $8 million mansion near the nation's capital and an $11 million mansion in Martha's Vineyard. Nevertheless, our 44th president, because he's never been a dictator, is inferior to Castro and highly unlikely to amass the phenomenal fortune that the Cuban humanitarian accumulated. As a lowly pinko on the ideological ladder, Michelle's husband will never reach the pinnacle of prestige by becoming a Red despot; and a near-billionaire one at that.

Most Republicans agreed with some prominent GOP members when the latter had stressed that "There is no place in the Republican Party for white nationalists and white supremacists" or words to that effect. In addition to this, yours truly will propose that "There is no room in the Democrat Party for communists, socialists and communist sympathisers." Now then, will any Democrat agree with me on this? If not...why not? How about any Republican? If the answer from both parties is "No" then it's because the mere personal/political opinions of white nationalists and white supremacists are UNACCEPTABLE while the very concept of actual socialism/communism is deemed admissible to the body politic and consequently becomes well-nigh respectable.

The American left resents Vladimir Putin for not being a communist. But the Russian president is neither a communist nor a fascist. Though, he IS a despot. General Secretary Xi Jinping of China IS a communist who is more hostile towards and a threat to the United States than Putin is. It's no wonder that most of those who support the Democrats never badmouth Xi Jinping.

The acronym LGBTQ stands for lesbian, gay, bisexual, transsexual, and queer, claims the left-leaning organization and its support for the aforementioned citizens. You'll notice how the second and fifth defining words conveniently eliminate any redundancy in their title. The letter "Q" for the term "queer" was at first, left out of the acronym but later on inserted because, apparently, leaving "queer" out was odd. And though LGBTQ will defend the five noted groups, they will not accommodate panhandlers. But the organization WILL, however, pander to pansexuals, especially pansexuals who like pancakes. The one group of identity-challenged that LGBTQ are NOT particularly fond of are the transvestites. Although, it could be that they think the transvestites and their incessant desire to reach the prestigious goal of victimhood status, is a real drag. The sexual identity that has dominated the news about LGBTQ and monopolized their attention over the past few years is the transsexuals. This quite common and tremendously vital species who are, incidentally, not subhuman, are finally getting the attention they've longed for and deserved. And the transsexuals (no relation to the hermaphrodites) have done some wonderful things for America. For instance, back in 1954, it was a transsexual who invented the *transistor* radio (it played both AM and FM). Anyway, one of the requests that the transsexuals have made is that if any of them are obese, he or she would prefer to be called *trans-fat*. If they insist, sure! But here's the burning question to the transsexual members of LGBTQ: You, along with the others, seem to like your organization title but need to explain it too often. Well, perhaps you can explain the following acronym....WTFRU?

CHAPTER **23**

Day Bee Lion 2

IT WAS FORMER Black Panther member, the late Eldridge Cleaver, who once said, "The Democratic Party harnessed black people to the Federal budget and left us in the lurch." But perhaps what Mr. Cleaver didn't consider is that without the Democratic Party being their umbilical cord and the government being their life support system, how will the black people of America survive? Who will care for God's chillun while their mammy and pappy are performing on the Chitlin' Circuit? Without the Democratic Party, who will cause the trees to bear fruit for our black people to eat? Who will plant the corn to be harvested in the fall? Who will knead the dough and bake the bread? Who will tote the barge and lift the bale? Who will fix the leaky roofs of liberal plantation shanties when it rains? The majority of blacks will counter that the reason they vote Democrat is because the Democrats are the party of civil rights. They're lying. That is not the reason why.

In 1964, at our nation's capital, 80 percent of the Republicans in Congress voted for the Civil Rights Act while 61 percent of the Democrats did. In the Senate, it was 82 percent of the GOP and 69 percent of Democrats. Democratic Senator Al Gore Sr. voted against it. For the 1965 Voting Rights Act, in the Senate, it was 94 percent Republicans and 73 percent of the Democrats that favored it. The House vote for the same bill was 82 percent GOP vs. 78 percent Democrat. The Ku Klux Klan was founded by Democrats. Bull Connor, a Democrat and KKK member, became infamous for ordering the use of fire hoses and attack dogs on black civil rights demonstrators in the early 1960s. The late Virginia Democratic Senator, Robert Byrd, was once a KKK member. J. William Fulbright, a racist segregationist, was a Democrat and mentor to former President Bill Clinton. Most black Americans will either be in denial about all this or try their very best to minimize it, thereby proving just how dishonest they really are.

Millions of black citizens vote by rote years after they're indoctrinated at an early age by their mother when she says to one of them, "Child, when you is an adult, don't you be votin for no Republican. You always vote Democrat because Republicans don't like blacks and poor folk, dey only like rich white people. Democrats care about you. Republicans don't." The percentage of white and black Americans on welfare are approximately the same, but the difference is that 39 percent of whites vote for Democrats mostly for the purpose of government supplementing and taking care of them, while it's more than twice as much (90 percent) of blacks voting Democrat for the same reason. Socio-economically speaking, the main difference between whites and blacks is that whites don't want to live off the money of blacks.

Quite simply, because black society is "owed," they have the right to live their lifestyle and whites have a duty to subsidize it via government enforced redistribution. Otherwise, American blacks' civil rights are being violated. Black people will condemn individuals stealing from the government but not vice versa. And unlike millions of white Americans, blacks hold no animosity toward the Internal Revenue Service. And why should they, since the IRS rarely bothers them. Back in the early 1800s, ACTUAL liberty was black America's best friend. Two centuries later, it is the main enemy that they dread. Blacks are repelled by liberty because it forces self-responsibility on them. Ergo, the more that economic freedom (i.e. LESS government bailing them out) is thrust upon black Americans, the more it compels them (along with Hispanics, as well as whites) to cut back on having illegitimate babies that they personally can't afford. This would consequently make it far more difficult for blacks to catch up with whites in US population, which in turn, isn't conducive to making "social change" happen. But whenever a candidate for political office gives a speech and then takes questions from the audience afterwards, more than any other race or ethnicity, a black person is likely to ask the candidate, "What are you going to do for me?" Translation: "Will you vote to have more government provide for me and take care of me?" In response, the candidate should ask that individual, "What is the definition of the word 'parasite'?" And "What is a leech?"

The "I want to keep what really is mine" attitude is right and appropriate. The "I want what was originally yours" is not. This latter disposition of too many blacks has harmed, not helped, them in the long run. The progressive left is well aware of this and the damage that the Great Society has done to the family institution and particularly, the black community. And they take glee in it. In the socio-political arena, the black person being a victim is a GOOD thing, not a bad one. The American far left enjoys the fact that the Federal government, with the Democratic Party as its agent, has supplanted the role of the black man as husband to his wife and especially father to his children. The left will then use the worsening condition of poor blacks (among other people) to help bankrupt the free enterprise system. To shift GOVERNMENT responsibility to SELF responsibility would be counterproductive in the minds of these progressives. They would like poor black people to believe that since their being destitute is society's fault, then it is pointless of them to try to improve their lives through their own efforts. Plus, black Americans as a whole need to be perceived by the public as being perpetual victims in order to keep the welfare gravy train chugging along down the track. In a choice between *freedom* and *free stuff*, most blacks will easily opt for the latter. Within the mindset of many blacks, it is NOT the case of which political party will actually make their lives better, but rather, which party will take care of black individuals so that each one won't have to be personally responsible for making a better life for him or herself.

The vast majority of black citizens would much rather have a liberal black man for president with an extremely high national 21 percent black unemployment rate as a result of his policies than a conservative white man as president with a super low three percent black unemployment as a result of HIS policies. In a not-at-all unrelated matter, one liberal black Hollywood celebrity once solemnly referred to President Barack Obama as "Our Lord and Savior." Now, what this famous actor said is, of course....true. Any disagreement with it constitutes blasphemy. To expound, if I may, on the Biblical accuracy of this celebrity's declaration: While in the Oval Office, Obama (aka the Messiah) successfully raised the unemployment rate of black Americans by two percentage points. But that's not his only achievement. In just three short years, the Messiah put a laudatory extra 47 million citizens on food stamps. He then accomplished racking up more debt than all the other presidents combined. Praise the Lord, indeed! Years from now, you, the proud reader, will be boasting about Him to your grandchildren.

Blacks exploit a solitary incident like, for example, a state capital flying the Confederate flag. They want America to concentrate on the symbolism of the Confederate flag so that blacks can use this subterfuge to take white society's focus off black society and the moral debasement and economic debt that blacks have inflicted on themselves and on the nation in general. Most black Americans, in regard to their socio-economic circumstance, are reluctant to place the blame on "the breakdown of the black family" because to do so would assuredly lead to the condemnation and discredit of the Federal government and subsequent indictment of the welfare state. They're determined not to let white people off the hook because that would indicate that black citizens, themselves, are the main culprits. No, blacks feel that it's more important and satisfying for them to nurture their vindictiveness against whites than to honestly address what they've done and continue to do to themselves. Ergo, government not only becomes their provider, but also their collaborator in bringing down white society and the nation in general. A lot of American blacks care about their country nowhere near as much as they care about their government. They look lovingly to "gubmint" in the same way black servants in movies of the 1930s and '40s looked up to their white owners. The term "Obamacare" initially became offensive to some blacks because it was a snide put-down of government. And "government," in this sense, is synonymous with black America's culture and values. Government subsidization of their lifestyle then becomes an integral component of their CAUSE.

And just what is their cause? Socialism – that's what. For almost a century it has been, ideologically speaking, the blacks' best friend and rescuer. Socialism is the very goal and tactical outcome of black liberation theology. Without a doubt, in the political arena, the black agenda is a socialistic agenda and vice versa. Quite simply, socialism is the PROMISED LAND. And what's especially attractive about the aforementioned utopian endeavor, is that even though it won't end racism, inequity and despair; it will at a minimum compensate for them. But then again, perhaps the slavery of socialism is the exact opposite of the noted latter three societal issues. Even better, it is, in all probability, the cure. Or at least, this is what millions of blacks and progressive whites insist on believing; otherwise, there is no hope. More than a few prominent blacks have said that Black America has definitely made progress in the last hundred years but that they still have a long way to go. But unless blacks are dreaming of the "promised land," they have already reached their destination. Many blacks want socialism not just because they would like to believe that it would be their emancipation, but that it's also an installer of racial "equity." Furthermore, for any white person to badmouth the egalitarian, benevolent slavery of Karl Marx's invention is to vocally attack the socio-political Savior of black society. Indeed, in the near future, any negative talk about socialism, verbal or written, by a white person will be denounced as, (SURPRISE!), *"racist."* If it's done by a black person then it will be labeled *"traitorous."* Just as intellectual dishonesty is intrinsic to black politics, socialism is ingrained in their culture and part of their identity. Presently, being black is more of an ideological philosophy than it is a race. At any rate, American blacks do NOT want to live under the TYPE of slavery that existed in our nation two centuries ago because THAT TYPE of slavery was racially unjust and unfair. The TYPE back then was a slavery of a black man by a white man for the benefit of a white man. That's not good and it's not right.

The GOOD type of slavery that the overwhelming majority of today's black citizens yearn to live under is the slavery of socialism. This is because it is a compassionate and caring slavery of both blacks and whites (and anybody else), administered by both blacks and whites (slave masters) for the benefit of both blacks and whites (the compliant slaves). Socialism is socio-political conformity and obedience to the benevolent State. It is racial equality and social justice. Socialism is slavery of the people, by the people, for the people. That's what is known as "fairness." If it isn't already, in the near future, socialism (or tenderhearted subjugation, if you want) will be considered a "civil right." It should be no surprise that people with this collectivistic mentality abhor the capitalistic, anti-slavery Tea Party. And the Tea Party is the Number 1 enemy of "civil rights" for present-day black Americans. What both white and black people should realize is that collectivism does not "bring the races closer together," but rather foments disrespect, distrust, and dislike, because it induces social groups to battle each other for government favoritism. Paradoxically, it is the practice of INDIVIDUALISM that empathetically "brings the races closer together." If each black person in the United States were to concentrate on improving his or her own life by doing right, then black society as a whole would become less impoverished and move closer to becoming socio-economically equal to white society. Alas, many if not most blacks would rather live under a system (socialism) where both races are equally miserable than live under a freedom-based economy that won't bring down white citizens (whom they envy and resent) and doesn't guarantee to upgrade the livelihood of black Americans. In a nutshell, socialism is not just potentially the great rescuer of Black America, but it is also the great punisher of white people (and Lord knows they deserve it, don't they?).

There are prominent black individuals who held or are currently holding political office, or in show business who are socialists. John Lewis (presently driving down the pine box highway) was and most of the Congressional Black Caucus are clandestine socialists. Civil rights activist and Board Chairman of the NAACP, Julian Bond (also pushing up daisies), was a socialist. Actor Danny Glover is a socialist, as was Paul Robeson protégé, the late singer/actor Harry Belafonte. Yes, there are conservative blacks who embrace a capitalistic (individualism and self-responsibility) philosophy: "It is plainly not in the interest of black leaders that blacks become individualistic no more than it was in the interest of slaveholders that slaves learn to read and write," says Associate Professor and author Anne Wortham. Then there's former Congressman

Alan West, a black anti-socialist (read: traitor and Oreo cookie). But these two and other "sell-outs" are to be shunned by the liberal and black establishment for challenging or defying the black person's best interest (socialism). In the opinions of both white and black folks on the left, though a black person has the indisputable liberty and the right to be a conservative, he or she is OUT OF LINE for being one. A white conservative is not out of line. That is, for a white person to lean to the capitalist right is understandable and acceptable. But blacks who lean to the right evidently don't know what's good for them and deserve to be rebuked and ostracized. They have betrayed their people.

From the penniless to the lower middle-class, some black folks figure----what's the point of being alive if the Marxist inspiration is no damn good? Of the black Americans who always vote Democrat, many if not most of them, insist on believing that socialism is the "heaven" that blacks would be living in before they die. Recent history tells us that there have been hundreds of American blacks who have already seen the Promised Land and received their deliverance. Once upon a time, there was a handsome, charismatic preacher from San Francisco known as the Reverend Jim Jones. Now, Jones wasn't at all a God-fearing religious man. But he was a communist. In the year 1976, Jones brought over a thousand members of a cult that he led called "The People's Temple" to the country of Guyana. His congregants came there to build a heavenly, socialistic paradise. But in November of 1978, while on their exploratory mission to find Heaven, they prematurely FOUND IT. Nine hundred and nine of them (including 304 children), the messianic leader's followers, committed suicide on his command by consuming a cyanide-laced flavored drink. As for Jim Jones, like his fellow socialist, Adolph Hitler, he took the smartest action that one could take. He shot himself in the head. Of the "Reverend's" devotees that drank the poison "Kool-Aid", 69 percent of them were black. Today, a sorry majority (90 percent) of America's blacks continue to drink the Kool-Aid.

Since the 1920s, black people have been useful pawns (sometimes aware of it) of American communism. They have always been a disproportionate part of the audience of communist speakers for a century. Though said pawns don't cerebrally indulge in conversations about dialectical materialism or any other communist crapola, they do adore that Marxist message of societal "change" and America moving "forward." It gives them *hope*. Blacks don't mind standing on the dock at the harbor waiting for their ship to come in. When the ship fails to appear, the noted pawns simply expire. "He who lives upon hope will die fasting." So spoke Benjamin Franklin. For too long, black individuals have been lying to themselves and taken for suckers by the liberal / left. How sad.

Moocher-mentality blacks and infantile white liberals denigrate our Founding Fathers as "dead white men" but elevate dead black communists to eminent status: The late black actor and singer, Paul Robeson, once declared, "If fighting for the Negro people and their trade union brothers, if that makes me the subversive that they're talking about in Congress, if that makes me a Red, then so be it." Well, no, it didn't make him a Red. But being a member, albeit secretly, of the Communist Party USA, did. This singing lackey to great Mother Russia once stated, "The artist must elect to fight for freedom or slavery. I have made my choice." He certainly did! Which the actor exemplified in his effusive 1953 eulogy entitled "To You Beloved Comrade" to the decomposing slave master, Joseph Stalin. Robeson remained slavishly pro-Stalin even AFTER he heard about the dictator's genocidal crimes and forced famine against the Russian people. The actor/singer was a smart, educated man. But he was apparently also a fool. Black NAACP co-founder W.E.B. DuBois joined the American Communist Party for the last two years of his life because he believed this organization represented an honest assessment and culmination of his politics. He was correct. A few years ago, both of these men were honored by the US Government with first-class postage stamps bearing their likenesses.

For some unknown reason, Barack Obama's mentor and role model, Frank Marshall Davis, has not received similar reverential treatment from our Federal government even though he was also a Communist Party member. Perhaps the US Senate should launch an investigation into this to find out why he hasn't been honored. If a certain prominent black American was an enthusiastic supporter of South African apartheid and wished it was the system here in the USA, he or she would be branded as an "Uncle Tom" and a "traitor." But a black person who is a communist is never even thought of as being either of the noted two slurs. And that's because communism, unlike apartheid, would be beneficial to American blacks. This is why Angela Davis, a former twenty-three-year member of the Communist Party USA and a popular lecturer on the college circuit, is lovingly referred to by one and all as a "civil rights activist" and "supporter of social justice." Our nation hasn't awarded Ms. Davis with her own postage stamp yet because US Government law stipulates that the honoree has to be deceased and, as of this writing, she's still alive.

When blacks vote for the GOP, they're said to be "not voting their interest" (read: to live in a country ostensibly moving in a socialistic direction). In white liberal opinion, blacks aren't supposed to be joyful and fulfilled, because that would cut down on people that white liberals feel they need to rescue. Some left-leaning blacks have such an intense dislike of Republicans of their own race that they label the latter the "happy negro." This slur is usually designated for the contented, non-political black middle-class husband and wife with three children and the family dog. They live a Norman Rockwell suburban small-town life in a nice two-story house with a wooden "Home Sweet Home" sign on their porch enclosed by a yard with a white picket fence. On the other side of the racial fence, leftist black militants have a seething hatred of white suburbia as well as Americana itself. They despise the wholesome, clean-cut *Leave It to Beaver* stereotype neighborhood of whites who OWN their homes (particularly the ones with the American flag flying on the front porch) and having backyard family picnics on Saturdays and going to church every Sunday. Do not misunderstand, hardcore leftists (Antifa, BLM and others) don't so much envy as they just outright hate the aforementioned citizens. Nor do they desire blacks to aspire to emulate said lifestyle that progressive black malcontents only seek to destroy. You see; the far left (pro-socialism) mob want their black pawns to be bitter, jealous, angry, and vindictive while living in dilapidated public housing and subsequently crying out for more government. The noted Marxist protesters/rioters would rather have blacks standing on an urban street corner with, if they can't find a crack pipe, a brand-new EBT card in their hand instead of the Bible.

When conservatives criticize the self-detrimental behavior of various black citizens, the progressive's retort will be that the political right is "blaming the victim" of SOCIETY. By "society," what they mean is socio-economic freedom (American-style capitalism) which allows whites to NOT come to the rescue and bail out blacks. Because liberty is intrinsically neutral and indifferent, it doesn't provide hope. But government coercion and collectivism (socialism) does. In essence, because liberty isn't slavery, then it is not helpful to black people. Black Democrats and their white left-leaning counterparts like to claim, "We're all in this together." No, we're not! Nevertheless, quasi-socialist political commentator Melissa Harris-Perry once lectured us, "We have to break through our private ideas that kids belong to their parents or kids belong to their families and recognize that kids belong to whole communities." The majority of black Americans will agree with her. Why should mothers and fathers fund the upbringing of and be held accountable for the behavior of their own children when they don't have to? The State absolving them of their economic and moral responsibility will make the parents' life so much easier. Plus, if their offspring do grow up to be incorrigible street hoodlums, it will consequently be the government's fault, not the parents'. A lot of blacks would like to believe that socialism will at least make amends for, if not become a veritable antidote to poverty and crime. But, like the old Indian proverb teaches, "You can't wake a person who is pretending to be asleep."

The difference between a socialist and a racist is that the latter doesn't necessarily want slavery for black people. American blacks, in the past five decades, have been more victimized by the term "racism" than they've been oppressed by actual racism, itself, over the same time period. Prominent black leaders that shout "racism" every time a white person breathes have concerns for their people's welfare, alright. They get their people addicted to a socialistic disease called WELFARE, only to prescribe socialist nostrums as a remedy. Their clients then continue to look to them for more "medicine" as these "leaders", in return, reap the financial and social status rewards; not totally unlike prostitutes hooked on dope going to their pimps for help. One question for the reader to ponder: Since contemporary liberalism is the road to socialism, and socialism is just slavery, don't you think it's ironic and even pathetic that nine out of ten black Americans continue to vote for liberal politicians?

FOOTNOTE: Those that lean to the left will cry "racist" (which, for them, is quite rare and unusual) in their response to this essay. But you'll notice that they never said that yours truly is wrong. This is because the liberal/left will then be compelled or expected to explain how I'm wrong and they will be unable to. Therefore, these progressives are de facto admitting that what this author wrote is true by their outright refusal to say that it's not true. Or why else would the disingenuous liars not categorically disagree with me when they so easily could have? So as soon as the juvenile left engages in name-calling and character assassination (and they will), they just conceded the debate by default. I win.

CHAPTER 24

Moderation in the Extreme

BACK IN THE 1980s, it was wishful thinking on the part of any conservative who said or believed that America had swung to the right. Yes, the people, particularly the young, became more patriotic. But patriotism comes and blows with a political wind. The liberal/left, during this stars and stripes era (1981-1983), told the truth when they mentioned that the American people like President Reagan personally, but don't agree with his libertarian economic philosophy (cut BOTH taxes and social spending). Reagan secretly concurred with this truth and so during his last five years in office, taxes were raised at least eleven times. And as this Republican president more than once bragged, domestic social spending went up. The former actor and Governor of California was elected in 1980 and 1984 to lead our nation because he was a likable man, an astute politician, and possessed good leadership traits. In his first three years in the White House, Reagan was something of an ideologue. He did what he thought was right (ideological pun semi-intended) regardless of whether it was liked or not. In the following five years, the First Lady, Nancy, and Republican moderates molded him into a PRAGMATIST so that he wouldn't alienate the American voters, thereby retaining his popularity and not jeopardizing House and Senate Republican re-elections, particularly those who hoped to ride his coattails.

The term "pragmatist" is flatteringly applied to a staunch Republican who is "tough but flexible" (a contradiction in terms) and therefore willing to compromise. A Democrat with a liberal agenda is NEVER called on by the media or the American people to COMPROMISE on a policy with a politician of conservative principles. A dyed-in-the-wool liberal Democrat in Washington, DC is helping to push the nation in a "progressive" direction and therefore doesn't need to compromise and surely isn't asked to be "pragmatic." A PRAGMATIST is always an elected Republican official who holds the line for a while on a conservative (i.e. capitalistic) policy that he or she knows is correct (cutting social spending and not raising taxes) but then capitulates to socio-political pressure for a quick fix (aka the expediency factor) to do just the opposite. That's when they become moderates. And a moderate's main mission is to "work with the Democrats" (translation: pass liberal legislation). Actual conservative legislation is to never be passed because it means LESS government, which isn't good because it diminishes a "fairer", benevolent command and control by the State.

Presidents Richard Nixon and Gerald Ford were both moderates. The same goes for George H.W. Bush and his first son. It was the younger Bush who made famous the term "compassionate conservatism." Actually, there is no such thing as "compassionate conservatism." It's an oxymoron. Or at least it is in an economic sense. The term is also a tactical modifier for "moderation." Presidential candidate George W. Bush knew, following a Democrat president (Clinton) that the electorate in the year 2000 would be hesitant to vote for a man perceived as a cold, heartless conservative and so he cleverly employed a safe-sounding modification. So, yes, this Republican candidate for president admits to being a conservative, but he's a COMPASSIONATE one. Kind of makes the medicine go down smoother, doesn't it? Bush was hoping that this gambit would help him win the year 2000 election and it worked.

Just as his immediate predecessor governed as a LIBERAL moderate, (though some would say that Clinton was a MODERATE liberal) Bush 43 did so as a conservative moderate. Many so-called moderates are actually just liberals who dislike the term "liberal." They become wolves in sheep's clothing and use "moderation" as a Trojan horse to push a progressive agenda and legislation. Actual moderates enjoy labeling themselves "conservative", e.g. "I consider myself to be a fiscal conservative", each of them will disingenuously boast. Doing so gives the moderate the pretense of having staunch integrity. Being thought of as a CONSERVATIVE by ones political peers, plus by the electorate, has a *gravitas* that being known as a "moderate" (read; "bland and submissive") just doesn't have. Liberal politicians at the nation's capital and the liberal media absolutely love moderate Republicans because moderates seek NUANCE. And nuance gives liberalism the opportunity for victory and redemption. In legislative debate and negotiations, the Democrat members realize that their moderate GOP colleagues will kick up a fuss, at first. But then later, the moderates will, albeit grudgingly, comply with the Democrats. And this is all fine and dandy with the liberal establishment. It was the moderate president, George H.W. Bush's economic adviser, Richard Darman, also a moderate, who got America's 41st CEO to renege on his famous 1988 pledge, "Read my lips, no new taxes." Much to the consternation of Republicans and to the malicious glee of Democrats, the elder Bush paid a heavy price for it when he lost his 1992 presidential re-election bid, largely because of this political transgression.

It was on the very same day (August 18th, 1988) as his "Read my lips..." that Bush Sr. made his second most famous quote, "I want a kinder and gentler nation." This was a repudiation of both Ronald Reagan's reputation and conservatism, itself. As a moderate, establishmentarian vice-president, Papa Bush, while campaigning for the White House, believed that it was incumbent on him to not just tacitly apologize for being associated with the present administration that he's been part of, but to reassure the country that, if elected as number 41, his next four years in the White House would be different than that of the 40th president. So, he wins the Presidency in 1988 and after almost four years in office as opposed to Reagan's eight, the voters proved Bush's prognostication true by rejecting him on Election Day November 3, 1992. Being a supposed conservative in the 1980s, Arizona Senator John McCain, in the following decades, became a moderate in order to spite conservatives who he thought wronged him and perhaps rub elbows with the donkey Party at Washington, DC social gatherings. From then on, he was affectionately referred to as a "maverick" by Democrats and the liberal media. Some on the right thought of McCain as being a NEOCON. A neocon or neoconservative, as the godfather of neo-conservatism, Irving Kristol, once famously declared, is a liberal mugged by reality. But McCain was never a liberal. In any case, a NEOCON is basically a moderate or a hawkish liberal.

The majority of Americans who are the least bit political prefer to think of themselves as "moderates," "centrists," or "middle-of-the-roaders." Those on the reactionary right and the radical left are inclined to think of them as being "cop-outs" or "fence-straddlers." Moderates enjoy the complacency of straddling the middle of the ideological spectrum. They offend no one. For them to take philosophical/ideological sides would be unfair to either side. Moderates probably figure that if they were to adopt a politically definitive stand, it wouldn't give ambiguity a chance. Nevertheless, they will disagree with liberals on more than just a couple of matters. For example, if all the Democrats in the House and Senate wanted the entire outside of the Whitehouse to be painted with brown, orange, green and purple stripes, every moderate Republican would put his or her foot down and shout a big, unequivocal "NO" to the Dems plan to paint the White House with purple stripes. Plus, if liberals wanted our nation's capital to raise taxes on all Americans by 25 percent, moderates would absolutely take issue with this too. They think that taxes should be raised on all Americans by 23 percent. That's all! Not one percentage more. And these moderates aren't going to budge (probably not). Alas, like a communist is just a socialist in a hurry and a liberal is just a socialist in a closet, a moderate is just a liberal who drags his feet on the road to socialism.

The centrist establishmentarian GOP's main goal is to amenably cross the aisle and shake hands and compromise with the liberal Democrats. The main goal of the latter is to make chumps out of the centrist establishmentarian GOP. Moderate Republican politicians are reluctant to criticize the Democratic Party but not at all hesitant to rebuke their own Party (they're weary of the opinions of independent voters). Unlike staunch conservatives, moderates accept the premise of liberalism. With a moderate GOP president, the foundation of liberalism remains strong. He or she will merely attempt to fine-tune liberal legislation, but a hard-line conservative president will try to kill it. Moderate Republicans are appreciated by the left-leaning media because they, the moderates, lack the intellectual dynamism to expose the innate dishonesty of liberalism. Abraham Lincoln's party is to be portrayed as having been "hijacked by the right" if the GOP isn't led by the ideologically mundane and ineffectual. Liberals like moderates because moderates rarely actually disagree with them. And why should they disagree, since moderation is not the opposite of liberalism. With such centrist Republicans, liberals don't have to resort to making intelligent arguments. Unlike the logic and truth of conservatism, the moderate mentality is no threat to the liberal left. And it's not just the media who wants the GOP to be dominated and controlled by moderates, but the American people in general, over the long run. This way, the ratcheting up of the nanny state will continue to get little, if any, real resistance. Moderation is just stealth progressivism flying in under the radar. But the country's electorate likes to think of MODERATION as the "wise, common-sense middle" only because outright liberalism is too darn conspicuous.

Liberals are very fond of moderate politicians even though moderate politicians are rather conservative in their approach to implimenting liberalism. Democrats desire to be in power at our nation's capitol. But RINOs (Republicans in Name Only) would rather be the minority opposition party. This way, they consequently avoid being detested and vilified by the liberal media and society in general because their Grand Old Party isn't in power and so cannot be held accountable if things go wrong, which could diminish their likability. The GOP middle-of-the-roaders feel much more politically comfortable battling liberal Democrats when the latter holds power. Sure, liberal bills are indeed to be passed and liberal legislation enacted, but the moderates are content in the knowledge that they are likely to retain their seats in the general election. This is because the electorate has expressed a noticeable lack of enthusiasm for manifest Constitutionalism, which moderates don't particularly care for either. It is moderate Republican lawmakers, not libertarian conservatives, who join with Democrats in supporting crony capitalism. And it is the American people who would rather have centrist GOP politicians at the Federal level than have hard-line libertarian conservatives there. The noted establishment Republicans may accept some hardcore conservative solutions, but only if they're not going to be controversial and dispiriting. What the establishment GOP in Washington really wants is moderation that will simply be labeled "conservatism." They will enact this facade for the purpose of placating the rigid liberty-pushing right-wing. Though, there ARE many Republicans who recognize that our country needs ACTUAL conservative government (deeds, not words) and not MODERATION. Said ideological/political centrism is appreciated by the establishment because it tacitly props up liberalism. It gives liberalism at least a modicum of plausibility, which is conducive to any success that liberalism has. In the opinions of most Americans who are at all political, the base of the Democratic Party is SUPPOSED to be LIBERAL, but the base of the Republican Party is SUPPOSED to be MODERATE. As a consequence of this happening, a centrist GOP majority will marginalize conservatism and give MODERATION the pretense of being the main rival of progressive Democrats, thus solidifying the actions of the latter. Hence, liberalism can thrive while appearing to have some resistance and eventually winning any battle that it has with moderates. Doing so helps to legitimize the progressive agenda. But especially, when moderation ultimately capitulates to liberalism, the centrist country club GOP will be complicit in any damage to America that liberalism has done. This is sure to give Democrats and their goal the cover that they're looking for.

Have you ever noticed that when an ostensibly right-leaning president gets the opportunity to choose an individual for the Supreme Court, liberals and Democratic politicians call on him to nominate a.....moderate, not a liberal? Why is this? It's because they know that the president will not knowingly pick a liberal and that a nominally moderate justice will, most of the time, turn left. This is progressivism's surreptitous way of stopping a Constitutional conservative from getting on the Supreme Court and instead electing some wimpy RINO (I wasn't thinking of John Roberts, honest, you gotta believe me). When George W. was president number 43, the Democrats, upon learning about a Supreme Court opening for a new judge, said that they wanted Bush to nominate a moderate because, like a jet plane, the highest court in the land "needs two wings to fly" (as in right-wing and left-wing). Frankly, that's a lousy metaphor. But what any curious person should ask is; if the Supreme Court were to be gifted with nine strict Constitutionalist conservatives, what's wrong with that? The liberal/left will retort, "No, that's too extreme." Gee, that's right. Not only is totally abiding by the Constitution "too extreme" but doing so will undoubtedly be considered un-Constitutional. Okay, the author will withdraw the question. Then I'll ask those within the port side of politics the following: (1) Would they also be AGAINST every Supreme Court judge being a solid liberal? No moderates and no conservatives. If so... why? (2) If Democrats and progressives are indeed in favor of having nine liberal justices on our nation's highest court, then forget the hypocrisy for the moment—on what basis can they claim that "it needs two wings to fly"? Why does it? (3) Will nine unabashed liberals on the Supreme Court make it "too extreme" or deleterious to our nation? If so, then how? Incidentally, if having nine rigid Constitutionalists on the Supreme Court makes the high court *too extreme*, doesn't that render the Constitution itself TOO EXTREME?

And what, pray tell, does "extreme" mean? Someone who is a VEGAN is believed by most of us to have a rather "extreme" diet. And it really is extreme. It's certainly a bizarre and somewhat uncommon life-style. But is it a wrong way to eat and live? Is a person who is a VEGAN in bad health? Or is he or she more likely to be in good health? Would it be too "extreme" or wrong for an individual with high blood sugar to drastically cut down on sugar and carbohydrate intake? "Extremism" is an adjective that has been abused to the point of meaninglessness. Calvin Coolidge was the president from 1923 to 1929. It was his auster-ity measures and pro-capitalism disposition which begat the economic dynamism of the Roaring Twenties. President Coolidge is considered to be "extremist." When he ran for the presidency in 1980, Ronald Reagan was thought of as an "extremist." Ditto, Jesse Helms who, as the sena-tor from North Carolina, had a 100 percent conservative voting record. It was Helms, and not John McCain, who was the real MAVERICK. Presently, an "extremist" is thought of as a conservative who merely adheres to conservatism and doesn't concede to liberal desires and demands like "conservatives" did in the past.

As the senator from Illinois, Barack Obama had a 100 percent liberal voting record. And as president, he was more liberal than President Reagan was conservative. But the public views Obama to a far lesser degree as an "extremist" than they do the famous B-movie actor or the late North Carolina senator. Yes, America's 44th Commander-in-Chief was deemed by many to be a "radical," but this adjective has more of an overzealous, though impish and lovable connotation to it. Plus, "radical" implies being BOLD, UNIQUE, and EXCITING and is therefore a word that the common folk and romanticists on the far left, embrace. Whereas the term "extremist" is felt to be more of a vilifying, incriminating slur, which most Americans believe that the former community organizer doesn't deserve. To wit, if a conservative politician wanted to CUT total domestic social spending by, say, ten trillion dollars, the majority of the people would look upon that as being "extremism" in a right-wing (capitalistic) direction. But if a liberal lawmaker wanted to do the exact opposite – INCREASE domestic social spending by ten trillion dollars, would the average American also regard that as "extremism," only in a left-wing direction?

The answer is "no," because it's compassionate, beneficent, and progressive. Now, some progressive spending may be labeled as unnecessary or WASTEFUL (such as the $535 million for the Solyndra solar panel manufacturer bankruptcy), but they are never thought of as "EXTREME," because such social spending is at least intended to nurture society, and for that reason should not be considered malfeasant or deserving of public scorn. Besides, progressive policies have long been Washington, DC's modus operandi since the heyday of FDR. They are therefore expected and accepted. As long as an economic course of action mandates government expansion that is ostensibly for the American people's own good, then most of us will never call it "too extreme." The word "extremism" is to be defined and thought of as a political agenda or laws that are NOT contributive to the comforting aura of socialism. Thus, economic policies that promote and push SELF-responsibility and INDIVIDUALISM on able-bodied citizens are "threatening," "dangerous," and "divisive." While those that necessitate GOVERNMENT responsibility and collectivism are "reassuring," "civil," and "inclusive" and therefore, are not the slightest bit *extreme*. Because capitalism is freedom, it doesn't accomplish coercive public bonding for the sake of our society. In the not too distant future, since socialism will have the potential (at least whimsically) to be our rescuer, benefactor and best friend and will "bring us all closer together," it will be totally unjustified and insulting to slap an "extremism" label on it. Indeed, it will be conservative Republicans who won't embrace "moderation" that are to be branded as "too extreme" because they're rejecting socialistic incrementalism.

Divulging a provocative or controversial TRUTH that the liberal/left would rather the public didn't know about, is also to be regarded and denounced as "extremism." For example, the premier fellow traveler of the 1980s was California Congressman Ronald Dellums. His protégé is former Congresswoman Barbara Lee, who is an outright communist. But it would be EXTREMIST to divulge this fact and so I won't. But this extremist writer will now sum up this extremist essay by introducing author and lecturer, Dan Millman, to share with us his extremist views on MODERATION...."Moderation? It's mediocrity, fear, and confusion in disguise. It's the devil's reasonable deception. It's the wobbling compromise that makes no one happy. Moderation is for the bland, the apologetic, for the fence sitters of the world afraid to take a stand to live or to die. Moderation is lukewarm tea, the devil's own brew." Quite simply, moderation is just liberalism with a veneer of conservatism to make it look respectable.

CHAPTER 25

Please Give Aid to Gays

A FEW DECADES ago, a doctor asked a gathering of three hundred medical personnel, "If you had the partner of your dreams available sexually and you knew that person was HIV infected, would you have sex with him or her depending on a condom for protection? If so, raise your hand?" No one raised his or her hand. Questions: So many have stated that AIDS is not a "gay disease." Then why was every protest march for more-government-funding-to-stop-AIDS led and dominated by gay men? Have you, the reader, ever seen, read or heard about any prominent homosexual men chanting for our government to find a cure for heart disease, leukemia, or cerebral palsy? Also, why was it that, prevalent in the 1980s, giant quilts were knitted for AIDS victims but not for victims of cancer, even though the latter had killed millions more people than AIDS did? And most important, is it true that dropping the proverbial bar of soap in the men's shower room has been the number one cause of AIDS-related deaths for males in America?

Columnist Mona Charen hit the bulls-eye perfectly back in the 1980s, with her comments about the statistics showing that ninety percent of AIDS is caused by behavior: "Aids activists don't want us to dwell on these facts. They want us to believe that we are all equally at risk of contracting Aids so that our prejudice against gays and blacks and drug users won't affect our willingness to fund research and treatment. They believe that if enough money is allocated, it will result in a miracle cure for Aids so that the licentious days of wild gay bathhouses can resume."

And about the fates of former pro basketball player Magic Johnson, the late tennis player Arthur Ashe, Hollywood actor Rock Hudson, and others, Charen writes, "Aids activists want every private tragedy caused by Aids to become a public spectacle. In the first place, it helps the fund drive. But especially, it makes society at large share in the blame, and Aids activists think that's only due, since the suffering of Aids victims is society's fault." Of the Americans who have contacted HIV since the early 1980s, two-thirds of them are gay men.

Beginning in the year 1986, government funding for AIDS treatment and research skyrocketed 170 percent (far more than that of cancer research) to about two billion dollars in 1992. But in that same year the homosexual/AIDS lobby expressed hatred of then-President George H.W. Bush and suggested that he didn't care about people dying from AIDS. But did they exhibit these same sentiments in election year 1996, against Bill Clinton? The answer is "no," or not nearly as much. And that's because President Clinton leaned to the left and therefore did not deserve their wrath, particularly with limited-government Republicans trying to retake the White House in said year. Smaller government, self-responsibility-espousing conservative lawmakers will not be as receptive to the gay lobby's grievances, let alone alleviate them. Furthermore, a Democratic administration's ostensible drift toward a bigger government-run society is considered just and virtuous compensation for NOT finding a cure for AIDS. In a nutshell, the AIDS/homosexual lobby is just another left-wing group screaming for socialism. With the exception of the Log Cabin Republicans, all AIDS/gay rights organizations lean to the left. A country going in a socialistic/secularist direction would considerably diminish *morality*, which largely disapproves of homosexuality. Secularism, being the enemy of "judgmental" Christianity, is the best friend of the gay rights lobby. Plus, a centralized government is more likely to subsidize their mainly hedonistic, "alternative" lifestyle. Though, homosexuality was actually ILLEGAL in the 1960s and 1970s in a country with a thoroughly left-wing socio-political system (Cuba), most American gay organizations have never denounced the island nation for their 1960-1979 law and never will. Now why do you think that is? In any case, if a cure were found for AIDS during a Democratic administration, that would only be icing on the cake. AIDS victims are the new addition to the list of political pawns (with blacks, Latinos, women, and the poor) to be exploited by the left in their "struggle" for a "more just, compassionate, equal, and especially *non-judgmental* way of life for our democracy." (Yes, it's the "S" word).

A young man who has had a lisp ever since he was a little boy and exhibits a gait that consists of quick, baby steps, is typically more likely to die from AIDS than any other American. But a lesbian of any age will never die from AIDS no matter how straight her figure or how short her hair is. Nonetheless, "Gay pride advocates applaud the courage of those who "come out" discovering their true nature as homosexuals after many years of heterosexual experience. But enlightened opinion denies a similar possibility of change in the other direction, deriding anyone who claims straight orientation after even the briefest interlude of homosexual behavior and insisting that they are phony and self-deluding. By this logic, heterosexual orientation among those with past gay relationships is always the product of repression and denial, but homosexual commitment after a straight background is invariably natural and healthy." To add to this spot-on analysis by author and political commentator Michael Medved, if a famous or prominent gay man wants to remain in the closet, it won't be the moralistic right that "outs" him, but the sophomoric left. To progressivism, the personal IS political.

Perhaps gay men and lesbians will one day accept that homosexuality should never be part of the norm simply because it is not the norm. This "alternative" lifestyle should be designated as just that. Like the porn industry, there is a place in a free America for it. But its *lesbigay* organizations and gathering places do not belong on suburban Main Street right next door to the schools and houses of worship. There is nothing detrimental to the homosexual lifestyle by remaining on the fringe of society. President Bill Clinton's signing of "Don't Ask, Don't Tell" into law during his administration was darn good policy. It allowed gay men and gay women to make a career out of serving in the military while quietly retaining their "sexual orientation" off-base. This "none of your business" legislation was advantageous to the morale and comradeship that military units need, just like it's conducive to the camaraderie within the Boy Scouts.

Before this writer goes any further, let me just point out that I think all homosexuals in our country are un-American and at least slightly retarded......No, no, I'm just joking! I sincerely DO NOT believe that they are un-American. And I'm not some knuckle-dragging, right-winger who thinks that all gay men and lesbians should be rounded up and deported. That's dumb. Where would they go? Antarctica is too cold, and all the other countries won't take them. But contrary to what many gay/left organizations proclaim, homosexuals are not 10 percent of our nation's population. They're a little bit less than 2 percent of it. A lot of gays think that the term "homo," which is short for "homosexual," is offensive and want the straight community to stop saying it. Conversely, the noted two syllable word does not dissuade gays from using the epithet "homophobic" to label people who they believe disapprove of their sexual lifestyle. In addition, *phobia* means "fear of." Fear of what? Homos, that's what! MEMO to the "QUEER" leadership in America: Immediately replace the term "homophobia" with "gayphobia." Followers of QUEER theory and students of QUEER studies will undoubtedly support this change.

It is not religious conservatives that want to "impose their beliefs" on the gay lifestyle but vice versa. Many proponents of the left-wing/gay agenda cry "homophobia" hoping to shame heterosexuals into relinquishing our centuries-old Judeo-Christian beliefs. These progressive activists try to malign and guilt-trip straight society into assimilating homosexuality into the mainstream, by portraying the latter's opposition to them as "hatred." Heterosexual resistance to homosexuals is NOT *hatred* of them but it IS dislike and non-acceptance of their socio-political pursuits. Gay men and lesbians would do well to ponder the following analogy: Do most black members in BLACKS ONLY student clubs at American universities HATE white people? But left-leaning gays utilize the term "hate" because it usually connotes a *malicious irrationality* and thus becomes more effective in indicting straight America. For progressive homosexuals to correctly intone that heterosexual society doesn't personally hate them is to abstain from the demonization of heterosexual society. But no can do, because if straight citizens didn't hate but merely disapproved and rejected the homosexual subculture as being a fundamental part of our largely Christian nation, then that would become a negative reflection on the gay rights agenda and NOT on the non-compliant straight community.

LESSON: Firstly, if you, the reader, are not a female, and a good-looking one, then pretend (for instructional purposes only) that you are. If the reader were in the women's locker room at a college or excercise facility, would it be okay with you to take a shower right next to a mincing MALE that you knew for a FACT, was one hundred percent homosexual? If not, why not? What's he going to do? Nancy-boy isn't going to ogle or stare at you, and why should he? The dude is light in the loafers, not a drooling sex fiend. He's not going to hit on you or ask you for a date. This lifelong friend of Dorothy isn't going to try to molest or rape you. If anything, you and the other women in the shower room would be more likely to rape him. And depending on what your definition of RAPE is, he might enjoy it.

In fact, the fellow is so gay, that if the two of you were stranded on an island in the middle of the ocean, he'd rather have sex with a crustacean (provided that it didn't have crabs) then to have sex with you. The guy is so "queer" that he makes the president of the Judy Garland Fan Club seem like, well, a homophobe. You'll reply, "But he's still a man and I'd feel uncomfortable with him seeing me naked." As this author previously imparted, why in God's name would he want to eyeball a pretty thing like you? And yes, the man has his sight and so he will fortuitously see you in the nude. So what's the problem? The women in the shower room are also not blind and they too, will see you naked. In fact, as an attractive heterosexual lady, you'd probably have very little if any problem taking a shower between two *out-of-the-closet* lesbians. How come? Who's more likely to accost you in the women's locker room or do something lascivious that you wouldn't like -- a skinny, effeminate gay man or a couple of fat dykes named Gertrude and Butch?

The reasoning of this parable is analogous to the time-honored propriety of Americans and their response to the socio-political agenda of leftist-homosexual rights organizations. They're both a case of TRADITION vs. LOGIC. The secularist left supports "gay rights" not so much because they're for equal rights. They are. But it's mostly because "gay rights" sticks its thumb in the eye of and erodes traditionalism. If the gay-rights movement thinks that the Federal government should consecrate same-sex marriage, then shouldn't the former also support a father's *"right "* to get married to his own daughter? The moral trajectory of our republic has always been one of Judeo-Christian values ever since our Founding Fathers established the Constitution. For this matter and for the future of our country, American TRADITIONALISM should win over LOGIC. In San Francisco, the city where men are men and the women are lonely, there is a club called the Gay Men's Chorus. Are straight men allowed to join this club? If not, why not? Straight society has Main Street USA and gay society has Castro Street, San Francisco. Long may they both live, prosper, and be happy within their separate cultures and lifestyles.

CHAPTER **26**

Opinionated Bits and Pieces Part 6

THERE IS NO truth to the rumor that a black woman in Chicago named her newborn twin daughters Ebony and Ebola.

For decades, the American people have been clamoring for "affordable" health care. Is a person who is single and in excellent shape, with no dependents, and making $40,000 a year, earning enough money to have *affordable* health care? And who's to say claim that this person's health will negatively affect his or her ability to pay for it? What about a man who is making $130,000 a year but with a wife and three children? Can he keep up with, say, $450 monthly health care payments among his other expenses? If he can't, why should that be the taxpayers' problem? Should our perpetually wise and fiscally prudent Federal government have the right to dictate what the hospitals can charge their patients? If the American people can't or won't stipulate what precise cost would be "affordable" to EVERY citizen, then it is perfectly reasonable for one to assume that the term "affordable health care" is just a subtle and surreptitious way of saying that they want FREE health care. But as the satirist P.J. O'Rourke famously stated, "If you think health care is expensive now, wait until you see what it costs when it's free."

In the year 2014, our commander-in-chief, Barack Obama, broke the law by trading five of the most dangerous and top-ranking terrorists-turned-prisoners at Gitmo, for traitorous and hyper-sensitive flake, Army

Sergeant Bowe Bergdahl. This action was taken under the guise of "not leaving our military personnel on the field, we bring them home." The 44th president said that he makes no apology for producing the release of an American soldier. Many Americans agreed with his decision. But they and Obama also believe that the United States SHOULD NOT and WILL NOT pay ransom to get back an American who is being held hostage in another country. What this means is that if the Taliban, who had Bergdahl as a prisoner, demanded fifty dollars (which does constitute RANSOM) from the US government, then the president and his supporters would tell the Taliban "no" because "America does not pay ransom." So here's the question for the reader to answer: Which would have been more advantageous for, and especially, the least detrimental to, the United States in the long run? The USA trading five captured barbarian, high-command terrorists for Army deserter and useless space cadet Bowe Bergdahl, or getting the latter back for fifty bucks and the five hateful but potentially informative terrorists remain in our prison at Guantanamo Bay?

No matter what your race is or politics are, whenever you hear the words "peaceful protest" in the news, it usually means "white people." However, when the reader finds out that there was a RIOT, you're more than likely thinking "black people," and correctly so. American blacks are more likely to violently EXPLOIT a demonstration over a perceived injustice. White liberals, on the other hand, are apt to demonstrate by walking around in circles holding picket signs, though liberals have also been known to walk around in circles WITHOUT holding picket signs.

Liberals delight in declaring that we had a robust economy during Bill Clinton's presidency. Yes, and the sun rises in the morning because the rooster crows. The progressive left would like the American people to believe that because there was a Democrat in the White House (1993-2001) that America's economic system was firing on all cylinders ostensibly because of liberalism. What the Democrats don't want the electorate to know is that those were prosperous times because Newt Gingrich and the Republican Party took over the House in 1994 and cut taxes and spending. But then the noted two fiscally conservative actions are anathema to liberals, who would like to think that proper "governing" mandates Washington, DC to MANAGE and CONTROL the marketplace.

We want what we CAN'T have and don't want what we CAN have. By doing this, we stave off potential disappointment and/or rejection. As a consequence, we stop the aforementioned two feelings from happening before we have to deal with the heartache of experiencing them.

Have you ever noticed that it's NEVER liberals and always conservatives or "those Republican types" who are accused of "wrapping themselves in the flag"? This is because Old Glory symbolizes *capitalism*, which in turn, denotes *freedom*. People who vote Democrat do not associate socio-political *virtue* and *decency* with freedom but with ever-expanding, benevolent GOVERNMENT. However, they do compensate for this attitude by associating the American flag and Independence Day with the GOP. So, in the end, all is fair and well.

And speaking of "fair" what is often overlooked is the liberal's use of the term. When the aforementioned say that they want "fairness" in governmental policies, it doesn't mean that they desire *neutrality* or *non-favoritism*. "Fairness," progressivism believes, is supposed to be rectifying the lowly little guys' lot in life. "Fairness," in essence, is SUPPOSED TO BE taking sides. Likewise, in a professional football game, the referee needs to root for and favor the underdog team that's losing by a score of 57 to 0 in order for him to be "fair." He should call no penalties on the losing team and wrongly call lots of penalties on the winning team for the aim of helping the losing team catch up. *Dishonesty* is the essential means that today's liberal-left employs so that they can achieve *the end* (equity). It's only fair.

The Ku Klux Klan is a non-partisan, non-ideological social group with an animosity toward black people. They are not on the political right, nor on the political left. But the left tries to portray the KKK as a "right-wing" organization because *conservatism*, the leftists either thinks or wants everybody else to think, doesn't "side with nor try to help" American blacks. Hence, right-wingers, similar to the Klan, aren't sociologically *"supporters of black society"* like progressives are presumed to be. The left is just trying to demonize and stigmatize the proponents of socio-economic freedom (the right) by associating said conservatives with the Ku Klux Klan because the latter two share a demeanor that doesn't propitiate black folks. But the Klan is actually more like the liberal left—they're obsessed with race. In any event, our citizens who wear pointed white sheets over their heads never get deep into discussions about the philosophical and economic liberty-based virtues of John Locke, Adam Smith and Milton Friedman. They downright couldn't care less about laissez-faire doctrine....that is, if they ever heard of it. The KKK has complained about black people. They have NOT complained about black helicopters.

If a conservative tells an outright boldface lie, the far left really won't detest him that much, if at all. They will even "understand" his prerogative to lie and practically respect and like him for it. This is because the far left themselves, are dedicated liars and can't really blame the conservative for employing a stratagem (lying) that has long been their own modus operandi. So, it's not any lying done by conservatives that progressives don't like; quite the contrary, it is conservatives speaking the truth that they can't stand. It's logic-fortified veracity that gets the far left seething. Like the ends justify the means, lying helps the socialist cause.

Many, if not most Americans are of the mindset that the United States economy is one large pie, not an infinitive number of pies, and that we're all supposed to share in that one large theoretical dish. But that the wealthy one percent is hogging seven-eighths of the dish of pie while the rest of us have to squabble over the one-eighth piece. We, as a nation, don't mind sports superstars, millionaire recording artists and sundry celebrities making $70 million in just two years, because they really are admiringly special, uniquely talented, obviously *superior,* not to mention adored by the masses, and for those reasons, deserve to be placed on a pedestal. For example, let's say that there's a beloved American female pop singer who's worth more than 800 million dollars. Most of her fans, because they adulate the noted entertainer, will

NOT desire for the government to confiscate more of the star's money. This, especially if they find out that she's a liberal. Though, our glorious State enacting a punitive tax on wealthy conservative celebrities will likely be embraced by the singer/idol's devotees. But it's the bosses of Big Businesses who make $7 million a year that receive our wrath because they're one of us humble, plain and ordinary, forty-work-hours-a-week, NON-famous common folk. Americans resent and dislike ultra-successful business owners who supply Americans with jobs and an income. We bite the hands that feed us and virtually worship those who merely entertain us.

In late 1964, President Lyndon Johnson had the American people (via taxation and redistribution) make a gigantic "investment" called "The Great Society," and after five decades this "investment" turned out to be devastatingly bad for black society. Nevertheless, prominent black Democrats constantly label domestic social spending *as* "investments." They would be loath to explain the difference between the term "investments" and "throwing money at the problem." But the term is not so much a euphemism as it is a misnomer meant to delude the public. A real INVESTMENT is something that a shareholder pays money into in order to reap dividends in the future. But there are no dividends for taxpayers when they "invest" their hard-earned income into EBT cards for husbandless welfare queens who are fond of referring to themselves as "the breadwinner of the family."

If communism is the opposite of Nazism, as the far left would like to think it is, then why, as seen on film of communist countries' parades in the past, do their soldiers always march in Nazi goosestep fashion? One would think that communism's supposedly ANTI-Nazism "leaders" would have put a stop to their own soldiers' goosestep marching immediately after it started.

Speaking of communism, yours truly was working in a store years ago when I was approached by a customer who initiated a chat with me that quickly segued into politics. At first perplexed, I figured that the man was undoubtedly an ideologue who just loved to talk, albeit with a political chip on his shoulder. Anyway, in our short conversation, the gentleman lamented that the US Post Office was one of the last vestiges of socialism (he was incorrect, the Post Office is not taxpayer funded) in our country and mentioned that the US military was also a bastion of socialism. The customer conveyed to me through the lingo he used that he was a communist. I asked him if his politics were in line with that of Gus Hall, the leader of the Communist Party, USA at that time. The guy confirmed that they were indeed and told this store clerk that he was surprised that I knew about Gus Hall when very few other people did. Curiously, he asked what the future author's name is and I told him. This fellow radical (only in a different ideological direction) said that he read one of my political articles in the town newspaper and that he "blasted" me in his write-up response to it. Said left-wing individual took care of business and, like Elvis, left the building. A few days later, it dawned on yours truly that my "comrade" customer actually spoke the truth when he stated that the US military was a bastion of socialism. But for an entity whose mission is to invade exotic lands, find exotic people and kill them, the military OUGHT TO BE socialistic. There should be, and there is, the following of numerous strict rules and regulations, the obedience to government edicts, the same pay for all individuals of the same rank, plus conformity in clothing and haircuts. It is a compliance that one has to abide by or he/she can be, and will be, punished. For this, military members will have jobs from which they can never be laid off, receive "free" housing, receive a "free" triad of square meals a day, receive a "free" clothing (uniform) allowance, and receive a free prostitute in every barracks on weekends with a free visit to the on-base infirmary the following Monday.

Those who have stated that there is no voter fraud in the United States are liars who always vote Democrat. Bearing in mind that obtaining an identification card costs nothing and is simple to do, there are millions of disdainful people in our country who object to being required to possess the noted verification document and that's because it would be more difficult for them to cheat. For young people to not have a photo ID would allow those of them who are underaged, to illegally vote. The same goes for a person who isn't a bona fide U.S. citizen. Plus, someone without an ID could surreptitiously vote multiple times. This must be the case, or the objectors (Democrats) would also take it as a personal insult that someone has to show identification in order to cash a check, get a job, enter a nightclub, check into a hotel, buy liquor, or board a jet airliner. But they don't object to the aforementioned six in the slightest bit. How come? Plus, if it's racist (*unfair*) to insist that black Americans obtain something (ID) that's FREE and EASY to get, then isn't it also racist to comply white Americans to do likewise? Or does the reader contend that treating blacks and whites the same would be racist?

Liberals always accuse conservatives of being JUDGMENTAL. Are liberals not being "judgmental" when they make that accusation? Aren't these left-leaning citizens being "judgmental," not to mention dishonest, when they say that conservatives hate the poor, that the GOP has declared war on women and "wants to impose their morality on everybody else?" Any person, no matter what their politics, is being "judgmental" if he or she verbally expresses their opinion about the behavior or actions of another. If no one were to be JUDGMENTAL, then nobody would be corrected on their perceived-to-be-wrong conduct, nor receive constructive criticism. What should matter is whether the "judgmental" statement that's being spoken is true. But the one deal that the entire liberal/left WILL NOT go along with is if they stop supporting government subsidy of dubious behavior (such as abortions or having illegitimate children) then the conservative right will stop being JUDGMENTAL.

In 2007, then Senator Barack Obama called for the Bush administration to stop spying on the American people. Six years later, the Obama administration was caught spying on the American people. But President Obama was in luck; he's a Democrat. The majority of the nation's citizens consider it more egregious when a Republican administration is spying on us than when a Democrat administration does. This is because a White House under the GOP isn't as much "for the common man" as are the Democrats. Mr. Obama spying on us was not a good thing, but because he's a Democrat, it also couldn't be that bad.

If a Republican White House is spying on the people, it will be thought of as an attempt to thwart the democratic desires and will of the humble, ordinary citizen. But if a Democrat President spies on the people, although disliked, the citizens figure that it's ostensibly for their own good. This same reasoning applies to an administration that is being SECRETIVE. Since a liberal Democrat's agenda, unlike a Republican's, is thought to be egalitarian, caring, and well-intentioned to begin with, the secrecy of or spying by the Democrats isn't considered to be as despicable or deplorable. Hence, it's the reason for the double-standard.

Margaret Thatcher once famously said, "The problem with socialism is that you eventually run out of other people's money." To augment this adage by the late Prime Minister of England: With socialism, if everybody is responsible for everybody, in good time, nobody will be responsible for anybody!

President Obama allegedly unfroze billions of dollars in Iranian assets and sent $400 million in cash on pallets to the Iranian government. He wasted $830 billion on what was to be a redistribution-to-the-needy stimulus package where the allocations instead went mostly to special interest groups. Our 44th Commander in Chief "invested" $535 million in the infamous money-losing Solyndra scandal. But the good news is that his ardent supporters were and still are very much elated that their beloved president DIDN'T use all this funding (over three quarters of a $trillion dollars) to build homes for the working poor, buy food for the hungry, repair roads and bridges for the nation, and finance other essentials. Nevertheless, the intended recipients of liberal do-goodism will continue to look up to progressive politicians even when the latter doesn't deliver on their promises. The mere symbolism of liberalism will suffice.

In the summer of 2011, New York Congressman Anthony Weiner was forced to resign from office after it was revealed that the Democrat, a married man, was *sexting* explicit pictures of his underwear-clad groin, via a mobile phone, to women. Directly after his departure, Weiner publicly confessed that he was "deeply ashamed" of himself. Then two years later, in his candidacy for New York City mayor, Mr. Weiner once again was compelled to admit that he was still sexting photos of his package to various females. The problem with the former representative from the Congressional 9th district, to be frank, is that he can't seem to stay away from his last name. Right in the middle of his race for mayor, which the man surely wasn't going to win, Weiner should have pulled out. His immediate withdrawal wouldn't have been that hard. But perhaps one day, the good people of Brooklyn will honor Weiner by having a statue of him erected. Provided that the ex-politician cleans up his act, of course!

Those who support Obamacare will not call out nor criticize the LIBERALS who are trying to escape from it; thereby proving the folly of said Affordable Care Act and the inherent dishonesty of its supporters. Similarly, most Republican politicians are loath to be asked, "If you repeal Obamacare like you say you want to, what are you going to put in its place?" The GOP lawmaker can't reply, "Nothing," because this office- holder knows darn well that the electorate will demand another type of reassuring government program (it can't be via the free-market or the people will reject it---too risky) to take the place of the Affordable Care Act. If the noted politician agrees to the demand, then it will only embolden the American voters to clamor for more legislation and new departments to plug up the financial areas where "the people who are trying to make a living are NOT GETTING BY."

Riddle: What's the difference between a conservative and a liberal? Answer: Only the former will agree that Nazism, communism, fascism, socialism, and apartheid are ALL unjust, oppressive, and morally and economically wrong. If that particular "conservative" does NOT agree, then he or she is actually no conservative. But what everyone, no matter what their politics are, should realize is that nobody in the history of the world has ever lived under the INTENTIONS of the five aforementioned socio-political systems; only under the REALITY of them. But to the liberal/left, intentions are supposed to supersede truth/reality. The further one leans to the left, the more sincere, dogmatic and determined one becomes when that person says or thinks that truth/reality doesn't matter.

Conservative political talk shows have long dominated talk radio. This is because conservatism is thought-provoking and offers numerous facets of logic, insight, and ideological validation which make it so appealing to the listener. Liberal radio talk shows don't do as well because they're mostly about feelings and emotion, which other media outlets provide. The left calls conservative opinion broadcasts "hate radio" because these broadcasters tell the truth and take political positions that are not conducive to socialistic thought and desires. Indeed, the libertarian conservative adage, "Truth is treason in the empire of lies" would aptly apply to living under authoritarian socialism.

Presently, one of the main differences between black Americans and white Americans is that the former will not apologize for their skin color.

Have you ever noticed that of the worriers who have been vocal about climate change, 90 percent of them do not and will not give their opinion on what PRECISELY should be done about it? He or she will invariably respond, "Well, I'm not a scientist or expert." But you don't need to be either one in order to present your idea on what YOU THINK should be done about it, stupid! The author of this book supports all the solutions to the wellness of this planet that the environmentalists want as long these solutions do not include government control of the people nor the diminishing of free enterprise, which probably means that I don't support anything that the environmentalists want. Incidentally, most of those on the environmental left don't really give a damn about the human feces (I mean these last two words LITERALLY, not figuratively) lying in the streets of San Francisco and Los Angeles.

If certain American citizens want to cause envy, resentment, and hatred of one racial group toward another and potentially provoke a nationwide race riot, all they have to do is get our leaders in Washington, DC to pass a law that favors one racial group over another. It is governmental neutrality and individualism that actually unites us, but governmental favortism and collectivism that divides us.

It never ceases to amaze this writer that millions of appallingly ignorant liberal and moderate citizens continue to call on our politicians in Washington, DC to make life better for them. They want the politicians to create millions of jobs by passing a bunch of papers (legislation to make employers provide us with work) for the president to sign. What this undoubtedly means is that if the politicians produce, not just *a few*, but A WHOLE BUNCH of papers to sign, it will create millions of jobs. The people, who usually vote Democrat, want our politicians to find alternatives to oil and coal. They want the politicians to eradicate poverty, build homes for all, put an end to suffering, provide everybody with free health care, and force the trains to run on time. But someone has to tell these Americans that our politicians at the nation's capital already have their hands full working on a cure for cancer, among other diseases. Do continue to give our politicians the veneration and aggrandizement that they deserve, but please also give the politicians more time; they're only human.

Some progressive labor unions of America are, for the most part, against the World Trade Organization (WTO), the North Atlantic Free Trade Agreement (NAFTA) and the Trans-Pacific Partnership (TPP). The leaders and the rank and file of these left-leaning unions think that the WTO and the two noted trade agreements will slow down American economic growth, decrease domestic wages, and induce our jobs to go to other countries. The noted labor unions are profoundly correct. Workers of the nation, unite! You have nothing to lose but your livelihood.

In their race for the 2016 presidency, Donald Trump was perceived as being bombastic, a braggart, a bully and a billionaire. Hillary Clinton had the reputation of being corrupt, dishonest, and untrustworthy. But, in an opinion poll taken five weeks before the November election, the Donald LOST to the Hildabeast by a score of 31 percent to 35 percent for being more honest and trustworthy. That's odd. Why does she get these better poll numbers, particularly taking in the fact that the former Secretary of State was infamous for being a liar? It's because the citizens who took this poll were thinking in terms of their socio-economic safety net. Hillary Clinton (liberalism) represents government-based security and reassurance. Donald Trump, who is far more conservative (liberty-based self-responsibility) than the former, does not. Thus, the Democratic Party will always, in the long run, be thought of by the electorate as being more "honest" and "trustworthy" than the Republicans, particularly in *handling* (read: safeguarding) entitlements and domestic social spending that the American people would like to think is a birthright and that they can't live without.

A whole bunch of Americans partook of a remonstrance in the summer of 2017 and summer of 2020 over some old Confederate monuments (e.g. Robert E. Lee). The noted protesters knocked over and demolished many of the large statues, and their demands that others be taken down had been granted. Some of the white soldiers of the past, like the aforementioned general, had blacks for slaves in the 1800s and were against civil rights for black people. Well, let's say that it was a fact that Martin Luther King, Jr. owned slaves for five years in the 1950s, when slavery was ILLEGAL, unlike the early and mid-1800s. If you, the reader, support the removal of these historic monuments, would you also support the revoking of the national holiday named for the Reverend King after hearing that he had white people as slaves working for him? How about if MLK owned black people as slaves? If you dodge these two questions by not answering each with either a "yes" or "no", then you're a cowardly piece of shit and you know it.

The socialistic left *desires* taxation mostly for the purpose of redistribution. The capitalistic right, on the other hand, *accepts* taxation almost entirely for our judicial system, the defense of our country, and maintenance of infrastructure. Liberals constantly complain about "tax cuts for the rich" economic policies. When they do this, the liberals are really expressing their resentment concerning a certain policy's cutback on *redistribution* from the affluent to the "needy." Raising taxes for the purpose of *redistribution,* these progressives tell themselves, is how we "pay our bills" in order to be fiscally responsible. Republican politicians, on the other hand, are politically scared to death of informing the electorate that redistributing money from the rich to the poor and middle class is wrong, immoral and anti-capitalism and that they, the GOP, intend to stop it. Indeed, grandstanding so-called conservative lawmakers who brag about their desire to CUT TAXES will never say a disparaging word about *redistribution*, because they are well aware that even their own constituents are very fond of it. The income and wealth of each American individual is just that. It is NOT "the people's money." Allowing the wealthy to keep more of their own money isn't "socialism for the rich" and it is NOT "redistribution from the poor to the affluent." The aforementioned two slogans are just LIES that the liberal/left has gotten away with promulgating because they've never been publicly called on it by the Party of Coolidge and Reagan.

When Donald Trump was running for the 2016 presidency, more than a few times he declared to our nation's black citizens as to why they should vote for him, "What the hell do you have to lose?" Left-leaning black political leaders went ballistic in their response to the seemingly innocuous query. Why? It's because the former real estate mogul's rhetorical question was an indictment of *liberalism*, the long-established bread and butter strategy of black politics. Nevertheless, most of black America believes that it is alright for a Republican running for political office to go into a district of black citizens and speak to them. The caveat from a conservative standpoint is that it is of the utmost importance that the GOP candidate doesn't "REACH OUT" to black voters by becoming more liberal. But, au contraire, his message absolutely has to be a liberal one, palatable to the angst, and which blames society, racism and government being derelict in not doing its duty to help blacks. Otherwise, this Republican office-seeker has insulted black America and deserves their wrath.

People who vote Democrat would like to think of the Affordable Care Act (Obamacare) as insurance when it's merely another redistributionist welfare program. Liberals in Washington, DC and the media have told us that the Affordable Care Act, as one liberal editorial put it, "is not close to being perfect and needs major revisions." The aforementioned disingenuous progressives never tell us what these *revisions* are, and that's because they honestly don't have any revisions in mind. The initial plan of millions of Obamacare supporters was to implement it, then wait for somebody to fix Obamacare, then abandon it and finally, hope for the best. Although wishful-thinking always works, it didn't work this time. As of the year 2010, not one politician or journalist has told the nation how to make the ACA fiscally sustainable. Most polls say that the majority of Americans want to keep Obamacare and not have it repealed. Hence, even though Obamacare is structurally unsound, has financially damaged the lives of millions, and will NEVER work, we should keep it because it's righteous. This, most of society will agree on. Alas, once you give the American people heroin, you cannot then turn around and give them cold turkey.

Besides Nazism being anti-Semitic, the only other real problem that American communists honestly have with Nazism is that it's anti-minority, anti-little guy, anti-underdog.

Nancy Pelosi said that she wants technological devices like drones and robotic dogs for migration enforcement on the Southern border rather than construct a wall. The House Speaker would like us to think that it is America's lack of proper surveillance that is the problem. She also tried to appear worried about the drugs and guns coming across our border. But the octogenarian Congresswoman with the whopping fun bags is skirting the real issue. Said San Francisco politician attempted to make contraband the main subject when she was darn well aware that it's the caravans of miscreants and non-criminal poor illegal aliens, who are flooding America "looking for a better quality of life" (read: living off the US taxpayers) in a country that they really don't give a damn about, that is our real concern. It is the STOPPING, not the monitoring of unlawful immigrants, that is the utmost national problem. Lastly, if not Donald Trump, but Hillary Clinton were elected president in 2016 and stated that she wanted a southern border wall built, Ms. Pelosi would have endorsed it and would have NEVER called the wall "immoral," and she knows it.

If the Federal government ever takes total command and control of our society, which millions of Americans desire it do; somehow, someway, the Federal government will attain mystical and magical powers to solve problems that it couldn't and didn't solve before.

Famed folk-singer and political activist Pete Seeger was honored by the Kennedy Center in 1994, conferred the National Medal of Arts award the same year and was inducted into the Rock n' Roll Hall of Fame (???) in 1996. No explanation was given for the last one. But then to be fair to the late Mr. Seeger, no explanation was given for the previous two, either. The perpetually proletarian-dressed, head-tilted-upward-while-singing musician was a communist most of his life and a self-declared one in his last few decades on earth. The organizations who bestowed the three congratulatory acts upon Seeger undoubtedly knew that he was a communist. But what if the famous fellow travelling troubadour was, instead, a Nazi? Would he have been celebrated in the same noted manner? Absolutely not! But the difference is that, unlike Nazism, at least communism has good-hearted intentions and should be judged solely for that reason and not by its historical reality.

Upon hearing the statement, "From each according to his ability to each according to his needs," the majority of Americans will agree with it and will think that this sentence is in the Constitution and/or Bill of Rights, and if it isn't, then the statement ought to be, because its' very concept is so extremely attractive. Although they will later very likely be disappointed to find out where the famous slogan actually comes from, many if not most of our citizens would still desire it.

Republican Senator John McCain getting shot down by the Vietcong while riding in a plane during the 1965-1975 Vietnam war, was very heroic. And his being captured by the noted foe was even more heroic. The Arizona politician's subsequent torture by Vietnamese soldiers was also, of course, heroic. But I suppose that's all water under the bridge now. What really matters is that we call the late John McCain a national hero because he was a victim of the enemy's brutality and deserves at least a verbal token of our sympathy.

Today's political handlers have instructed their clients/candidates (Hillary Clinton, etc.) that just as they arrive at the podium to give their speech, to look out at the audience, smile and exclaim, "WOW!" as a reaction to the crowds' applause and cheering. Doing so doesn't just signal to the audience that the candidate appreciates their enthusiasm, but also conveys to those watching back home on TV that this concerned citizen seeking political office is "genuinely" flattered by how popular he or she is ("WOW!") and that the crowd's response will hopefully influence the television viewers to like and support this candidate. Just like back in high school, popularity breeds popularity. Well, in political races, a candidate's rousing reception and seeming likability within a throng of fans will convince the fence-sitting voters observing it on TV, to hop on the popularity bandwagon (no need to think about the issues) which in all likelihood, would transfer into votes.

Our former president, Barack Obama, engaged in some frivolity at Nelson Mandela's funeral. He was caught on film in December of 2013 taking a selfie with attractive Danish Prime Minister Helle Thorning-Schmidt, clearly enjoying the moment. That the president did this and kissed the hand of the pretty blonde is, in and of itself, no big deal. I mean, it's not like he was making out with her (Mr. Obama's wife, Michelle, was sitting right next to him). It was the occasion that magnified the incident. The subject is not so much the ex-president's behavior, but his adoring acolytes. Could you just imagine their histrionics if a white Republican president committed the exact same act? Black Americans and white liberals would have accused him of being at least insensitive if not racist for "dissing Nelson Mandela." To this, they would reply "Well, of course that white Republican president would diss Nelson because he (the white Republican) don't like black people." If that's the case, then what's Obama's excuse? What he did should be considered more flagrantly offensive because then-President Obama is also black, and to an extent, shared the late South African president's ideological philosophy. In any case, Nelson Mandela must have rolled over in his coffin. So now he shall surely rest in peace.

I don't mean to wax metaphorical (that's not true) but has anybody ever noticed that the toilets in government buildings are a lot more powerful at flushing than the toilets that are used in the privacy of one's own house, built by free enterprise for the homeowner? You, the reader, can now add your own metaphor like you know you're going to.

Liberalism must perpetuate itself in order to make up for the damage it has done. Similarly, the bigger and more powerfully deleterious that "responsible" government gets, the more the American people will call on government not to leave them to fend for themselves. If, in the near future, say year 2030, the Federal government makes life absolutely miserable for the American people through social engineering, our citizens will, quite naturally and immediately, call on government to fix the problem....."Everything is worse now than it was before. "Don't just stand there; government, do something!" they will anxiously implore. We, the American people, need to be guided. We need to be managed. We need to be marshaled. We need to be commanded. We need to be controlled. Having such courses of action are the only way that we can be rescued.

Lies and truths are the exact opposite of each other. But they do have something in common: they both tend to hurt the target they're aimed at—for example, someone that's telling lies about conservatism/capitalism or another telling the truth about liberalism/socialism. In both cases, the ends justify the malicious means.

Most Americans of any political stripe would agree that our nation's conservative citizens are more religious than and go to church more often than liberals do. But those on the port side of politics also need a diety to look up to. Observe what the Democratic Senator from New York, Charles Schumer, said three weeks after his party lost the November, 2014 election. "Democrats must embrace government. It's what we believe in; it's what unites the party." Plus, "If we run away from government, downplay it, or act as if we were embarrassed by its role, people won't vote for our pale version of the Republican view." It should be of no surprise that the New York Senator and his ideological counterpart on the west coast,

California Senator Barbara Boxer, will never admit that economic policies that lead to the slavery of socialism are no damn good. And that's due to the fact that the religion of both of them is Presbyterian.

It was Democrat presidents who got the United States into WWI, WWII, the Korean War, and the Vietnam War. But a public consensus would see it differently. If there was a poll taken and the American people were asked, "Who was the politician who was mostly responsible for getting us into the Vietnam War," there's an excellent chance that the majority of them would answer "Richard Nixon." Society unfairly associates the Republican Party with our nation getting into wars around the globe. Why? Well, it can't possibly be because of the aforementioned four biggest battles that America entered into during the twentieth century. It's because (1) the people associate Ronald Reagan's political Party with being more hawkish and patriotic and thus more likely to defend the sovereignty and national interest of America if they felt that our republic was being threatened. So, in a sense, the Republican Party IS "America," if you catch my drift. (2) This being the case, it will be correctly assumed that the GOP will want to spend more money on defense than the dovish Democrats will. As a consequence, the everyday citizen will resent it when these "war" expenditures don't go to domestic spending programs and "entitlements" like they believe it should have. Even if the Democrat Party entered our country into World War III, most of the public would still scapegoat Republicans as the WAR PARTY. The citizens' blatant dishonesty and blaming the GOP would be their way of getting back at them for not being the social spending Party, like the Democrats are. Incidently, the Constitution calls for the common defense of the nation. What that necessitates is that IF Washington, DC needed to spend FIVE trillion dollars a year (YES, THAT'S RIGHT!), every year for eternity on our military / defense in order to adequately protect our country, its sovereignty and America's interest around the world, then that, and no less, is precisely what our Federal government must do.

If the taxpayer doesn't want to be a HATER of immigrants, then you will have to be IN FAVOR of the government allowing untold millions of poor, uneducated illegal alien parasites to take advantage of the American citizenry. It's the least you could do for the noted invaders.

Has anybody ever noticed that all the punters and kickers in the National Football League are white? Well, it's because this entire sport organization is RACIST (e.g. all of their football fields are filled with WHITE lines and WHITE numbers but NO lines or numbers of COLOR) and so you can surely bet that their caucasion punters and kickers are WHITE nationalists and WHITE supremacists. This is a serious matter that needs to be investigated..

There are two types of radicals on the left, each with a different reason as to why they call conservatives "fascists." The IGNORANT soft radical erroneously conflates conservatism with fascism because he believes that the latter is the opposite of socialism. It's not the opposite, but conservatism is, hence their smearing of conservatism. On the other hand, the hardcore radical, (a communist or a socialist and communist sympathiser) is well aware that conservatism really isn't a relative of fascism and that it's actually just capitalism. But the hardcore radicals won't label the conservatives as capitalists because that doesn't disparage conservatism. However, branding the aforementioned capitalistic ideology as "fascism" would influence the naive, deceivable Americans to intuitively disagree with conservatism and then promptly disavow it. And so the soft radicals don't know what they're talking about and the hardcore radicals just flat out LIE when they try to associate conservatism with fascism.

The surreptitious view of contemporary liberals is that the expression "our democracy" is merely their code words for SOCIALISM, or any action or policy that takes our country in a socialistic direction. To the liberal/left, socialism is *democracy* perfected. When "democracy" rules, a State-mandated conformity follows, which subsequently begets the peoples' even stronger desire for more governmental edicts to rectify what THEIR "democracy" has done. A dictatorship is soon born. In the opinion of our citizens that mostly or always vote Democrat, electing a genuine DICTATOR really wouldn't be so bad as long as we're living under an ostensibly benevolent socialism. The "democratic process" (e.g. voting and state rights) in and of itself, is all well and fine. But all Americans, when speaking or writing, should replace the second word of the term *"our democracy"* with the word *"republic"*.....that is, if they want to keep it.

Evidently, some people believe that they need to be super-sensitive in order to find something trivial to get upset about. It is now considered to be politically incorrect and offensive to refer to the master bedroom as the "master bedroom" because of the racial and gender connotation of the word "master." In the not-too-distant future, the only time that an American citizen will be allowed to utter the word "master" is when that person addresses the Internal Revenue Service as such, after he or she was summonsed. Likewise, it may also become against the law for a white man (unless his name is Cheeta) to refer a banana republic named Zambia as... .a *banana republic*. And speaking of verbal political incorrectness, lately there's been a lot of hot air about global warming (sorry). Although, this writer has actually experienced global warming. One February, I was outside in bone-chilling fifteen-degree weather. And then in just five short months, the temperature shot up SEVENTY degrees. I kid you not!

Joe Biden's policies of destructive liberalism have caused monumental inflation due to trillions of dollars in profligate social spending. Even worse, was the 46th president's allowing of the Taliban to confiscate 85 billion dollar$ worth of American weapons in Afghanistan. And especially, in just two years, Biden permitted some SIX MILLION mostly impovershed, illiterate, illegal aliens (any person who calls them "asylum seekers" is a liar) cross over into the country thus damaging American sovereignty while causing much grief, despair and utter chaos among our citizens living near the southern border. Particularly harmful was the smuggling into this republic of more than seven tons of Fentanyl pills, causing over one hundred thousand American deaths. Nonetheless, our nation's cognitively-challenged Commander-in-Chief, with the superb support of the California Cackler (i.e. the vice-president), HAS made millions of progressive Americans insanely happy by implementing the infamous Clowerd/Piven strategy, nation-wide.

Hey, yours truly has come up with a humorous racial joke (don't worry, it's still legal to tell one) for the mirth and merriment of his readers. Here it is: What do you call a black man who is an advanced calculus professor, a neurosurgeon, or an astronomer? Answer: An Oreo cookie, an Uncle Tom or a white-acting handkerchief head....Now, most blacks won't think this rib-tickler to be particularly funny. But that's alright, as long as the majority of them agree with it. And they will!

The 2022 Supreme Court has outlawed abortion in all 50 states. Due to the fact that a female is now unable to get a legal abortion anywhere in America, it is of the utmost importance that drug stores all over the country, immediately start making available for purchase, birth-control pills and condoms.

The vast majority of white Americans agree with the slogan "Black Lives Matter" but won't also publicly agree that "White Lives Matter" because to do so sounds antagonistic toward blacks. You see, white folks want to avoid being labeled the dreaded "R" word. And it is far more important for whites to NOT be detested by today's woke culture and polite society on the left, than it is to concur with an incontestable truth. Hence, in order for them to go along to get along, our Caucasian citizens believe that they need to wave the white flag.

Politically conservative news, statements and opinion in the media are a threat to the people because they champion one's freedom and autonomy. But pro-government news and progressive propaganda are NOT a threat to your well-being because they are the opposite of conservatism. They advocate providing for, taking care of, and bailing you out. In essence, GOVERNMENT should be viewed as a quasi-GOD. Most Americans who vote Democrat will agree with me on this.

If the GOP doesn't take back the White House and the Senate in November 2024, it will be for three reasons. (1) The electorate didn't like Donald Trump's personality. (2) Twelve million illegal aliens were allowed to vote and (3) Americans have thrown in the towel and resigned to living under a benevolent subjugation administered by the glorious State.

CHAPTER **27**

Bush vs. Obama

GEORGE WALKER BUSH: Saddam Hussein, super nice guy and great humanitarian that he was, had nothing to do with 9/11. In September, 2002, President Bush was told by his CIA director, George Tenet, that the aforementioned Iraqi president did NOT have weapons of mass destruction. Six months later, the United States invaded Iraq. Bush and his successor kept American troops there for over eight and a half years. At the end of the war, 4,487 of our military personnel were killed; 32,223 were wounded; more than 2,000 attempted suicide; six billion dollars had been stolen by Iraqi government thieves; ten billion dollars had been wasted or mismanaged; and about four *trillion* dollar$ had been spent on the entire debacle. This author believes that Bush dismissed what his CIA director had told him because he, our commander-in-chief, was itching for someone to go after in response to the terrorist attack on the two World Trade Center buildings a year and a half earlier. Osama Bin Laden, the real culprit, was roaming around somewhere in the vast mountainous landscape of Afghanistan and was too hard to find.

But Saddam Insane was an evil cartoon character, and better yet, a stationary one. He was easy pickings. It was bad enough that our president scapegoat the Iraqi leader of the Arab Socialist Ba'ath Party. But what is even more egregious is what George W. Bush didn't do: When we invaded Iraq on March 20, 2003, within three weeks, Saddam was out of office, on the run, never to return, and a statue of his likeness was toppled. At that point, Bush should have ordered the soldiers to pack up and leave. If he had done that, just a couple of billion (a pittance by war standards) would have been spent, and moreover, all loved ones waiting anxiously stateside would have been happy to know that there were no body bags coming back. That's because in those three weeks of battle, there were ZERO American casualties. That's right. Not even one death. Mission accomplished. Bush would have saved billions of dollars, thousands of lives, and he would have saved face.

As for what may have happened in the aftermath, the new government of Iraq would have to deal with it. The United States initially thought (or pretended to) that Hussein was the villain of 9/11 (he wasn't), but after his departure, we should have followed. Any subsequent invasion by an enemy would have been engaged by the Iraqi army with the help, by request, of US drone strikes and/or cruise missiles on enemy compounds. But many a concerned citizen has said that we are not the world's policeman – and it's true. As a result of this 2003 through 2011 Middle East misadventure, the American people have had to deal financially and emotionally with the suicidal and physical basket cases that have returned. Numerous Republican and some Democrat politicians, among many citizens, recognize the immense sorrow that our country's combat personnel were going through. And so, to compensate for our wounded warriors' grief, the lawmakers, parents, and others call them "heroes" and "brave young men and women who have fought for their country." We must not allow these "brave heroes" to believe that their invasion of Iraq and Afghanistan was all for naught, lest our soldiers think that they were just cannon fodder. The 43rd US president would agree.

The enormous Federal debt of the years 2001 through 2009 was the fault of George W. Bush spending money like a drunken liberal in order not to be despised like a sober conservative. He was never an economic conservative (like father, like son) and proved it in just eight years. But first of all, those who said that there was a surplus at the end of the Clinton presidency are lying. At the end of Clinton's last fiscal year budget (September 2001), there was a $133 billion national DEFICIT. In his two terms in office, Bill Clinton raised the debt ceiling four times to support big spending, the debt INCREASED by $1.5 trillion and he left us with $5.8 trillion in DEBT. In the following eight years of Bush's fiscal budgets, starting in October of 2001, W raised the debt limit SEVEN times in order to fund two wars and allowed even more Congressional spending than Clinton did. Spending increased by $4.9 trillion by the end of the former Texas governor's second term in the White House; leaving us with $10.6 trillion in debt and a $407 billion national deficit.

And now, yours truly will tell you, the reader, something that the liberals won't and the conservatives neglected to. As you already know, a presidential veto is a tool that is used to eliminate what is usually, but not always, liberal legislation for a new gratuitous social program, pork barrel government spending, costly regulations, and the like. Naturally, vetoes are more likely to be done by a Republican in the White House. Well, in his eight years as president, and not at all bad for a Democrat, Bill Clinton vetoed thirty-seven legislative bills. That's three times as many as George W. Bush did with his twelve vetoes, the least amount of any president since Warren G. Harding. And these twelve vetoes came only in his last three and a half years in office. Bush very likely figured that, now in his second term and not up for re-election, he could politically afford to veto a few items like others before him did and it wouldn't tarnish his legacy. But unbeknownst to most, Bill Clinton governed more fiscally conservative than Bush 43 did. That's why the economy of 1993 through 2000, (especially because of the Republicans' Contract with America), was better than that of the years 2001 through 2008. Clinton correctly deduced that, as a Democrat, he could get away with being more fiscally responsible (miserly). As president, W saw the way that fellow Republican president, Ronald Reagan, was treated by millions of malcontents ("Reagan hates the poor") and he, George W. Bush, in regard to fiscal policy in his entire first term, wanted to avoid that at any cost. And he succeeded.

Nobody ever thought of President Bush as being a bully, and that's because Obama's immediate predecessor was passive and didn't want to fight back against the Democrats, the liberal media, and the establishment because he, George Junior, was worried about aggravating them and hence, squandering the very little popularity that he had. Indeed, many times during a Congressional recess, the Democrats would tell W to hand over his lunch money to them and Bush would meekly oblige. The political left and the American people in general detested the second George Bush in regard to his war in Iraq juxtaposed with his obtuse, aw-shucks demeanor and penchant for malapropisms. But they never derided this president's spend-happy fiscal irresponsibility. During his years in the White House, Republican politicians did the republic no favors when they refrained from criticizing the Texan's complicity with big spending. They foolishly abided by Reagan's asinine eleventh commandment, "Thou shall not speak ill of thy fellow Republicans." This dictum evidently excludes GOP primary debates and negative political advertisements against fellow Party members. Also, our 43rdpresident was well aware that the American people really are fond of domestic social spending, and he knew that the Democrats, the liberal media and the voters would tie Republican candidates for political office, with "the president's cruel, heartless cutting of much-needed programs."

What Bush and the rest of the Republican Party didn't foresee is that the citizens would conflate their "Republican" (presumedly *conservative* but actually not) economic policies with the cause of the massive debt and deficit, when the real blame goes to the liberal tax and spend policies that the GOP president and most of his Party embraced. Later on, White House-bound Barack Obama effectively exploited the ignorance of the public by using this conflation in his censure of President George W. Bush. When presidential candidates John McCain (2008) and Mitt Romney (2012), failed to contradict Mr. Obama and his assertion, they tacitly agreed with the 44th president and politically accepted the blame. The voters noticed this, and it sealed the fate of these two Republicans. For America's biggest-spending president ever, Obama takes home the trophy and the W comes in second place. While president, Bush was displeased that he was so disliked by the pop culture of America and the largely liberal media.....both holding socio-political clout. Post presidency and concerned about his legacy, President 43 wants so very much for Americans in the future to look back and say "Hey, you know what, when Bush was president, I didn't like him very much, but because he comes off as a moderate and was friendly with

Barack and Michelle, maybe he's not such a bad guy after all and he even seems to be pretty cool." Nowadays, Republican George W. Bush has publicly criticized fellow GOP members but has not and will not say anything negative about the Democrats, particularly Barack Obama.

BARACK HUSSEIN OBAMA: In grading the American economy since 1981, there was the Reagan era, which merits a "B+" for a grade. Then came the George H.W. Bush / Bill Clinton years and they score a "C" for a grade. And then we had the George W. / Barack Obama period, which gets a "D-" for a grade. In eight years, Bush 43 racked up enormous debt, not just because of the two wars, but also by his complying with the profligate spending by the House of Representatives. But his successor, Barack Obama and his administration, actually INITIATED the profligate spending and he beat Bush's debt in just THREE years. Deficit spending under George W. was $410 billion a year. Obama's yearly deficit spending in not quite the same time frame and yet to include Obamacare, was more than three times as much ($1.4 trillion). The 44th president was clearly determined to out-liberal Bush, and he prevailed. In his 2012 re-election campaign, the former community organizer said about his immediate predecessor's economic policies: "We just tried this. What they're peddling, we have tried. It didn't work." Correct. And that's why, as president, Obama took whatever Bush tried, but didn't work, and TRIPLED it, much the same way that one drills holes in the bottom of a rowboat on a lake to compensate for the holes that are already in the boat.

Barack Obama (the Honolulu Mulatto) is a socialist. He is, at the very least, a quasi-socialist, if not a clandestine one. Mr. Obama is a democratic socialist, to be exact, but a socialist nevertheless. Some folks have called him a NAZI. They're not only wrong, but dishonest if not outright irrational. Many think that the Illinois ex-Senator's a communist. They too are in error. Indeed, Barack Obama's closer to being a fascist than to being a communist. But he's neither one. Others have claimed that our forty fifth president's a *SOCIAL DEMOCRAT* who wants America to be like Europe. But then, a *SOCIAL DEMOCRACY* is essentially a socialism that just lacks confidence. Proponents of the former are the ambivalent sort. They want socialism; but on the other hand, they don't want it. At any rate, Barack Obama was born on an island in the Pacific Ocean and then he was born-again (politically speaking) in the house of a communist terrorist (Bill Ayres).

The 44th president is, of course, a citizen of the United States, but considers himself to be a citizen of the world, first and foremost. While in the White House, Obama didn't want an elite, powerful USA but a humble one. This way, we don't offend or alienate third-world countries whose approval he sought. When our then newly elected president went on his world apology tour in 2009 and bowed to the leaders of unfriendly countries, Obama was, in essence, asking them for forgiveness. Tyrants, on the other hand, saw it as weakness and disrespected him for it. And like all socialists, Obama feels an affinity with the BASIC, not entire, Communist economic system, but disapproves of many, if not most, Communist social policies. But the pinko who lived in the White House had given a few too many verbal tell-tale signs ("spread the wealth") for one to honestly think otherwise about his socialistic intentions. About the occupations leaving our country for Mexico and elsewhere, the former and least corrupt political resident of Chicago famously stated, "Those jobs aren't coming back" in June 2016 and then asked the GOP presidential nominee, "What magic wand do you have?" President Obama, who had the word "HOPE" as part of his motto in his 2008 candidacy, was clearly throwing in the towel on job creation as he tried to convince the nation's citizens that they might as well give up on any *hope* for free-market capitalism to provide employment and improve their lives. But then again, when Obama mentioned the word "hope", what he thinking was *centralized government*. Plus, Jimmy Carter and Bill Clinton were both Democratic presidents, but they never said that they wanted to "fundamentally transform America." If this quote plus Obama's repeated clarion call to give everybody, particularly the underdog, "a fair shot" doesn't signify America living under socialism or at least going in its direction, then what do they mean? At one particular moment in his 2012 presidential debate with Mitt Romney, Barack Obama responded to the former Massachusetts executive head of state and his firm anti-Russia political stance; "Governor, when it comes to our foreign policy, you seem to want to import the foreign policies of the 1980s, just like the social policies of the 1950s, and the economic policies of the 1920s." What were very likely unbeknownst to Mr. Romney and the majority of Republicans, is that Mr. Obama was belittling actual conservatism (capitalism). Michelle's husband was unabashedly disparaging the "paranoid" (read: "unjustified") ANTI-communism of the 1980s, the clean-cut patriotism with its ensconced Judeo-Christian morals in the 1950s, and the libertarian/laissez faire philosphy of American society in the Roaring (socio-economically speaking) 20s. Now, there have been some prominent conservatives who have pointed out, a few derisively, that Barack Obama is not a socialist. Would these same conservatives also concur that he, as president, was adamantly AGAINST our country going in a socialistic direction? If they won't agree with this; why not?

The charlatan savior from Illinois said that he wanted government to invest in people. But if this were to happen, it would be only an investment in government, not individuals. Mr. Obama also told us that America moves forward ONLY when we do it together. Wrong. America moves forward when each of us moves forward independently. We are not cogs in the wheel of one big unit, nor one big family. The socialist shyster disingenuously likens individualism with collectivist cant and equates the word "values" with *liberalism*. To wit: "Hard work, personal responsibility – these are values. But looking out for one another, that's a value. The idea we're all in this together. I am my brother's keeper; I am my sister's keeper, that's a value." That's right, it is. But it's a different kind of value that requires government-based collectivism, redistribution, and the people's reliance on the omnipotent State and its acceptable coercion of them. The messiah added, "Our journey is not complete." Well, no, of course not. We're not living under socialism yet. Now, a few of my colleagues on the capitalistic right will respond that America is ALREADY living under socialism. That's not true. It's hyperbole, and they know it is.

Barack Obama has postulated that there IS American *exceptionalism*, but only insofar as citizens of all countries believe in their own exceptionalism. Now this would only render the exceptionalism of the USA virtually meaningless. But then, that was precisely president 44's intent. Liberal journalists portrayed Obama as being remarkably smart; this way, alluring but elusive socialism gets the intellectual gravitas that that they would like to think it deserves. But the dominant left-leaning media and the electorate that voted for Obama tried to convince us that he's a moderate because our redistributionist-in-chief didn't loudly proclaim that he's a socialist. Any man (such as cartoonist Garry Trudeau) who calls President Che Obama and his one hundred percent liberal rating a "moderate", must be, himself, a socialist. It was the March 2009 edition cover of *Newsweek* magazine that warned (or was it "bragged"?), "We are all socialists now!" Obama attended socialism conferences in the early 1980s, where he likely learned about the infamous (or is it beloved?) Cloward-Piven strategy! The president's January 2009-January 2017 LET'S-BANKRUPT-AMERICA strategy that he was pushing had been working. This negates my conservative brethren who have called Obama a failure. A fraud! Yes. A failure! No.

Our Food Stamp President was also a snake oil salesman and a superb one. In his 2008 presidential campaign, he told a riveted audience of thousands, "What the naysayers don't understand is that this election year has never been about me, it has been about you." Beautiful! The emotionally drained listeners gobbled it up and failed to recognize Obama's ingratiating statement for the inane platitude that it was. All elections are about the people and their wants and needs, not the candidates. The Anointed One, circa 2007-2010, often scampered up to a podium in front of an audience and whipped his passive facial expression into a crowd-pleasing megawatt smile. Men became enraptured, women fainted, and blacks cried out "Praise the Lord!" It's as if the glistening from Obama's teeth were enough to put supper on their dining room tables. He's the emperor that wore no clothes, but his fans declined to notice it.

If, in 2008, the former community organizer had been a strict conservative Republican, his charisma notwithstanding, much of the American people wouldn't have been so enthralled by Obama due to the fact that his philosophy wasn't socialism-based. Because Obama (aka "Dear Leader") represented empathetic nanny government coming to their rescue, his flock believed that their idolatry of him was absolutely essential. Although, for some strange, unknown reason, the impressionable school children who performed the adoration chant, "OBAMA, MMM, MMM, MMM," were noticeably NOT wearing red scarves around their necks?? But President Obama was clever. There were a few times that he mocked detractors who labeled him a socialist. I'm paraphrasing Mr. Obama...."There have been those who think that I'm some wild-eyed, tax and spend socialist." The 44th president would like us to think that his mere mockery of some people calling him a socialist constitutes being a denial. It doesn't. But the public had been conned into believing that it WAS a denial, and so his verbal stratagem worked. In any case, the reason why the former Illinois senator is a socialist is because he is a liar, and vice versa.

Barack Obama, who has been rumored to have once been the leader of the free world, has never said that he's not a socialist and furthermore, has never uttered a bad word about socialism and never will. If a reporter were to nail Obama to a wall by asking him, "Mr. President, why shouldn't the American people live under socialism? Why are you against it?" there is an excellent chance that Obama's answer will be the old Jackie Gleason "homina-homina-homina" routine. There have been both sides of the ideological spectrum who have mentioned that the ex-president is not a socialist because he hadn't tried to nationalize the banks, or because we still had private property and a free-market economy while he was in office. In the year 2007 when the Wizard of Uhhs started his campaign for the presidency, he had no illusions that in his one or two terms as the country's chief CEO, that the American people would be living under the "caring and compassionate" authority of centralized government. And that was perfectly fine with Obama. It takes time, maybe decades. But his goal was to lock them into that direction with the Affordable Care Act as the main linchpin and impetus.

To augment this, a poll showed that, although most Americans didn't originally want Obamacare, the majority are against the REPEAL of it. This suggests that our citizens didn't like the initial website glitches and flubbed White House rollout of Obamacare, but they do like the concept and noble intention of its very creation. Just by the virtue of being another government program, the ACA deserves a chance and the people's support, and so they oblige. Indeed, a probable majority of those who enthusiastically embrace Obamacare would also support a statute that decrees doctors to stay in their profession or that the government would penalize them if they quit. Many Americans who voted for President Wealth Spreader will forget about and forgive him for lying to them ("You can keep your health care plan") and reneging on his pledge that no family making less than $250,000 a year would see any of their taxes going up, not one dime. His acolytes probably figure, that if Chairman Maobama needed to bamboozle the people into voting for more government control over them, then so be it. But then, to these Obama supporters, his saying that their taxes WOULD NOT GO UP isn't the main reason why they voted for him. The majority of those who supported the socialist shyster really don't give a damn about higher taxes, the debt, the deficit and the ultimate fate of the nation in general, if they wanted to be quite honest with themselves. The Annointed One's wife said about her huband, that "He knows we are going to have to make sacrafices; we are going to have to change our conversation, we're going to have to change our traditions, our history. We're going to have to move into a different place as a nation to provide the kind of future that we want desparately for our children." And so folks, we the people need to "change our history." Great idea! Let's reverse time somehow and expunge the truth and facts of the past. And remember that America needs to "move into a different place" in order to "provide the kind of future we want." What in the hell is this "different place" and "kind of future" that the woman is talking about? Oh.....wait a minute.....I know, it's the "S" word........SHIT. Which, believe it or not, the stench of stinks almost as bad as the stench of SOCIALISM.

CHAPTER 28

Exercise in Analysis

POPULAR TUNES BY young ladies singing about their rivalries with other girls, and reverence for boys, seemed to be the predominant trend on radio in the year 1963. One such song had the female artist singing about how the bad boy that she adores never feels the least bit remorseful when he treats her cruel. Since then, not much has been written about why females between the ages of fourteen and thirty four, are so smitten with the bad boy. Some have suggested that American girls like the bad boy because he's callous and emotionally unavailable. The reader may have watched movies or television shows where the teenage girl, regarding a certain boy, says something like, "Ooh, that Johnny Jones makes me so angry. He's the most stubborn, egotistical, arrogant boy that I've ever met in my entire life and I never want to see him again!" Translation: She likes Johnny and wants him to remain being her boyfriend. The young lady doth protest too much, me thinks. A few thinking individuals have opined that young females associate the bad boy's attitude with masculinity, which in turn, makes her feel protected and secure when she's with him. Others have offered that the good guys are dull and boring and not sexy like the bad boy is, and also that the latter's unpredictable behavior offers mystery, raises the young lady's dopamine and presents her with an exciting challenge to tame him. All of the aforementioned reasons are fairly correct.

This author will now provide further insight as to why young females, particularly the attractive ones, desire the bad boy: Have you ever noticed that, in high school, there are girl cheerleaders for boys' sport teams but no boy cheerleaders for girls' sport teams? This is because throughout history, when men went off to war, the womenfolk were kept off the battlefield while rooting for their men's victory and their safe return, not vice versa. From the dawn of mankind, and in all cultures, the woman has played a subordinate role to the dominant male. Since teenage maidens consider their male peers to be the superior sex, at least athletically, they disdain the high school boy taking a supporting role of cheering girls on in their sport. High school girls, especially the comely ones, really don't appreciate or want the boy who is deferential to and supportive of them. They desire the bad boy who, unlike the other boys, is indifferent to her and doesn't fawn all over a girl. Young, very attractive females have no romantic feelings for guys who put them on pedestals, only for guys who contemptuously knock them off their pedestals. Example: There's a group of five boys, each of them with average looks. Four of them are super nice to the lovely young lady and treat her like a queen. The one lone boy talks rude to noted teenage dream and treats her like dirt. Guess which one in this group of five male youths, that she will take a fancy to for a boyfriend?

You guessed it. It's the lone boy that the girl wants precisely because he doesn't seem to desire her. And she likes him for it. Ever since this young lady was six years old, infatuated boys would pay her more attention because of her cute face. The reader may recall that in their youth, it was almost always the attractive coquette who was called "stuck-up" by various boys, and that's because she was rejecting their advances. But then, this beguiling babe knew that she could afford to be "stuck-up" because so many boys wanted her. Anyway, out of the blue, here comes one young man whom the winsome kitten figures must be special and better because he doesn't adulate her like the other boys do and have for much of her life. The attractive high school queen likes to be flattered by ordinary guys (toadies) but desires to be dated and controlled by the bad boy—not just because her overprotective parents warned her to stay away from his kind, but mostly because, unlike the good boys, the bad boy, she believes, is her superior. Also, NAUGHTY is what a prim and proper Miss was taught not to be and SEX (naughty) is what she was not supposed to have until she got married. For this reason, the naughty (bad) boy becomes, if you will, sexually appealing forbidden fruit and thus, is more alluring. Plus, a delectable doll in her teens or early twenties doesn't like a fellow who always pleases and agrees with a girl, because then there's no gender tension between them that she finds intoxicating. In a young woman's mind, there is supposed to be a "war between the sexes," or a young man isn't worth having. Furthermore, pretty girls just plainly do not like boys who respect them. For a boy who respects or reveres a girl validates her dominance over him.

"Girls are sugar and spice and all things nice" while boys are "snips and snails and puppy dog tails" is just an old nursery rhyme to most, but an allegory to some. If this allegory were converted into an early 1960s pop song with a young lady singing about why she's so crazy for the bad boys, the lyrics might go something like this: "Bad boys rouse the libido in me, good boys don't. Bad boys will hurt me, good boys won't." Sleeping in bed late at night, it is extremely rare for a sixteen-year-old babelicious cheerleader to have nocturnal emissions dreaming about the upright, goody two-shoes, boy-next-door. In high school, the honeys with the come-hither looks are enthralled by the bully, not repelled by him. This is because the bully's character is one of power and strength. The pretty girl desires a boyfriend who will, every so often, get mad at her and make her cry. Otherwise, she won't be drawn to him. But such a comely cookie doesn't want a guy to simply hold her hand. She needs for him to grab it and lead her. She finds it curiously captivating if her boyfriend humiliates her in front of others. Said teenage girl has now become a craver of punishment and emotional abuse.

As one anonymous young lady opined, "In order for a girl to be a good girl, she needs a bad boy." When trying to pick up a stunning teenage knockout, if a nice, clean-cut lad uses the "flowers and candy" approach of surprising her with a present, he'll get shot down in flames. The ravishing dish will conscientiously reject him instantaneously, albeit diplomatically, as she says, "Oh, how sweet of you." But, if the lucky kid does happen to land her, he should realize that in order for this good-looking chick to remain his girlfriend, he's going to have to be pleasingly amiable one moment (though, no reciting romantic poetry) and then hot-tempered and mean the next. Germane to the general topic of this article; there is a movie called *The Last American Virgin* (snicker if you must). It's about a good boy in high school who is lovesick over an enticing female student, who in turn, likes a bad boy. The denouement of this film is surprisingly true-to-life and refreshingly UNHOLLYWOOD.

When the fairer sex is out in public, the prettier she is, the better her peripheral vision (she's slyly observing if a guy is checking her out). Though, it's the eye candy between eighteen and thirty-four years of age who gravitates toward the ruffian while the Plain Jane seeks the bland, ordinary Joe. And it is this easy-on- the-eyes lassie who is wildly attracted to a man who will put a woman in her place by slapping her down, at least verbally, if not physically, every now and then. In doing so, he manipulates the lady and thus, dominates her. She simultaneously respects him for this and is "turned on" by it. It keeps HER off-balance and HIM intriguing. If a man doesn't subordinate his lovely damsel, she won't feel, biologically, like the woman that she is and the "inferior" second-class citizen that our patriarchal system has long conditioned her to be. The guy who IS her *equal* is NOT her *superior* and therefore becomes undesirable. Many, if not most, beauteous babes in their twenties would much rather have a physically UNATTRACTIVE man who is a dominator than a "drop-dead gorgeous" guy who is not. Such women don't want men who will be good TO them but good FOR them. The more fetching a never-married wench is, the more she craves marriage as a deterrent to predators (men on the make). Dichotomously, she also likes to fantasize about being raped by a stranger.

But the pretty twenty-three-year-old doll does not want a guy who aims to make her happy, though she does have an itch for one who doesn't give a damn if she's happy or not. The noted bombshell dislikes being propitiated by a man when, from her standpoint, it is supposed to be the other way around. If said young female does get into an argument with her bruiser boyfriend, she wishes to be told off by him, even if she's right and he's wrong. Initially, the good-looking dame may be miffed by his verbal slapdown, but shortly later, will find his bullying demeanor to be irresistible and endearing. If her steady constantly hits her, the woman will convince herself that she is at least partly to blame. This way, the beauteous babe provides herself with a justification to keep him. As a matter of fact, some females remain attracted to a ruffian NOT in spite of his beating them but BECAUSE he beat them. Now, if this brutish beau strikes her and does so too much, the twenty-three-year-old lassie will eventually break up with him. When this happens, she will not date another man that she knows for sure is a bruiser, for at least another month. But there's nothing that beautiful, youthful broads consider to be more pathetic and repulsive than the nice guy (even if he's handsome) who loves the lady and wants to passionately yet tenderly make love to her. Indeed. She yearns to be banged by the bad boy! Having it rough or feeling "sexually violated" will be her punishment for being pretty (and perhaps spoiled) in the first place. Only when these fine-looking gals reach middle age (40), seeking companionship and aren't being led by their hormones (they're chasing mere romance and not "mind-blowing" orgasms) will their masochism subside. It is then that they long for the kind and easy-going man for a real friend, lover, and partner in simpatico. Maybe it just never occurred to the feminists of yore that the young, attractive women of America generally do not desire gender equality.

CHAPTER **29**

Racism Doesn't Matter

"RACISM IS NOT dead, but it is on life support -- kept alive by politicians, race hustlers and people who get a sense of superiority by denouncing others as racist." Thomas Sowell.

Racism is said to be deleterious to America. A seventy percent black out-of-wedlock birth rate has certainly proven to be just that to black Americans. It could even be that the deed of having a illegitimate child is FACTUALLY and demonstrably racist, but that it's nevertheless acceptable to society. If the aforementioned is true, then it would merely confirm that racism doesn't matter. Back in 1987, when asked by a poor black woman for him to get her more government assistance (money), the Mayor of Washington, DC, Marion Berry, scolded her, "Why don't you stop having so many babies, I'm serious." Good answer and a rare one coming from someone who was neither conservative nor white. This being the case, the mayor's put-down became not an insensitive remark coming from a racist, but rather, "constructive criticism coming from someone who cares." It's unfortunate, but sometimes the truth only becomes the TRUTH depending on who speaks it. Twenty two years later, numerous concerned, patriotic citizens at town hall meetings argued angrily with their Democratic senators or Congresspersons over the latter's support for President Obama's initiative to implement the Affordable Care Act (ACA), later to be known by most as Obamacare. These incensed individuals were clearly worried about their eroding liberty and made it the main complaint to their respective representatives.

But progressives across the country lied when they said that the enraged folks at the town hall meetings were just going against Obama because he's black. This accusation by the left is plainly false because (1) All of these patriots gladly support Judge Clarence Thomas being on the Supreme Court (Thomas is 100 percent black while Obama is half white and half black). But every white liberal has vehemently opposed Thomas being on the nation's highest court. (2) What if Barack Obama had, all of a sudden, become a right-winger, changed his mind, stopped supporting the ACA, and instead embraced a free-market solution championed by conservatives? Would that mean that all whites on the liberal/left immediately became racists because they turned against Obama? (3) If the predominantly white Tea Party, which the town hall meetings begat, is racist; then doesn't that make every white person who DIDN'T VOTE FOR Obama, a racist? Indeed, it does. And (4) Progressives realize that conservatives' anxiety about loss of economic freedom and their dislike of Obamacare are perfectly legitimate political issues to address. But because the pro-socialism left concurs with the 44th president's economic philosophy, they lie and make Obama's race the subject in order to dissuade anybody from opposing him. White progressives' exploitation of race has become very convenient to them, an act which black America mostly supports.

Black former Olympic track and field sprinter Michael Johnson opined in 2012, "Over the last few years, athletes of Afro-Caribbean and Afro-American descent have dominated athletic finals. It's a fact that hasn't been discussed openly before. It's a taboo subject in the States but it is what it is." He also spoke of the "superior athletic gene" of his race. What Mr. Johnson proclaims about his race is not absolutely true, but it is possibly true. At least it is in sports. The Olympic multi-gold medal winner asks why we can't discuss it. Well, actually, some of us can. Blacks can talk about and even brag about any alleged racial/athletic prowess of theirs. Whites are not permitted to speak publicly, a la Mr. Johnson, in the same manner because they own America's power structure, and for this reason, it would be elitist, condescending, repugnant, and, of course, "racist" for whites to do so. However, the politically correct crowd will not redress DARK-skinned blacks boasting that they're genetically and racially superior to LIGHT-skinned blacks (or vice versa) because that's a conflict that doesn't involve whites, proving that there is some racism that just doesn't matter.

But for a white person to simply COMPARE blacks with whites, let alone mock or disparage blacks, is considered taboo and frowned upon by the socially conscious. An example: for a Caucasian to say that blacks can SPRINT faster than whites because they, the blacks, have stronger and longer legs (one inch), is deemed by society to be at least "racially insensitive." For the record, American whites can generally run long distances (over a mile) faster than American blacks. But for that white individual to say that whites can swim faster than blacks because whites are more buoyant (blacks are said to be naturally more muscular, carry less body fat and have heavier, denser bones, which makes their entire body more solid which, in turn, accounts for blacks being less buoyant) is to be lambasted as being "outright racist." Whether it's true or not is banned from discussion and completely disregarded. If talk about race FEELS uncomfortable and merely SEEMS racially dissonant, it automatically becomes "racist." But there are exceptions. A few decades ago, there was a movie that came out called *White Men Can't Jump* (alluding to the game of basketball). NOBODY regarded the title of this film as "racist." Indeed, the movie-going public condoned it, not just because the title is accurate, but because it compliments blacks (the underdog minority) as being better than whites (the *"privileged"* majority) at something. And that's okay. Divulging the fact that most black professional basketball players and most black professional football players don't know how to swim (athletic as they are) is not okay. But not to worry, they will never produce a movie entitled "Black Men Can't Swim." Liberal Hollywood is well aware that they can belittle whites but NOT disparage blacks. This is because the latter are the down-trodden pity-inducing second-class citizen while the former are the opposite. Thus, it would feel uncomfortable and reactionary to go against black society even if they're in the wrong. The American mindset is that the little guy/underdog is supposed to be rooted for and needs to win regardless of the truth and integrity of the matter at hand. Blacks are socio-politically allowed to boast about any alleged superiority over whites but not vice versa. Hence, Michael Johnson's talk of a "superior athletic gene" would be racist only if he were white. Avoidance of truth for the sake of racial harmony may keep the conscience clean but it doesn't help society's economic and social problems (such as not asking questions like the one Marion Berry asked that black woman).

Of course there is racism in America and throughout the world, and there always will be. But demagogues have thrown around the epithet "racist" with such reckless abandon that any fight against REAL racism becomes less effective. A game hunter who shoots too many decoys not only wastes his ammunition but also loses his credibility (à la Joseph McCarthy). Blacks spew out the invective "racist" ad hominem (not to mention ad nauseam) to deter whites from blaming black people for the problems of blacks. Guilt-ridden white liberals commit "reverse" racism, like a reluctance to hold black citizens accountable for their actions in order not to feel like they, the white liberals themselves, don't like blacks. For instance, liberals like to say that poor blacks commit crimes because they're poor. This cannot possibly be true because, by far, most poor black Americans DO NOT commit crimes. As for the liberal mantra "Blaming the victim"---the victim of what? Are they the *victim* of a mostly socio-economically free society or victim of the Great Society? If it isn't conducive to the drive toward social and economic equity, it's "racist." Advocating individualism and self-responsibility (the dreaded bootstraps theory) is borderline "racism." Just like the intention to cut back on the welfare state also is. To be against the redistribution of wealth from the rich to the poor has "racist overtones." Liberty is intrinsic in capitalism, and since liberty isn't the rescuer of blacks or the punisher of whites, then liberty is, well, racist. Any plans or policies that will help install bona fide socialism in America, are NOT racist. But even if they are, the inate authoritarianism of socialism will simply counteract if not eliminate, any type of racial unfairness. Socialism/communism don't be racist but liberty/capitalism do be.

Unlike five decades ago, today's cry of "racism" is employed mostly as a socio-political cudgel to deter any battle against the liberal left's agenda. Their contemptible scheme has been successful. Our present day dumbed-down society will fallaciously agree that a racist is a white person who has a disagreement with what the vast majority of blacks seem to want, regarding society. If some blacks tell white America "Don't be racist" what they're really saying to white people is "Don't DISLIKE what we like" and "Don't LIKE what we dislike." If the current cultural Marxism commonly known as *political correctness* or *wokeism* gets any loonier, it won't be just hockey teams that are considered to be borderline racist (they're 98 percent white) but also barbershop quartets and Caucasians sun-bathing at the beach (they're attempting to darken their skin in order to impersonate black people just like whites did in the minstrel shows of the mid 19th century). And what, pray tell; exactly is this racist "system" or "institution" that constantly emanates from the mouths of the more chronically disgruntled blacks? They never explain. When malcontent blacks complain about the "system," are they referring to the old Dewey Decimal System at the public library? And what is this "institution"? Are they talking about the institution your crazy Aunt Bertha presently resides at? Can these militants and other leftist losers name a country on earth that has millions of whites and millions of blacks in it, but no racism? If they can, are the blacks in this particular country, with its lack of racism, living just as well as American black people? Nigeria and Siberia have no anti-black racist system in them. Would each of these two territories be a better place for a black American to live? Also, if the United States should rid itself of this so-called racist "institution" or "system," then what precisely do we put in its place? Would the solution that they have in mind involve more government expansion and subsequent control of the people, or less of it? Which one?

The black Americans who always vote Democrat are quite fond of repeating their dogma, "Because white America run the INSTITUTION, only whites can be racists. Black people can be prejudiced, but we can't be racists because we not in power." This can only mean that if American society were to somehow invert itself with the black population becoming significantly bigger than the white population, placing blacks in power (as in they now overwhelmingly dominate the higher echelon positions of government, corporations, academia and private enterprise), then ONLY BLACK Americans can be RACISTS. It would be impossible for white people to be racists because they're not in power. A member of the Ku Klux Klan can be prejudiced, yes, but he can't be a racist (even if he wants to be) because his race (white) doesn't own the INSTITUTION.

At least 80 percent of black America would dodge answering ALL of the following questions: (1) Can the United States get rid of most of, if not all of, racism and still remain a capitalist country? Yes or no? (2) Cuba has, similar to America, a population of 65 percent white citizens and 10 percent black. Does it have systemic racism? If not, why not? (3) If our nation has "institutionalized racism" then how does one explain the fact that almost half (46 percent) of black society, is a thriving middle-class community? Why didn't "systemic racism," or "institutionalized racism" from the very beginning, stop this 46 percent dead in their tracks from moving upward? (4) If the United States has had racist government ever since its birth in 1776, should we all strive for MORE government or LESS government? Which one? And lastly, can a white American who is an avowed, dedicated communist, be a racist? Yes or no? Speaking of Reds...the late Marxist-Leninist revolutionary Che Guevara once opined, "The Negro is indolent and lazy and spends his money on frivolities, whereas the European is forward looking, organized, and intelligent. The Negro has maintained his racial purity by his well-known habit of avoiding baths." Now, there has to be well over four hundred black Americans who consider what this communist thug once stated, to be racist. But nevertheless, millions of American blacks, upon hearing about what he said, will continue to wear T-shirts emblazoned with Guevara's image, and they will do so with pride. A praiseworthy act, if ever there was one! And better yet, they prove that racism doesn't matter.

In our politically correct society, a black individual is acclaimed by the general public if he or she loudly asserts, "I like being black." But it is almost against the law for a white person to even whisper, "I like being white" (hate speech). You see, blackness is intrinsically cool and culturally chic; whiteness isn't. The former is admirable and endearing because it rebels against the "whiteness" of *Americana* (culture that's appreciated mostly by whites, the respect for law and order, the diety and patriotism). Quite simply, blackness deserves to be revered because it is antithetical to whiteness. In a perverse bit of self-flagellation, white liberals, particularly the young, like to bash various groups (the Republican Party, Mormons, the sport of hockey; wholesome, clean-cut suburbanites, and others) as being "too white." These liberals warm to the guilt-easing self-indulgence of disparaging white people like themselves. This, the lighter-pigmented ones believe, allows them to "be down with" their "black brothers." As a result, said conscientious white liberals feel secure in the knowledge that their contrition is on full display for the public (particularly blacks) to notice. The noted compunctious do-gooders especially know for a fact that they, as progressive whites (black America's best friend) have been sufficiently inoculated from being perceived by anybody (including themselves) as not liking black people. No siree, there ain't no way that these empathetic Caucasians are racists. They proved it and are quite satisfied with themselves. It doesn't matter that the ramifications of white liberal guilt haven't bettered the relationship between black and white America. What's really important is that these narcissistic whites who lean to the left have been vindicated by their belief that they are racially irreproachable for any adverse plight of black America. Blacks, too, play mind games. Blacks mostly employ the all-purpose besmirching label "racist" as a bullying tactic to deter whites from truthfully criticizing blacks plus keep the former intimidated, guilt-ridden and off-balance; the better to extract concessions from them. This psychological con job by blacks and the left is used under the guise of "trying to stop racism" in order to browbeat a timid, gullible and "eager-to-get-along" white America into submission. Their ruse has been successful. In any event, from now on, when anyone cries RACISM, that person should be called upon to explain how what he or she is indicting is RACIST; otherwise, this individual should be called a LIAR and then IGNORED.

With the possible exception of public education, our country does NOT have *systemic* racism, and any government oppression ended in 1965. Anyone on the liberal left who thinks or says otherwise is really just conveying that actual FREEDOM is racist because it doesn't force racial and economic equity on the nation as a whole. In essence, if it isn't conducive to placing blacks under the veritable slavery of socialism, then it's racist. The majority of American blacks and progressives would like to think, and would like all of us to believe, that racism is prevalent in our country only, not most of the world. This way, their vengeance remains aimed not so much against racism itself, as it does against the United States. If racism is viewed as a common personality trait affecting the denizens of all seven continents, then that would only make it more culturally and politically difficult for blacks and left-wing subversives to isolate any racial iniquity as being ingrained solely in the USA, and subsequently harder for them to undermine our Constitutional republic. To paraphrase an anonymous but wise man, "Racism is seen only by those who look for it. Live your life like racism doesn't exist and racism will slowly fade away. Keep harping on it and racism creates its own power." But, alas, to a lot of black people and their white counterparts on the liberal/left, RACISM is mostly something to exploit and perpetuate, NOT diminish. But hard-line progressives want to prolong racial animus to the point that it effectuates tyrannical statism in order to sufficiently punish white America and bring down the "system" created by them. If this is NOT the case, then it behooves those who constantly shout the R-word to tell us exactly how the United States can eliminate "systemic racism" WITHOUT going in a socialistic direction. If they decline to tell us, then the American people should be suspicious of their racial portrait of our nation and consider their alleged war against REAL racism to be null and void. Unfortunately for the far left, their desire and demand for more racism vastly exceeds America's supply.

On many college campuses, young black students strive for diversity by demanding that their learning institution provide clubs, organizations and graduation ceremonies for BLACKS ONLY. And they receive them. In good time, these black students will progress to having their own separate drinking-water fountains. On the other side of the academia race fence, the rules are different. Because whites are "privileged first-class citizens" and are in the majority, a "whites only" club at a university would be looked upon as being superfluous and elitist. This would only anger an already alienated black society. As a consequence, said aggravation could form into something more than just a mild protest, and for that reason, a "whites only" club is verboten. College organizations exclusively for blacks, however, offer a respite from white society and are therefore acceptable to both races. Since blacks are the "oppressed" and "downtrodden" minority, they have a legitimate right to be provided a forum in which to not only celebrate their heritage, but vent and perhaps alleviate any anti-white resentment. This being the case, any falsehoods that are uttered at these meetings will be "understood" and "excused." I digress ever so slightly.

The American people, perhaps under the influence of political correctness and wokeism, have a bad habit of thinking that RACIAL plus CONTROVERSIAL equals RACIST. It doesn't. Various whites believe that if a member of their own race speaks about black people in a negative or unflattering manner, then it automatically constitutes "racism." This attitude is both craven and dishonest. But nevertheless, the cry of "racism" does become handy as an escape hatch for anybody to not have to deal with the racial truth. The nation's repressive racial discourse, and the people's inability to understand the word "context," has reduced many of us to thinking that non-blacks merely uttering the word "nigger" is automatically racist with very few of us asking, "How so?" The 1884 novel by Mark Twain, *"The Adventures of Huckleberry Finn"*, mentions the word 217 times. Does this make Twain's book racist? In 1974, the comedian Richard Pryor released a comedy album entitled *"That Nigger's Crazy"* and then reissued it the following year. The album won a Grammy award and sold half a million copies. Very few Americans were offended by the title. Also in the early 1970s, there were *blaxploitation* movies with titles like *"Boss Nigger"* and *"The Legend of Nigger Charley."* There was minuscule if any outcry or denunciation (particularly from the media) of these two films when they came out five decades ago. Nor were there any protestations from black America. In addition, newspapers across the nation back then DID advertise the aforementioned movies' titles, synopses, reviews, and show times at local theaters. The white media and white theater owners were very rarely if ever, called *racists*. How come?

"I'll have those niggers voting Democratic for the next 200 years" said Lyndon B. Johnson while he was the POTUS of America. Currently, if another white liberal male Democrat running for national political office said something racially very similar to what President Johnson said, he would NOT get the usual 90 percent of the black vote but only 86 percent. Or maybe said candidate would do real lousy with black voters on Election day and have to settle for a super-low 81 percent of their support. Today, the N-word is utterly derogatory if it is used to label or refer to a person as such. Some blacks claim that the infamous insult, if it's coming from them, is a "term of endearment." Though, how it became endearing or complimentary, no one knows. Other racial groups think that this negative term is the worst name that blacks can be called. It isn't. The slurs, "coon," "porch monkey," "spear chucker," "jungle bunny", and "baboon" are far more demeaning than the pseudo-notorious "N-word." They must be, because you never hear blacks calling each other those names. Otherwise, the five noted, more egregious words would, themselves, become "terms of endearment" and socially acceptable for blacks to use. From the 1960s through the 1980s, the derogatory names "honky" and "cracker" were bandied about by various blacks against whites. It's incredibly rare for white people to call one another "honky" or "cracker." This is apparently due to them having *WHITE PRIDE*. In any case, such Freedom of Speech from either race has never been found to be deleterious to our society.

Left-leaning whites and blacks say that it's white people who are responsible for eradicating racism. How then, are white individuals going to end "systemic racism"?......Oh, I get it. Saying that white Americans are the ones responsible for stopping racism is just an oblique way of calling for the omnipotent State (which just happens to be run mostly by whites) to take command and control of the country (especially of its white citizens) via coercion and collectivism which would increase socio-economic equity and eradicate *"institutionalized racism"* (i.e. socio-economic liberty). If you, the reader, regardless of your race or ideology, had to label one of these two men as a RACIST, strictly because of his economic philosophy and policies; would it be the late conservative Republican, Ronald Reagan, or the late liberal Democrat, Ted Kennedy? Many, if not most of you just thought to yourself, "the former president." Why? It's because a capitalistic/libertarian economic policy pushed by a conservative is a harsh, demanding and disciplinary (you're on your own, fend for yourself) course of action that FORCES blacks, along with everybody else, to practice self-reliance and personal responsibility. Thus, since it doesn't mollify or mollycoddle black citizens, it's automatically perceived as an animosity toward them. White people, like Reagan, who harbor this "animosity" are resented, then vilified with the R-word in the hope of dissuading them, the whites, from supporting liberty-inducing social and economic policies that compel blacks to stand on their own two feet.

Racism Doesn't Matter: And I'll prove it. Do not dodge this next question by replying "But it's not a fact" because you're a dishonest coward if you do. IF it were a FACT that getting food stamps, welfare checks, Medicaid and Section 8 housing were racist, would the black people of America turn against the four of these? The correct answer is "Nope, absolutely not." It would be one hundred percent alright with the predominance of them that receiving such benefits is RACIST. They couldn't care less that it is, thereby proving that racism doesn't matter. Bitter black Democrats have been heard to admonish black Republicans: "White people in your party are calling you nigger behind your back." Not only is it a lie and a vile one, but even worse, it's hypocritical. Surely, black America has heard about former President Bill Clinton's "colorful" language while he was the Governor of Arkansas? Larry Patterson, a former Arkansas State Trooper, was Governor Clinton's driver from 1986 until 1993. Dolly Kyle Browning was Clinton's girlfriend throughout the 1980s. According to them, Bill Clinton frequently referred to the Reverend Jesse Jackson as a "nigger." While being chauffeured through town; speaking to his driver about a Little Rock black man who was standing on a sidewalk protesting the governor, Clinton uttered "There's that god damn nigger" and often made snide and scathing comments about black people behind their backs. Now then, is Clinton's gutter language racist, and does it make him a racist? Maybe---but it doesn't matter. And if you don't believe me that it doesn't matter, just ask any black person who voted for him.

A white male conservative Republican candidate for national public office goes up to the lectern in a small, mostly white town; and before he gets into his speech about small government, support for the Second Amendment and touting family values, he tells the crowd, "Ladies and gentlemen, there's something that I've noticed about black people. I've noticed that they have darker skin than us white people." Could you just imagine the phony outrage performed by the far left liars, the liberal media and black America? "He's a racist!" "He made a shocking and hateful racial comparison before a lily-white audience." "He's a dangerous bigot." But what if a white male, liberal Democrat candidate, also running for national political office, stood up at the podium and solemnly declared into the microphone, "My fellow white Americans, I seriously and whole heartedly believe and proudly proclaim that we whites are genetically and intellectually superior to black people and for that reason, they ought to be our slaves." The entire liberal/black establishment would be grasping at straws, vainly trying to vindicate him with the flimsiest of excuses---"Well, he simply misspoke."..."His statement wasn't supremacist, what he said was just kind of dumb, that's all."..."It was a regrettable choice of words that he used, taken out of context."...."Uh, it's not his fault that his speechwriter gave him the wrong script."...."He didn't mean it; the man was just feeling irritable because he hadn't moved his bowels yet."

No accusatory mention of the word "racist" by the progressive establishment because that could jeopardize the man's election. But nevertheless, said liberal Democratic candidate would still EASILY (though only 85 percent and not the usual 90 percent) win the black vote. Why? It's because the vast majority of black voters will play down what he said, publicly forgive him, and dare not even hint at the R-word. The blacks will rationalize that this white Democrat at least compensates for himself (deeds ARE stronger than words, after all), by advocating and safeguarding government expenditures and pushing the State to care about and provide for them. And isn't that, not "trivial campaign rhetoric," what's really important? Also, blacks figure that their voting for a political candidate that society at large has deemed obviously racist would only appear contradictory and thereby undercut the black voters' presumed opposition to racism. They realize that if the white population noticed that hypocritical blacks were supporting and rallying behind the obviously bigoted Democratic office seeker, it would damage black America's credibility.

Plus, sincere black people will infer, how can blacks, like themselves look in the mirror if they vote for a white person that they privately acknowledge is definitely a racist. It would only be discomfort to the conscience and reflect negatively and shamefully on their own individual character. For these reasons, black citizens who will indeed go vote on election day, absolutely need to be in denial and cannot, and will not, publicly label the Democrat candidate a racist even though they know, deep down, that he really is one, thus, proving that racism doesn't matter.

Fomenting racial discord is evolutionary to installing "social justice." Thus, it is liberal chic to try to sensationalize and stigmatize anything that ever so slightly involves race. To the ninety percent liberal media nowadays, almost no subject is simply "race-related," "race-based," "racially-sensitive," or even just plain "racial." Nope. Virtually every headline has to yell "RACIST." Doing so accomplishes three things. (1) It stokes black citizens' resentment and animus toward white America. The longer that black citizens remain perpetual malcontents, the faster they will get to the *"PROMISED LAND"* simultaneously with white society being punished by authoritarian decree. This, much to the malicious glee of progressive journalists. (2) It grabs the reader's attention due to the fact that Americans presently live in a race-obsessed culture and we're constantly looking to be entertained by controversy. And (3) the liberal journalist who cried "RACIST" gets to tell himself that he's a good Samaritan who has done his civic duty in divulging and alerting us to something that he hopes will be construed by the public as "RACIST"; quickly followed by a nationwide denunciation of the racial incident and by extension, America in entirety. For example, in one news item, there was a food menu at a school in California that listed fried chicken, cornbread, collard greens, and watermelon. The food menu listing was actually stereotypical or race-related. But, no, the liberal storyline branded it as a "RACIST LUNCH MENU." Modern-day liberalism believes that it must be hypersensitive and dishonest in order not to be racist.

Never mind if it's erroneous or not, is it racist to assert that Sleep n' Eat (aka Willie Best) was America's greatest black actor in our nation's history? Likewise, is it racist to proclaim that Aunt Jemima made the best pancakes ever? Is it racist to have the freedom to shout "basketball" in a crowded Apollo theater? Is it racist for a white gardener to say, "I needed to dig up some dirt but I couldn't find the shovel, and so I had to use a spade?" And especially, is it RACIST to merely taunt individuals who display an exaggeration of being offended, or mock their pretentiousness on matters of race? The correct answer to all five questions is "No."

The liberal/left wants RACE to be the issue as much as possible so they can win the socio-political debate with ad-hominem attacks and without actually engaging in honest dialogue. This way, without using intelligent analysis and conservative solutions, the lives of blacks will not improve. And in far left doctrine, that's a good thing. But America will make faster genuine progress when it's explained how whatever person or subject that blacks and progressives are condemning…is racist. For instance, the following is NOT a racist joke (or riddle) and nobody will be able to explain how it is:…."What's black and yellow and screams?……..A school bus full of niggers going off a cliff!"…..Keeping in mind that one's contrived umbrage is not a substitute for reason, here's more, and it's no joke. Just because a man is the Grand Wizard of the Ku Klux Klan doesn't indicate that what he's saying about blacks is WRONG. Moreover and especially, it doesn't mean that the statements that he's making about black people are RACIST.

If a white restaurant owner wants to discriminate against black customers from dining there, is it racist? It doesn't matter. If this restaurant owner will not allow people to eat there because they're black, then that's unjust, oppressive, and wrong (morally and economically) and should be against the law for that very reason. Whether it's RACIST or not is immaterial. Again, using logic, let's say, for instructional purposes, that white discrimination against our black citizens is unjust, oppressive, and wrong, but it IS NOT RACIST. Would you then say that racial discrimination against black people by whites is perfectly alright because, hey, it isn't racist? Of course not! Conversely, let's maintain that the action taken by the restaurant owner WAS definitely RACIST, but it was NOT factually unjust, oppressive, or wrong. That being the case, what's the problem? You will be unable to explain what the problem is. And that's because there is no problem, thus rendering "racism" irrelevant. Besides, blacks should be AGAINST the complete eradication of racism in America. Because, if racism is completely gone, how would blacks proclaim themselves victims?

CHAPTER **30**

Opinionated Bits and Pieces Part 7

SOME SAD NEWS: Nancy Pelosi recently had scalp surgery performed on her. The doctors said that they had to open the California Congresswoman's head to find out what was in it. May she get well soon!

Sometimes, Republicans too, can be absent-minded. Like, for example: When Republicans ask, "How is it that, for decades, liberal Democrats have owned and controlled cities like Chicago, Newark, and Baltimore, but have only made living conditions and life there in general, worse, not better?" without even realizing that they just answered their own question.

Barack Obama as President, parroted by millions of his supporters, had bragged more than a few times that his administration "got Osama Bin Laden." He was correct. It was the CIA Director, Leon Panetta, who was 30 percent responsible for the orders to kill Bin Laden. It was the president's senior advisor, Valerie Jarrett, who was 65 percent responsible for the Muslim terrorist's death. And it was Obama, himself, who chipped in 5 percent. It's been reported by an unnamed source in the Joint Special Operations Command, that he, our commander-in-chief, went to Ms. Jarrett three times and requested her approval for the United States to launch a military strike on Bin Laden. She said "no" each time. On the fourth time that Mr. Obama asked, Jarrett finally gave him permission to have Bin Laden killed and then our president relayed her "OKAY" to the CIA and Navy SEALs to eliminate the Al-Qaeda founder. It is because of the commander-in-chief's stellar leadership in this matter that Osama Bin Laden, who was America's number one enemy, is dead. As the leader of our country, Obama could have abstained from telling the military and the CIA that Valerie Jarrett gave them the green light to carry out their objective. But he didn't. Therefore, President Barack Obama deserves credit and praise for his initiative and decisiveness in a US combat mission that turned out to be splendidly successful.

We are not a nation of immigrants! Though, the opposite was somewhat true for a century starting in 1840. Even so, today it is irrelevant. Presently, we are a nation of 87 percent native born citizens. But the liberal/left wants to brainwash America into believing that the mass migration to the United States of over one hundred years ago somehow validates current entry into our country. It does not. If people of various other places go to live in Botswana, Japan, Madagascar or Switzerland; does that make the noted four "nations of immigrants?" No, it doesn't. Actually, this three-word platitude is just liberalism's way of conflating the immigrants of, say, the 1880s, with the foreign invaders of the years 2019---2024 for the purpose of bringing in poor left-leaning (read: socialistic thinking) minorities to help increase the size of the welfare state via the voting booth and give eternal power to the Democrats. Progressives are AGAINST legal immigration law if there's a Republican in the White House because it means that the noted President, as delegated by the US Constitution, has the power and the legitimate right to regulate and thus, TERMINATE any immigration. Consequently, this enables the United States to deny the requests or demands of the world's people, especially the destitute, to live here in America or preventing them from trespassing over our borders. Such actions thwart the left's Cloward-Piven strategy of bankrupting and destroying the social safety net of America via government dependency, which would ultimately result in a socialistic totalitarianism—precisely the goal of the far left. Incidently, the term "socialistic" and the phrase "the browning of America" have a symbiotic relationship. If all minorities practiced individualism and self-responsibility, there wouldn't be a "browning of America."

As everybody knows, there is a difference between capitalism and socialism. But what, pray tell, is the difference between CRONY capitalism and CRONY socialism? The answer: Nothing. And they're both unethical. America has had too much crony capitalism because of government growing over the last century and politicians in both parties arranging government sweetheart deals with, and bailouts of, corporations. President Obama had the government bailout of General Motors auto industry (crony capitalism) and the overwhelming majority of the liberal establishment approved of it. What the pro-capitalism Tea Party and the pro-socialism anti-Wall Street protesters have in common is that they're both solidly against crony capitalism. The former is, of course, also against crony socialism, but is the latter? They ought to be. In the Soviet Union from 1917 to 1991 there were practitioners of economic corruption called the *Nomenclatura*. In contrast to the common Russian citizen, its members were rich, had nice homes, and just plain lived the good life while buying luxury items off the black market (underground capitalism). Most of the Nomenclatura were partisans of the Communist Party and they lived off the backs of the oppressed, proletariat masses like the greedy capitalist pigs that they were. Those of all political stripes in America should be against ALL types of cronyism.

On many occasions that a RINO member of the GOP is running in the primary for national public office, when asked about his politics at a town hall forum, the Republican candidate gladly proclaims to his constituents, "Well, I consider myself to be a fiscal conservative" or "I'm proud of my conservative values" and "You elect me as your representative and I'll go to Washington, DC and do battle with those crazy liberals." The man is full of large amounts of hippopotamus turd. For there is an excellent chance that the specious boilerplate employed by the aforementioned pseudo-conservative is really just a ruse for his desire to get elected. Which would, in turn, allow him to enjoy the monetary perks and privileges of government and engage in some friendly cocktail party back-slapping in the Swamp at our nation's capital. The man is also probably aware that a good enough number of GOP voters want conservative lip service from their candidate ("I'll vote to put an end to wasteful spending.") but that said constituents will actually be AGAINST most of if not all domestic social spending CUTS. It would not at all be a shock if thousands of common Russian citizens in Moscow took notice and referred to participants in this American activity as, the *Nomenclatura*.

Liberals lament the McCarthyism of the early 1950s because, they claim, it ruined the lives of many people. Indeed it did for a lot of individuals who were either innocent OR guilty of being communists. But if McCarthyism is thought of or defined as accusing or revealing any American in, say, the year 1952, as being a Red, then that person is deemed by many to have been unfairly persecuted. If an American in 1942 was secretly a member of a pro-Nazism organization in our country, would it have been an unfair persecution to OUT him or her? Yes or no? Are there any bona fide Nazi countries today that are a threat to the United States? Were there any communist countries in 1952 that were a threat to ours?......Precisely!......Case closed......May God bless Joe McCarthy!

In the opinions of those who voted for Barack Obama, it really is alright with most if not all of them that his lovely and gracious wife, Michelle, spent $467,000 on a vacation trip to Spain in 2012, which was paid for by the taxpayer. However, it is not the least bit okay with these voters and many if not most Democrats that First Lady Nancy Reagan, in 1982, spent $210,399 on a new set of china for the White House that was paid for solely with contributions from the friends of President Reagan and Nancy, not one dime from the taxpayer. This is because contribution-funded opulence and ostentation by a Republican administration is to be exploited, denounced, and contrasted with the plight of the poor for political reasons, while publicly financed extravagance and luxury by a Democratic administration is to be ignored and excused. It is perfectly acceptable to our nation's plebian masses and the liberal left that an empathetic, progressive monarch and his even more empathetic queen take lavish taxpayer-funded vacations because at least they, Barack and Michelle, purportedly REPRESENT solicitous government coming to the rescue of the marginalized and underprivileged working-class commoners. And isn't having faith in this empathetic couple's politically driven pretense of caring for the proletarian people all that really matters?

Past head honchos at the United Nations and their progressive supporters have called its participant, the United States of America, a "deadbeat" donor country. The USA, with the help of its *deadbeat* taxpayers, provides 22 percent of the UN's operating cost, while China chips in 2 percent and Russia and India, practically zero. But the entire liberal/left will not denigrate China, Russia, and other "deadbeat" countries that have not paid their "fair share." America's "union dues" to the virtually useless United Nations should be whatever our membership in it is worth to us. Though some will say that a thousand dollars a year is too much, I disagree. We can fiscally swing it. And if the organization's Secretary General doesn't like our new annual payment, then he can move the whole conglomeration to Libya, noted to be the hottest country on earth. If its petulant members still object, well then, planet Earth does have a hotter place. The United Nations can start digging immediately. America will provide the shovels.

The civilization of mankind is a false yet fascinating dichotomy. We can accomplish a lot when we do things together, but we can also accomplish a lot if each person does things alone.

If Bill Clinton's estranged wife WASN'T a liberal, much of the electorate in 2016 wouldn't have been so proud and excited that we "elected our first woman president" had she won. A female president, our nation's first, who is a hard-line conservative, wouldn't validate her gender because she's not an advocate of the almighty maternalistic State. Said lady would therefore NOT count as the FIRST woman leader of the United States. If Little Miss Chipmunk Cheeks (aka Hillary Clinton) had become our 45th president, many Americans, particularly women, would have been eager to overlook the corruption, scandals, and lack of achievements that permeated her resume, and overjoyed that the nation got its first female POTUS. But if liberal Hillary were to do a 180-degree ideological turn after her first day in the Oval Office, the former First Lady's fan club's joy would quickly dissipate into extreme disappointment because only progressivism/idealism (activist government nurturing its people) reinforces the notion that she will be "a great president." Just like her immediate predecessor obviously was. Incidentally, whenever you hear various voters say that "It would be great for America to have a woman president," it almost always means that they would be dead set AGAINST her being a *conservative* Republican. Such is the electorate's pseudo-virtuous and ulterior way of saying that they want a LIBERAL for President (but preferably, it should be a woman). Quite simply, a woman president absolutely needs to be a liberal; otherwise, what's the use of having a woman president?

With the advent of Barack Obama's 2008 election as president, much had been said about some rather irate citizens during his two terms. Angry white men were angry because, unlike most angry black men, they didn't want to live under or even move toward the slavery of socialism, Obama's ultimate goal. The difference is that the phrase "angry white men" is a pejorative, while the phrase "angry black men" is not. White anger and rebellion are unreasonable and uncalled-for. Whites should just calm down and submit to a socio-political system that purports to be for their own good. Black anger and rebellion, however, are admired, respected, and justified because American blacks simply yearn to live in the "PROMISED LAND" that they have long been denied.

Liberals are not deep-down as happy as conservatives, because liberals spend a good portion of their lives fretting over how to achieve more social engineering in order to install egalitarian social order and make everybody *equally* melancholic. Such societal urgency, they believe, necessitates their fatalistic demeanor. The liberty-loving right adopts the attitude of live and let live (you're on your own). It's a war of socio-political opinion with the progressive OFFENSE vs. the reactionary

DEFENSE, if you will. Conservatives, particularly of the libertarian kind, instinctively recognize that each one of us really is figuratively living in his or her own world, and we focus on it. By the same token, Americans who are not at all political are generally happier than either of the two noted dissonantly ideological opposites. As the line in the Rick Nelson song "Garden Party" teaches us, we can't please everyone so we have to please ourselves.

Speaking of songs—Dean Reed was an American singer, actor, and self-proclaimed Marxist who cut records and made movies while living in the Warsaw Pact nations in the 1970s and 1980s. He was a superstar adored by legions of East Europeans and was sometimes referred to as "the Red Elvis." What's sad about the Dean Reed story is that even though he opposed America's economic system and its foreign affairs, he loved and missed the country he grew up in and never renounced his citizenship. But then on one occasion, Reed made a fatal mistake. In an April 1986 *60 Minutes* interview, he expressed his support for the Russian invasion of Afghanistan, compared President Ronald Reagan to Joseph Stalin, and claimed that the East Berlin Wall was built for the self-defense of East Germany. The ideologically progressive entertainer was called a traitor and received numerous hostile letters from non-fans in the United States. A month and a half later and estranged from his third wife and their two young children, our internationally famous celebrity, augmented by an overdose of sleeping pills and both wrists slit, drowned in a lake in East Germany. Some people had theorized that he was killed by the American CIA or the Russian KGB. But it was neither of them. Dean Reed (age forty-seven) committed suicide. It is sheer conjecture on the part of this author, but a despondent Mr. Reed felt that he ruined his chances of living in his beloved USA again, after carelessly verbalizing his "strong" opinions on American nationwide television for one too many patriotic citizens to witness. Before the interview, he was virtually unknown here in the United States. Dean Reed surmised that, although a mediocre talent, he could have come back home, be lovingly embraced by the denizens of left-wing culture, play the college circuit, and just plain enjoy the good life while living off the millions that he made from his fan base in communist countries. But, no! The man, who was every so often called "Comrade Rock Star", had to open his big mouth. Nevertheless, may God bless Dean Reed!

Over the decades, more than enough of us have hurled the insult "dictator" with utter abandon in order to demonize presidents that we disagree with or just plain dislike. President Trump was not a dictator, nor was President Obama. Neither gentleman made an effort to be or even desired to become a dictator. But the name-calling by various left or right leaning citizens is just a wee bit more dishonest than it is puerile. ANY president, present and hereafter, would be delusional and hare-brained to even attempt to abrogate the Constitution, the embodiment of eternal liberty. Though, it IS far from being an impossibility that the United States could live under a dictatorship in the not-too-distant future. And to bring this about, all we would need to do is undermine or reject actual liberty-based proposals, and we've got our despotism. Most Americans foolishly believe that our nation is more likely to live under a dictatorship if a conservative Republican is president rather than a liberal Democrat. This is because the noted citizens ignorantly conflate "the cold, heartless, uncaring cruelty" character of despotism with their opinion of the seemingly indifferent, self-responsibility/individualism philosophy and austerity of conservatism. The people's love for domestic social spending, redistribution and their desire to "stick it to the rich" will never be blamed for any foreboding dictatorship, because to do so is to blame themselves for its imposition. If the United States had as its' leader, a genuine left-leaning DICTATOR with a very likable personality, most liberals and some moderates would yearn for his leadership and depend on his guidance, the actual results of his policies being irrelevant. In the minds of too many Americans, in order for our nation to avoid ever living under a dystopian despotism, we must strive for more well-intentioned, compassionate government expansion and its humane and selfless control of our society. Henceforth, the socialism awaiting us somewhere down the pike MAY be *democratic*....at first. But it will soon become totalitarian. It will have to. Freedom/liberty is the antithesis of a dictatorship. It's just unfortunate that this truism needs to be drilled into the American mindset.

Shortly after the 2016 presidential election, black TV news commenter and self-declared communist Van Jones said about Donald Trump's win over Hillary Clinton, "This was a whitelash against a changing country." And "It was a whitelash against a black president, in part." Come again? If the white John McCain had beaten the black Barack Obama in 2008 for the presidency, then it would be somewhat credible for Jones to call it a "whitelash against a changing country" and completely understandable that this far left media personality was upset. After McCain lost, four years later, it would have also been plausible that white man Mitt Romney's win and the American voters NOT re-electing current leader, Barack Obama "was a whitelash against a black president in part" as Mr. Jones put it. But how, pray tell, does WHITE person, The Donald, and his electoral drubbing of WHITE person, The Hildabeast, constitute being a "whitelash" in any sense of the word? It's because, in the back of Van Jones's mind, "whitelash" means a rejection of progressivism. If a presidential candidate's social and economic policies aren't progressive (read: socialistic) then they are "pro-white" and are therefore, not advantageous to blacks. We, the People, are supposed to be enacting a socio-economic agenda that benefits racial minorities for the long run. This is something that the *white-lashing* (capitalistic) economic policies of President Trump, did not do. If, in the future, the black conservative South Carolina Republican Senator Tim Scott were to triumph over the black and Red Democrat, Van Jones for President in the November election; that too would be deemed a *whitelash*.

Actors Ronald Reagan, Jon Voight, and James Woods were once liberals who became conservatives. Media mogul Ariana Huffington, political commentator William Kristol, and morning TV talk show host Joe Scarborough were formerly conservatives who became liberals. The first three simply became more intellectually honest over time. The latter three were merely nominal conservatives who made the transition to liberalism because it's culturally more popular and socially prestigious and they longed to be part of the *in-crowd.* Inside the political/celebrity arena, although superficial, it is far more gratifying for one to become a status-seeking, social-climbing butterfly than it is to have conscientious integrity.

Many American gentiles are well aware that it is considered automatically anti-Semitic for them to talk about Jews, whether what they say is critical of Jews or not. The only statements that non-Jewish Americans are allowed to make about Jews have to go something like this: "The Holocaust was a horrible tragedy in human history, and let's never let it happen again. It wasn't a hoax. It was real and evil and heinous. Always remember the Holocaust." While saying this, for a gentile to cry crocodile tears brought on by guilt and sorrow, is perfectly welcome. What is not welcome is humor from gentiles about Jews. For example if the following joke's opening line, "Three Jews walk into a bar..." is told by a non-Jew, then it is to be instantly labeled ANTI-SEMITIC. It does not matter that the joke-teller didn't even get to the punch line. It becomes automatically "anti-Semitic" strictly because Jewish people FEEL uncomfortable when gentiles tell jokes about them. Indeed, the mere mentioning of the word "Jew" in a joke told by a non-Jewish individual seems like an on-coming verbal attack by said gentile. But if a well-known Jewish comedian told the riddle, "What's the difference between a loaf of bread and a Jew?" Answer:...."The loaf of bread doesn't scream when you put it in the oven," very few would admonish him for it and some may even call him a "comedy genius." However, if the same meant-to-be-humorous joke is told by a white Christian, then it somehow becomes a hatred of Jews. Though it's NOT an intrinsically anti-Semitic riddle, it alienates most American Jews due to the fact that they're a minority in a largely Christian country.

If the Jew vs. Christian population roles were reversed and Judaism were the dominant majority religion in the United States, Jews wouldn't feel so *persecuted* by macabre humor about them made by a person in the miniscule two percent Christian minority. Most, if not all Jewish Americans don't like the "Jews are cheap money-grubbers" kind of jokes made about them, and rightfully so. The question is, why not? Jews will reply that such jokes perpetuate a myth, an unfair stereotype, or an outright lie about them and for those reasons, non-Jews who may be influenced by these jokes will dislike Jews and treat them cruel and unfairly. But if that's the case, and it undoubtedly is, then what it means is if there is anybody, professional stand-up comic or not, who should NOT be telling "Jew jokes," it's the Jewish person. If the person who is telling a humorous but disparaging anecdote about Jews is known to be Jewish, then that joke that he/she is telling will more than likely be thought of by gentiles to be TRUE, since the noted Jew "knows what he or she is talking about." Jewish people's self-deprecating jokes have far more credibility and hence, influence because they have lived the Jewish life. On the other hand, if a comedian who is known to be an Irish Catholic makes negative jokes about Jews, he can and will be easily dismissed as being anti-Semitic, prejudiced, or a bigot who speaks from ignorance about or has a dislike of, Jews. As a consequence, the Catholic comedian, unlike the patently believable Jewish comedian, isn't as convincing in his demeaning remarks about Jews, and as such, his words should therefore be considered more permissible and forgivable...and justifiably so.

Regarding those on the liberal/left, being "woke" is the newfangled expression of their solidarity with the oppressed *marginalized* who are suffering from "social injustices" (read: socio-economic freedom or *capitalism*). Although, an American who is definitely "woke" will not feel the least bit hurt or indignant after hearing a poor black lesbian communist state that she hates rich, white people and would like for them to die from AIDS. Indeed, the *woke* American would very likely take malicious delight in the latter's statement. For a citizen who is extremely "woke" usually has a dislike of people who are not "*woke*" and wishes fascistic oppression on them. Accordingly, it is absolutely 100 percent impossible for someone to definitely be "woke" and at the same time be dead-set AGAINST socialism. Alas, when about fifty percent of the nation does NOT disapprove of *political correctness, identity politics, cancel culture, virtue signaling, critical race theory, wokeism* and any other Marxist/cultish behaviors; then almost half of the people of the United States are, perhaps inadvertently, buttressing the left's hatred of our country and their desire for its ultimate destruction.

In April 2018, two young black men were sitting down at a Starbucks coffee shop in Philadelphia. Because they wouldn't buy anything, which constituted loitering and is against company rules, the manager called the police on the two violators. Their arrest was filmed by a patron, resulting into a response of over six dozen protesters in the City of Brotherly Love and the scene quickly became a national embarrassment and public-relations nightmare for the famous coffee chain. The white lady who was the manager of the noted coffee shop was fired. The coffee giant's executive chairman, Howard Schultz, was scared to death of bad publicity and a national boycott by blacks and left-leaning organizations. Such action by the latter two groups has the potential to do long-term financial damage to the Starbucks brand. In order to avoid this happening, Schultz made darn sure of trying to placate black America by pouring his abundant contrition on real thick: "I think what occurred was reprehensible at every single level." What, precisely, are these "levels," and how many of them are there? About the incident, the chairman added, "I think I take it very personally, as everyone in our company does." Wow! That's 175,000 of their employees in America who "took it personally." Just think, countless Starbucks baristas (most of them teary-eyed) across the country got on the phone and called this former CEO to express their shame and sorrow, and as well, they should have. After all, what the lone Philadelphia store manager did was partly their fault.

Howard "I know nothing,...nothing" Schultz, in proving that he really does empathize with blacks, said, "The announcement we made yesterday about closing our stores, 8000 stores closed, to do significant training with our people is just the beginning of what we will do to transform the way we do business and educate our people on unconscious bias." First of all, instead of closing 8000 coffee shops and shutting off some $12 million dollar$ in revenue, why not just send all of them a FAX blast or e-mail blast telling the shop managers to immediately terminate Starbucks' present loitering policy? Plus, because of one isolated incident (it's never been reported to happen at any other Starbucks) why do roughly 175,000 Starbucks employees, including blacks, need "SIGNIFICANT training?" Also, approximately how many hours of instruction does it take to learn how to be nice to minority customers and not call the cops on them for loitering? No, what's going on here is that the head honchos at Starbucks speculated, perhaps correctly, that they had to prematurely capitulate to what they believed to be an imminent socioeconomic threat by the *cancel culture* mob and their minions. Hence, a couple of twenty-three-year-old male citizens were offered a college education as compensation, not so much because they were unfairly treated but because they are black. Howard Schultz consequently wasn't so much apologizing to the store-evicted gentlemen as he was racially assuaging the "Black People of America." The executive chairman merely felt compelled to make a big production number out of his penitence in order to EMPHATICALLY express earnestness. If the two men who were arrested for a loitering violation were WHITE, it wouldn't have been an "injustice" that Mr. Schultz cared about and was anxious to rectify in order to counter any negative perception of the incident by the public. Although, the two white men WOULD probably have received a free coffee. In sum, Howard Schultz figured that he had to engage in some major virtue-signaling in order to make up for the rule/ law violation that the lady manager never committed. Finally, does guilt-ridden liberalism and a disinclination to use intelligent analysis constitute being "unconsciously biased" (a contradiction in terms) for certain high-level members of Starbucks?

Blue states will sometimes elect a Republican for their governor (such as Vermont, Massachusetts, Rhode Island, Connecticut, and Hawaii) because every so often even their voters desire at least some degree of fiscal sanity to sometimes redress fiscal recklessness. But when it comes to the Federal government as opposed to State government, the citizens of a Democratic state want a "fighter" (read: spendthrift) as opposed to an "accountant" (read: tightwad) to go to Washington, DC, and bring home the bacon. For this reason, the humble author of this outstanding book knew that liberal Democrat John Kerry would beat moderate Republican William Weld in the 1996 race for Massachusetts senator and that socialist Democrat Mazie Hirono would win going up against GOP centrist Linda Lingle in the 2012 race for the next Senator of Hawaii. Both Weld and Lingle were once governors in their respective states. For the most part, a blue state will tolerate a MODERATE Republican as their governor but NOT as their senator.

The difference between capitalism and socialism is that under capitalism, there are millions of rich people who are NOT politicians, and under socialism there are NO wealthy people who are NOT politicians. With the nation barreling ahead in a progressive (a euphemism for "*socialistic*") direction and reaching the final destination, in order for an American to be financially well-off, he or she will have to hold public office in Washington, DC so said person can pass laws that not only take care of the nation's citizens, but also manipulate their lives. Such humanitarian social control is sure to gain the appreciation and respect of the lawmakers' constituents in which they will undoubtedly reward the aforementioned by re-electing him or her. So it's not so much the "good life" per se, that the noted voters covet, but rather, the caring government "management" of the people that they HOPE will provide them with the good life. The American electorate mindset is not totally unlike that of certain forlorn citizens of communist countries. When communist dictators Mao Zedong (1893-1976) of China and Kim Jong-il (1941-2011) of North Korea died, millions of their grieving citizens were crying hysterically. This is because even though the two countries were oppressive, murderous enslavements, their "Dear Leaders" were posthumously given respect, love and appreciation from the nation's forlorn denizens because the deceased tyrants deserved it. Whether it's America, China or North Korea; as long as a nation's lawmaker purports to be benevolent, it is acceptable that the law he or she supports is actually deleterious. For any progressive law, no matter how bad or unnecessary it is, provides HOPE by simply REPRESENTING comfort and security. And the Democratic party does just that. It does NOT have to deliver on it.

The illegal immigrants heading toward the United States have been instructed to claim asylum once they get here and when doing so, taught what sentences to vocalize. Though, a foreigner can claim asylum in America ONLY if he or she is being religiously or politically persecuted by their own government. Individuals from abroad CANNOT claim asylum because they want to escape poverty, flee from their abusive relatives, because they're bored, nor particularly, to simply live a better life. But our dishonest liberal news media likes to disingenuously refer to the illegal aliens from South America as "asylum-seekers" in order to draw sympathy from the American people. You see, if the "migrants" are portrayed and viewed as seeking *asylum* presumedly because they were oppressed or unfairly persecuted by their government, then that is more likely to evoke America's pity and hopefully make their invasion appear legitimate and warranted. Liberals flatter themselves by desiring the poor people of other nations to come here and live off our generous welfare state that liberalism itself begat. Liberals just know that poor minority immigrants will be so impressed with our enormous social safety net that compassionate do-goodism has created. It will be true unsung praise and a testimony to liberalism. Then, there is the unlawful act DACA (Deferred Action for Childhood Arrivals) to benefit those commonly known as "Dreamers." These anxious young individuals presently living here are mostly south of the border alien minors or ABHP (Anchor Babies for Hispanic Parents) who purportedly dreamt about and desired to become proud, happy, genuine citizens of America—Land of Opportunity. BFD! Millions of *"dreamers"* rich and poor, all over the world fantasize about and want to live in the United States. The aforementioned, along with American liberals and moderates, desire the same thing....Comprehensive Immigration Reform..(read: AMNESTY).

Many politicians, especially Democrats, say that they want to UNITE our country. When a liberal running for the presidency says that he (or she) will UNITE the nation if elected, rarely does it not involve governmental coercion and collectivism. In essence, we must move in a profoundly socialistic direction in order to be a *united* people. An utter recipe for disaster! Only implementing more personal liberty and fiscal austerity, which forces individualism on the American people, will *unite* the country by getting our citizens to practice and appreciate self-responsibility. Society will then be "united" via everyone respecting and supporting the autonomy of each individual.

In the summer of 2020, there were some protesters carrying picket signs saying that if you support Donald trump, then you support "white nationalism" and "white privilege." What they were thinking but refrained from speaking out loud, is that President Donald Trump is pushing conservatism, which is buttressing capitalism, that in turn, defines socio-economic freedom which benefits whites though is detrimental to blacks and other minorities. Naturally, if America were to live under totalitarian socialism, it would eradicate "systemic racism." If this were to happen, never again would there be any more institutionalized oppression keeping blacks down and making their lives miserable. For socialism IS racial justice and is the remedy to, and exterminator of, "white nationalism" and "white privilege." The castle of socialism, with totalitarianism as its moat, will protect the proletarian villagers because it is the duplicitous enemy of a liberty that allows "white nationalism" and "white privilege" to exist.

Prelude: It is not the obvious lack of timeliness of the below two paragraphs about Donald Trump that is relevant but their wisdom and lucidity.

If it bothers the reader that our current POTUS doesn't do what our allies want him to do, is mean to people and insults them, sports a horrendous hairstyle, is constantly tweeting and "always wears that same red tie", then you really ought to do your very best to be a little more petty. People who make such complaints would not detest Donald Trump in the slightest bit if he were a liberal president enacting a socialistic agenda, and they know it. Whether the President of the United States is a Democrat or Republican, his personal peccadilloes, idiosyncrasies, and "bad behavior" matter nowhere near as much as how his ideology and especially his policies, affect the economy, the stability and security of our Constitutional republic and the lives of the American people in general. Indeed, it's the character of a nation's CITIZENS which is more important than that of its leader, since it is they who elect the winning presidential candidate to lead, and lead only. But then, there are too many of us who can't or don't want to see the forest for the trees. If Barack Obama, while president, picked his nose every night at the dinner table, doing so had no effect on the economy, the country or the public's well-being. The man placing his fingertip in his nostrils every 24 hours would be undoubtedly gross and offensive to family members and visitors alike, but it should have been of no concern to the average person who will never even meet Mr. Obama.

Similarly, if you the reader, consider our 45th Commander in Chief, Donald J. Trump, to be brash, vulgar, disturbingly outspoken, offensibly assertive, politically successful, and for that you just plain hate him, then after the former real estate magnet leaves office, simply avoid living right next door to him. If you somehow can't do that and neighbor Trump comes over to your house, knocks on the front door, you open it and he asks to borrow a cup of sugar, shout "NO" and then promptly shut the door. If the big bad Orange Menace is strolling down a sidewalk and he says "Hi" to you, DO NOT greet him back. Just ignore him. If, in November of any year, private citizen Donald Trump calls you up and asks you to come over to his home for Thanksgiving, tell the ex-president, "Forget it, not a chance!" and then hang up on him. Stop employing emotion and feelings when judging somebody. Stop longing for the almost perfect mentor for you to idolize, because Donald J. Trump (or anyone else) just isn't going to cut it. Live as if the personality of our nation's leader doesn't make your own life better, because it doesn't and isn't supposed to.....STUPID! Barack Obama can vouch for this. In essence, you should put faith in a POTUS who implements beneficial, effective POLICIES, both foreign and domestic, and who does not necessarily possess a likable demeanor, to be your guide.....STUPID! President Trump operated like a superb doctor achieving excellent results, but displaying a sometimes atrocious and cringeworthy bedside manner.

Prelude again: Exclude, just for the moment, the far more serious threat of Chinese expansion as the author delves into the pertinence of the following paragraph. For a frame of reference, it was written in 2015.

As of the early 1990s, Islamic extremism has supplanted expansionary communism as being more of a threat to the United States. Supporters of the latter dormant Marxist-Leninist religion don't have nearly the vicious hatred of the American way of life as the deranged strain of religion emanating from the Middle East. Agents of communism, foreign or domestic, have never strapped bombs to their chest and walked into a restaurant or other place of business and blown themselves up. Communists don't claim that the God they worship (in their case, the spirit of Vladimir Lenin) had instructed them to commit suicide by flying passenger jets into tall buildings. But the far left in America has more of an intense dislike for traditionalist conservatives who are law-abiding than they do for radical Muslims who want to kill us. These bitter progressives condone the intentions of Islamic extremism—to tear down America, just as they, the former, aim to do. But the difference is that the far left wants SOCIALISM (which in their view would be a 50/50 combination of *punishment* (for rich, white, Christian men) and *emancipation* (for everybody else) of society as the ends to their means and not SHARIA LAW.

The capitalistic right is more "paranoid" and engages in conspiracy theories (black helicopters, Agenda 21, strange-looking clouds, fluoride in the toothpaste is a communist plot, etc.) far more than the socialistic left does. This is because the liberty-loving right doesn't want to live under ANY type of government domination, no matter how well-meaning it is, and believes that we are NOT "all in this together" via centralized control. The seemingly delusional right-wing organizations (e.g. the cultish on-line group, "Q-Anon") are merely concerned about their freedom and societal independence regardless of whether their "paranoia" is justified.

Although the United States is a free country and stands a fair chance of remaining so until the year 2028, it doesn't give a white banker the right and the liberty to NOT LEND black citizens money because of their race. Such action would hinder the potential prosperity of black citizens, would be a violation of their *negative rights* (or negative *freedoms*) and deleterious to our republic in general. *Positive rights* (or positive *freedoms*), on the other hand, are conducive to a pure democracy, which this nation isn't and should never, ever be. In a *democracy,* a word that our Constitution and Declaration of Independence doesn't mention, the people would clamor for so many *positive rights* that the Federal government would soon be compelled to take away most of, if not all of, their *negative rights.* The Tea Party is more hated than liked, not just because they're against *positive rights,* but also because this right-leaning, grass-roots movement has conscientious integrity, which the advocates of *positive rights* don't have. The rectitude of the former political gathering of patriotic concerned citizens and their love for the Constitution, plus their pro-capitalism philosophy, grate on the nerves of those who continually refer to America as "our democracy." A person who supports *positive rights* and sneers at the Tea Party and its ideology is a person who has never and will never say a bad word about coercive collectivism. Likewise, citizens who think the world of the term "our democracy", will never diss socialism. And that's because socialism IS the paragon of a "democracy."

Of some 200 million American citizens who own guns, there are at least a dozen of them who are deranged and quite possibly dangerous. But when well-meaning liberals say that they want to make shopping malls and other areas "gun-free zones," it would only make said lunatics delirious with delight. Indeed, it would MAKE THEIR DAY! Many gun owners have stated that Americans need a militia in order to defend their God-given rights. In response, some of the gun-control groups have offered, "America doesn't need a militia, we already have the military." Do these anti-Second Amendment advocates not fathom what they just said? If a foreign or domestic homicidal yet powerful despot were to somehow take ironfisted command of our country, the gun-control zealots may want to walk back those words, and then soon afterwards, they should put a large neon sign on top of their house with the words, "Gun-Free Zone." But all seriousness aside, if there's one place that should NOT be a gun-free zone, it is jet airliner cockpits. If pilots on passenger aircraft were allowed to carry guns for the past one hundred years, *nine/eleven* more than likely would NOT have happened.

Is it not a harbinger of the USA's socio-economic system in the not-too-distant future, when we celebrate a national holiday for a socialist (MLK), elect a clandestine socialist for president in 2008, commemorate American communists (W.E.B. DuBois and Paul Robeson) with their likeness on first-class postage stamps and fly the American flag at half-mast to honor a dead communist, (Nelson Mandela), even though he wasn't an American? What's next, political correctness becoming the law of the land and the state of Texas turning electorally purple? These are rhetorical questions that need to be answered.

Many, if not most American Indians are not really offended by the term "squaw." But that doesn't deter do-gooder liberals from taking vicarious umbrage. For over a century, refering to a young native American woman as a "squaw" was about as derogatory and hurtful as calling a white person "paleface." The "outrage" over the psychologically traumatizing label...."squaw", (e.g. "Squaw Valley Ski Resort") is primarily employed as a political devise by progressives to convince Indians to feel victimized as the latter seeks sympathy from other citizens. But the hyper-sensitive left speakum forked-tongue. What's more offensive; someone saying about an attractive Indian girl, "Hey, there's that pretty little squaw" or someone saying "Hey, there's that god damn motherfucking Indian bitch!"

Besides coffee, some poetic justice has been served. The lady manager at that Starbucks coffee shop in April 2018, who told two black loiterers to leave the store, was compensated for her unfair involuntary departure. The court ordered the famous coffee chain to pay the lady $25 million for firing her because she's white. If only said woman was black, Starbucks wouldn't have had to shell out $25 million because they'd never have fired her. Although, the young black men told to vacate the premise WERE directed by the judge to be given a dollar by the wealthy coffee corporation. Perhaps the multi-billionaire Howard Schultz, out of pity and if he can afford it, will donate $25 million to each of them.

Has anybody ever noticed that progressives accuse politicians on the freedom-based, capitalistic-right of wanting AUTHORITARIANISM? The noted ideologues on the left are the same ones that complain about conservatives trying to CUT BACK on governmental *edicts, regulations* and *restrictions*!!! Those who call Donald Trump a dictator are actually LIARS who would absolutely welcome a Democrat president for a dictator because then we'd all be living under authoritarian socialism and to the noted Trump detractors, that's a good thing. The vast majority of liberals and some moderates desire a strict, but compassionate and caring autocrat to command the American people and make them obey. Authoritarian socialism really is the logical outcome of contemporary liberalism. No liberal has ever said a negative word about socialism and they never will. Why is that?

Liberal journalism and the liberal media constantly refer to conservatives as "the far right" or "the right." They would be loath to explain the difference between the two. That is, on what issues does the "RIGHT" disagree with the "FAR right" on? The liberal-left would like the American people to think that if conservatism is not actually fascism/Nazism (the far-right), then it is very close to being so (the right). Progressivism has been winning because most political citizens erroneously conflate "the far right" with fascism/Nazism. Going back to at least the 1930s, Europeans associated the despotic couple with the ideological RIGHT because the noted two isms were perceived as having the exact opposite of a kindly and benevolent nature, which was the demeanor and reputation of socialism/communism (the LEFT).

Some late-breaking news: The doctors that performed open-head surgery on Democratic Congresswoman Nancy Pelosi said that nothing malignant or deleterious to her health was detected and that all they found were a few crumbs. Godspeed, Mrs. Pelosi. Your Party needs you.

CHAPTER **31**

Social Values

"AMERICA, IT IS said, is suffering from intolerance. It is not. It is suffering from tolerance. Tolerance of right and wrong, truth and error, virtue and evil, Christ and chaos! Our country is not nearly so overrun with the bigoted as it is overrun with the broadminded." Thus spoke Catholic Archbishop Fulton J. Sheen. Domestic social issues are an area where conservative intellect isn't as well defined as it is with economic philosophy and American foreign policy matters. It's an area where the liberal/left has politically exploited the perceived intolerance and puritan aura of the religious right. Fundamentalist Christians, and the like, care primarily about morality, mostly of stopping abortion and putting the freedom to pray back in the public schools. In the vocabulary of the religious right, "atheistic communism" is ONE word. Because Marxism believes in no God is primarily the reason why they're against it. The fundamentalists, and others on the social values right, come underneath the banner of CONSERVATIVE TRADITIONALISTS.

There is nothing in our Constitution that calls for the separation of church and State. Nonetheless, we do have a SECULAR Federal government, and rightly so. But we are also a Christian nation with Judeo-Christian values, and rightly so. It's not the conservative right that's "trying to impose its values on the rest of us," but the liberal left via the government. If an American is a member of a certain house of worship and comes to dislike its' beliefs, he or she has the freedom to leave it. But in order to escape ever-expanding government, one would eventually have to leave the country. The lawmakers of Washington, DC allowing peaceful religious institutions the freedom to thrive, is not an endorsement of or partnership between the government and the church. But those on the anti-religion left disingenuously try to portray it as such. These progressives want to brand Christianity somehow as a government-enforced religion precisely because it isn't statist secularism. They want your allegiance to the glorious State (man), not to the deity. But as the Rabbi Marc Gellman explains, "The desire of people to worship God is far greater than their desire to live in a failed state that hates a loving faith." The American left would rather not recognize that their virtual worship of the Federal government is, in itself, a form of religious devotion. They desire not individuality, but for society's collective belief to be *bundled up* (nationalized group-think) in the aim of being advantageous to the left's "progressive" (socialistic) agenda. Though, as Rabbi Gellman points out, "We must be bundled not just to each other but also to the Truth, which in my view comes from both reason and God. The Nazis bundled millions of Germans into a murderous bundle of genocidal hate. The problem therefore is to carefully evaluate the moral virtue of your bundle and if it falls short of its ideals, to speak and act in such a way as to return it to its collective virtue."

In the United States, people who are NOT religious are far more likely to HATE those who ARE religious, than vice versa. Peaceful religion in our country, particularly Christianity, is a threat to the secular left if it does not banish itself strictly to inside the church and home. That is, if religion makes its presence known in the socio-political arena and becomes too popular, it may inspire most voters to look to the heavens above for their salvation. Henceforth, the American electorate will be more likely to embolden, consciously or not, individualism and self-responsibility by voting in conservative lawmakers. This, progressivism cannot tolerate. The absence of religion in the public square, the secular left correctly believes, would create a vacuum that they could exploit and a cultural war that they would more easily win. The left is well aware that those who believe in God and not the great State are far more likely to adopt a Bible-based propriety and be opposed to what practically amounts to criminality, governmental COLLECTIVISM (economic coercion) and REDISTRIBUTION (legalized thievery). Some liberals have exploited Jesus Christ by claiming that the Son of God had beckoned us to take care of our fellow man (via taxation and redistribution). That's INDIVIDUALS through his or her own initiative that Christ was referring to. NOT collectivistic government, STUPID!

To believe in God is to believe in faith, morality, and individual liberty. On the other hand, to genuflect at the altar of the almighty State is to tacitly endorse authoritarianism and a rigid societal conformity. A lot of us desire to look to government (man) as our veritable "savior." This assumes that man is not just infallible but well-nigh saintly. As for atheism, it is not immoral to be an atheist. But it IS immoral to be a militant atheist extremist who wants to subvert America's liberty-based, Judeo-Christian values. Atheism is perfectly fine as a personal preference but not as a State-enforced doctrine. Although, militant atheist extremism would do well to ponder as to whether itself is outright HATE, the Godless quasi-religion should at least accept that most Americans don't believe in atheism. But when left-wing atheists and progressives hear a religious conservative speak emphatically about "family values," they get that awful feeling that said right-winger is leaving government out of the equation. The liberal/left has filched the term "values" from the lexicon of traditionalist conservatives. The former's version of *values* tends to veer away from the deity and moral decency and closer to nihilism and hedonism. Progressives also disingenuously employ the term "values" to undercut legitimate opposition by the political right. For instance, liberal college students will try to block a conservative author from speaking on their campus because said writer's belief "goes against their values" (read: it opposes liberalism). But then, liberals' "values" are usually personified in shallowness. They love to say that government can't legislate morality (true); though nevertheless, liberals will continue to call for laws of harsher punishment for those that conscientiously commit "crimes of hate." It's the thought that counts, you see. Now, liberals and leftists won"t hold your feet to the fire of having decent morals, but they will advocate the government subsidize your shameful behavior. The entire left rejects the moral standards of traditionalists and the religious right and replaces them with moral relativism. But then that's only characteristically par for the course, since moral relativism is intrinsic to socialism; which in and of itself is immoral. The high priest of socialism, Karl Marx, famously proclaimed that religion is the opiate of the masses. If that's true, then as long as it's peaceful and makes them happy, it is the very best drug that people can administer to themselves.

If you, the reader, are a supporter of moral relativism, would it be okay with you if totally uncensored profanity were permitted on daytime AM/FM radio? If not, why not? Would you disapprove of X-rated movies being shown on public network television on Saturday mornings, right alongside the kiddy cartoons? If so how come? If you champion same-sex marriage, shouldn't you also back the legalization of polygamy? If your reply is "no," then who are you to say that a man can't have seven wives all at the same time? Are he and his wives a threat to you? By rejecting their rights to happiness, you must be a polygamistophobe! Plus, as long as a ten-year-old boy has written permission from both of his parents, why would you object to him marrying a thirty-five-year old man? What have you got against love? Also, if a mother and father say that it's perfectly alright with them that their daughter becomes a porn star at the age of thirteen, what's it to you? Why should there be a law against it? Furthermore, what's so bad about the noted thirteen year old girl having sex on film? As long as she gets paid at least minimum wage, her partners wear condoms and the bed is comfortable-----what's the problem?. By being against her human right to enjoy something that's done in the bedroom, you come off as a prude. And what about a farmer and one of his sheep? Shouldn't he-----well, never mind.

Some liberals have asked how traditionalist conservatives can be so hypocritical by being pro-life, in regard to abortion, but also support the death penalty. Well, it's probably because a cold-blooded murderer really is guilty and deserves an EYE FOR AN EYE punishment, while a seven week old fetus really is innocent. The secular left has long exploited the seemingly hypocritical factor of various Republicans (an adulterer politician) or religious men (a pedophile priest) as a political tool to bludgeon morality. But what these progressives won't tell you is that only an INDIVIDUAL who "preaches" one way and behaves another can be a hypocrite. No, the secular left seeks to blanket the entire religious right as hypocritical in order to impugn all of Republicanism, religion, and morality. If one is not cognizant of this, then one will be deceived and accept the left's false narrative. But it's not an absolute that the left-wing fringe is always wrong nor the right-wing fringe always correct. The majority of ostensibly open-minded American voters impulsively reject these two fringes on the political spectrum, but they shouldn't. What should be rejected is any demonstrably deleterious fringe of ideology or societal behavior in its attempt to become the norm.

Libertarians should accept that if corruption and decadence are indeed parasitic to the so-called VICIMLESS crimes of prostitution, organized gambling, and certain illegal drug possession, then maybe these type of liberties are not compatible to our republic and to the liberty that libertarians espouse. Genuine liberals (as opposed to socialists who pretend to be ordinary liberals) should comprehend that their drive for social equality can actually bring about something that they've long had a reputation of being against: social control. Traditionalists should ponder that if abortion is murder, as they say it is, then shouldn't these moral conservatives agree that the abortionist doctor receive the death penalty and that the consenting mother-to-be get life in prison? If not, why not? Pro-choice women should answer the following question, "Does having an abortion at being eight months pregnant make you the mother of a dead baby?" Yes or no! Just the same, any plans that a female may have, to make the termination of her pregnancy a form of birth control, should be aborted. Same-sex marriage supporters should admit that the real reason they want it is mostly because homosexual matrimony would undermine the stability of the nuclear family and America's traditionalist core that they have come to resent or detest. Or why else are civil unions (which nearly everybody supports) not good enough for them? Yes, the country's high divorce rates have made a bit of a mockery out of traditional (heterosexual) marriage, but nevertheless, wedlock between a man and woman only, is an institution that should be respected and aspired to. We mustn't throw the baby out with the bath water; unless, of course, you're a pro-choice woman.

The vast majority of Americans should adopt the clean-cut, morally upright values that embrace peaceful religion and rejects all enmity. Anything else is the *fringe,* and on the *fringe* is where it should remain. But if there's anything that should be "imposed" on the American people, it's freedom. It is liberty-inducing LESS-GOVERNMENT that will persuade individuals to choose a lifestyle that behooves, not forces, them to embrace religion or at least have a healthy respect for the deity. To do so, in turn, is more likely to influence them away from debauchery. *"Liberty cannot be established without morality nor morality without faith."* -- Alexis de Tocqueville. Quite simply, the more freedom that human beings have, the more religious that they become. The more religious that humanity becomes, the more freedom that it achieves. But on all social value issues, what must be ascertained by every adult citizen of any political stripe is: What precepts of morality should be enforced by laws that do not fundamentally erode our personal liberties? And what personal liberties can be tolerated that do not fundamentally erode our moral fabric? In any event, we should all realize that morality and freedom really do go hand in hand. The complete erosion of either could mean anarchy or despotism.

CHAPTER 32

The Jewish Question Revised

"THE LOPSIDED JEWISH voting pattern resembled that of the blacks, the unemployed, and persons in households earning $10,000 a year, even though Jews in no way resemble those groups or share their social and political interests." So wrote the late scholar and historian, Lucy Davidowicz. As the old aphorism goes, "Jews earn like Episcopalians and vote like Puerto Ricans." Although a poor Jew is more likely to vote Republican than a rich Jew. This is because a lower-class income Jewish man recognizes his economic status but is earnestly climbing the financial ladder to success and wants to keep as much of his monetary reward as possible. The rich Jew, on the other hand, has already made it and feels guilty and more compelled to compensate for his or her wealth by voting Democrat, much like the millionaires living in the Hamptons. And government economic engineering, via the Democratic Party, is the Jews best way to manifest their compassion and caring for the forlorn little guy. In 1984, the Republican Presidential candidate, Ronald Reagan, received only 31 percent of the Jewish vote. He did exceptionally well. But of all America's ethnic and religious groups; the Jews are disproportionately the richest, the most successful, and the most intelligent (e.g. scientists, doctors, lawyers, professors). And yet, roughly 77 percent of Jewish Americans continue to vote for liberal Democrats.

Within the boundaries of the United States, Jews really don't so much mind, anti-Semitism coming from the liberal/left. Most of God's Chosen

People in our nation's political arena, for ideological reasons, desire that the charge of *anti-semitism* be used solely against conservatives. In particular, the more ideologically progressive that a black American is, the far LESS likely that Jews will condemn any outright anti-Semitism displayed by that black individual. In 2013, some black teenagers on a train bound for Brooklyn taunted a yarmulke-wearing white Jewish man. One of them said to the Jew, "They should have killed all of you," in reference to the Nazi extermination camps. Many Jews and non-Jews on the liberal/left regretted that it happened and didn't want to talk about it. This is because the taunter was black and, more than likely, a Democrat. Left-leaning Jewish Americans want so very much to believe that there is a political alliance between blacks and Jews. The harassment of the Jewish passenger by a black man serves only to undermine this desired political alliance. You see, blacks are the victims of society, Jews are their prime rescuers, and socialism is the Emerald City. If a Jewish man in our country is ever physically or verbally attacked again, most Jews and liberals will hope and pray (well, hope) that his attacker is a white, evangelical Christian conservative who just recently graduated from the late Jerry Falwell's Liberty University. Unfortunately for the Jewish left and the liberal media, there is extremely little chance of this happening. But oh, the politically exploitative fun that they would have with it if it did!

Many, if not most, Jews care nary a whit about the success of Israel to remain a Jewish State, for more Jewish Americans to go to synagogue every week, or for themselves to marry other Jews in order to better preserve the foundation and sanctity of their religion. The majority of liberal American Jews (such as singer Bette Midler) despise the Tea Party and their smaller government, anti-socialism philosophy (Midler calls it "hate"). And with liberalism being the road to socialism, this subsequently begs the question: Why, since the 1920s, has the vanguard of the American far left's advocacy of socialism/communism been Jews? It's because these two ideologies have always held an idealistic appeal to individuals (Jews) who are socially concerned and want to identify with the downtrodden and disfranchised. For over eighteen centuries, the Jews have proudly been the religion of *care-for-and-support-the-little-guy/*

underdog. Also, a lot of Jewish Americans insist on believing that in order to get as far away from Nazism as possible, that they have to become what they would like to think is its exact opposite, and that's socialists if not outright communists. This, plus the "struggle" toward a compassionate and egalitarian utopia offers Jews a heroic role in the making of history.

With noble overtones, the goal of socialism and its complementary component, SECULARISM, relieves them of the feelings (contrived or not) of being outcasts of the largely Christian society that America is. Secularism mitigates Christianity to the extent our Jewish citizens contemplate that their small religion won't be bullied and persecuted by larger denominations like it has been for well over a thousand years. But the majority of the nation's Jews aren't inherently religious. And they are the ones who are convinced that the non-spiritual "Judaism" that they desire will flourish under secularism. These particular Jewish Americans believe that a Christian country is religiously unethical. To the former, piety from any predominant denomination can't help but become biased and unfair to others. Jews will tell you, and not without merit, that Christian Americans wouldn't like it if their positions were reversed; if 78 percent of America were Jewish and only 2 percent were Christians. And both religions WOULD NOT tolerate an Islamic United States instilled with Islamic values.

Christianity isn't a threat to our nation's Jewry. But many, if not most, of American Jews would like to think that it is, which explains their fixation on "the separation of church and State." Christianity vs. the People: if you will. Thus, of the entire American left, Jewish citizens are disproportionately attracted to secularism because it's an adversary of Christianity and "Christian values." If a religious Bible-toting churchgoer mentions something about "Judeo-Christian values", then left-leaning Jewish individuals will only feel the need to close their hands over their ears. Perhaps, sometimes it is more comforting to feel like an outsider than to join in. Or as Mrs. Davidowicz once put it, "The answer, it seems to me, has to do with the powerful residual hold of the universal mindset, a hold so encompassing that it has led to an alienation of the Jews as a political group from their rightful place in the

American consensus."

Unfortunately, there are more Jewish Americans interested in a manifesto written by a self-hating Jew than there are who are interested in the Torah. Though Karl Marx and his partner Fredrick Engels; being the only communists that had any influence on the denizens of the United States, is plainly not the case. There was a mass migration of communist Jews from Russia and Europe to America, from 1860 to 1914. Starting in the early 1920s, they established far left organizations in (surprise!) New York. The garment industry in New York City was dominated by communist Jews, particularly women. That was also the decade that their indoctrination youth camps came into being and begat the "Red Diaper Babies." It was a joyous era with impressionable, mostly Jewish youngsters singing proletarian folk songs and playing games of cooperation, not competition.

Now Judaism is not at all essential to socialism/communism; but socialism IS an integral part of Judaism, in the minds of the majority of Jewish citizens, just like the Democrat Party is part and parcel of the identity of black Americans. In a nutshell, to most American Jews, socialism IS Judaism and vice-versa. They are synonymous. There is not a religion in the United States that is fonder of or more passionate about socialism and communism than the Jews, and nobody will be able to name one. I guarantee it. In fact, about half of Jewish Americans are socialists, albeit clandestine, and the Jews participation in the Communist Party USA has always been far disproportionately higher than that of any other religion in our country (roughly 40 percent membership even though Jews are just 2 percent of the population). Even AFTER Stalin died (1953), many American Jews ignored the Gulag of Russia and the regime's oppression and murder of its people from 1919 (the same year that the CPUSA started in America) up through the 1980s. The problem with too many left-leaning Jews is at the same time that they rightly excoriate Nazism, they've got their arm around their good friend, communism. It's analogous to a guy who shouts at the notorious criminal Charles Manson as the latter is being taken away in handcuffs, "You're a bad, wicked, evil scumbag, Manson, and you deserve your punishment,"—this being said while the guy has his arm around best pal and drinking buddy, serial killer, Ted Bundy. In essence, a lot of our nation's Jews primarily don't support Nazism only because it's not the exact same type of subjugation as communism. That is, they are not the least bit against Nazism BECAUSE it's oppressive or *totalitarian*. For oppression and totalitarianism to even slightly be part of the reason would become an indictment and condemnation of communism. No, Jews don't like Nazis primarily because Nazis don't like them. Even moderate and genuinely liberal Jews who are against communism and never want to live under it, are extremely reluctant to disparage communism because they realize that to do so would be an oblique repudiation of their fellow Jew. But isn't it a shame that, today, an inordinate amount of Jewish Americans feel more of a kinship and compatability with communism/socialism than they do with Christianity, even though throughout the twentieth century, Christianity had been far, far nicer to Jews?

As long as it isn't Nazism, a lot of American Jews would welcome an absolute despot for a leader who will install religious neutrality (secularism). This, they would like to think, will rid them of their alienation. Many of our Jewish citizens are super-sensitive because they believe that they need to be, in order to FEEL persecuted by American gentiles. They desire to be "victims" because it validates their being Jewish. This, the same Jews would like to think, will then become an indictment of gentiles. If a Christian lady makes the comment "Jews are smart with money and have made wonderful lawyers and scientists for our country," numerous Jewish Americans will insist on being offended and taking what she said as some kind of underhanded insult (via reaction formation). The same Jews will subsequently employ the "anti-Semite" moniker to deter any future verbal slight, criticism of, or disagreement with them by non-Jews. They would rather not acknowledge that such a tactic could only foment REAL anti-Semitism. But a gentile's demeanor toward God's Chosen People is mostly irrelevant. Only what he or she wants for Jews and, especially, for the USA's friend and ally, the State of Israel, is what's important.

THE HOLOCAUST: Firstly, the basic definition of "the Holocaust" is "the slaughter of people and the destruction of livelihood on a mass scale." If one were to add harrassment, persecution and oppression to millions of Jews plus others in the 1930s and early 40s, it would be the quintessential description. But if one were to ask relatively knowledgable individuals the question "What is the date that the Holocaust began?", ninety five percent of the time the answer would be *January* 30th, 1933. This answer is wrong. Adolph Hitler was elected chancellor of Germany on that date but the Nazi officially-authorized harrassment, persecution, oppression and murder of Jewish people didn't happen BECAUSE Hitler took office, per se. Also, the aforementioned government-sanctioned human atrocities against the Jews didn't take place on the 30th of January, 1933, nor the next day. Furthermore, they didn't occur at all in February. No, perhaps unknown to all but one person, the infamous human cruelty and genocide initiated by the notorious dictator was very likely set into motion on March 9th, 1933. So, the Holocaust as we know it, actually commenced five weeks and four days after Hitler was installed as the head of Germany. The Nazi genocidal death camps (aka the Final Solution) began in December 1941. It was also at this time that President Franklin D. Roosevelt became aware of it. In the summer of 1942, our 32nd president declared, "The Nazis will not succeed in exterminating their victims any more than they will in enslaving mankind." History disagrees. But there are many Roosevelt defenders who will protest that there was nothing that he could have done to end the brutal subjugation and mass slaughter. Okay. Let's review that. Accepting that FDR was privy in the first quarter of 1942 to the abominable mass genocide taking place, his defenders will concur that in said time frame, (1) The United States was right not to have declared war on Germany because they weren't attacking us, (2) We would have been wrong to invade their extermination camps and liberate the prisoners without a declaration of war, and (3) Declaration of war or not, it was smart of America to refrain from dropping bombs on or near their killing centers because hundreds if not thousands of Jews would have died. If all this is true, then doesn't it render moot the Jewish sacrosanct catchphrase "Remember the Holocaust?" It does indeed. Holding back our military power to halt this human atrocity in the last month of 1941 truly does become an indictment of the Roosevelt administration, which was informed about and DID BELIEVE the news about the Nazis building a murderous gas chamber, but decided against trying to destroy it.

So it's not at all a factor of "Remembering the Holocaust" and to "Never let it happen again" but rather, acknowledging an ongoing horrific event and next deciding what to do about it THEN AND THERE. Hence, the two noted slogans are not the slightest bit logically applicable to stopping a re-enactment of the infamous factual occurrence of the past. Let's pretend, for instructional purposes, that the Holocaust gas chambers barbarity never happened. And let's say that a mass killing equally horrible as the *Nazi death camp myth* was presently taking place in another country and the United States found out about it. Even though there were no "Final Solution" of long ago to REMEMBER and thus, supposedly base our course of action on, would our leaders in Washington, DC still be capable of implementing a plan, in all probability military engagement, to stop today's human enormity? Yes, of course we would. Ditto, early 1940s America! If President Roosevelt had ordered the immediate bombing of Chelmno, the first of the half dozen Nazi death camps, as soon as it went into operation (early December 1941) or within the next few weeks; numerous innocent prisoners would have also perished as a result. But then, some two million, seven hundred thousand Jews, destined to be murdered in the ensuing three years and five months, would have never become prisoners in the first place. This is because the destruction of the initial gas chamber center would extremely likely have deterred the other five extermination camps from being built over the next forty one months because the noted death centers, had they proceeded to being erected, would have been soon obliterated by American or Allied bombs. Very likely, when the Fuhrer took note of FDR and his counterparts in Great Britain, France and Russia's abstain from decimating Chelmno, that told the dictator that he had the green light to proceed with the construction of more extermination prisons. Otherwise, with such a bombardment unleashed a day after the one at Pearl Harbor, there would have been no Auschwitz as we know it, for any revisionist to deny that there was. Government/military action is, and should be, predicated on CURRENT knowledge and decision, not remembrance and pity. To expound; before the year 1933, there were NO mass subjugation and maltreatment of a multitudinous amount of people along with genocide/extermination camps in a country that was friendly with America, for our 32nd Commander in Chief to have "LEARNED FROM." So, as a logical consequence, because there wasn't a similar genocide that happened in the year 1932 or earlier for Franklin D. Roosevelt to have remembered and retrospectively RESPONDED TO, then it wasn't possible for him to even attempt to halt the on-going 1933-1945 Holocaust that ended up killing six million Jews. There now, isn't that right?

Presently, the entirely emotion-based slogan "Never Again" is relevant only if American Jews need to be consoled and American gentiles need to do penance. Most of our country's left-leaning Jews, regarding oppression of their ancestors by the Third Reich, are eager to rationalize Franklin Roosevelt's negligence or minimize altogether the heedlessness of America's early 1940s commander-in-chief. In fact, FDR remains the Jewish American's favorite president ever, in spite of his abandonment of their European kindred (excluding the SS St. Louis affair). Why? It's because FDR was a liberal who initiated Social Security (America's best-loved Ponzi scheme) and the New Deal (America's precursor to centralized planning). These particular Jews believe that to castigate and demonize a liberal lion like Roosevelt would do collateral damage to liberalism itself. In their opinion, outrage over our 32nd president's tacit permission of an abhorrent and nightmarish occurrence induced by a nationalistic socialist (Hitler) should take a back seat to their veneration of a quasi-socialist (Roosevelt).

As everybody knows, Nazism is government command and control of the people. This writer wonders what percentage of the US Holocaust Museum's frequent visitors, support NON-Nazism command and control of the people and what percentage are against it. There were 150,000 Jews in Hitler's military. Today, if a Jewish American was to become a member of the US Nazi Party, that person would be branded a self-hating traitor because the Third Reich had a history of, to put it very mildly, not treating Jews well. But if a Jew is a member of the Communist Party USA, then he or she would NOT be thought of as a "Judas." This is because communism has always been good to Jews. Though, in all fairness to communism, it has a widely acclaimed reputation of treating *everybody* well, not just Jews. But all seriousness aside, anybody who thinks or says that Nazism is the polar opposite of communism is a liar. In 1939, the communist Soviet Union made a friendship pact with Nazi Germany. After hearing about this and the Russian Gulag, thousands, if not millions, of American Jews, over the next half century, remained sympathetic to and enamored of the Soviet Union. Jews are not so much against Nazism because of its crimes and atrocities but merely because it's viciously anti-Semitic. The Third Reich, in its twelve years, was reponsible for the deaths of some twenty million people while communism killed about one hundred million people in seven decades. Today, conversation about the Jews and Nazism is welcome. But, conversation about the Jews and communism is taboo for some reason that no one can figure out. Nonetheless, with Nazism and communism merely being two sides of a bad socialist coin, how do America's left-leaning Jews live with themselves?

Now, a negative demeanor by an individual against a certain group of people doesn't necessarily mean that what he/she is saying about them is wrong. If it seems that our republic's conservative (capitalistic) right is acrimonious toward American Jews, it's because of the latter's socialistic mindset. Although, it's also the Jews' woe-is-me disposition despite the fact that a good many of them are well-to-do. But God's Chosen People were wildly attracted to socialism before the Fuhrer could even grow a mustache. America's mournful, progressive Jewish citizens want so very much to think that "anti-socialism" is synonymous with "anti-Semitism." It isn't....and....it is! But the vast majority of them would have absolutley no qualms about voting for an AVOWED dyed-in-the-wool socialist, gentile candidate for public office who is unequivocally anti-Semitic, than vote for a free-market conservative that not only is not anti-Semitic, but is also staunchly pro-Israel. This proves that most Jews' concern with anti-Semitism to be utterly insincere and superficial.

In conclusion: Yours truly is well aware that many will try to, as a diversionary tactic, associate this essay with centuries-old tales (as in "tall") about the "Jewish international conspiracy," "Jew bankers" and "secretive, evil Jewish cabals." My article has nothing whatsoever to do with preposterous canards (and my detractors know it doesn't), but with the Jews' natural ideological inclination, dating back to at least the mid nineteenth century. The writer also realizes that any criticism of or disagreement with the American Jewish establishment, from gentiles, is to be considered automatically anti-Semitic particularly if it conflicts with the progressive goal and agenda. There will be individuals who, after they read this essay, will have a conniption fit and engage in name-calling, cry "paranoia," and call me a "Jew hater." But you will notice that they didn't dispute anything that this author wrote. And they won't. So, in lieu of that, my perturbed opponents, for the purpose of dissuading agreement by the reader, will snivel "anti-Semitism" and "McCarthyism" or the like. In doing so, they will be de facto admitting that what I wrote is true by their outright refusal to argue that it's not true. This must be the case, or why else would these dishonest critics not say that yours truly is wrong when they so very easily could have? And that, folks--is what's known as CHECKMATE!

CHAPTER 33

The Beatles Were Jewish

OKAY NOW, PLEASE don't be prejudiced by the previous article into thinking that this writer doesn't like Jews. I'll have you know that some of my best friends are actually friends with someone who is Jewish. In fact, I myself like to visit a family of Jews every December 25th and try to cheer them up. And countless times, I have joyously driven my car in the vicinity of Brooklyn. Why, my favorite recording artists of all time, the Beatles, were Jewish. Yes, that's right. Though, this was never divulged perhaps because it would have jeopardized their popularity. Some may doubt me, but I will explain in a wee bit, just how the Fab Four were (secretly) Jewish.

In October 1957, seventeen-year-old John Lennon welcomed fifteen-year-old Paul McCartney into his skiffle / rock n' roll group in Liverpool, England. Four months later, George Harrison, who was just a couple of weeks away from turning fifteen, joined, and the band was finalized in August 1962 with the addition of Ringo Starr. It was also that year the Beatles hit the big time in Liverpool. They hit the big time in England in 1963 and then took the world over musically in 1964. England's finest had their first number one hit, "Please Please Me" the same month that their youngest member, George, stopped being a teenager and the band broke up three months before their eldest member, Ringo, turned thirty years of age. The Beatles went on to become the biggest, the best, and especially, the most influential recording artists of all time. This, while they were still in their twenties. Now, you'll notice that I didn't say that the Beatles were "one of the best." That would be a cop-out that most people would commit. But the Fab Four are not the best because they were the leaders of the British Invasion or because of the quartet's personalities, haircuts, or clothes. Nor was it due to any "deep meanings" in the lyrics of their compositions.

No, the Beatles are the best because they have a cornucopia of the catchiest, most infectious and memorable pop songs that there ever were. Think about it. And what the majority of even the pop rock group's most ardent fans don't realize is that every one of their albums released from 1963 to 1970 is worth getting, due to most, if not all of the songs, on each and every album. It wasn't a case of a "New Hit Single" on an album pulling a bunch of drab, forgettable ones, like it was with all the other artists. Nobody with three or more albums in any music genre has ever achieved this. Indeed, the Mop Tops had unsung, overlooked gems such as *"There's a Place," "I Call Your Name," "It Won't Be Long," "When I Get Home," "I'll Be Back," "Another Girl," "Think For Yourself," "She Said, She Said," "Rain," "And Your Bird Can Sing,"* etc.

Any other band at that time would have killed for these mostly unknown songs and have insisted that they be marketed as singles, where these catchy tunes would have undoubtedly reached the Top 10 of the Billboard 100. But the Beatles treated the aforementioned songs as "filler," "working songs," or "throwaways." Such was the power of their vast catalogue. In one particular case, the Fab Four declined to release a certain "filler/throwaway" as a single. But their subsidiary in America, Capital Records, liked this "forgetable album filler" enough to distribute it as a single where, sure enough, it soared to Number 1 in February 1965. That song: "Eight Days a Week."

More books have been written about the Beatles than any other show business artist/artists. Many of these books have delved into their recording sessions (the time and date, what instruments were used, how many takes, and more.). The lyrics of their songs have been dissected more than those of any other musicians. And the "Beatles sound," (ear-grabbing guitar hooks, super-melodic tunes, unorthodox but brilliant chord structures, two- and three-part harmonies) have been revered by numerous students of many a musical genre. Even absolute non-musicians are familiar with the brand names Rickenbacker, Hofner, Gretch, and Ludwig, and what pop rock band these instruments are in reference to. England's finest band has reached such an iconic status that even the manner of their 1964 stage presentation is now rock n' roll folklore: Ringo, with his head cocked downward and to the left; Paul, a little bit knock-kneed, playing a left-handed violin-shaped bass guitar; George, in the middle and slightly bow-legged, sometimes doing a little jig; and in the music world's most famous stance, John, with his legs far apart, feet at a 45-degree angle, and body gently bouncing up and down. His stance and guitar played on his chest (not on his pelvis like today's guitarists) was widely imitated by guitarists in many Merseybeat groups. Even Ed Sullivan's "really big" introduction of the Fab Four on his television variety show (February 9th, 1964) has become famous and practically iconic.

During their music reign beginning in late 1962, the Beatles had fifteen Number 1 albums and twenty Number 1 singles. This feat will remain unbeaten in pop music for eternity. Another remarkable achievement that will never be repeated is that they owned the TOP FIVE songs on the Billboard Charts (the first week of April 1964). Moreover, and especially, no one is even close to having the song craftsmanship, musical inspiration, and supremacy that the Mop Tops had and still have. In absolute greatness, they come in first place and Elvis Presley comes in second place. The King didn't write his own songs or play any instrument for most of them. Nor do Presley's songs have as many memorable melodies or the inventiveness of those of the world's most famous quartet. Furthermore, the Beatles, in regard to recording, accomplished it all three times faster than the rock n' roll idol from Tupelo, Mississippi (seven and a half years vs. twenty-three years). All other music artists have to contend for third place. According to the record Industry Association of America, from 1991 to 2007, the leaders of the British Invasion sold more records than Mariah Carey, Celine Dion, and Metallica. John Lennon was correct in 1966 when he remarked that the Beatles were more popular than Jesus Christ. It could very well be the case today. More than five decades after they officially broke up on April 10, 1970; John, Paul,

George, and Ringo still sell more records than most of the current musical artists. Utterly phenomenal!

P.S. "I Want to Hold Your Hand" is the song that originally made the Beatles world famous when it became their initial Number 1 seller in the USA for the first month of 1964, a seminal year in pop music. In fact, the tune was primarily credited for bringing the Fab Four over here a few weeks later on February 7th. "She Loves You" became the nation's Number #1 song two months later. Now, Paul McCartney has sung "All My Loving" and "I Saw Her Standing There" numerous times on stage since the early 1980s. Neither of these songs reached Number #1 in our country or England. But what most of the Beatles aficionados and "experts" don't know is that the last time the famous bass player performed the more musically/historically important "I Want to Hold Your Hand" and "She Loves You"(the latter launching Beatlemania in England in August 1963) to an audience of thousands was in.....1964. By contrast, the prolific former Beatle, over recent years, has sung some of the group's more obscure tunes like "Things We Said Today" and "The Night Before." Also, Mr. McCartney has performed on stage "Please Please Me" which was originally written by John Lennon who also did the lead vocal like he did on their first American Number 1 hit. But with the Beatles being already halfway to a reunion, perhaps Sir Paul can enlighten us about his curious neglect of performing the Beatles second biggest hit, *"I Want to Hold Your Hand"* (seven weeks at number one on the Billboard 100) that initially endeared them to America; before the world's best musical quartet's final get-together comes to fruition.

And now as promised: The Beatles originally employed titles of their songs that centered on or around their religion, Judaism. For example, John Lennon was heard singing "Baby, You're a Rich, Fag Jew" in reference to their manager, Brian Epstein, a homosexual. But for the record-buying public the world over, the name of the song was changed to "Baby, You're a Rich Man Too." And that is what's heard today when you listen to it. As with the rest of their song repertoire, the four Liverpool musicians, at first, gave these well-known tunes Hebrew titles (song names) relating to Judaism. But you'll never see any Beatles records with such titles because the world's best rock n' roll band ever, perhaps with the goading of their WASP-like producer, George Martin, converted them into names of songs that the predominantly gentile fans could relate to, appreciate, and purchase. Here are just fifty of the songs that we have all come to know and love, though with their original but unfamiliar titles. The following are in, NOT exact, chronological order:

1. Love Hebrew
2. I'll Get Jew
3. She Loves Jew
4. From Me to Jew
5. All My Scrimping
6. I Want to Hold Your Ham
7. This Goy
8. I'm Happy Just to Dance with Jew
9. I Shoah Known Better
10. I Feel Fineberg
11. I Don't Want to Spoil the Lobster
12. Talmud to Ride
13. You're Goering to Lose That Girl
14. If I Needed Bacon
15. Day Kippur
16. Eleanor Rabbi
17. Got to Get Jew into My Life
18. Doctor Josef
19. Treblinka Fields Forever
20. Penny Lane
21. Sergeant Birnbaum's Lonely Hymies Club Band
22. When I'm Sorbibor
23. Sheeny's Leaving Home
24. Lucy in the Bed with Goebbels
25. Being for the Benefit of Mr. Kike
26. I Saw Himmler Standing There
27. You've Got to Hide Yourself Away
28. With a Little Zyklon B From My Friends
29. I'm Only Decomposing
30. Dig a Body
31. Run for Your Life
32. HELP
33. Kabbalah Mystery Tour
34. All You Need Is Pork
35. Your Mother Should Shuckle

36. The Fool on the Hillel
37. I Am the Torah
38. Hey Jew
39. Lady Mennorah
40. Everybody's Got Something to Buy Except for Me and My Money
41. While My Dachau Gently Weeps
42. Eichmann's Silver Hammer
43. Happiness Is a Warm Oven
44. Don't Let Me Burn
45. Carry That Corpse
46. She Came in Through the Broken Glass Window
47. The Ballard of Jonah and Yarmulke
48. Mean Mr. Matzah
49. Why Don't We Do It in the Temple
50. Here Comes the Schmuck

Now, here are the same 50 tunes only this time with their more internationally known gentile and genteel titles.

1. Love Me Do
2. I'll Get You
3. She Loves You
4. From Me to You
5. All My Loving
6. I Want to Hold Your Hand
7. This Boy
8. I'm Happy Just to Dance with You
9. I Should Have Known Better
10. I Feel Fine
11. I Don't Want to Spoil the Party
12. Ticket to Ride
13. You're going to Lose That Girl
14. If I Needed Someone
15. Day Tripper
16. Eleanor Rigby

17. Got to Get You into My Life
18. Doctor Robert
19. Strawberry Fields Forever
20. Penny Lane
21. Sergeant Pepper's Lonely Hearts Club Band
22. When I'm Sixty Four
23. She's Leaving Home
24. Lucy in the Sky with Diamonds
25. Being for the Benefit of Mister Kite
26. I Saw Her Standing There
27. You've got to Hide Your Love Away
28. With a Little Help From My Friends
29. I'm Only Sleeping
30. Dig a Pony
31. Run for Your Life
32. HELP
33. Magical Mystery Tour
34. All You Need Is Love
35. Your Mother Should Know
36. The Fool on the Hill
37. I Am the Walrus
38. Hey Jude
39. Lady Madonna
40. Everybody's Got Something to Hide Except For Me and My Monkey
41. While My Guitar Gently Weeps
42. Maxwell's Silver Hammer
43. Happiness Is a Warm Gun
44. Don't Let Me Down
45. Carry That Weight
46. She Came in Through the Bathroom Window
47. The Ballard of John and Yoko
48. Mean Mr. Mustard
49. Why Don't We Do It in the Road?
50. Here Comes the Sun

CHAPTER **34**

What is to be Done

A SPECTER IS haunting America – the specter of socialism. But merely not wanting to live under socialism or being against communism will not stop the USA's decline into a veritable slavery. One must be cognizant of what's going on and act accordingly. That does not necessarily include being PATRIOTIC. The use of an equivocal term like "patriotism" doesn't bode well for "the American way," whatever the heck that means. In and of itself, patriotism is inefficacious. Besides this humble writer, there are very few people in this country who realize that "patriotism" is just the frosting on the cake of American-style capitalism (socio-economic freedom). But just like being "patriotic", each and every US citizen can plausibly claim to be "pro-America." All of our nation's hardcore Marxist-Leninists are "patriotic" if they claim they are. If said communists had their druthers, the United States would live under the same system that the denizens of the old Soviet Union enjoyed under Stalin, Khrushchev, and Brezhnev. Why would the noted American comrades want this? Because these "patriots" purportedly want to help the people of our great nation, that's why. And we would still be called "*America*" and live "the American way." Though, if this (communism) were to happen, Neanderthal right-wingers (aka conservatives) would be put into zoo cages for patrons to stare at as what was once part of Americana. As for our liberals, they will be liquidated and made into coffee tables.

During the Cold War of 1947 through 1991, many liberals were somewhat uncomfortable with American PATRIOTISM because they felt that this word couldn't help but foment an alienating nationalism that was antithetical to peace, harmony, and world unity (globalism). Overt patriotism, they believed, only served to pointlessly agitate the USSR, an adversary that, liberals would have liked to think, could have been our friend. Today, if the nation of Brazil sold the United States a shipload of rancid coffee beans, we could declare war on them and invade the shores of Rio de Janeiro like it was Normandy Beach. If various Americans enthusiastically supported our military invasion while waving the flag, they would duly be called "patriotic." But would such an incursion be the right thing to do? That is all that should matter. "Don't you dare question my patriotism," Senator John Kerry once admonished Republicans. President Ronald Reagan was famous for being sufficiently patriotic. But the quality or quantity of the patriotism of both gentlemen is irrelevant. Being PATRIOTIC is about as meaningful as the nationwide truism, "I'm an American".... yes; and the point is? Julius and Ethel Rosenberg were AMERICANS and they were "patriotic." The couple "loved their country" and "wanted to make it better." They truly were red, white, and blue—minus only the last two colors.

As for the American flag, waving or saluting the flag is just as helpful to our country as burning the flag is harmful to it. Many flag-burners realize this, but unfortunately, most flag-wavers do not. Burning or desecrating the American flag is not a crime, nor should it be. The flag really is just a piece of cloth that symbolizes one's own notion of "America." Being FOR or AGAINST the American flag is not what it's all about. Being FOR or AGAINST economic freedom (capitalism) and its ramifications is the issue. Show me a patriot who waves the flag, repeatedly chants "USA" in singsong unison with friends, loves a Memorial Day parade, and enjoys cookouts and fireworks on the Fourth of July, and I'll show you a person who would be aghast that anybody would want to abolish the IRS and the Department of Education, among others; and privatize Social Security. Patriotism, by itself, will not save America. Furthermore, it can be either good or bad (patriotism in the USA 1941-1945 *equals* GOOD; vs. patriotism in Germany 1933-1945 *equals* BAD). The American left has long sneered at patriotism, and not without merit. But there is one thing that patriotism and the left have in common. They are both intellectually void.

Most members of the media lean to the left (yeah, I know, "Ooh, big surprise!"). In college, they majored in journalism because as idealistic students, they wanted to be in the "people business." The future journalists' forte was their INTEREST in people. This "interest," augmented by sympathy, eventually segues into trying to help the common folk. "It is the duty of the newspaper to comfort the afflicted and afflict the comfortable." From the 1960 movie "Inherit The Wind." Many in the media erroneously assume that the job of journalism is to "protect our democracy." It is not. Although, the media DOES flatter themselves. Today, the liberal journalists' incidental job is to report the news, but their primary "responsibility," they believe, is to advance and improve society, and that's where the government comes into the picture. The liberal media knows for a fact that they are wiser than and superior to the average American, and so it's incumbent on them to manifest this notion by supporting central government command and control through most aspects of the ordinary people's lives in order to make them better. The left-leaning journalists and news anchors' main mission, from their perspective, is to influence the American voters via progressive propaganda. For social activism is not just their desire, it is their calling. Hence, in their pursuit to rescue the perceived underdog/downtrodden, DISHONESTY becomes the creed of liberal journalism, because it's entirely necessary in battling the capitalistic right. It subsequently behooves these do-gooders to destroy conservative lawmakers and their policies, plus help leftist politicians. One liberal column in the newspaper once pleaded with our Democratic president (Obama) to GET MAD when pushing his progressive agenda. The writer of the noted column, surely among many, would like to think that anger will at least compensate for liberalism if not outright propel it. To him and others, it is liberalism's PASSION that matters, not its adverse consequences.

To counter and discredit conservatives who are weary of looming government hegemony via excessive domestic spending and social programs, progressives inject subterfuge: "We already have Social Security and Medicare, but that doesn't mean that we're a socialist country, does it?" No, it doesn't. Nor does it mean that we should exploit the two programs as a basis for more expansive government. Social Security, Medicare, Medicaid, and the like are not "socialism" per se, but they are *socialistic*. There is a difference. The former S-word is the ends. The latter word in italics is the means or going in said ideological direction. Those who continually vote for the donkey Party always extend society's advocacy of government services, to activist government bankrolling the citizens' lives. Countless times, staunch Democrats have explained to us, "For many years, the government has been taking care of roads, bridges, city parks, and public beaches for the people, so shouldn't government also provide us with free college tuition and affordable housing?" It's a case of "Give the Democrats an inch and they will demand a mile."

They're perhaps unknowingly conflating local government services (town infrastructure) and Federal government services (interstate highways) with nanny state responsibility. The government can INVEST in infrastructure because it's conducive to the success of commerce and free enterprise. But the government cannot "invest" in people, as it will only subsidize them and their livelihood. For over at least a half a century, when the electorate opted for GOP control of the House and Senate every so often, this was not a pro-Republican stance per se, but a protest vote against the Democrats for being scoundrels and not delivering (via government) on their promise to improve the lives of the people. It is Democratic politicians, not liberalism; that the electorate is going to punish. Various Democrat lawmakers will have to become scapegoats because for the people to blame liberalism, is to blame themselves and their own desires. But with the overall trajectory that the nation has seemingly embraced for over a century, the Democratic Party, for the most part, will remain more popular than the Republican Party and will grow exponentially in the near future. But party time for America is over because liberals have failed liberalism.

True 1960s-type economic liberalism involved government taking care of the poor, the homeless, and the needy. But over the last five decades, there have been progressive but corrupt Democratic politicians voting for frivolous pork barrel projects, allocations for unnecessary military bases in their home states, bailing out corporations, subsidizing unions with taxpayers' money, and just plain throwing trillions of dollars away on the unessential. But has the common everyday liberal voter ever publicly or even privately criticized or repudiated the moral and economic wrongdoings of these Democratic "leaders" or threaten not to vote for them? The answer: Absolutely not. Billions wasted on the totally inane, needless, and counterproductive when we, the people, could have had very little difficulty funding temporary unemployment benefits and decent, "legitimate" social programs (operating in the black) if it weren't for the squandering of liberal lawmakers and their complicit supporters. Not to mention that our nation could have very easily afforded the monetary clean-up of natural disasters (hurricanes, tornadoes, earthquakes, Nancy Pelosi) that we would have bankrolled WITHOUT going bankrupt. The liberal voters, over half a century, have disgraced honest-to-goodness liberalism.

Already, some Americans have been conditioned to think of ever-expanding government as merely "growing pains." They tend to agree with the first female Speaker of the House and like-thinking lawmakers that we have a BUDGET problem, not a SPENDING problem. Many citizens really are apathetic about a potential catastrophic financial collapse of our country. The majority of our voters are against real domestic spending cuts, but they don't mind vague generalities about "cutting spending" coming from the nation's capital. That is, they nonchalantly accept a politician speaking about having "lean, streamlined, reduced government" just as long as he or she isn't serious about it. The voters' lack of more fiscally stringent demands, renders the very term "reform" ineffectual, which is the desired result of liberal and moderate politicians. The American electorate, in general, wants the omnipotent State to be designed and built by the Democratic Party but prefer it to be managed by the Republicans. Their hope is that the GOP with their pro-business reputation and fiscal acumen will then be compelled to "run our (enormous) government efficiently," and so, said Republicans will consequently forget about any fiscally conservative goals of trying to chop it down. This will give the American people the respite and contentment that they seek. Our nation's tax-payers would find it most convenient if the government subsidized their *cost-of-living* expenses as much as possible while they, the citizens (government clients), mainly finance their pursuit of a leisurely life, which is what they long for. But the bigger that the government grows, the bigger that it needs to grow. To the media and the public in general, only a Republican President with a Democratic Congress diligently fighting his freedom-inducing budget cuts can be properly termed a "dictator" with a "my way or the highway" attitude. But Democratic voters themselves, really do yearn for a benevolent tyrant who is an advocate of strict but compassionate centralized government. And if the Republicans in Congress don't go along with this progressive "dictator" president and give him all he covets, then the former are to be viewed as "obstructionists."

In getting "wonderful" things done, we the people have a bad habit of conflating "that American-know-how and can-do-spirit" with the legislative action of Washington DC politicians and not with ordinary American individuals. Many of our citizens are well aware that CONSERVATIVE GOP lawmakers going to Washington, DC and making conservative (liberty-inducing austerity) legislation the law of the land, will make our free-market financial system stronger and more beneficial to the nation. But they still vote Democratic (not taking any chances) in order to protect their entitlements. For it is security that they crave, not a robust economy. The public believes, and correctly so, that the Party of Ronald Reagan is more likely to take away "their" government checks (a cutback on redistribution), oblivious to the fact that it's not theirs, it is the government's. And then there are the 51 percent of Americans who advocate raising the minimum wage to $15 an hour but are unable to explain why it shouldn't be raised to $17.50 an hour or $20.00 or for that matter, $22.50 an hour. Better yet, let's make it a nice, even $25 an hour, which would be great for kids working in a fast-food joint, become a veritable living wage for adults, and fantastic for the country because it will give the working class more money to spend to stimulate the economy…right? Why would the truly caring be AGAINST this $25 an hour recommendation? But, paradoxical as it seems, our economy and the American worker would be better off if the minimum wage were ZERO. Our society disapproves of the "fat cats" in the private sector who provide us with jobs, far more than they disapprove of the FAT CATS in government who take our earnings. This is because the government ostensibly takes care of the people and LOOKS OUT FOR THEM while the private sector does not. You'll realize that the republic is in trouble when its denizens extol the virtues of big government even when most of them will privately acknowledge that big government isn't virtuous.

Journalists and voters don't ask, and the politicians don't want to be asked, precisely what social programs or entitlements should be cut or eliminated. It's not just Social Security anymore, but all entitlements, social programs and Federal agencies that have become the Third Rail of politics. During the Reagan/Bush Sr. years, the National Endowment for the Arts was on the chopping block for elimination, though unfortunately, that turkey was saved. But then, very little, if anything, was cut or eliminated during that "conservative" era. The American people should realize that when they call on government to subsidize their well-being as much as possible, then it has the right to control them, and the people are wrong to say that it doesn't. Yes, that's correct! When you insist that the government provide for you and take care of you from cradle to grave and give you lots of free stuff, the powerful State would be negligent NOT to make a virtual slave of you. This, coming from yours truly, a nationalistic libertarian, a laissez-faire capitalist; a veritable Ayn Rand Objectivist!

There have been a FEW Republicans who have spoken about THE POINT OF NO RETURN in regard to America's free-market economic system. "The Point of No Return" is when more than 50 percent of the citizens of the United States are permanently living off the government, the Feds more than soak the rich who provide jobs for the non-rich, private enterprise virtually ceases to be and the USA snowballs toward a catastrophic bankruptcy far worse than that of Greece. There is an analogy about a frog that has often been told by the libertarian, liberty-loving right. This fable about our amphibian friend is owned and patented by us. It is against the law for liberals and moderates to tell it, and so far, they have never broken this law: A frog is put into a pan of cool water. The contented amphibian proclaims, "This human being who put me in here is very kind." The pan is put on the stove and the temperature is put on low. The little creature, which is still capable of hopping out, says to himself, "I can feel the water getting soothingly warmer. This man must really care about me." The stove knob is turned to very warm. Now, the frog is still relatively comfortable but is a little worried that something wrong is happening. The cook then sets the temperature on high and secures the lid on the pan of water.

"The only difference between communism and socialism is its method of imposition. Communism is forced upon the people against their will. Socialism, on the other hand, is entered into voluntarily by the majority of voters. Even though the goals are the same, socialism is much more dangerous because it gradually enslaves the people without the use of visible force while artfully disguising its evil motives with a variety of so-called noble causes." Author: unknown. Socialism is not sustainable. Capitalism IS because it has no system of overgrown statism to sustain. An upper-middle class family consisting of husband and wife with eight adult children, seven of them are on their own and doing splendidly while one of them, a son, is unemployed, dependent on hard drugs and living off his parents, is nevertheless, a SUSTAINABLE family. However, if five of the son's siblings join him in his lifestyle, then this family is NOT sustainable. With almost pure free-market enterprise, there's very little, if any, government economic collectivism of the people in order for government to depend on them. As for the middle class, it has always been prosperous under American capitalism. Socialistic economic policies only lead to an oppressive statism where there is no thriving middle class, only the rich elite and the government-dependent lower-class. Besides, a free society focusing on the thoroughly meaningless *gap between rich and poor* only foments envy and not upward mobility for those of lower-class income to middle-class status. Furthermore, government closing the gap between the two opposite economic classes on each end, and building a stronger middle class via redistribution, is a LIE that too many Republican politicians have never rebutted and that a gullible public wants so very much to believe in.

Demopublican politicians always flatter the American people by telling them that they're smart… as one of them would say to his or her opponent: "The American people are smart. You can't fool them. They know what you're up to and they don't like it one bit. The American people agree with me because, unlike you, I'm in the common-sense, mainstream center, just like they are." This phony compliment is just a ruse to charm the listening audience into backing that politician, but it does work. It really is alright with the public if various members of the House and Senate lie to them or at least refrain from divulging a truth that they don't want to hear. This is because the people themselves are liars, and liars are attracted to politicians who lie. They admire lawmakers and political candidates who artfully dodge hard-ball questions. In order to attain social and economic equality, many (especially those who vote Democrat) believe that the facts must be dismissed and the intellectually honest must be demonized and shunned. The further the United States slides to the left, the more the ideological truth is detested and denounced.

There are some 12 million more members of the Democrat Party than there are of the Republican Party. Does that not tell you that the socialistic philosophy and policies (government will provide for you and take care of your major problems) of the former are more popular than the capitalistic (liberty-based, you're on your own) attitude of libertarian conservative Republicans? In future elections, the independents and moderate voters will feel snubbed by the Democratic Party on a certain issue or two and begin a flirtatious though fleeting romance with the GOP. But said voters will eventually "come home" to the Democrats, the party of safety and security. In doing so, these de facto Democrats will surmise...why should they vote for some establishment Republican, who is merely a pale pastel version of the real thing, a liberal Democrat, when they can have the latter in office doing a better job of "looking out for them" and "sharing their concerns"? The everyday, independent-minded Joe Citizen only needs to tell himself that the superficial empathy of progressive political candidates will somehow make his life better. One should look for the Democrat Party to gradually, but assuredly, ratchet up their power in the nation's capital over the next two decades with a few minor mid-term setbacks.

Since the late 1980s, there are no states that used to be Democrat but are now Republican. But there WAS big-time political change. In the presidential elections over the last five decades, New Hampshire was solidly Republican through the 1970s and '80s, but since 1992, with the exception of the year 2000 presidential election, has voted Democrat. From the year 1968 until 2004, Virginia voted the Republican ticket for President. It is now firmly Democrat. Arizona went from being solid GOP to a swing state. Nevada once was a toss-up state; it's now leaning Democrat. North Carolina used to be a red state but is currently a purple state. On a radio talk show, a Republican candidate running for political office in Minnesota claimed that his state is NOT blue (Democrat), but purple. He lied and lost. It wasn't even a close race. Georgia was once dependably conservative but not anymore. Today, the Peach State is moderate and probably on the way to becoming more liberal. Colorado and New Mexico used to be battleground states. Today, they are medium-to-dark blue, politically. From the 1950s through the 1980s, with the exception of one presidential election (1964), the state of California, which carries the nation's largest electoral vote, was a dependable GOP region. It is currently, and forever more, dependably Democrat because of both legal and illegal Hispanic influx. Conservative Ronald Reagan's former place of residence has gone so far to the left that the corpse of former Venezuelan president Hugo Chavez is being exhumed and will be flown into Sacramento to become the Golden State's next governor. Right-wing extremist and present governor, Gavin Newsom, will be dragged out of office and executed. Florida used to lean Republican, but it is now a prime electoral-vote area that went blue in 2008 and 2012. For more than twenty years, Pennsylvania has been solidly Democrat, NOT a toss-up state. But that didn't deter the last four GOP nominees for president (this is before Trump in 2016, the rare exception) from foolishly boasting, while on the campaign trail, "We're going to win Pennsylvania!" One should not whistle "Dixie" while standing in Northeastern territory. So, since the early 1980s, one dozen formerly Republican states have gone mostly Democratic while the party of Lincoln has picked up ZERO states that used to be Democrat. Get the picture? With the help of the influx south of the border, it should be no surprise if the Lone Star state is on its way to becoming number 13. But never, in the years to come, will a blue state become a red state. This is not the case, vice versa.

Our country is becoming more PROGRESSIVE (a euphemism for "socialistic"). The majority of American voters insist on equating SOCIALISM with MUSHROOMS. That is, sure, there's such a thing as POISON mushrooms that one could get sick or die from eating. But there are also the healthy and delicious mushrooms that we buy in a grocery store and eat with our steak. If you, the reader and quintessentially average, independent-minded citizen, were to be asked, "Are you for or against socialism?" you will be predisposed to reply, "Neither. I'm not for it and I'm not against it." Correct. And the reason that you're NOT against socialism is because there is no reason to be against it. Since this is the case, then why not be all for it? You will be unable to explain why not. If I asked you if you think that socialism is unjust, oppressive, and wrong; would you precondition your answer with, "Not necessarily. What do you mean by *socialism*? It depends. You have to be careful with that word." Why the equivocation? It's because you must first ascertain precisely WHAT KIND of socialism that this author has in mind. Hence, if it's a GOOD socialism, then you will be all for it. And if it's a BAD one, then you will be against it.....just like that of mushrooms. But, socialism, at least subjectively, needs to be given the benefit of a doubt that you would like to think it deserves. That makes you a de facto socialist, since you refuse to answer with a definitive "yes" to my question. Let's put it this way. If I asked you if you think that Nazism is unjust, oppressive, and wrong, would you have replied with a lame "Not necessarily, it depends on what you mean by *Nazism*? It's got to be a certain type." Or, how about if I asked you the same question about fascism, would your retort be a namby-pamby "Well, maybe, maybe not, I don't know, what kind of *fascism* are we talking about here?"

Alright then, how about apartheid? Is your answer a dithering "You have to be careful with that word; although I think that a little bit of *apartheid* would be good for America, but not too much of it" And what is your opinion about communism? "Oh, I think it would be wonderful to live under *communism* just as long as our leader isn't the Joseph

Stalin type, because he wasn't a very nice man. Nor that Pol Pot guy in Cambodia, he was a communist but was kind of kooky and dangerous." Unfortunately, too large a chunk of our society believes that it needs to equivocate on actual socialism because its' very concept is so extremely enchanting and worth romanticizing about, that the Marxist religion should at least be given the benefit of a doubt, otherwise there is no hope for mankind. Socialism deserves to be viewed as being neither black nor white but just a grey area merely needing diligent, patriotic and non-corrupt economic experts, with that American can-do spirit, to properly run socialism like the beautiful human machine that is its potential. Why should individuals be responsible for their own life decisions and monetary problems when they don't have to be? Americans find it very comforting and convenient if the Federal government will relieve citizens of their BIG financial obligations with free cradle to grave health care, subsidized housing and assuring them a job with a livable wage and more, while the common people would pay for their leisurely pursuits (vacations, sporting events, new barbecue grills, etc.). Besides, under socialism, if a certain individual does fall into financial dire straits and the government doesn't bail him or her out, then the government is negligent, not the individual. That's most enticing. It will legitimately be the government's fault if that person's life isn't going well. The preceding statement is not just an alibi or excuse but a REASON, because it's the truth. And if massive government creates even more problems for the American people, the people will simply clamor for the government to solve them. Only this time, they'll be putting more effort into hoping that government does a better job than it did before. The more control that Big Brother has over society, the more society will look up to it and respect it, and be ever so grateful when Big Brother DOES grant their requests and maybe allow them some liberty. The sheeple will ultimately believe that their rights come from the Omnipotent State, not the Almighty. And they will be correct.

Most political Americans are imperceptive and unable to connect the dots that it is LESS domestic social spending, lower taxes for EVERYBODY and the drastic cutbacks on regulations and restrictions that create an economic dynamism and a prosperity that benefits all the citizens, especially the non-wealthy. On the other hand, the people should try to understand that in order for all of us to make socialistic economic policies more effective, we will need to engage in absolute pretense about their effectiveness. Understand? In 1930s Germany, the Jews were vilified and made the scapegoats by Hitler's regime for the country's moribund economy. And the Fuhrer did this with the support of citizens who were NOT members of the Nazi Party. Today, the hated "one percent" in the USA gets the blame for our severe debt and deficit. This lie about the rich being responsible for our bankruptcy has to be contradicted (no Republican in Washington, DC has done such) and the truth must be told: It's the representatives and their extravagant spending AT THE BEHEST OF THEIR CONSTITUENTS, that is responsible. At town hall meetings across the nation, the voters will tell their representatives to SAVE sundry and "essential" social spending, never ELIMINATE it.

Whenever you think that government makes your life better, you are then susceptible to allowing it to tacitly subjugate and control you. The public has to be educated by the Republican Party that it's the dynamism of monetary FREEDOM that is the catalyst for prosperity and job growth, not a politician's pleasant personality or gift of oratory and certainly not the central command of Washington, DC. It has always been because of Constitutional conservatism and never liberalism that the United States became a rich country in the first place. But a probable majority of our citizens would like to think that it is government management and manipulation of our economic institution that provides for the people's well-being. If these patriotic citizens feel that way, then they should advocate for not just a few more rules, regulations, and restrictions, but rather, total command and control of the economy. This way, the powerful State can run things to perfection. The American people are going to have to be told that the POPULARITY of an economic policy doesn't necessarily mean that it's a good one. Otherwise, the Feds allocating exactly one million dollars to every adult citizen who isn't already wealthy would be a rousing accomplishment and stimulating remedy that would end poverty and homelessness; plus grow the economy and stave off a recession. To add to this mindset, most of us think that "compromise", "ending gridlock" and "bipartisanship" are automatically beneficial to the nation and that passing bad legislation (usually conducive to socialism) is better than passing none at all. More and more, our society is being conditioned to believe that an individual who is the enemy of the omnipotent State is also the enemy of the people. If we, the People, don't view socialism as an oppressive, miserable hell-hole to be avoided at any cost, then we will quite naturally, inexorably and quickly gravitate in its direction....and why shouldn't we?

What Is to Be Done? First and foremost, the God-awful monstrosity known as "Obamacare" needs to be stabbed to death in its infancy, stuffed back into its uterus, and permanently clamped shut with heavy-duty, industrial-strength staples. Can America accomplish this? To quote the mother who gave birth to the bastard, "YES WE CAN!" Already, the three stages of its festering growth has gone something like this: In the first five years starting in 2010, the majority of American citizens hated Obamacare, insulted it, made jokes about it, and sneered at it. The next five years, Obamacare was merely disliked by the public but grudgingly accepted and the criticism of it diminished. And now in the third decade of the 21st century, much, if not most of the people will be dependent on and cherish what is now sometimes called the Affordable Care Act. But woe-betide the lawmaker or candidate for political office who threatens to abolish "THEIR Obamacare." It will have gone from disgraced abomination (circa 2013) to beloved beauty in less than two decades. And don't think that its creator, the Socialist Shyster, isn't gleefully aware of it. In 2010, our 44th president was abundantly sure that the ACA would bankrupt the healthcare insurance industry and that too many Americans with way-above-average intelligence would consequently call for the Federal government to rectify the problem (read: take total control of the healthcare industry). The un-Constitutional and redistributive Obamacare is the stepping-stone to a single-payer system (aka socialized medicine) and one/sixth of the economy. The former community organizer stated back in 2003, "I happen to be a proponent of a single-payer universal health plan." In that year, Obama spoke the truth. And if you like this truth, you can keep it. Period!

Here's more truth from the late author and columnist, Joseph

Sobran: "Liberals have a new wish every time their latest wish is granted. Conservatives should make them spell out their principles and ideals. Instead of doing this, conservatives allow liberals to pursue incremental goals without revealing their ultimate destination. So thanks to the neglect of their opponents, liberals control the terms of every debate by demanding "more" while never defining "enough." The predictable result is that they always get more and it's never enough."

If various Americans aren't put on the spot by telling them the truth, spoken especially from self-proclaimed "conservative" politicians, then the people are being allowed to get away with being dishonest. Have you ever noticed that conservative pundits on political news shows and talk radio may have upbraided various politicians for not cutting domestic social spending, the cause of our massive debt? But the noted purveyers of right-wing opinion have not condemned the government-loving general public that elected the noted lawmakers into office in the first place. For it is at the behest of these voters that the socio-economic philosophy of the Democratic party, with the assistance of recreant Republicans and their strong desire to be liked by not rocking the boat, that domineers Washington, DC. About a third of our country insists on giving the machinations of leftism the chance to work its magic. A few years ago, there was a gallop poll survey showing that 53 percent of Democrats and 23 percent of Republicans approve of socialism. This is even more dreadful. These ignorant individuals find the "dream" of the Marxist invention to be emotionally uplifting and satisfying but would rather not be told or learn about the reality of it. The prevalent attitude is: Let's install socialism NOW and then just fix any flaws that it may have, in the future. Even many Republicans (especially irresolute moderates), when asked if America should live under socialism, will reply, "No, we can't afford it!".....This is not because socialism is unjust, oppressive and wrong, mind you, but merely because "We can't afford it." Which means that if we COULD AFFORD socialism—like say in a couple of years or a few months down the road;—then we should definitely live under it. LAME! But apparently, the people want to have their cake and eat it...while blindfolded. There ought to be another survey that asks the aforementioned RINOs and like-thinking ambivalent Americans to name a country with a socialist economy (with the exception of Venezuela, which has been a phenomenal success) where life is better than the nation that they're living in. Incidentally, Sweden, Denmark, and Norway are NOT socialist countries....so don't even think it. Indeed, the three of them have NO government-mandated minimum wage. Yes, that's right!

What else needs to be done in order to stave off a catastrophic socio-economic collapse in America? Starting in junior high school, make it a prerequisite for children in public schools to be taught about the socio-economic evils of socialism, despite the vociferous objection by the National Teacher Association. Shut the government down the first Wednesday of every month. Enact the Fair Tax. Elect to political office strict Constitutionalist libertarian conservatives, NOT go-along-to-get-along establishmentarian Republicans. Eliminate several subsidies (farms, Amtrak, Planned Parenthood, corporate welfare, and the like). Abolish the Department of Commerce, the Department of Energy, the Department of Housing and Urban Development and the IRS. Also, eliminate ten percent of the more than two thousand Federal government agencies. This will necessitate no less than two hundred of the least important agencies. We must raise the Social Security retirement age and Medicare eligibility age to seventy. Today's sexagenarians and septuagenarians are far healthier than those of six decades ago. Also, pass a law that ceases all earmarks and pork barrel projects. Keep US military bases only in world hot spots that are in OUR best interests. Plus, stop building weapons that we don't need and our military generals don't want. But especially, it is imperative that we slash all ACTUAL domestic spending (not just the rate of growth) by five percent each and every year at least until the United States totally eliminates its debt and deficit. It should be mandatory that all candidates running for national office, must sign a pledge stating that America SHOULD live under socialism...OR, that we the people must NOT live under it. Although many of them for some unknown reason will object to such a ruling, the noted political aspirants have to officially choose just one or they will be disqualified from holding public office. Our lawmakers need to be put on the spot about a serious subject,...the fate of our country. And finally, implement term limits. Let's make the Congressional and senatorial residency that of the presidency, two terms of four years each. But not to worry, folks; even with these term limits, our distinguished office-holders in Washington, DC will still have time for avarice and malfeasance, much to the chagrin of the American people. This you can depend on, because they are our leaders.

So who's to blame for the nation's bankruptcy and the fact that the Federal government is still on a spending binge? The answer: Conservative politicians, particularly, the Republican Party. Nobody votes for a Democrat for the purpose of his or her marching over to the US Capitol and putting an end to massive government spending. Politician Joe Liberal is just doing his job as a tax and spend, bring-home-the-bacon champion. His constituents expect it and appreciate it. He has done nothing politically wrong. But while left-leaning lawmakers have been ECONOMICALLY irresponsible; conservative lawmakers have been POLITICALLY irresponsible. They have abandoned REAL leadership and have forsaken their libertarian/self-reliance economic principles by not rubbing the truth in the collective face of American citizens that it's not the government's job, obligation, or responsibility to provide for or take care of them.

This intentional neglect by the Grand Old Party is all in the hopes of being re-elected. A GOP lawmaker is well aware that, to the voters, raising taxes is disliked but deemed, in the long run, ACCEPTABLE. However, CUTTING domestic social spending is absolutely despised and totally UNACCEPTABLE. Though the Republicans' pusillanimity doesn't let the Democratic Party entirely off the hook, because, if there's anybody who could cut social programs and entitlements, which would put our budget back in the black and make America super prosperous with no debt; it's the Democrats. No, the Democratic constituents will not like their Party's new-found austerity, but they're certainly not going to check the ballot box for their even more fiscally conservative opponents. The entire liberal/left establishment will just have to grin and bear it while supporting Democratic candidates, who, on Election Day, would probably win, as the economy would definitely win.

And so the bottom line is this: If a CONSERVATIVE Republican is not elected the president of the United States in November 2024, preferably with a GOP Senate and GOP house, our country will tumble over the ideological precipice and fall quickly into absolute ruin. By and large, the public likes the word "capitalism," but they do not like capitalistic (individualism/self-responsibility) economic principles. On the other hand, most of the common citizens don't care for the word "socialism" because of its bad reputation, but they're extremely fond of socialistic economic policies themselves. American-style capitalism (socio-economic liberty) is the truth that puts us on the spot, which we don't like. Socialism, on the other hand, is a utopian fabrication that excuses and subsidizes society's adverse behavior and allows us to get away with self-deceit, which we don't mind doing. If the majority of the adult population were to be perfectly sincere, what they want to live under is a democratic socialism that will allow for a free-market and some property rights. Americans want politicians, particularly Republicans, to be "pragmatic," "mainstream," and "bi-partisan," that will pay lip service to fiscal accountability but yield to the electorate's appetite for increased domestic spending and nanny government. They want their creeping socialism in small, gradual increments so they can pretend not to notice its encroachment. But what too many of the USA's 330 million citizens DO NOT want is Paul Revere type ideologues who alert the people that more government services and subsidies will only mean more authoritarian control over them (and rightfully so). Otherwise, they wouldn't be able to feign ignorance and escape the blame if America ever descended into an oppressive totalitarianism. So you see, socialism is not just an emotion and a lie, but it is also the epitome of selfishness and failure.

Quite simply, in the realm of life, socialism really is THE PHILOSOPHY OF SURRENDER! Think about it.

Printed in the USA
CPSIA information can be obtained
at www.ICGtesting.com
LVHW040837070824
787572LV00004B/26